# Eastward
# bound

◖◗

Published in our
centenary year
∼ 2004 ∼
MANCHESTER
UNIVERSITY
PRESS

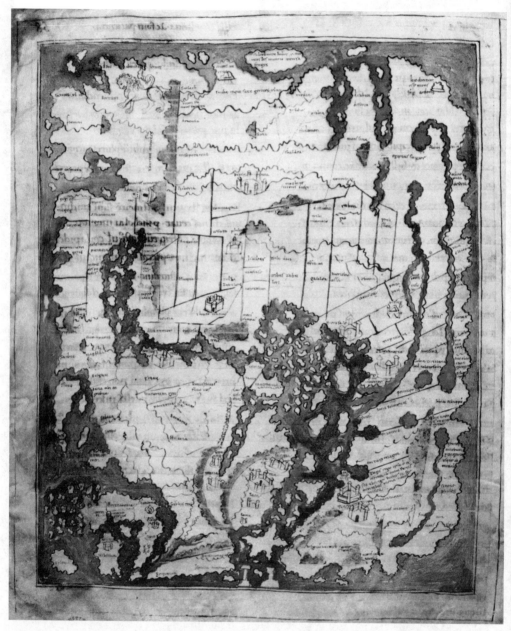

Map of the world, *c.* 1050. The Anglo-Saxon (Cotton) map illustrates the Christianisation of a geographical map (probably derived from copies of a Roman prototype) nearly a century before the earliest known *mappamundi* proper. East is at the top, and the Mediterranean Sea forms the vertical axis in the bottom part of the map. The boundaries are those of Roman provinces, but the territories of the Twelve Tribes of Israel are also named. 21 × 17 cm.

# EASTWARD BOUND

*Travel and travellers,*

*1050–1550*

❨❩

edited by
Rosamund Allen

Manchester University Press
Manchester and New York

distributed exclusively in the USA by Palgrave

*Published by* Manchester University Press
Oxford Road, Manchester M13 9NR, UK
*and* Room 400, 175 Fifth Avenue, New York, NY 10010, USA
www.manchesteruniversitypress.co.uk

*Distributed exclusively in the USA by*
Palgrave, 175 Fifth Avenue, New York, NY 10010, USA

*Distributed exclusively in Canada by*
UBC Press, University of British Columbia, 2029 West Mall,
Vancouver, BC, Canada V6T 1Z2


*British Library Cataloguing-in-Publication Data*
A catalogue record for this book is available from the British Library

*Library of Congress Cataloging-in-Publication Data applied for*


ISBN 0 7190 6690 5 *hardback*

0 7190 6691 3 *paperback*


First published 2004

13 12 11 10 09 08 07 06 05 04    10 9 8 7 6 5 4 3 2 1


Typeset in 10.5/12.5pt Minion
by Graphicraft Limited, Hong Kong
Printed in Great Britain
by CPI, Bath

*For*
*Marianne Wynn*

◖◗

# Contents

❰❱

CONTENTS

# Figures

(•)

# Contributors

**()**

ROSAMUND ALLEN studied English at Royal Holloway College and has taught in the University of London since 1965, at Bedford and Westfield Colleges, and now in the School of English and Drama, Queen Mary, University of London. She has published on the Middle English mystics, medieval romance and Lawman's *Brut* and Malory. She is currently working on metre in Middle English texts.

NIALL CHRISTIE received his undergraduate degree in Arabic from the University of St Andrews, Scotland, in 1995. In 1999 he completed a PhD in medieval Islamic history from the same institution, concentrating in particular on Levantine responses to the early crusades. He is currently a Research Associate and Sessional Lecturer at the University of British Columbia, and is continuing research on Muslim responses to the early crusades, focusing in particular on the presentation of the Franks in Muslim sources and (with Professor Deborah Gerish of Emporia State University, Kansas) comparative study of medieval European and Islamic calls to holy war.

SUZANNE CONKLIN AKBARI was educated at Johns Hopkins and Columbia Universities, and is currently Associate Professor of English and Medieval Studies at the University of Toronto. She has recently published a book on optics and allegory, titled *Seeing through the Veil* (Toronto: University of Toronto Press, 2004), and is currently at work on *Idols in the East: European Representations of Islam and the Orient, 1100–1450*. She has published articles on western views of Islam in *Scripta Mediterranea*, *Islam and Christian–Muslim Relations* and *The Dante Encyclopedia*, and on western views of the Orient in *The Postcolonial Middle Ages* (ed. Cohen, 2000), *Chaucer's Cultural Geography* (ed. Lynch, 2002) and *Orientalism and the Jews* (ed. Kalmar and Penslar, 2004).

CATHERINE DELANO-SMITH graduated, and gained her D.Phil., from the University of Oxford. She is editor of *Imago Mundi: The International Journal for the History of Cartography* and Research Fellow at the Institute of Historical Research, University of London. She was formerly Reader in Historical Geography at the University of Nottingham. Her book on *Western Mediterranean Europe: A Historical Geography of Italy, Spain and Southern France since the Neolithic* (London and New York: Academic Press, 1979) was followed by publications on prehistoric maps and on a number of aspects of the history of pre-modern cartography. She has co-authored *Maps in Bibles* (1991, with Elizabeth Ingram); *English Maps: A History* (1999, with Roger J. P. Kain) and *Plantejamentos i objectivos d'una història universal de la cartografia: Approaches and Challenges in a Worldwide History of Cartography* (2001, with David Woodward and Cordell Yee). She has an essay 'Map signs on printed topographical maps *c.* 1470–

*c.* 1640' in David Woodward (ed.), *The History of Cartography*, volume iii: *Cartography in the European Renaissance* (Chicago: University of Chicago Press, forthcoming).

EVELYN EDSON is a Professor of History at Piedmont Virginia Community College in Charlottesville, Virginia. She is the author of *Mapping Time and Space: How Medieval Mapmakers Viewed their World* (1997). She is currently working on a book on the transformation of the world map between 1300 and 1500.

BERNARD HAMILTON is Professor Emeritus of Crusading History of the University of Nottingham. His recent publications include: *Prester John, the Mongols and the Ten Lost Tribes*, edited with C. F. Beckingham (1996) and the collected studies *Crusaders, Cathars and the Holy Places* (Aldershot: Ashgate, 1999) and *The Christian World of the Middle Ages* (Stroud: Sutton, 2003). He is now preparing a monograph, *The Crusades and a Wider World*, for London Books.

ANDREW JOTISCHKY is Senior Lecturer in History at Lancaster University. He is author of *The Perfection of Solitude: Hermits and Monks in the Crusader States* (1995) and *The Carmelites and Antiquity: Mendicants and their Pasts in the Middle Ages* (2002), and articles on aspects of the relations between Franks and Greek Orthodox Christians in the Crusader States.

ANNE SIMON is Senior Lecturer in Mediaeval German at the University of Bristol. Her research interests include medieval German travel literature, especially that on pilgrimage to the Holy Land; the history of the book; and the relationship between text and image in the late Middle Ages. Her major publications include *Sigmund Feyerabend's 'Das Reyßbuch deß Heyligen Lands': A Study in Printing and Literary History* (Wiesbaden: Reichert, 1998) and, with Helen Watanabe-O'Kelly, *Festivals and Ceremonies: A Bibliography of Works Relating to Court, Civic and Religious Festivals in Europe, 1500–1800* (London: Mansell, 2000).

BARRY TAYLOR is curator of Hispanic Collections, 1501–1850, at the British Library, London. His publications include *Cultures in Contact in Medieval Spain: Historical and Literary Essays Presented to L. P. Harvey*, edited with David Hook (London: King's College, 1990); *Latin and Vernacular in Renaissance Spain*, edited with Alejandro Coroleu (Manchester: Department of Hispanic Studies, 1999), and over thirty articles on Don Juan Manuel, Juan de Mena and wisdom literature in Old Spanish, Old Catalan and Latin.

SHAWKAT M. TOORAWA is Assistant Professor of Arabic Literature and Islamic Studies in the Department of Near Eastern Studies, Cornell University. He has taught at the University of Pennsylvania (where he received his PhD), Duke University and the University of Mauritius. He is a co-author of *Interpreting the Self: Autobiography in the Arabic Literary Tradition*, edited by Dwight F. Reynolds (2001), and author of *Ibn Abi Tahir Tayfur and Arabic Writerly Culture: A Ninth Century Bookman in Baghdad* (forthcoming from RoutledgeCurzon).

ROSALYNN VOADEN works primarily on late medieval women visionaries and saints' lives. She is the author of *God's Words, Women's Voices: The Discernment of Spirits in the Writing of Late-Medieval Women Visionaries* (1999), and is currently at work on a study of holiness in the domestic setting entitled *Household Saints: Holiness and Domesticity in Late-Medieval Europe.* She is co-editor of the forthcoming *Yale Guide to Medieval Holy Women in the Christian Tradition.* She teaches at Arizona State University.

ELKA WEBER recently finished a Ph.D. in Middle Eastern Studies at New York University, where she wrote a dissertation comparing late medieval travel accounts of Muslims, Christians and Jews. Her article 'Construction of identity in twelfth-century Andalusia: The case of travel writing' appeared in *The Journal of North African Studies,* and she is now researching the relationship between British colonialism and the translation of medieval pilgrimage accounts into English around the beginning of the twentieth century. She teaches at Fairleigh Dickinson University in New Jersey.

# *Acknowledgements*

**( )**

This collection of commissioned essays took its origin from a suggestion by Professor Marianne Wynn, who has published work and organised conferences and seminars on travel for a number of years. The work is respectfully dedicated to her in gratitude for her inspiration. It has been a pleasure to work with the contributors, who have not only written their own chapters with enthusiasm but have also suggested other contributors, twice at short notice when a previously engaged author was obliged to step down. Evelyn Edson suggested the title for the book. The advice and support of Professor Paul Harvey is gratefully acknowledged. Brian Place, Queen Mary Arts Computing Manager, and Joe Elwood, Computer Support Officer, have given much appreciated assistance. I thank Queen Mary and Westfield College for allowing me to spend part of a semester's teaching remission in completing the preparation of the book. The editor and contributors are grateful to the following libraries for permission to reproduce images from manuscripts: The British Library, London, the Bodleian Library, Oxford, the Master and Fellows of Corpus Christi College, Cambridge, the Bibliotheca Estense, University of Modena, and the Österreichische Nationalbibliothek, Vienna and to Columbia University Press for permission to quote from P. K. Hitti, *An Arab–Syrian Gentleman and Warrior* in Chapter 4. My grateful thanks are extended to the readers for the press for their supportive and informative suggestions, and to the staff at Manchester University Press for their prompt and tireless work on behalf of the press in preparing the book.

Rosamund Allen
Queen Mary, University of London

# Note on Arabic transliterations, Arabic names and Islamic dates

**(  )**

The Arabic transliteration used in this volume is a simplified and more literal form of the system used by the *International Journal of Middle East Studies*. Thus, all macrons and dots are omitted; *'ayn* (') and medial and final *hamzah* (') are retained; *ta' marbutah* is rendered (-*ah*) but (-*at*) in construct.

Specialists will have no difficulty in recognising words and names. Non-specialists are asked to note that in *The Encyclopaedia of Islam* the leading reference work in the field of Islamic studies, (j) is rendered (dj), and (q) is rendered (k).

In names, 'ibn' means 'son of' and is lower-case. When its first letter is upper-case it indicates descent of more than one generation. Thus, Ahmad ibn Majid means that Ahmad is the son of Majid, but 'Ali Ibn al-Munajjim means that 'Ali is a descendant of al-Munajjim.

Common Era dates are used but, where relevant, Islamic (Hijri) dates are provided before the Common Era ones, e.g. (d. 629/1231).

# *Abbreviations*

**( )**

| | |
|---|---|
| *AFP* | *Archivum Fratrum Praedicatorum* |
| BCE | Before the Common Era (= BC) |
| BEFAR | Bibliothèque des Écoles Françaises d'Athènes et de Rome |
| *c.* | circa |
| CE | Common Era (= AD) |
| CICO | Pontificia Commissio ad Redigendum Codicem Iuris Canonici Orientalis Fontes |
| d. | died |
| gen. ed. | general editor |
| *fl.* | floruit (active) |
| MGHSS | Monumenta Germaniae Historica, Scriptores |
| MOPH | Monumenta Ordinis Praedicatorum Historia |
| *PL* | *Patrologiae Cursus Completus, Series Latina* |
| r. | ruled; years in office |
| RHC Docs Arms | Recueil des Historiens des Croisades, Documents Arméniens |
| s.l. | sine loco (without place of publication) |
| s.n. | sine nomine (without printer's name) |

# Introduction

**CD**

## Rosamund Allen

> Pilgrymes and palmers pliȝten hem togidere
> For to seken Seint Iame and Seintes at Rome;
> Wenten forþ in hire wey wiþ many wise tales,
> And hadden leue to lyen al hire lif after.
> (William Langland, *Piers Plowman*, Prologue, lines 46–9)[1]

(Pilgrims and those standing in for pilgrims, making a mutual contract to go to visit Compostela and the shrines in Rome, set off on their route with many learned instructions, and so were authorised to tell lies for the rest of their lives.)

T HIS SATIRICAL comment on pilgrimage from *Piers Plowman* reflects William Langland's deeply conservative mind. He did not approve of social or geographic mobility; travelling to obtain pardons whether in person or by proxy was unnecessary and provoked tall tales. Langland would have disapproved of many of the narratives in this book, tales about and by travellers who often claim to be eyewitnesses but who are often recycling accounts by classical or medieval writers. Like Langland, the modern reader has difficulty with a first-person account which is plainly not based on factual personal observation.[2] But the medieval veneration for sources, written and oral, accepts the probity of an inherited account and seeks only to pass on the information. Miracles, marvels and monstrous creations, all must exist as all things are possible under God. The travel accounts which we may read as entertainment were directives to wisdom.[3] The kind of 'knowledge' we use for the London taxi driver's familiarity with actual places had its medieval equivalent in the shipmaster's knowledge of the coastal waters he navigated,[4] and the local guides' familiarity with terrain across deserts and round the established pilgrim route for the holy sites. Pilgrims relied on personal direction rather than maps for finding their way. Written descriptions of the sites did exist, but were as much advertisements as route guides.[5] Accounts of what could be seen in the orient (as far as the writer was concerned at least) form a different type of narrative, though as *The Book of Sir John Mandeville* shows there is much blending of genres. Billie Melman comments that travel writing is diverse, and has also changed over time. She surveys two dominant models for writing of the Middle East from the western (British) perspective, 'the pilgrimage[,] and the domestic ethnography focused on Muslim every-day life'. Pilgrimage remains the dominant mode of travel even after the Reformation, and in modernised form continues, despite political turmoil, though since the eighteenth century it has co-existed with interest in Islamic private life and with narratives of exploration of the 'wilderness' hinterland of the Arabian peninsula.[6]

Unlike that of the modern vacation traveller, the pilgrim traveller's im-perative was not release from pressure of work but release from the pains of impending infernal torment. Those who were already too old or sick when the horror of coming doom took hold would enlist professional pilgrims, the 'palmers' whose palm was the badge of Holy Land pilgrims. For the medieval pilgrim the journey usually began soon after Easter and lasted a great many months. The crusades were also first 'proposed as a devotional act of pilgrim-age' and were continually being declared, 'at least one crusade summons being directed at each generation in the twelfth and thirteenth centuries', to reinforce and then restore the holy places and to tap the resources of Egypt.[7] Sanudo was preparing a crusade proposal as late as the fourteenth century (see Chapter 7). Merchants travelled even more extensively, and merchant explorers like Marco Polo were (apparently) absent for years.[8] St Brendan fictitiously travelled west from Ireland into the Atlantic,[9] Henry the Navigator (1394–1460), grandson of John of Gaunt, promoted Atlantic exploration by the Portuguese, the Canaries were explored and exploited from the four-teenth century, even as the hinterland of Africa and the sources of the Nile were beginning to be discovered. But the majority of travellers went east-wards, as pilgrims, missionaries, crusaders, envoys and merchants, towards what the *mappamundi* presented as the centre of the world: Jerusalem.[10] A minority went further east, as ambassadors, like Clavijo, on embassy to the Great Khan Timur (Tamerlane), or as merchants on the trade routes for silk, spices, pearls, perfume and other luxuries. Pegolotti's advice on travelling to Cathay for silk was to grow a beard, take a native speaker and travel in a caravan of sixty men for safety.[11]

Today's eastward-bound travellers are urged to be careful about finance, exchange rates, insurance, dress codes and, sadly, disease, terrorism, scams and theft and personal safety, yet one third travel without advance planning.[12] Those who do not travel simply to 'party' relish differences in climates and cuisines of the lands visited, and phrase book to hand savour the food, sites and relics. Medieval travel was not undertaken lightly; it was dangerous, painful and expensive, and it had an objective – pilgrimage, trade, learning, crusade or warfare – and an end product – salvation, wealth, knowledge, prestige, conquest or restoration. Even Tafur (Chapter 11), who sought to gain chivalric prestige from his lengthy travels, did so for social advancement – and he obtained some slaves as well. Modern ideas of travelling to 'broaden the mind' do not operate to any noticeable degree in this collection.[13] Indeed, it appears from previous travellers' accounts, written and oral, and from diagrams and maps (Chapters 6 and 7), that many travellers to Jerusalem had already formed a clear idea of how the Holy Land would look and what they would find. And they found what they expected to: a familiar narrative of biblical texts extended over and buried within the very ground they trod. Jewish pilgrims to the Land of Israel (Chapter 2) found the tombs of the patriarchs, and Christian pilgrims (Chapters 9, 10, 11) identified places with the life and death of Jesus. Both sets of shrines were mainly managed by people of a different religious faith from the pilgrims' own: Muslims, and eastern-rite Catholics, Greek Orthodox Christians and Coptic Christians.

The medieval travellers in this book are more conscious of difference in dress and religious belief than of language, foodstuffs and culture. They are impressed by luxurious clothes, furniture and buildings as an index of status. Yet pilgrims' awareness of the Other is secondary to the impact on them of the long-distant past: like a transparent membrane, the historical plane overlies the geographical, and they find themselves closer to the long-dead founders of their faith than to the local inhabitants with whom they negotiate for food, shelter and access to the shrines. These travellers are concerned about identifying the Other, not always to marvel at difference but to define more securely their own belief system, which had been their main motive for leaving the safety of the familiar home or conventual routine.[14] Nor, despite misunderstanding of the Islamic faith, was there 'a developed hatred of Islam and all things Muslim',[15] though the travelling friars (Chapter 4) are on missions to convert Muslims and non-western-rite Christians, and they meticulously identify those who are in fact Christians in Arab garb. Clothing is identity: Clavijo on embassy to the Mongol Great Khan is impressed by the sumptuous attire at his court (Chapter 11); disguise will enable him to gain access to otherwise prohibited sites (Chapter 2).

Medieval pilgrims had to take with them enough to support their expenses for food, footwear and appropriate clothing. They might appeal for funding to their parish, and the 'overdraft' would be paid in the prayers for bene-factors offered at the destination shrine and in a vicarious share of the pilgrims' reward for suffering Christ's own pains on the journey. They also needed the equivalent of passport and visas, and had to obtain royal permission to cross the sea and permits to enter hostile territory. They needed money to pay to visit shrines, but were supposed to be exempt from certain tolls. Such permits and freedoms could not, however, be relied on.

Travellers' torments from hostile climates and lack of means of subsistence are not prominent in their accounts, though the impetuous Margery Kempe does expose herself to privation and infestation with vermin. But their immediate responses do not go unrecorded. Encina and Tafur (Chapter 11) and Hans Tucher (Chapter 10) are aggrieved at being exploited by the locals. Margery Kempe (Chapter 9) is distressed over money after giving away hers and her companion's in misguided charity. Like us they are anxious about their safety – about brigands and shipwreck, disabling illness and being stranded. The Bedouin are a threat, but Tafur feels a momentary pity for their miserable lifestyle (Chapter 11).

Strange surroundings may seem familiar if they recall a known significant moment in religious history, or are made imaginable by comparing them to known landmarks such as European cities or buildings. Even the totally exotic is not necessarily frightening: unfamiliar animals and plants provoke wonder, and suggest the possible existence of huge variations in human physicality, wholly extraordinary and monstrous forms of human life, men with eyes in their shoulders, huge lips or one huge foot. The variety in God's universal creation presents a careful balance of opposites (Chapter 8). Such marvellous forms of creation were thought to exist in what was once called 'the Orient', the lands on the edges of the *mappaemundi* where the 'wonders of the East' were drawn. As people gained knowledge of the East and failed to find them in India the monstrous races were relocated (Chapter 1) to 'Africa', itself then thought to extend into the Indian Ocean (Chapter 5).

The writer known as 'Mandeville' (Chapter 8), having described the Holy Land and access to it, moves from instructions for alternative routes to Jerusalem by an abrupt transition to the lands east of Israel as far as India, where he locates the monstrous forms. Like so many, he bases his 'observations' on learned sources and on actual travellers like Friar Odoric of Pordenone. Travellers from the regions of Syria, Iraq and Iran, on the other hand, are the most factually accurate of the medieval travellers in this book. From the other side, they observe the distinctions between their own culture and that of the *ifranj*, the 'French' crusaders. Usamah Ibn Munqidh (Chapter 4), a trouble-seeking character, records his outraged impressions of the invading Franks and their females, but is more tolerant of the many other women he encounters. 'Abd al-Latif, with prodigious intellectual energy, travels to learn and later to teach law, medicine and theology (Chapter 3) and rejects the spurious. These men observe the ordinary vagaries of human nature, the common disasters of plague, warfare and brigandage.

Unlike Tafur, eyeing the private parts of Greek women in the Constantinople baths and exciting his readers' imagination, most medieval travellers record their experiences to edify others. Those who record their visits to the Jewish shrines in the Land of Israel (Chapter 2) do so for the spiritual benefit of their successors. Hans Tucher (Chapter 10) aims to provide a guide for Christian pilgrims; Ludolf von Sudheim and Margery Kempe follow a tradition in which a clearly measured out and described account of the holy places becomes for the devout reader a virtual pilgrimage in itself. Reading and absorbing others' accounts of the world beyond home (even though we and Langland would call them 'untrue') gives them an imagined reality: in this way they endorse the truth and power of the Creator, with whom all things are possible.[16] This book examines the ways in which medieval travellers engaged with their world.

In 'The Impact of the crusades on western geographical knowledge' (Chapter 1), Bernard Hamilton provides an overview of the knowledge of the Middle East in the period after the seventh century. The rise of Islam prevented eastward travel but Arabs allowed pilgrims access to the Holy Land, and these pilgrims supplied information on the shrines in the Holy Land and on Egypt. Few left written records, however, and Africa and Asia were known of through late classical, romance and biblical accounts, partly fabulous. There were marvels in India according to Honorius Augustodunensis, writing in the early twelfth century of lands from Africa to Asia. More accurate knowledge of the Holy Land was available after the First Crusade; more pilgrims visited and described the shrines on the pilgrimage route. William of Tyre was born and died in the Crusader States, about which he supplied for his patron a detailed and widely circulated history, but he knew little of Asia. Burchard of Strasburg travelled from Cairo to Damascus as ambassador to Saladin in 1175–76, and reported on Muslim culture and the animals of Egypt. The legend of Prester John, an oriental Christian and supposed conqueror of the Persians, produced the hugely influential 'letter of Prester John' which told of the wonders of the East, using information from apocryphal, classical and perhaps oriental sources. Actual events in Africa and Asia were known to Muslim and Jewish travellers, but not available to readers outside those language communities. With the Muslim reconquest of the Crusader States in 1187 the pilgrim routes altered in the thirteenth century and more accounts of the area were written. Jacques de Vitry and Oliver of Paderborn, who took part in the thirteenth-century Fifth Crusade, brought knowledge of the Coptic Church and of Nubia and Ethiopia back to Rome, and Joinville, biographer of Louis IX, recorded a report of an expedition to find the source of the Nile (though his account of the Mongols in Asia was mixed fact and fantasy). Contact with Asia along the spice trade routes produced reports of Genghis (Chingiz) Khan in the west by 1219–21, though it was assumed that the Mongols were Christians until embassies by Dominican friars arrived. Vincent of Beauvais incorporated the resulting *History of the Mongols* in his *Speculum maius*. Franciscan missionaries to the Mongols included William of Rubruck, who found neither Prester John nor the monstrous creations of fable. Trade and clerical activity continued in Asia throughout the mid-thirteenth-century contest for power between Mongols and Mamluks, and the pagan (later Muslim-convert) Mongols in Persia restored access by Christians to India and even China by sea. By the end of the crusading era a factual account of Asia had been produced by Jordan Catalani, who describes Indian culture and reports at second hand on the flora and fauna as far east as Cambodia and the East Indies, relocating Prester John as King of Ethiopia and the monstrous races to the Horn of Africa. The Hereford *mappamundi* of *c.* 1300 locates them in India and Africa. The newly accurate information about Asia and Africa was put to the practical purpose of preparing (unrealised) plans for crusades in the fourteenth century.

Fantasy is absent from the factual narratives of Jewish travellers described by Elka Weber in Chapter 2. From Spain, France, Italy and Germany they travelled to the Land of Israel as pilgrims and traders, describing the holy shrines they visited, usually in Hebrew. They used their scriptures to interpret what they saw (as Anne Simon also demonstrates for the Christian pilgrims in Chapter 10). In the commandment of 538 BCE three or more annual visits to Jerusalem were required, but after its destruction in 70 CE, Byzantine rule, and later Muslim rule, permitted only one visit, to mourn that fall, for which a ritual developed. By the fifteenth century, Jews, Christians and Muslims travelled for their respective festivals in spring and early summer. Jewish pilgrimage was less on a set pattern than Christian: many visited the Patriarchs' graves, though Benjamin of Tudela in the late twelfth century also saw Christian and Muslim sites. Pilgrims had additional interests: Meshullam of Volterra may also have been on a business trip, and Isaac Chelo sought rare Hebrew books in Jerusalem. The Jewish pilgrim Jacob haCohen even quotes Pliny on crocodiles. Predecessors provide advice on the route to follow, and biblical events determine the sights to seek, which have intrinsic significance as a teaching aid, their ambiance created by use of Arabic terminology to engage reader response; the pilgrims' personal reactions are not explored. Genuine sites, some not shown to Christians, are sought out, even by the paradoxical expedient of disguise as Christian or Muslim. The importance of the sites is shown by God's miraculous interventions to protect them. Many Jewish holy sites were also venerated by Christians and Muslims; there was mutual tolerance of other faiths and admiration of their architecture.

Tolerance also marks the travel narratives in Shawkat Toorawa's account of medieval Islamic travelling scholars (Chapter 3), despite the personal and political dangers they faced. Toorawa extends the previously categorised forms of Islamic travel (for knowledge of Islamic traditions, pilgrimage to Mecca, exploration and trade) to include travel with or because of patrons and travel by non-Muslims in Islamic territory. Early travelling poets and court attendants initiated a system of patronage whereby scholars and writers travelled to seek patrons among caliphs, regional governors and wealthy people, who gained in prestige as patrons even if they were themselves illiterate. Poets moved to seek better takings, climates or political safety. The highly learned and hardworking 'Abd al-Latif travelled in his youth to obtain instruction and knowledge and in maturity to obtain or please patrons. His studies began with oral and written information and religious texts and extended to science, medicine and law, which he taught from dawn till dusk in Cairo, Damascus and Aleppo, pursuing his own studies and writing at night. He died in Baghdad at the age of sixty-nine. Toorawa concludes by proposing a taxonomy of medieval Islamic travel.

Niall Christie's Muslim traveller, Usamah Ibn Munqidh (1095–1188), of Bedouin origin, travelled widely throughout Egypt, Syria and the Holy Land (Chapter 4). Exiled from Syria, he went from Damascus to Egypt and back. He composed poetry now lost and collected an anthology of his poetry at the court of Qara-Arslan, and spent two years in Saladin's court. His remarkable propensity for getting himself embroiled in politics wherever he went gave him much experience of the invading *ifranj* and the Muslim rulers he served. He records in his 'memoirs', the *Kitab al-I'tibar*, his scornful impressions of the crusaders, their inadequate medicine and their dissolute womenfolk, and often misunderstands their humour. He describes his far more complimentary impressions of other women, including many, especially those in his house-hold, who are active in a variety of roles, supporting their sons and charges, asserting themselves politically, socially and in combat, preferring death to dishonour. The vigour of his style enhances the assertive roles of the many women he met on his travels.

Andrew Jotischky's travellers in the Islamic states (Chapter 5) are teachers like 'Abd al-Latif, but their aim is to convert. Franciscan and Dominican missionaries founded convents throughout the Near and Middle East and beyond. In the Crusader States they encountered Christians of other rites as well as Muslims, and extended their mission to them. Their experiences were recorded by their biographers and in their own accounts; some were martyred. One significant ministry was the visitation of Christian prisoners of war, and after the fall of Acre friars readily obtained travel permits from the Muslim authorities for the Jerusalem pilgrimage, but had to pay tolls to enter cities and visit shrines, and needed to avoid attacks by brigands and even their own guides. Writing in the second quarter of the fourteenth century, the Irishman Symon Semeonis, James of Verona and Niccolo da Poggibonsi furnish detailed accounts of differences they encounter in dress and religious practice from the 'norm' they know at home. They follow a tradition of reporting established in the twelfth century and adopt the papal practice of associating 'schismatic' Christians with Muslims: papal injunction requires the friars to preach to eastern-rite Christians as well as Muslims, though they themselves were more tolerant than the papal admonitions.

How the friars and other pilgrims reached the Holy Land, before full knowledge of Ptolemy's Almagest and Geography was regained, is the subject of Catherine Delano-Smith's 'The intelligent pilgrim' (Chapter 6). Biblical narrative provided a prospective pilgrim with an outline of what he would see, as it did for Weber's Jewish pilgrims. The medieval *mappaemundi* (unlike late Roman topographical maps) were not route plans. They were summaries of sacred history and Christian doctrine, which gained prominence as pilgrim numbers increased from the tenth century, and fell out of use by the late fifteenth century as increasing knowledge of the Far East made them too inaccurate. A *mappamundi* was a learned encyclopaedia for devotional reflection in closet or monastery, and contemplation of Jerusalem positioned at its centre might substitute for actual pilgrimage. Regional maps of Palestine, updated from travellers' and crusaders' reports, would serve a potential pilgrim better for locating places. Knowledge of Arabic texts had already enabled Roger Bacon to produce a superior world map constructed from tables of latitude and longitude, and the 'Anglo-Saxon' (or Cotton Tiberius) map (*c.* 1050) is based on a lost Roman map: it combines classical and Christian information. Sanudo's grid map of Palestine is considerably clearer than Burchard of Mount Sion's account and accompanying map in a later copy. Local plans of Jerusalem from the crusader period replace the stylised earlier plans in symmetrical circular form with pictures of the holy sites. Actual plans of the sites dated back to Adomnán and Bede in the seventh and eighth centuries, and later Christian and Muslim travellers carefully recorded measurements of the sites, with maps to aid future pilgrims. For the journey itself, however, not maps but group guides and written accounts were their route finders. Even mariners did not have Mediterranean charts before the early twelfth century: as late as 1483 Felix Fabri was amazed to see a portolan chart covered in rhumb lines.[17]

As Evelyn Edson shows in Chapter 7, in the fourteenth century, maps based on or influenced by portolan charts were produced in close collaboration between the Venetian Marino Sanudo and the Genoese mapmaker Pietro Vesconte, a collaboration so close that the extent of Sanudo's own contribution to the maps, particularly that of the Holy Land, is still uncertain. These maps aimed at physical accuracy and in some manuscripts were supplied with gridlines. They were not devotional aids like the *mappaemundi* nor guides for potential pilgrims, but were part of Sanudo's impressive plan to regain the Holy Land after the fall of Acre in 1291, presented to the Pope as 'two books', one of which may have contained the maps. According to the plan, supplies to Egypt would be cut off in a blockade of Alexandria by experienced mariners supplied with ships, food and materials. The regional maps of the Eastern Mediterranean are to aid the attacking forces. Thus, although the pictures in the Jerusalem city map illustrate Jesus's life, the water supplies of the city, vital in time of siege, are closely detailed. The inclusion of a world map sets the scene. Two manuscripts include marine charts identical to those made by Vesconte at other times. They are navigational aids for the crusade, giving distances and directions as Vegetius had advised in classical times. However, Sanudo's crusade campaign, fuelled by his religious fanaticism, and adapted to changing political circumstances, never bore fruit. He researched the depicted locations, and his distances were accurate, derived from portolan directions: the crusaders could have planned their route from these to minimise danger and achieve victory. Sanudo died still believing in his proposal.

Another form of travel which remained unrealised is represented in the travel accounts of the Far East. These include the *Itinerarius* of Johannes Witte de Hese,[18] and the famous *Book of Sir John Mandeville* discussed by Suzanne Conklin Akbari in Chapter 8. The author, writing in French *c.* 1360 and using the pseudonym 'Iohn Maundevylle, knight . . . of Seynt Albones', was an armchair traveller drawing on a variety of sources. Even more than Witte's book, *The Book of Sir John Mandeville* was instantly popular, and was translated, adapted and re-issued until the mid-seventeenth century, and unlike Witte's, Mandeville's *Book* remains popular as fantasising fraud. Akbari shows how the *Book* presents people 'on the edge' of humankind and of the *mappaemundi*. Bodily ideals are found in temperate zones, the monstrous races occur in climatic extremes, with a full range of human diversity in between. *The Book of Sir John Mandeville* presents 'a kind of virtual journey' which arouses the reader's wonder at the diversity within unity of God's creation. The *Mandeville*-author's classification of geographical, cultural and bodily difference constructs a balanced order of creation, following Pliny, rather than the theological explanation of 'monstrosity'. Bartholomaeus Anglicus in *De proprietatibus rerum* added an astronomical dimension to the medical opinion that the temperate body is the ideal, and favoured the northern climate; the *Mandeville*-author adopts Bartholomaeus's system of complementary opposites: heredity and climate determine physiology, as is seen in the contrast between western European and Indian physiques. Far from denigrating those 'on the margins', the *Mandeville*-author expresses wonder at the differences encountered in his 'virtual journey' eastwards. Amazement and puzzlement are compounded in his attitude, epitomised in his account of India, which he terms 'Albanye' because of the inhabitants' unexpected paleness. England is India's 'contrarie', and its lushness, complementary to the lush lands of 'Prester John', produces natural explorers who seek to dominate others. The *Mandeville*-author departs from his source, Friar Odoric of Pordenone's account written thirty-one years earlier, by viewing England

and India as microcosms of the world, producing a new opposition of north-west/south-east, and thus the Orient replaces the south as the extreme of heat. England, seen as the epitome of normality, makes the world-view Anglo-centric from an extra-terrestrial vantage point where the 'traveller' is both a close eyewitness and a distant assessor of terrestrial diversity.

Although some claim that Margery Kempe was another armchair traveller, Rosalynn Voaden sees her in Chapter 9 as indeed adopting the spiritual discipline of pilgrimage, inspired by narratives of Christ's life and the allure of travel drawn from her location in Lynn (King's Lynn) on the Norfolk coast. At home and on the travels which formed her as a holy woman Margery was vilified, especially for her loud 'roaring' grief at Christ's passion. Her various pilgrimages and the new religious ideas entering England from northern Europe through the port of Lynn give Margery's spirituality a con-tinental basis. Unlike the friars and Jewish pilgrims to Jerusalem, Margery as a woman of forty ran additional physical as well as financial risks in travelling so far. Her role model, Birgitta (Bridget) of Sweden, went there in her late sixties. After travelling from the Netherlands and apparently, and without comment, crossing the Alps in winter, Margery took ship at Venice for Jaffa. On this outward journey she may have learned of the Beguines of Liège and Marie of Oignies, and on her return via Assisi she may have heard of Angela of Foligno. But Margery entirely avoids the sin of *curiositas*, and does not describe the world she traverses: suffering, not scenery, is her narrative. Unlike Marco Polo and the *Mandeville*-author, she places herself strongly before the reader, filtering her experience of the Holy Land through her emotional responses to the sites. Her return home is unremarked – there was no literary model for this, nor for her later travels in northern Europe in 1433. For these later travels we have authentic-sounding details of the experi-ences of the now sixty-year-old Margery, short of money, injured and without a clear destination. She did visit two shrines, but the focus of the pilgrimage was Margery herself and her persecutions. She often travelled alone. On her return, she dictated her *Book*; its shape and her self-presentation throughout was largely formed on her northern pilgrimage experience.

Hans Tucher, one of two pilgrims leaving the north for the Holy Land in Anne Simon's account (Chapter 10), also records his own reactions, notably his responses to the Other. Ludolf von Sudheim in Westphalia and the nobleman Hans Tucher of Nuremberg wrote in the fourteenth and fifteenth centuries respectively. Both were impressed by the stench of the Dead Sea, though their record of this unhappy experience is derivative on earlier accounts, and Tucher himself echoes Ludolf closely. Like many western pilgrims, they view landscape through Bible narrative, but both also observe the societies they encounter. Ludolf travelled between 1336 and 1341 and his Latin account, first published around 1468, is the earliest pilgrimage report printed in Germany; it became very popular. Like Sanudo, Ludolf hints that the Holy Land should be regained through a crusade. He uses written and oral sources which he regards as reliable and outlines the procedures for going on pilgrimage, from obtaining papal permission to possible routes and attendant risks; the trials of pilgrimage enact a form of *imitatio Christi*. The point of departure, unusually, seems to be Genoa rather than Venice, and Ludolf's route jumps from Alexandria to Tripoli and back down the coast to Cairo via Bethlehem and Jerusalem, an uncommon route dictated by the destruction of Jaffa, but which nevertheless recalls to readers both Old and New Testaments. Ludolf's description of the Jerusalem shrines echoes the history of salvation from Abraham to Judgement Day. This route is encyclo-paedic rather than a prescription for travel, though Ludolf describes the elite classes on Cyprus and disastrous wranglings in Acre, and is aware of the trade routes from India. Besides classical authors, he uses sailors' accounts. This digest of information includes miracles and fabulous beasts and is not coloured by subjective response; unlike Margery's, Ludolf's focus is the land-scape that validates the biblical past, which the reader will then invest with pious devotion. Despite his interest in the crusades, he is tolerant of Muslim belief. Hans Tucher spent ten months from 1479 to 1480 on pilgrimage to the Holy Land with Siebald Rieter; his very popular account was first printed in 1482. It is in two parts, covering the trip to Jerusalem followed by an account of the desert of Sinai and Cairo, with historical and practical information, derived from both earlier sources and oral report. Unlike the Spaniard Tafur, he structures his account round specific dates.

Completing the survey of travellers bound for the East, Barry Taylor in Chapter 11 looks at four journeys (two beyond the Holy Land) undertaken by Spanish travellers. Clavijo travelled from 1403 to 1406 in an embassy to Tamerlane's court in Samarkand and wrote, or collaborated in, a narrative of the long journey. Thirty years later, Pero Tafur travelled via Rome and Venice to Jerusalem and Egypt, returning via Constantinople, Venice, Germany, Poland and Hungary, reaching Sardinia (where the extant account ends) in 1439. His aim was to acquire knightly prowess by learning of other states. Less familiar are Tarifa and Encina, pilgrims who travelled independently to Jerusalem in 1518–20 and 1519 respectively, joining company in Venice. All four travellers visited Venice, about which Tafur wrote a long account, while the court poet Encina described its wonders in his *Tribagia*, a narrative of his voyage in *arte mayor* metre.[19] Tafur's narrative survives in a single incomplete manuscript, but the other three accounts each survive in more than one manuscript, and Tarifa's and Encina's were printed in 1521. Tafur's anecdotal narrative is the most subjective of the four. All four refer to Christian relics, and both Clavijo and Tafur recount the political history of the states they visit. Even Clavijo includes marvels and the monstrous races, however, and is naively surprised at many of the sites he actually observes. Tarifa is more discerning, and attributes information about marvels to a traveller's report. Unlike Egeria long before (and Ludolf nearly a century earlier), Encina observes directly and does not see the landscape as corroboration of biblical history. He is severely critical of extortionate traders, of the state of buildings and of eastern-rite religion, and includes a poem to the Pope urging renewed crusade. Clavijo maintains a diplomatic objectivity. All four travellers write in diary form. All indicate spatial measurement, referring to famous European buildings for comparison. These writers are aware of classical models and earlier travel writings but provide eyewitness accounts which include dress, marital customs and exotic (but real) animals. All travelled with a practical objective which they accomplished, but they returned home unchanged by their travels.

## NOTES

1 William Langland, *Will's Visions of Piers Plowman, Do-Well, Do-Better and Do-Best*, ed. George Kane and E. Talbot Donaldson (London: Athlone Press, 1975).

2 Hakluyt believed, in contradistinction to his own editorial practice, that travel accounts should consist of the travellers' own testimony, eyewitness accounts; distinguishing fact from fiction in the sixteenth century 'was made much more difficult by the *topos* of the claim to empirical truthfulness so crucial to travel stories of all kinds, both factual and fictional' (Peter Hulme and Tim Youngs, introduction to Peter Hulme and Tim Youngs (eds), *The Cambridge Companion to Travel Writing* (Cambridge: Cambridge University Press, 2002), pp. 3–4.

3 The medieval belief in religious miracle and secular (but God-created) marvel developed from the seventeenth century in Europe into the 'curiosity' cabinets and rooms; the motive of the collectors was understanding and ordering the universe. See Patrick Mauriès, *Cabinets of Curiosities* (London: Thames and Hudson, 2002).

4 Information which was beginning to be recorded from the fourteenth century or earlier on the portolan charts discussed by Evelyn Edson in Chapter 7.

5 For largely eyewitness guides to the Holy Land (and other eastbound travel material in Middle English) see Christian K. Zacher, 'Travel and geographical writings', in A. E. Hartung (gen. ed.), *A Manual of the Writings in Middle English, 1050–1500*, 4 (New Haven, CT: Academy of Arts and Sciences, 1967–), vii (1986), xix, pp. 2235–54: items 6, 'Advice for eastbound travellers'; 9, 'Purchas's pilgrim itinerary'; 10, 'The way unto Rome . . . and to Jerusalem'; 13, 'The itineraries of William Wey'; 14, 'The stations of Jerusalem' (much used in 17, 'Information for pilgrims'); 20, 'The pilgrimage of Sir Richard Guylford' (adapted in 21, 'The pilgrimage of Sir Richard Torkington').

6 'The Middle East/Arabia; "the cradle of Islam"', in Hulme and Young (eds), *The Cambridge Companion to Travel Writing*, pp. 107–21.

7 Marcus Bull, 'Origins', Chap. 2 of Jonathan Riley-Smith (ed.), *The Oxford Illustrated History of the Crusades* (Oxford: Oxford University Press, 1995), pp. 13–33, at pp. 25, 36–7.

8 Marco Polo, *The Travels of Marco Polo*, trans. Ronald Latham (Harmondsworth: Penguin Books, 1958).

9 Brendan's 'travels' were probably composed before 1000 CE and recounted by Irish missionaries who drew on the missionary activities of St Columba and on folktale

sources from many cultures (W. R. J. Barron and Glyn S. Burgess (eds), *The Voyage of Saint Brendan: Representative Versions of the Legend in English Translation* (Exeter: University of Exeter Press, 2002), pp. 1–2. Barry Cunliffe makes a case for Pytheas's account (*c.* 320 BCE) as the earliest narrative of Atlantic travel as far as Iceland (Thule) (*The Extraordinary Voyage of Pytheas the Greek: The Man who Discovered Britain* (London: Allen Lane, 2001)). Westward exploration was probably being conducted by merchants from Bristol from the early fifteenth century at least, motivated by their existing trade with Portugal and Iceland; records of their discoveries are scanty, however, before the end of the century (Zacher, 'Travel and geographical writings', p. 2248).

10 The author of *The Book of John Mandeville* also claims world centrality for Jerusalem. As Iain Higgins shows, this notion derived ultimately from a biblical gloss by Jerome but gained in popularity from the First Crusade until scholars began adopting Ptolemaic geography in the fifteenth century (Iain MacLeod Higgins, 'Defining the earth's center in a medieval "multi-text": Jerusalem in *The Book of John Mandeville*', in Sylvia Tomasch and Sealy Giles (eds), *Text and Territory: Geographical Imagination in the European Middle Ages* (Pennsylvania: University of Philadelphia Press, 1998), pp. 29–53.

11 Francesco di Balduccio Pegolotti, *La pratica della mercatura*, cited in Robert S. Lopez and Irving W. Raymond, *Medieval Trade in the Mediterranean World: Illustrative Documents Translated with Introductions and Notes* (London: Oxford University Press, 1955), pp. 357–8. My thanks to Jonathan Wooding for this reference.

12 British Foreign Office guidelines, reported in *The Times* (1 May 2003).

13 If travel itself seems to have had a negative influence on the mindset, its effect on the contemporary imagination was profound: both *The Book of Marco Polo* and *The Book of John Mandeville* were used by fourteenth- and fifteenth-century romance writers. Moreover, as Jennifer Goodman shows, there was a two-way influence, since exploration itself is 'a natural outgrowth of the medieval "cult of knight-errantry" ' with an 'interplay between fiction and historical narrative' (*Chivalry and Exploration, 1298– 1630* (Woodbridge: Boydell Press, 1998), esp. pp. 6, 23, 45). Goodman's study illustrates in detail how medieval exploration narratives, including Rustichello da Pisa's *Book of Marco Polo* (quoted *ibid.*, pp. 83–103), are structured on romance motifs.

14 To have examined too closely other places and lifestyles would have constituted the sin of *curiositas*, the desire to know for the sake of self-advancement (see Rosalynn Voaden in Chapter 9). Even in the eighteenth century, 'curiosity' was an unstable term, connoting variously 'the wonder aroused by distant lands' on a proprietorial or on a commercial basis, and the means to 'philosophical articulation of "foreign" singularities'; only this last would have constituted *sapientia* (wisdom) in medieval theory. (See Nigel Leaske, *Curiosity and the Aesthetics of Travel Writing, 1770–1840* (Oxford: Oxford University Press, 2001), reviewed by David Womersley, *Times Literary Supplement* (19 July 2002).)

15 Marcus Bull, 'Origins', p. 17.

16 'The *Mandeville*-author offers his audience a final, reassuring account of the Christian God's mysterious omnipotence': Iain Higgins, 'Imagining Christendom from Jerusalem to Paradise: Asia in *Mandeville's Travels*', in Scott D. Westrem (ed.), *Discovering New Worlds: Essays on Medieval Exploration and Imagination* (New York and London: Garland Publishing, 1991), pp. 91–114.

17 Richard Pflederer discusses the portolan charts and their use in 'Portolan charts: Vital tool in the age of discovery', *History Today*, 52:5 (May 2002), 20–7.

18 Edited, translated and discussed by Scott D. Westrem, *Broader Horizons: A Study of Johannes Witte de Hese's* Itinerarius *and Medieval Travel Narratives* (Cambridge, MA:

The Medieval Academy of America, 2001). Westrem comments that Witte, like Marco Polo and John of Plano Carpini, is 'a narrator given more to observation than self-reference', and, like the *Mandeville*-author, writes not from experience but from a variety of literary works (*ibid.*, p. 39), which include 'The letter of Prester John' and the St Brendan legend; 'Mandeville' was a master compiler (*ibid.*, p. 38). As Westrem notes elsewhere, Sanudo and Ludolf von Suchem [Sudheim] also 'lifted' passages, from Burchard of Mount Sion and William of Boldensele respectively, 'but no one has questioned the integrity of their accounts' ('A medieval travel book's editors and translators: Managing style and accommodating dialect in Johannes Witte de Hese's *Itinerarius*', in Roger Ellis and Ruth Evans (eds), *The Medieval Translator*, 4 (Exeter: University of Exeter Press, 1994), pp. 153–80, at p. 174 n. 7).

19 Venice also impressed the English travellers Richard Guylforde and Robert Langton (Zacher, 'Travel and geographical writings', pp. 2252–3).

# 1

## The impact of the crusades on western geographical knowledge

**( )**

### Bernard Hamilton

ALTHOUGH IT IS sometimes said that in western Europe before 1100 knowledge of a wider world was derived from ancient sources imperfectly known and uncritically used, such a view is misleading. Adam of Bremen, for example, included a full description of the lands in the north Atlantic recently settled by the Vikings in the history of his archbishopric completed in 1075.[1] It was more difficult for people in the West to gain up-to-date information about Africa and Asia after the foundation of the Arab Empire in the seventh century. Although intermittent trade contacts were maintained, the Arab authorities seldom allowed western merchants to travel beyond the Mediterranean ports; but an exception was made in the case of pilgrims to the Holy Land, for the Muslims understood the concept of pilgrimage, which occupied a central place in their own faith.[2] Western scholars were interested in the information which pilgrims like the Irish monk Fidelis gave about Egypt, through which he travelled to Jerusalem in *c.* 762–65,[3] as well as in the very detailed information which Bishop Arculf gave about the shrines of the Holy Land under Muslim rule in the years 679–88.[4] It was, of course, a matter of chance whether such experiences were recorded; the monk John of Montecassino spent several years in the Mount Sinai monastery in the tenth century, before returning to become abbot, but did not leave any description of his travels in the East.[5] Moreover, although there was a great increase in western pilgrimage to Jerusalem after 950, none of the participants wrote a full account of what they saw.[6]

But if accounts of the Holy Land available in the eleventh-century West were fragmentary or out of date, there was no recent information at all about the rest of Asia and Africa. Western scholars still relied on the accounts given by writers such as Pliny the Elder (d. 79 CE), the Church historian Orosius (*fl.* 417) and the encyclopaedist St Isidore of Seville (d. 636), augmented by the mixture of fact and fable in the description of men and of animals given by Solinus (*fl.* 238 CE). These sources were augmented by the accounts of the marvels of Asia contained in the Romance of Alexander the Great, of which various versions circulated in the West, derived from the translation made in 936 by the archpriest Leo of Naples of the Greek text of pseudo-Callisthenes.[7]

Western people had no empirical means of evaluating these sources because they could not visit the regions which they described. Yet as Charles Beckingham has rightly commented: 'It is in fact easy and often tempting to underestimate geographical knowledge in medieval Europe . . . The blemish in so many medieval geographical works . . . is that reliable information is mingled with the utterly fabulous.'[8]

Thus Erathosthenes's calculation that the circumference of the earth was *c.* 25,000 miles (252,000 *stadia*) was quite widely known in the medieval West through Macrobius's *Commentary on the Dream of Scipio* (*c.* 400 CE),[9] while Pliny's assertion that all the water systems of the world were interconnected by a network of underground channels was also generally accepted.[10]

Medieval scholars accepted the Bible as authoritative, but its geographical data did not conflict with their other sources of knowledge. There was no agreement about the location of the Garden of Eden, except that it was inaccessible to men, though many scholars thought it was in the extreme east. According to Genesis four great rivers had their source there: the Tigris, the Euphrates, the Gihon (universally identified with the Nile) and the Phison (often identified with the Ganges). It was congruent with accepted scientific opinion that the four rivers of Paradise could run underground from wherever Eden might be and emerge in widely different places.[11]

The picture of Asia and Africa prevalent in the West in *c.* 1100 is exemplified in the *De imagine mundi* of Honorius Augustodunensis. The river Don marked the boundary between Europe and Asia, the Nile that between Asia and Africa. Asia was divided by a series of mountain ranges which stretched from the Black Sea to the eastern ocean. Scythia and the mountains of the Hyperboreans, Bactria where Alexander had campaigned and the land of Seres from whence silk came, all lay to the north of these ranges. South-west Asia consisted of the Greek lands of Asia Minor, Syria, the Holy Land, and Arabia, the source of incense, Mesopotamia, where the ruins of the Tower of Babel stood, Georgia and Armenia, where Noah's Ark had come to rest on Mount Ararat. Further east was Persia, the home of magic, beyond which was India with its two great rivers; the Indus in the west and the Ganges which flowed eastwards into the outer ocean. The Indian Ocean was bounded by Africa, not only to the west, but also to the south; it contained many islands including Taprobane (Sri Lanka), which was densely populated, and the uninhabited isles of gold and silver where mountains of precious metal were guarded by dragons and gryphons.

Honorius described Egypt and the north African coast very briefly but reasonably accurately, but knew very little about the rest of the continent. The Atlas mountains were in southern Morocco and beyond them lay the two Ethiopias, one to the south of Egypt, the other in the extreme west, bordering on the Atlantic. The Nile was thought to rise in the west, to the south of the Atlas, and flow towards the east for hundreds of miles before going underground again and emerging near the Red Sea to circle eastern Ethiopia before turning north and flowing through Egypt to the delta. The Nile had been, it would seem, conflated with the Niger, reports of which must have reached the Mediterranean.

Africa and Asia were indeed lands full of marvels. Eels 100 metres long swam in the Ganges, while the tortoises of the Indian Ocean were so huge that one of their carapaces might be used to make a spacious dwelling. The traveller might meet Cynocephali, men with dogs' heads, or Sciapods, who had only one large foot which at need they might use as a parasol. There were also unusual forms of wildlife such as the Monoceros, which had the head of a stag, the body of a horse and the feet of an elephant. It was armed with a single very long horn; it howled horribly, was extremely fierce, and transfixed anyone who stood in its path.[12]

By the time Honorius had completed the first version of his text in 1110, an arc of territory stretching from northern Mesopotamia to the Sinai peninsula had come under western rule through the success of the First Crusade (1095–99) (see Figure 1). Consequently huge numbers of western pilgrims came to the Holy Land each year, and some of them wrote accounts of what they saw there. Although at first they tended to rely heavily on earlier authorities,[13] some of them were concerned to emphasise how up-to-date their own knowledge of the holy places was.[14] Some accounts were designed to be read by people living in the West; John of Würzburg, who visited Jerusalem in c. 1170, dedicated his narrative to his friend Dietrich and added: 'I have paid particular attention to the Holy City, Jerusalem, in order to describe all the facts about it in detail . . . if you . . . are not going physically to see them you will have greater love of them and their holiness by reading this book.'[15] In this way accurate information about the contemporary state of the Holy Land became widely available to people in western Europe. Nevertheless, such reports were limited, for, as John Wilkinson has pointed out, most pilgrims followed set itineraries. None of them is known to have visited Caesarea Philippi, for example, when it was in crusader control from 1140 to 1164, despite its important associations with the life of Christ (Matthew 16:13–20), and the pilgrim guides have little to say about sacred sites outside the Holy Land such as Antioch, where Jesus's followers were first called Christians (Acts 11:26).[16]

Information about other places in the Crusader States reached the west through the writings of historians who lived there, the most important of

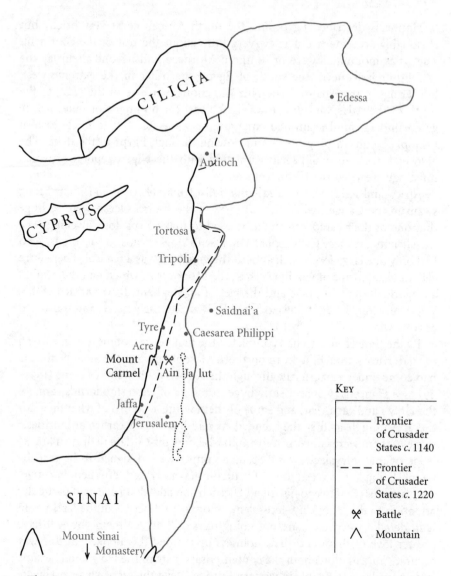

1 The Crusader States. Edessa is now Urfa; Antioch is now Antakya; Tortosa is now Tartus; Tyre is now Sur; Acre is now Akko; Caesarea Philippi is now Baniyas. Other names remain the same. Saidnai'a is a few miles north of Damascus.

whom was William of Tyre. He was born in Jerusalem in *c.* 1130, studied in the schools of Italy and Paris and returned in 1165 to the East, where King Amalric commissioned him to write a history of the Crusader States. He later became Chancellor of the kingdom and Archbishop of Tyre, and died in 1186.[17] He gave a long description of Edessa, for example, held by the crusaders from 1098 to 1144. It had important religious associations; it had formerly been called Rages and was mentioned in the book of Tobit (Tobit 1:14); Christ himself had written a letter to King Abgar of Edessa, as the church historian Eusebius records, the Apostle Thaddeus had preached there, and the inhabitants had all remained Christian since that time.[18]

William also gave good accounts of some places which had remained under Muslim rule, such as Damascus, which he describes as standing in the midst of green meadows and orchards through which abundant waters flow in ancient irrigation channels drawn from the nearby river.[19] He was particularly well informed about Lower Egypt, where his patron, King Amalric, had campaigned several times in the 1160s. He explained how the Fatimid caliph Meezedinall (Muizz li-Din Allah) had made Cairo his capital in 969 CE, and he gives what is, I believe, the only detailed western account of the Fatimid court when he describes the meeting between the ambassadors from Jerusalem, Hugh of Caesarea and Geoffrey Fulcher, a Templar knight, with the Caliph al-Adid in 1167.[20] William had little to say about more distant Islamic cities like Baghdad (which he called Baldac), though it is possible that he wrote more about them in his *History of the Oriental Princes* – which has not been preserved.[21]

William seems to have known almost nothing about the lands beyond the Islamic territories. He thought that Egypt was bounded to the south by Ethiopia, by which he seems to have meant Saharan Africa.[22] The only other current information that he gives is that spices, pearls and other eastern luxury goods from Arabia, Saba, both Ethiopias, Persia and both Indias reach Upper Egypt through the port of Aidabh on the Red Sea and are then taken down the Nile to Alexandria.[23]

William wrote in Latin, but his work reached a large audience in western Europe because it was translated into Old French in the early thirteenth century as the *Estoire d'Eracles*, which was widely read.[24]

A contemporary of William's, Burchard, Provost of Strasburg, was sent by the western Emperor Frederick Barbarossa as ambassador to Saladin in 1175–76. He visited Alexandria and Cairo, and then travelled overland to Damascus, and in his report he detailed not merely the topography of these regions but the way of life of the people who lived there. He noted how Muslim men prayed five times a day and the ritual ablutions they performed, how Muslim women were veiled in public and how great ladies lived in harems guarded by eunuchs. He also remarked on how the Nile not only contained innumerable crocodiles but 'nutrit equos indomitos sub aqua latitantes et sepe foras egredientes' ('is home to wild horses which hide beneath the waters and often emerge from them') – that is, hippopotamuses.[25]

Burchard is the first western writer to mention Nubia: 'Item in Nubia psitaci abundant, qui veniunt de Nubia. Distat autem Nubia a Babylonia per viginti dietas, et est terra christiana, habens regem sed populus eius incultus est et terra silvestris.'[26] ('There are many parrots in Egypt which come from Nubia. Nubia is twenty days' journey from Cairo and is a Christian land with its own king, but its people are uncivilised and the land is uncultivated.') There were two Christian Nubian kingdoms at that time. Burchard was presumably referring to Makuria, which bordered Egypt, but beyond that was Alwa, with its capital at Soba on the Blue Nile. These societies were far from barbarous: they were defended by well-built fortresses and full of churches and monasteries decorated with vivid frescoes, in which the Greek liturgy was sung.[27]

There was considerable interest in western Europe in the presence of Christians in the lands beyond Islam. When in 1122 a Bishop John, who claimed to come from India, visited the papal court and described the wealth of his Christian kingdom, watered by the Phison, which brought down jewels from the earthly Paradise, and blessed by the thaumaturgic relics of St Thomas the Apostle, his account was widely circulated despite the scepticism of Calixtus II.[28]

The Franks in the Crusader States were aware that there were independent Christian states in Asia, because pilgrims came to Jerusalem from all the oriental churches.[29] The crusader princes of Antioch did establish contact with King David III of Georgia (1089–1125) when he attacked the Saljuq rulers of northern Syria.[30] This interest in finding eastern Christian allies, which existed both in the Crusader States and in western Europe, gave credence to the legend of Prester John.

He is first mentioned in the universal history which Otto of Freising, the half-brother of Emperor Frederick Barbarossa, completed in 1147. Two years before, Otto had met Bishop Hugh of Jabala in the principality of Antioch at the papal court, who told him how a few years earlier John, Priest and King, known as Prester John ('presbyter Iohannes'), a Nestorian Christian ruler living in the Far East beyond Armenia and Persia, had defeated the rulers of Persia in battle. The Priest King was very rich and had an emerald sceptre, and he was said to be descended from the Magi who had come to worship the infant Christ. The factual basis of this story was an attack by the Kara-Khitai, some of whom were Nestorian Christians, on the lands of the Saljuq sultan Sinjar situated beyond the river Oxus, but Hugh of course was not aware of this.[31]

In c. 1165 a letter purporting to be written by Prester John began to circulate in western Europe in a Latin text. The Priest King claimed to rule in all three Indies, to have a vast army recruited from his seventy-two provinces, and to count among his subjects giants forty cubits tall, satyrs, Amazons, pygmies and dog-headed Cynocephali as well as the Ten Lost Tribes of Israel. He had an elaborate mirror in the courtyard of his palace which enabled him to see everything that was happening in his dominions. Among the many marvels of his kingdom was the Fountain of Youth; this did not confer immortality but ensured that those who drank from it would enjoy perfect health and look as though they were thirty-two for the rest of their lives. The authorship and purpose of this letter remain controversial, but it clearly incorporates material about the wonders of the East drawn from the apocryphal Acts of St Thomas, the work of Solinus and the Alexander Romance, and it may also have drawn on some oriental sources.[32]

The letter was immensely popular. It was translated into most western European languages and successive copyists added fresh material to the catalogue of marvels it contained.[33] It met a two-fold need: it fuelled popular imagination with extravagant stories of the fabulous East, but it also encouraged western people to hope that a powerful Christian ally might help them against the resurgent forces of Islam.

A reasonably accurate and detailed account of the topography of Asia and Africa was made by the Spanish Muslim scholar al-Idrisi for King Roger II of Sicily (r. 1130–54), but because it was written in Arabic it was little read outside the Sicilian court, and it is difficult to determine what indirect impact it may have had on western geographical awareness. The *Itinerary* of the rabbi Benjamin of Tudela, who travelled extensively in the Near East in *c.* 1159–73, reaching Egypt and Baghdad, was not read at all outside the Jewish community because it was written in Hebrew.[34]

Because of what were effectively cultural limitations most educated western people in the twelfth century were ignorant of what was happening in most of Africa and Asia. Richard of Poitou, a monk at Cluny, exemplifies this. He concludes his world chronicle:

> De rege autem de Marroch ... et de rege Bugie et de rege Numidie et Libie et Cyrene et de rege Ethiopum tam rara et tam pauca audivimus quod fere prorsus ignoramus quid ibi agatur ... Similiter autem et de soldano Persidis propter terre longinquitatem et alienationem christianitatis et linguam pauca novimus; preter quod dicunt, ultra Perses et Medos et Macedones christianos reges esse ... Illi autem valde vexant gentiles regionum illarum. Rex quoque de Avesguia et rex Nubianorum, sicut audivimus, hoc idem faciunt ... Is status erat rebus humanis anno ab Incarnato Verbo 1172.[35]

> (Concerning the king of Morocco ... and the King of Bugia and the King of Numidia and Libya and Cyrene and the King of the Ethiopians we have heard so few things and so seldom that we are almost completely ignorant of what is happening there ... Similarly we know very little about the Sultan of Persia because his land is very distant, and is cut off from us by language and religion, though they do say that there are Christian kings beyond the lands of the Medes and Persians and the Macedonians ... They strongly attack the pagan nations in those parts. We have also heard that the King of Georgia and the King of the Nubians do the same ... This was the state of human affairs in the year 1172 of the Incarnate Word.)

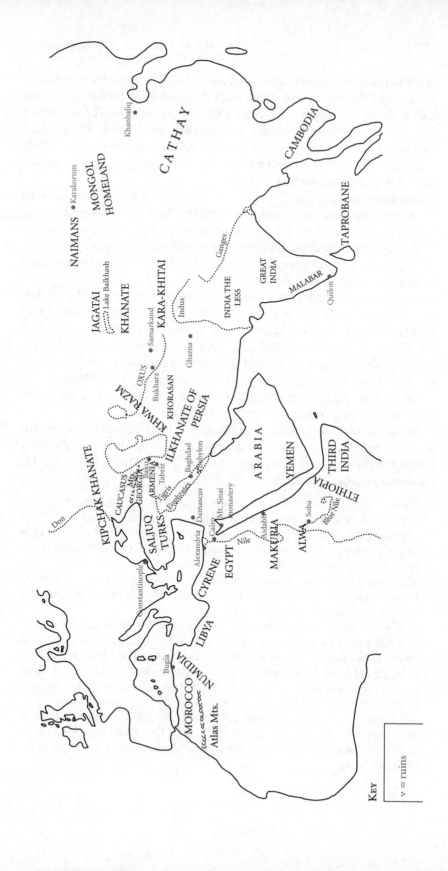

In 1187 Saladin defeated the Frankish army and conquered most of the Crusader States, and the Third Crusade succeeded in 1192 only in negotiating the return to Frankish rule of a strip of coastal territory from Jaffa to Antioch. Although the frontier sometimes changed, these lands remained the nucleus of Frankish power throughout much of the thirteenth century (see Figure 2).

Western pilgrims continued to come to the Crusader States in large numbers, but there was a shift in the itineraries they followed. The new capital, Acre, occupied a central place because the papacy gave many of its churches special religious privileges.[36] Among other new focuses of devotion were the Church of Our Lady of Tortosa and Mount Carmel, where an order of Latin hermits had recently become established.[37] Pilgrims who wished to visit Jerusalem had to obtain a papal dispensation to live in Muslim territory.[38] Some of those who did so also visited the Orthodox shrine of Saidnai'a near Damascus, which had a miracle-working icon of Our Lady revered both by Muslims and Christians.[39] Some thirteenth-century pilgrims wrote accounts of their travels, so that people in the West were kept informed about the state of the Holy Land and the surrounding regions.[40]

After 1192 neither the Franks in the East nor the papacy were resigned to the loss of Jerusalem, and began to look for eastern Christian allies. Celestine III (1191–98) successfully negotiated the union of the Armenian Church with Rome, hoping in this way to strengthen the western alliance with Leo II of Cilicia, while Innocent III established diplomatic contact with King George IV of Georgia in 1211.[41]

This concern to find eastern Christian allies was shared by some of the churchmen who took part in the Fifth Crusade and therefore lived in Egypt from 1218 to 1221. They presumably learned about the kingdoms of Nubia and Ethiopia from talking to Copts, who formed the main Christian community in Egypt, for the Coptic Patriarch was recognised as head also of the Nubian and Ethiopian churches. Although the West already knew a little about Nubia it knew nothing about the present state of Ethiopia. Ethiopia had been converted to Christianity in the reign of King Ezana (325–52), and this was known to some western scholars from Rufinus's History of the Church, but little was (or is) known about events there between c. 700 and 1150. This period of obscurity was brought to an end by the vigorous rule of King Lalibela (1172–1212), who impressed the Egyptians by sending an embassy

facing] 2 The wider world in the age of the crusades. Bugia is now Bejaia; Aidabh is now Aydhab; Constantinople is now Istanbul; Ghazna is now Ghazni; Khanbaliq is now Beijing; Taprobane is now Sri Lanka. Seba is on the Blue Nile, not far from Khartoum, but now a ruin. Babylon was ruined even at the time of the crusades. Karakorum, capital of the Mongol Empire, was south of Lake Baikal.

to Cairo in 1209, bringing a crown of pure gold for the Coptic Patriarch and an elephant, a giraffe, a hyena and a wild ass for the sultan.[42]

Jacques de Vitry, Bishop of Acre, who took part in the Fifth Crusade, included a section about the Coptic Church in his *Historia Orientalis*, saying that, while some Copts live under Muslim rule, 'alii autem proprias absque infidelium consortio occupaverunt regiones: scilicet Nubiam, quae contermina est Aegypto, et magnam Aethiopiae partem et omnes regiones usque in Indiam, plus quam quadraginta regna, ut asserunt, continentes.'[43] ('But others live in their own lands where there are no infidels: that is true of Nubia, which borders on Egypt, and of a great part of Ethiopia and of all the regions as far as India which are made up, so it is said, of more than forty kingdoms.') By India Jacques means the Third India, the Horn of Africa, the point of departure for the sea crossing to the Indian sub-continent.[44]

Oliver, head of the cathedral school of Paderborn, who had also taken part in the Fifth Crusade and wrote a history of it, also described the Nubians and Ethiopians who belonged to the Coptic Church and lived, he thought, beyond Leemania (i.e. the Yemen).[45] Both Jacques de Vitry and Oliver of Paderborn were later made cardinals, so their knowledge of the independent Christian kingdoms of Africa was thus available to the Roman curia.[46]

In 1249–50 Louis IX of France also campaigned in Egypt at the head of a crusade. His biographer, John of Joinville, says nothing about Ethiopia and Nubia, but gives an account, presumably told him by an Egyptian, about an expedition sent by a sultan to find the source of the Nile: 'They reported that they had explored the river and had reached a high mass of precipitous rocks which it was impossible to climb. The source of the river was in this cliff. There seemed to be a great profusion of trees on the mountain above, and they said that they found marvellous wild animals of different kinds, lions and snakes and elephants which came and watched them from the river bank while they ascended the stream.' This bears a considerable resemblance to modern descriptions of the headwaters of the Blue Nile, which descends through impenetrable gorges from Lake Tana.[47]

But although more became known about the interior of Africa in thirteenth-century western Europe, that knowledge remained second-hand. So far as I know, no western traveller reached Nubia then, and once Makuria had come under the suzerainty of the Mamluk sultans of Egypt towards the end of the thirteenth century it ceased to be a potential ally for the western powers.[48] Although the West would have liked to make contact with the King of Ethiopia, it could find no means of doing so until an embassy from King Wedem Ar'ad reached Europe in *c.* 1310.[49]

Western contacts with Asia in the thirteenth century followed a very different pattern. In 1220 Prince Bohemond IV of Antioch received from spice merchants coming from the East a report written in Arabic about the activities of King David, reputed to be Prester John's great-grandson. Bohemond sent a copy to Jacques de Vitry, who was with the Fifth Crusade in Egypt, and who had a Latin translation made of it. The *Relatio de Davide* tells how King David had attacked the Great King of Persia and captured Bukhara, Samarkand, Ghazna and Khurasan among other places. As Jean Richard has shown, this is an early and independent account of the campaigns of Genghis Khan and the Mongols against the lands of the Khwarazm Shah in 1219–21. This text received wide publicity since Jacques sent copies to Pope Honorius III, Leopold Duke of Austria and the Chancellor of the University of Paris, as well as to various friends.[50]

By 1245, when Innocent IV was planning a new crusade, he was aware that the Mongols were not the Christian subjects of Prester John. By that time the Mongol Empire stretched from China to Russia, and in south-west Asia included northern Persia, the Caucasus region and the Turkish lands of Asia Minor. The West did not know very much about them and the Pope therefore sent a number of embassies to the Mongol leaders which were, in effect, fact-finding missions. Two of them were directed to the Mongols in western Asia, and both were led by Dominican friars. Andrew of Longjumeau's party reached Tabriz and held discussions with Simeon Rabban-Ata, a Nestorian monk who had been a religious advisor of the Great Khan Ogedai (r. 1227–41).[51] The other mission, led by Friar Ascelin, met with Baiju, the Mongol commander in south-western Asia; though it was a diplomatic failure, this mission achieved its objective in terms of fact-finding. Simon of St Quentin, one of Ascelin's companions, wrote a *History of the Mongols* which gave an account, based on the evidence of eyewitnesses, of how they had conquered south-west Asia, and Simon also described the appearance, characteristics and social organisation of the Mongols on the basis of on his own observation. His work became available to western scholars because many passages from it were incorporated by Vincent of Beauvais in his great encyclopaedia, the *Speculum maius*, completed c. 1259.[52]

Andrew of Longjumeau joined St Louis when he came to Cyprus on crusade in 1248, and was sent by the king on a fresh embassy to the Mongols. There was an interregnum and Andrew travelled to Lake Balkash where he met the regent, Oghul Gamish, widow of the Great Khan Kuyuk (r. 1246–48), but his mission was a failure because the regent treated the gifts which Louis had sent as tribute and the king was offended. John of Joinville talked to the envoys on their return, but the information he included in his *Life of St Louis* added nothing to western knowledge of the Mongols. It is a strange mixture of accurate detail and fantasy.[53]

A Franciscan, William of Rubruck, who may have belonged to the province of the Holy Land, wished to undertake a religious mission to the Mongols. St Louis supported him, though he would not give him formal accreditation because he feared that the Mongols might interpret William's mission as another act of homage. William left Syria in 1253 and travelled by way of Constantinople and the Crimea across central Asia to the Mongol capital at Karakorum. He returned through the Caucasus and Armenian Cilicia, where he took ship to Cyprus. He was not the first European envoy to reach the Mongol capital, his fellow Franciscan, John of Plano Carpini, having gone there in 1245–46 on a mission from Innocent IV, but he was the first Latin Christian to go there from the Crusader States. The report which he wrote for St Louis is, in my opinion, one of the great travel books of all time.

At the Mongol court William met Chinese subjects of the Great Khan. The Mongols called China Cathay, and William correctly identified it with the land of the Seres, spoken of by classical writers as the source of silk production.[54]

William was also concerned to find out the truth about Prester John. His conclusion was a piece of shrewd detection:

> Now on a plateau among these highlands there lived a certain Nestorian, a mighty herdsman, and a ruler over the people called the Naiman who were Nestorian Christians . . . The Nestorians called him King John, and only a tenth of what they said about him was true. For this is the way with Nestorians who come from these parts: they create big rumours out of nothing . . . In this way was broadcast the impressive report about King John.

William concluded that after John's death his people had been absorbed into the Mongol Empire.[55]

William had expected to meet fabulous creatures and men in Asia, but when he failed to do so: 'I enquired about the monsters or human freaks who are described by Isidore and Solinus, but was told that such things had never been sighted, which makes me very much doubt whether the story is true.'[56]

On his return journey William travelled through Armenia and stayed near Mount Ararat. He commented: 'Many have attempted to scale it, but without success. The [Armenian] bishop told me about a monk who was very eager to do so, and how an angel appeared to him and brought him wood from the Ark, telling him to make no further efforts; they used to keep that wood in their church, so they told me. To judge by its appearance the mountain is not so high that men could not well climb it.'[57]

Although William's report was not widely read, his fellow Franciscan Roger Bacon incorporated much of the geographical information it contained in his encyclopaedia, the *Opus maius*, which he presented to Pope Clement IV in 1267–68.[58]

Soon after William's return to Syria the Mongols launched a great attack on south-west Asia led by Hulegu Khan. They captured Baghdad in 1258 and swept into Syria, but in 1260 they were defeated at Ain Jalut in Galilee by the Mamluk Sultan of Egypt, who re-occupied all the Syrian lands west of the Euphrates. This was the first serious defeat the Mongols had ever suffered since the rise of Genghis Khan, and led Hulegu to seek an alliance with the papacy and the western powers against Egypt. Although these negotiations were cut short by Hulegu's death in 1265, they were resumed by his son Abagha (r. 1265–82), who was very well disposed towards the Christian West, and sent representatives to the Second Council of Lyons in 1274, at which a new crusade was discussed.[59]

Despite the Mamluk resurgence in Syria, the Mongols continued to be recognised as overlords by the Turks in Asia Minor and the Armenian King of Cilicia, and western travellers reached Persia through the ports of southern Asia Minor. Abagha and his successors allowed western merchants to trade freely in their dominions, and they also allowed western Catholic clergy to work there. The early Mongol Il-Khans were pagans and treated members of all religions on terms of equality. The new Orders of Dominicans and Franciscans were the main participants in these missions; they had a zeal to evangelise the non-Christian world and were willing to learn eastern languages in order to do so. Consequently during the second half of the thirteenth century people in western Europe had access to much better sources of information about the lands of the Persian Il-Khanate than ever before. Moreover, western visitors to the Il-Khanate were able, if they wished, to use the ports on the Persian Gulf. For the first time since the rise of Islam, Christian merchants and missionaries from the Mediterranean world could take ship on the Indian Ocean. Many of them reached India, and some, like the Franciscan John of Monte-Corvino (d. 1328), the first Catholic archbishop of Khanbaliq (Beijing), even travelled to China by sea.[60]

Plans for joint military action against Egypt continued to be discussed by the western powers and the Il-Khans, even after the Mamluks had expelled the crusaders from their remaining strongholds in Syria in 1291. It was not until 1322 that the Il-Khan Abu Said made peace with the Mamluk sultan. The Il-Khan Ghazan had become a Muslim in 1295, but this did not lead to any restrictions on the presence of western missions in his territories.[61]

Among the Catholic clergy who travelled in Persia and beyond in the early thirteenth century was the Dominican Jordan Catalani, who was appointed Bishop of Quilon in south India by Pope John XXII in 1330. His account of the East, the *Mirabilia descripta*, when compared with Honorius's *De imagine mundi* provides some indication of the ways in which western European knowledge of Asia and Africa had changed during the crusading era.[62]

Despite its title, much of Bishop Jordan's work is not concerned with marvels, but is a sober factual account of Asia. Henry Yule, who translated his book, remarked about Jordan's description of an elephant: 'I doubt if a better is to be found until long after his time.'[63] Jordan records that the land of the Turks is the most westerly province of Asia,[64] and that beyond it lies Armenia. Unlike William of Rubruck, Jordan considered that the summit of Mount Ararat really was inaccessible.[65] He gives a brief factual account of the Il-Khanate of Persia, which stretched from Tabriz to northern India,[66] but he gives a detailed description of India, the country which he knew best. While observing the traditional distinction between India the Less (i.e. northern India) and Great India (southern India), he admits that they share many characteristics. The marvels which he reports are natural phenomena, such as the *anilea*, a fruit 'like a plum . . . so sweet and delicious as it is impossible to utter in words', which is in fact a mango,[67] and the 'two cats having wings like the wings of bats' seen in his own diocese, which were the flying squirrels of Malabar.[68] Jordan displays an interest in Indian society; he was amazed that the people of north India ate rice as their staple food even though wheat was grown there;[69] he reported how the Parsees buried their dead in towers of silence;[70] and he was impressed by the devotion of Hindu widows who were prepared to commit suttee on their husbands' funeral pyres.[71] He also gives a vivid description of the fleet of ships going to the pearl fisheries of south India and Sri Lanka.[72]

Although he had not travelled further east himself, he had heard how elephants were put to work in Cambodia, and gives a detailed and accurate description of how they were caught and trained.[73] He also knew a little about the many islands of the East Indies from which spices came.[74] He reported that people in the dominions of the Great Khan (the Mongol emperor of China) used paper money, and that the emperor favoured priests who wore red hats and capes, a correct description of the Buddhist lamas of the *Sa skaya-pa* Order.[75] In this empire he relates there are 200 cities 'larger than Toulouse',[76] and he adds that China is famous for the beautiful pottery vessels it produces.[77]

Jordan was less well informed about northern Asia. He knew that there were two other Mongol provinces there, the Kipchak and Jagatai khanates,[78] and that the Caucasus was the home of the Christian and warlike Georgians.[79] He had also been told that at Baku on the shores of the Caspian Sea there is 'extracted and drawn a certain oil . . . called *naft*, and it is a very warm oil of medicinal virtue and it burneth passing well'.[80]

Jordan had been to Arabia, but admits that he knows very little about it 'except that there grow there choice incense and myrrh . . . This Arabia hath very great deserts, pathless and very dry.'[81]

When writing about Asia Jordan did not mention the monstrous races and fabulous beasts which figure so largely in traditional accounts of that continent.[82] But he believed that such marvels were to be found in the Third India, the Horn of Africa. He was the first writer to identify Prester John with the powerful, but unknown, Christian King of Ethiopia.[83] He had never been there, and his accounts are based on hearsay. He tells us that in the land of Prester John dragons flew around with jewels in their foreheads, there were unicorns which could only be caught with the help of virgins, and Ethiopia was the home of the roc, a bird so great that it could seize an elephant in its talons and carry it through the air, as well as of 'certain animals like an ass, but with transverse stripes of black and white', in other words zebra.[84] Bishop Jordan also located the Earthly Paradise in Africa, the unknown continent, along with all the other marvels of his world.[85]

The Hereford *mappamundi* of *c.* 1300, which has been described as 'the largest, most detailed and most perfectly preserved medieval map in the world',[86] provides excellent information about the main trade routes and pilgrim routes in contemporary western Europe, and even includes a symbol of Caernarvon Castle, which was not built until 1283.[87] Yet the information which it gives about Asia and Africa shows no awareness of the range of new knowledge made available in the previous hundred years. The only exception is found in the description of southern Africa: 'Gens nibie ethiopes – christianissimi' ('the Nubian peoples of Ethiopia are very Christian'). Otherwise Africa and Asia are shown, in the early medieval tradition, as the home of monstrous races, exotic and often mythical animals and biblical sites such as Noah's Ark, the Tower of Babel and Joseph's Barns (now known as the Pyramids).[88]

Yet although the Hereford map is a reminder of how unevenly new information became available in the western world before the invention of printing, nevertheless such knowledge could be tracked down and used if need arose. An example of the detailed local knowledge of the East which could be made available is the memorandum known as *La devise des chemins de Babiloine*, giving detailed information about how to approach Cairo through the Nile delta by a variety of routes. It was a lack of such data that had been largely responsible for the failure of St Louis's crusade almost sixty years before, and Robert Irwin has argued convincingly that this document was drawn up in *c.* 1306–7 for the Order of St John, which was planning to attack Egypt.[89]

It was also possible to marshal the new knowledge of Asia and Africa in a much more comprehensive way, as Marino Sanudo Torsello showed in his *Liber secretorum fidelium crucis* produced before 1321. His thesis was that Jerusalem could best be recovered by a carefully directed attack on Egypt, but that that would be successful only if it were preceded by a prolonged economic blockade. Sanudo argued that such a blockade was feasible because all the eastern luxury goods the West imported from Egypt could be obtained from other sources, and he gave details of where they were. Sanudo displays a sound knowledge of the history and topography of the Mongol Empire,[90] and a detailed knowledge of the topography of the Levant that Norman Housley has suggested 'was probably unequalled in his time'.[91] He presented copies of his work to Pope John XXII, King Robert of Naples and Charles IV of France.[92] Crusading therefore played some part not merely in the collection of data about Asia and Africa, but also in its dissemination even after the fall of Acre.

## NOTES

1 Adam of Bremen, *Gesta Hammaburgensis ecclesiae pontificum*, ed. B. Schmeidler, MGHSS, rerum Germanicarum in usum scholarum, 51, 2 vols (Hanover: [s.n.], 1917).

2 Hugeburc, *The Life of St. Willibald*, c. 12; trans. John Wilkinson in *Jerusalem Pilgrims before the Crusades* (Warminster: Aris and Phillips, 1977), pp. 124–38, at p. 126.

3 Recorded in 825 by Dicuil, *Liber de mensura orbis terrae*, VI. 12; ed. J. J. Tierney and L. Bieler (Dublin: Dublin Institute for Advanced Studies, 1967), pp. 62–3.

4 Adomnán, *De locis sanctis*, ed. L. Bieler, Corpus Christianorum series latina, 175 (Turnhout: Brepols, 1965), pp. 175–234, but see Thomas O'Loughlin, 'Adomnán and Arculf: The case of an expert witness', *Journal of Medieval Latin*, 7 (1997), 127–46.

5 Leo Marsicanus, *Chronicon monasterii Cassinensis*, II, 28; ed. W. Wattenbach, MGHSS, 7 (Hanover: [s.n.], 1846), p. 645.

6 Wilkinson describes the narrative of Bernard the Wise, c. 870, as 'the best full account of a pilgrimage before the crusades': *Jerusalem Pilgrims before the Crusades*, p. 13.

7 Pliny, *The Natural History*, ed. and trans. W. H. Rackham *et al.*, 10 vols (London: Loeb Classical Library, 1938–62); C. Julius Solinus, *Collectanea rerum memorabilium*, ed. T. Mommsen (2nd edn Berlin: Weidmann, 1895); Paulus Orosius, *The Seven Books of History against the Pagans*, trans. R. J. Deferrari (Washington, DC: Catholic University of America Press, 1964); Isidore of Seville, *Etymologiarum sive Originum libri XX*, ed. W. M. Lindsay, 2 vols (Oxford: Clarendon Press, 1911); F. Pfister, *Der Alexanderroman des Archipresbyters Leo* (Heidelberg: Carl Winter, 1913). The complicated textual history of the Alexander Romance is examined by G. Cary, *The Medieval Alexander* (Cambridge: Cambridge University Press, 1956).

8 C. F. Beckingham, *The Achievements of Prester John: An Inaugural Lecture at the School of Oriental and African Studies, London, 1966* (London: School of Oriental and African Studies, University of London, 1966); repr. in C. F. Beckingham and B. Hamilton (eds), *Prester John, the Mongols and the Ten Lost Tribes* (Aldershot: Ashgate Publishing Ltd, 1996), pp. 1–22, at pp. 17–18.

9 Macrobius, *Commentary on the Dream of Scipio*, II, vi; trans. W. H. Stahl (New York and London: Columbia University Press, 1952), p. 207 (and cf. appendix B, pp. 251–2).

10 Pliny, *Natural History*, book II, LXV; J. K. Wright, *The Geographical Lore of the Time of the Crusades: A Study in the History of Medieval Science and Tradition in Western Europe*, American Geographical Society Research Series, 15 (New York: American Geographical Society, 1925); republished with additions (New York: Dover Publications, 1965), p. 27.

11 Genesis 2:8, 10–14. St Jerome had translated Genesis 2:8 as 'Plantaverat autem Dominus Deus paradisum voluptatis a principio, in quo posuit hominem quem formaverat.' ('At the beginning of time the Lord God had planted a garden of delight in which he placed the man whom he had fashioned.') The alternative reading 'The Lord God planted a garden of delight towards the East' was known to medieval churchmen

(A. Graf, *Miti, leggende e superstizioni del medio evo*, 2 vols (Turin: E. Loescher, 1892–93) i, pp. 1–192).

12 Honorius Augustodunensis, *De imagine mundi libri tres*, book I, cc. viii–xxi, xxxii–xxxiii, in J.-P. Migne (ed.), *PL*, 172 (Paris: apud Garnieri Fratres, 1895), pp. 123–8, 130–1; V. Flint, 'Honorius Augustodunensis, *Imago mundi*', *Archives d'Histoire Doctrinale et Littéraire du Moyen Age*, 49 (1982), 1–151. The identity of the author is discussed by E. Edson, *Mapping Time and Space: How Medieval Mapmakers Viewed their World* (London: The British Library, 1997), pp. 111–13.

13 e.g. Saewulf, who made the pilgrimage in 1101–3, relied heavily on Bede's work on the holy places (Saewulf, 'A reliable account of the situation of Jerusalem', ed. and trans. in J. Wilkinson, with J. Hill and W. F. Ryan (eds), *Jerusalem Pilgrimage 1099–1185*, The Hakluyt Society, 2nd series, 167 (London: Aris and Phillips, 1988), pp. 94–116.

14 e.g. the author of the guide appended to Baudri of Borgueil's *Historia Hierosolymitana* written in *c.* 1110, *Qualiter*, in Wilkinson, Hill and Ryan (eds), *Jerusalem Pilgrimage 1099–1185*, pp. 90–1, at p. 91.

15 Wilkinson, Hill and Ryan (eds), *Jerusalem Pilgrimage 1099–1185*, p. 244.

16 *Ibid.*, p. 79.

17 P. W. Edbury and J. G. Rowe, *William of Tyre: Historian of the Latin East* (Cambridge: Cambridge University Press, 1988), pp. 13–22.

18 William of Tyre, *Chronicon*, IV. 2; ed. R. B. C. Huygens, Identification des dates par H. E. Mayer et G. Rosch, Corpus Christianorum Continuatio Medievalis, 63, 63A (Turnhout: Brepols, 1986), pp. 234–5.

19 *Ibid.*, XVII. 3; ed. Huygens, pp. 762–3.

20 *Ibid.*, XIX. 21 (Cairo), 18–19 (Fatimid court), 23–4 (land of Egypt); ed. Huygens, pp. 884–5, 887–9, 894–8.

21 *Ibid.*, XIX. 15; ed. Huygens, pp. 890–2; Edbury and Rowe, *William of Tyre*, pp. 23–4.

22 By 'regnum Ethiopicum' William seems to mean the Nubian kingdom of Makuria (*Chronicon*, XIX. 24; ed. Huygens, p. 896).

23 *Ibid.*, XIX. 27; ed. Huygens, p. 903.

24 *L'estoire d'Eracles empereur et la conqueste de la terre d'Outremer*, in *Guillaume de Tyr et ses continuateurs*, 2 vols, ed. P. Paris (Paris: Librairie de Firmin-Didot et Cie, 1879–80); J. H. Pryor, 'The *Eracles* and William of Tyre: An interim report', in B. Z. Kedar (ed.), *The Horns of Hattin* (Jerusalem: Yad Izhak Ben-Zvi and London: Ashgate, 1992), pp. 270–93; J. Folda, 'Manuscripts of the *History of Outremer* by William of Tyre: A handlist', *Scriptorium*, 27 (1973), 90–5.

25 Burchardus Argentoratensis, *De statu Egypti vel Babylonie*, c. 4; in S. de Sandoli, *Itinera Hierosolymitana Crucesignatorum (saec. xii–xiii)*, 4 vols, Pubblicazioni dello Studium Biblicum Franciscanum, 24 (Jerusalem: Studium Biblicum Franciscanum, 1978–84), ii, pp. 392–414, at p. 402.

26 *Ibid.*, c. 4, pp. 402–4. I take 'terra silvestris' to mean 'wild land', rather than 'wooded land'.

27 W. Y. Adams, *Nubia: Corridor to Africa* (London: Allen Lane, 1977); G. Vantini, *Christianity in the Sudan* (Bologna: EMI, 1981).

28 *De adventu patriarchae Indorum ad urbem sub Calisto papa IIo*, ed. in F. Zarncke, 'Der Patriarch Johannes von Indien und der Priester Johannes', *Abhandlungen der philologisch-historischen Classe der königlich sächsischen Gesellschaften des Wissenschaften*, 7 (Leipzig: bei S. Hirzel, 1879), 837–46; repr. in Beckingham and Hamilton (eds), *Prester John*, pp. 29–38. On the jewels of Eden, see Ezekiel 28:13.

29 Described in *c.* 1170 by John of Würzburg (Wilkinson, Hill and Ryan (eds), *Jerusalem Pilgrimage*, p. 273).

30 Walter the Chancellor, *The Antiochene Wars: A Translation and Commentary*, ed. and trans. T. S. Asbridge and S. B. Edgington (Aldershot: Ashgate, 1999), II, 16, pp. 168–70.

31 Otto of Freising, *Chronica sive Historia de duabus civitatibus*, VII, 33; ed. A. Hofmeister, MGHSS, rerum Germanicarum in usum scholarum (Hanover: Hahn, 1912), p. 366; Abu l'Fida', *Annals A. H. 536*, ed. M. Reinaud, Recueil des Historiens des Croisades, Historiens Orientaux (Paris: Académie des Inscriptions et Belles Lettres, 1872) i, p. 25.

32 F. Zarncke, 'Der Briefe des Priesters Johannes an der byzantinischen Kaiser Emanuel', *Abhandlungen der Philologisch-Historischen Classe der Königlich Sächsischen Gesellschaft des Wissenschaften*, 7, 873–934, repr. in Beckingham and Hamilton (eds), *Prester John*, pp. 40–102; D. Wasserstein, 'Eldad ha Dani and Prester John', in Beckingham and Hamilton (eds), *Prester John*, pp. 213–36.

33 B. Hamilton, 'A note on the manuscripts of the Latin text of the Prester John letter', in Hamilton and Beckingham (eds), *Prester John*, p. 39.

34 Benjamin of Tudela, *The Itinerary of Benjamin of Tudela*, ed. and trans. Marcus Nathan Adler (London: H. Frowde, 1907); al-Idrisi, *Géographie d'Edrisi traduit de l'arabe en français*, ed. P. A. Jaubert, 2 vols (Paris: Imprimerie Royale, 1836–40).

35 Richard of Poitou, *Chronica*, ed. G. Waitz, MGHSS, 26 (Hanover, 1882), p. 84. 'Macedones' appears to refer to the Greek kingdom of Bactria.

36 *Pelrinages et pardouns de Acre*, ch. ii, in H. Michelant and G. Raynaud (eds), *Itinéraires á Jérusalem*, Société de l'Orient Latin (Paris: Société de l'Orient Latin, 1882), pp. 229–36.

37 e.g. *Les pelerinaiges por aler en Iherusalem* (c. 1231), cc. i, ii, xxi; in Michelant and Raynaud (eds), *Itinéraires à Jérusalem*, pp. 89–103; Andrew Jotischky, *The Perfection of Solitude: Hermits and Monks in the Crusader States* (University Park, PA; Pennsylvania State Press, 1995), pp. 101–51.

38 D. Webb, *Pilgrims and Pilgrimages in the Medieval West* (London: IB Tauris, 1999), p. 104, no. 15(a).

39 B. Hamilton, 'Our Lady of Saidnaya: an Orthodox shrine revered by Muslims and Knights Templar at the time of the crusades', in R. N. Swanson (ed.), *The Holy Land, Holy Lands, and Christian History*, Studies in Church History, 36 (Woodbridge: The Boydell Press for The Ecclesiastical History Society, 2000), pp. 207–15.

40 De Sandoli, *Itinera Hierosolymitana*, iii and iv.

41 B. Hamilton, 'The Armenian Church and the Papacy at the time of the crusades', *Eastern Churches Review*, 10 (1978), 61–87; Innocent III, *Regesta Innocentii III*, book xiv, no. lxviii; in J. P. Migne (ed.), *PL*, 216 (Paris: apud Garnieri Fratres, 1855), p. 434.

42 J. Perruchon, 'Notes sur l'histoire d'Ethiopie: Extrait de la vie d'Abba Jean, 74e patriarche d'Alexandrie, relatif à l'Abyssinie (texte arabe et introduction)', *Revue Sémitique*, 7 (1899), 81–2.

43 James [Jacques] of Vitry, *Historia Orientalis*, c. 76; printed edn (Douai: Balthazar Bellerus, 1597), p. 144.

44 Beckingham, 'The achievements of Prester John', 17–19.

45 Oliver may be reflecting reports that some of the vassals of the King of Ethiopia were Muslims: Oliver of Paderborn, *Historia Damiatina*, c. 62; in *Die Schriften des Kölner Domscholmasters, späteren Bischofs von Paderborn und Kardinal-Bischofs von S. Sabina Oliverus*, ed. O. Hoogeweg, Bibliothek des Litterarischen Vereins in Stuttgart, 202 (Tübingen: Litterarischer Verein Stuttgart, 1894), p. 264.

46 Oliver became Cardinal Priest of S. Sabina in 1225, Jacques Cardinal Bishop of Tusculum in 1229.

47 John of Joinville, *The Life of St Louis*, section 190; trans. R. Hague (London: Sheed and Ward, 1955), p. 71; A. Moorehead, *The Blue Nile* (London: New English Library, 1972), pp. 291–3.

48 Adams, *Nubia*, pp. 525–9.

49 C. F. Beckingham, 'An Ethiopian embassy to Europe, *c.* 1310', *Journal of Semitic Studies*, 14 (1989), 337–46; repr. in Beckingham and Hamilton (eds), *Prester John*, pp. 197–206.

50 We have only the translation which Jacques commissioned of this text, which, as Jean Richard points out, may contain glosses inserted by the translator: Jacques de Vitry, *Lettres de Jacques de Vitry, 1160/70–1240, Evêque de S. Jean d'Acre*, ed. R. B. C. Huygens, Corpus Christianorum Continuatio Medievalis, 171 (Turnhout: Brepols, 2000), letter VII, pp. 624, 634–44; J. Richard, 'The *Relatio de Davide* as a source for Mongol history and the legend of Prester John', in Hamilton and Beckingham (eds), *Prester John*, pp. 139–58.

51 D. Sinor, 'The Mongols and western Europe', in H. W. Hazard (ed.), *The Fourteenth and Fifteenth Centuries*: K. M. Setton (gen. ed.), *A History of the Crusades*, 6 vols, 2nd edn, iii (Madison, WI: University of Wisconsin Press, 1975), pp. 513–44, at p. 521.

52 Simon of St Quentin, *Histoire des Tartares*, ed. J. Richard (Paris: Librairie Orientaliste Paul Geuthner, 1965).

53 Joinville, *Life of St Louis*, sections 479, 492; trans. R. Hague, pp. 146–9.

54 William of Rubruck, *The Mission of Friar William of Rubruck*, ed. P. Jackson with D. Morgan, The Hakluyt Society, 2nd series, 173 (London: Hakluyt Society, 1990), p. 161. The identification of Cathay with China was not universally accepted until the Jesuit Bento de Goes proved it by his epic journey in 1602–7 (C. Wessells, *Early Jesuit Travellers in Central Asia, 1603–1721* (The Hague: M. Nijhoff, 1924)).

55 William of Rubruck, *Mission*, p. 122.

56 *Ibid.*, p. 201.

57 *Ibid.*, pp. 267–8.

58 *Ibid.*, p. 51; Roger Bacon, *Opus maius*, ed. J. Bridges, 3 vols (Oxford: Clarendon Press, 1897–1900).

59 J. A. Boyle, 'The Il-Khans of Persia and the Christian West', *History Today*, 23:8 (1973), 554–63.

60 J. Richard, *La papauté et les missions d'Orient au Moyen Age (XIIIe–XVe siècles)*, Collection de l'École Française de Rome, 33 (Rome: École Française de Rome, 1977).

61 D. O. Morgan, *The Mongols* (Oxford: Basil Blackwell, 1986), pp. 183–7.

62 Jordan Catalani, *Mirabilia descripta: The Wonders of the East*, trans. H. Yule, The Hakluyt Society, 1st series, 31 (London: Hakluyt Society, 1863).

63 *Ibid.*, p. 26 n. 1.

64 *Ibid.*, c. xvi, pp. 57–8.

65 *Ibid.*, c. ii. 1, pp. 3–4.

66 *Ibid.*, c. iii, pp. 7–11.

67 *Ibid.*, c. iv. 7, p. 14.

68 *Ibid.*, c. v. 9, p. 29.

69 *Ibid.*, c. iv. 3, p. 12.

70 *Ibid.*, c. iv. 23, p. 21.

71 *Ibid.*, c. iv. 22, p. 20.

72 *Ibid.*, c. v. 6, p. 28.

73 *Ibid.*, c. v. 37–40, pp. 37–9.

74 *Ibid.*, c. v. 1–16, pp. 30–1.

75 *Ibid.*, c. viii. 2, 3, p. 46.

76 *Ibid.*, c. viii. 7, p. 47.

77 *Ibid.*, c. viii. 10, p. 48.

78 *Ibid.*, c. xiv. 9, p. 54.

79 *Ibid.*, c. xiii, p. 52.

80 *Ibid.*, c. xi. 2, p. 50.

81 *Ibid.*, c. vii. 1, 3, p. 45.

82 Except in his description of the ruins of Babylon, which he had seen, and which he reports were infested by sinister monsters. Yule suggests persuasively that this may reflect Jordan's expectation that the prophecy of Isaiah 13:21–2 would be fulfilled (Jordan, *Mirabilia*, c. ix. 1–4, p. 49). On perceptions of 'Asia' see Suzanne Conklin Akbari in Chapter 8 below, pp. 166–70.

83 Jordan, *Mirabilia*, c. vi. 2, p. 42; B. Hamilton, 'Continental drift: Prester John's progress through the Indies', in Beckingham and Hamilton (eds), *Prester John*, pp. 237–69.

84 Jordan, *Mirabilia*, c. ci. 1–4, 11, pp. 41–3, 44. The roc (or *rukhkh*) is described by Ibn Battuta, *The Travels of Ibn Battuta, AD 1325–1354*, trans. H. A. R. Gibb and C. F. Beckingham, 5 vols (index vol. ed. A. D. H. Bivar), The Hakluyt Society, 2nd series, 110, 117, 141, 178 and 190 (London: Hakluyt Society, 1958–2000), 178, pp. 911–12.

85 Jordan, *Mirabilia*, c. vi. 6, p. 43.

86 P. Whitfield, *The Image of the World: 20 Centuries of World Maps* (London: The British Library, 1994), p. 20.

87 Edson, *Mapping time and space*, pp. 139–44.

88 N. R. Kline, *Maps of Medieval Thought: The Hereford Paradigm* (Woodbridge: Boydell Press, 2001); *Nibei* inscription, p. 143, no. 4.

89 *La devise des chemins de Babiloine*, in Michelant and Raynaud (eds), *Itinéraires à Jerusalem*, pp. 237–52; R. Irwin, 'How many miles to Babylon? The *Devise des chemins de Babiloine* redated', in M. Barber (ed.), *The Military Orders: Fighting for the Faith and Caring for the Sick* (Aldershot: Ashgate, 1994), pp. 57–63.

90 Marino Sanudo Torsello, *Marino Sanutus dictus Torsellus: Liber secretorum fidelium crucis*, in J. Bongars (ed.), *Gesta Dei per Francos*, 2 vols (Hanover: Typis Wechelianis apud heredes Johannis Aubrii, 1611); repr. with introduction by Joshua Prawer (Toronto: University of Toronto Press, 1972), III. 13. iii–x, pp. 234–42. Evelyn Edson describes Sanudo's plans in Chapter 7 below, pp. 133–6.

91 *Ibid.*, III. 14, pp. 243–62.

92 N. Housley, *The Later Crusades, 1274–1580: From Lyons to Alcazar* (Oxford: Oxford University Press, 1992), pp. 36–7.

# 2

## Sharing the sites: medieval Jewish travellers to the Land of Israel

❰❱

Elka Weber

Now the Lord said to Avram, Get thee out of thy country, and from thy kindred, and from thy father's house, to the land that I will show thee. (Genesis 12:1)

JUDAISM IS a religion born in travel. From Abraham's leaving his ancestral home to the exodus from Egypt, motion has been an element of nation building. In fact, the entire narrative flow of the Hebrew Bible concerns a people en route to their promised land. Over time, Jews lost political control of their land and were dispersed, first in the Middle East and the growing Roman Empire and then throughout the known world. Until the emergence of a modern Jewish state, most of Jewish history takes place in a diaspora setting. Despite the overwhelming presence of landlessness as a leitmotif in the sweep of Jewish history, the role of travel in the cultural life of the Jews has received almost no scholarly attention.[1] Travel was a given, a necessary by-product of dispersion, but rarely a subject of study in its own right. This chapter analyses how twelfth- to fifteenth-century Jewish travel writers related to their writings, to their audiences, and to the holy places they visited.

The body of medieval Jewish travel writing is not large. While Jews travelled and sometimes wrote letters that recorded their impressions, there is virtually no writing that focuses on the experience of travel until the twelfth century. The travel writing that emerges in this period (roughly the later crusade era) is based on western Christian *itineraria* of the Holy Land. The writing is more factual than fantastic, with little attention to topography, flora or fauna. There is no Jewish counterpart to Mandeville.

From the twelfth through the fifteenth century, there are some fourteen full-length Jewish travel accounts, and about twice as many letters and fragmentary writings. The travellers cited in this chapter include the two best-known names in Jewish travel, Benjamin of Tudela and Petahia of Ratisbon (Regensburg). Benjamin and Petahia left from Spain and Germany respectively at the end of the twelfth century and travelled extensively through the Middle East. A contemporary of theirs, Jacob haCohen, probably travelled to crusader Jerusalem from Provence. Samuel ben Samson was attached to a delegation of prominent French Jews who visited the Land of Israel in 1210. In the middle of the thirteenth century, a French rabbi named Jacob travelled on behalf of Rabbi Yehiel of Paris, a major religious figure of the age, as a fund-raiser; Jacob the Emissary, as he is known, wrote a description of the Land of Israel as well as a list of holy grave sites. The Aragonese Isaac Chelo wrote about Israel in 1334, after settling in Jerusalem. A highly personal and descriptive account was written by the Italian Meshullam of Volterra about his trip from Italy in 1481. Many travellers describe holy sites within the Land of Israel, although the longer travel accounts include descriptions of other places as well. Benjamin of Tudela writes an engaging and detailed description of some of the churches of Rome.

Most Jewish travellers, however, wrote about matters closer to home. Meshullam of Volterra wrote an account of his trip that includes many of the elements common to late medieval Jewish travel writing. His book is in Hebrew and focuses on Jerusalem, but the voyage that inspired the book was probably made for financial as well as religious reasons. Though he thanks divine providence for his good fortune, he rarely moralises and instead uses his authority to advise future travellers on practical matters (e.g. he recommends bringing lemons for squeezing onto insect bites). Deeply grieved at the loss of a Jewish Jerusalem, he nonetheless admires the architecture of its Muslim rulers and takes some measure of comfort in their respect for Jewish holy sites.

Travellers have a particular power to express who they are and how they differ from others. The very fact of going from the familiar to the unknown forces the travel writer to distinguish himself from others. Travel writing becomes an extended form of self-definition. To define someone as Other, though, the definer needs to be in a position of cultural power. The reader needs to share the assumption of the writer's power to determine who is 'us' and who is not, and to accept the mechanism of the 'Othering' process – in this case, a travelogue. Travel writers make the effort to establish themselves as reliable sources, capable of standing up to their readers' scrutiny.

Since the travellers are Jews, people whose primary identification is as members of a society which is constructed and defined through adherence to sacred text, the travellers already have a privileged text which defines Self and Other in its most necessary form. But where the privileged texts are taught and reproduced in limited and authorised ways, the non-privileged text is more accessible. Travel writings are non-privileged texts arrogating some of the rights of the privileged text. Writers use their understanding of their holy books as a starting point – but not their only referent – in their constructions of people they meet. The travellers take for granted that they bring with them the ideal practice of their religion.

There is a long history of Jewish pilgrimage to Jerusalem. In the period of the Second Commonwealth (538 BCE to 70 CE), Jewish pilgrimage to Jerusalem was a communal obligation in response to the biblical commandment for all males to visit the city three times a year for the festivals (Deuteronomy 16:16). The city was equipped to handle the influx.[2] Further ritual obligations might entail a visit to Jerusalem at other times of the year as well. After the Second Temple in Jerusalem was destroyed in 70 CE, some Jews who lived near Jerusalem continued visiting in fulfilment of rituals such as tithing that did not require a standing temple.[3]

From this point onward, visiting Jerusalem was a voluntary act, not a religious requirement. By the beginning of the Byzantine period (324–638 CE), Jewish visitors came to Jerusalem almost exclusively to mourn its destruction. They were allowed to visit the Temple Mount only on the ninth day of the Hebrew month of *Ab*, the anniversary of the Temple's destruction. An anonymous Christian pilgrim from Bordeaux reports in the fourth century that on this one day, Jewish visitors 'bewail themselves with groans, rend their garments, and so depart'.[4]

Mourning the loss of the Temple and its rites required rituals of its own. The rabbis of the Talmud, while setting out the rules of mourning, discussed precisely how the Jewish visitor to Jerusalem ought to behave. He should recite verses from Isaiah and Jeremiah relating to the destruction of the city and he should tear his garments. The Temple and the city should be mourned separately as two distinct entities.[5]

Over time, the ritual expanded. Some people had a specific liturgy for each of the city's gates.[6] A text from the Cairo *Geniza*, the great treasure-trove of medieval social history, shows a set medieval ritual that combines mourning with thanksgiving.

> If you are worthy to go up to Jerusalem, when you look at the city from Mount Scopus [you should observe the following procedure]. If you are riding on a donkey step down; if you are on foot, take off your sandals, then rending your garment say: 'This [our] sanctuary was destroyed' . . . When you arrive in the city continue to rend your garments for the temple and the people and the house of Israel. Then pray saying: 'May the Lord our God be exalted', and, 'Let us worship at his footstool . . . We give you thanks, O Lord our God, that you have given us life, brought us to this point, and made us worthy to enter your house' . . . Then return and circle all the gates of the city and go round all its corners, make a circuit and count its towers.[7]

By the seventh century, Jerusalem had come under Muslim rule and Jews returned to the city. More Jewish pilgrims came to visit, but not exclusively for mourning. The Jerusalem Yeshiva led an annual assembly on the holiday of *Hoshannah Rabbah*, the seventh day of *Sukkot* (Tabernacles), in which a procession of Jews would go through the city, around the Temple Mount and up the Mount of Olives for singing and prayer. Permission for this ritual was expensive, but it continued even after the Fatimid conquest in 970 ushered in a general decline in the city's Jewish life. The last known *Hoshannah Rabbah* procession in Jerusalem was held in 1062.[8] Often the medieval pilgrim was called a *hogeg*, 'pilgrim celebrant'. Many tried to be in Jerusalem for the high holy day season in the autumn.

Under the crusaders, as under the Byzantines, Jews were presumably not allowed to live in Jerusalem. With Christian control, Jews from Muslim countries had a difficult time visiting, while Jews from the Christian world benefited from easier maritime access. As the crusaders lost ground in the Middle East, fewer Jews visited from Christian Europe. In the Muslim world, Jews at all levels of society visited holy places, especially tombs of the sages, during the Jewish holidays. At first the visits were timed for the autumn holiday of *Sukkot*, like the *Hoshannah Rabbah* festivities of the early Muslim era. In the fifteenth century, Jews usually visited in spring and early summer for *Pessah* (Passover) and *Shavuot* (Pentecost). Perhaps they were influenced by Christians coming to celebrate Easter and by Muslims arriving for the *Nebi Musa* pilgrimage to a site near Jericho venerated as the tomb of Moses, or perhaps Jews simply took advantage of caravans heading for Jerusalem.

The Jewish holy sites were clustered around the Temple Mount in Jerusalem and the Tomb of the Patriarchs at Hebron. At Jerusalem, the travellers may have ritually visited each of the gates of the city and prayed.[9] Jerusalem was not the only locus of Jewish pilgrimage, as evidenced by the Talmudic discussion of what to say in certain places marked by famous historical events. The Mishna (*Berakoth* 9:1) says that a blessing should be recited in a place where special things happened to the Jewish people. The Talmud discusses what to say if a person sees the place where the Jews crossed the Red Sea, the place where the wall of Jericho stood before collapsing, or the pillar of salt that Lot's wife had become.[10] Obviously, these places were considered known and 'visitable' to Jews of the Talmudic era, roughly between the fourth and sixth centuries CE. In the later Middle Ages, much of the tour was spent in the northern Galilee region.

Medieval Jewish pilgrimage, whether to Jerusalem or especially to other areas of the Holy Land, was not a regular, ongoing and organised system, as it was for Christians in the Holy Land or Muslims in the Hijaz. Jewish pilgrimage does not re-enact a history or follow a set path. Rather, Jewish pilgrims look to history and historical personalities for inspiration that the future redemption will come, and with it the rededication of the Temple with its obligatory pilgrimage rites.[11] When medieval Jews explain their travels, they usually write, as did the French Rabbi Jacob the Emissary in the thirteenth century, that they 'wish to contemplate and pray at the graves of the Patriarchs, the righteous and the saints of the Holy Land, and to our holy and glorious Temple wherein our fathers prayed in Jerusalem. May it be rebuilt, and established soon in our days.'[12] Apparently the major burial sites were along well-known routes. Petahia of Ratisbon got from a certain Rabbi Samuel, head of the academy at Nehardea, a list of all the grave sites of the famous sages of the East as well as a safe-conduct pass or letter of introduction. Unfortunately for future readers, Petahia lost the list of graves along the way.[13]

The most famous of all medieval Jewish travellers has kept people guessing for generations about his motivation. Benjamin of Tudela did not set out from Spain at the end of the twelfth century simply to do a standard 'tombstone tour' punctuated with sites of miracles. Benjamin points out industries, taxes and Jewish populations in the towns he visits. He tours the Great Mosque of Damascus and the Coliseum in Rome. He writes about the grave of Ali and the Abbey of St Aegidius, once the home of an eighth-century hermit more commonly known as St Giles, and 'a place of pilgrimage of the Gentiles who come hither from the ends of the earth'.[14] Unlike them, however, Benjamin was not simply planning a pilgrimage. He visits and then leaves 'Trani on the sea, where all the pilgrims gather to go to Jerusalem; for the port is a convenient one'.[15] His discussion of Jerusalem is barely focused on religion and ritual. He offers very specific information about a pearl fishery in Qatifa in the Persian Gulf which belongs to the king, but is managed by a Jew.[16]

Benjamin is as interested in the present as in the past. This has led to some speculation about the purpose of his trip. Was he a jewel merchant or a textile dyer? Was he scouting new areas of settlement in the East should Christian Europe become too difficult a place for Jews to stay or was he simply writing to console Jews by showing them how well their co-religionists lived in other places? All these suggestions are predicated on the idea that people visit the Middle East to discover what was. A traveller concerned with the present must have some hope of tangible gain, or else why would he visit? Benjamin's nineteenth- and twentieth-century editors almost automatically rule out the possibility of ethnographic and/or geographical interest. It may very well be true that Benjamin was on a trading voyage, especially when one considers his near-obsessive attention to the waterways close to all the cities he visited, but the exclusion of travel for the sake of curiosity says something about twentieth-century images of the medieval mind.[17]

The Italian Meshullam of Volterra does not tell his readers exactly why he went on his voyage either. Because he mentions wearing a ring that he took as a pledge, he may have been transacting business. But, upon leaving Egypt, ullam writes: 'may it be the Almighty's will that I may reach Jerusalem ⎱lfil my vows [*'va'ashalem nedarai'*], and that he may let me go back to ⎱use in life and joy and peace'.[18] Mixing business with pilgrimage seems to have been completely natural to him. Certainly, he was prepared to visit Jerusalem: when he arrived he tore his clothes according to custom 'and in the bitterness of my heart recited the appropriate prayer which I had in a small book'.[19] Jerusalem is clearly the focus of his trip. When Meshullam leaves Jerusalem for Beirut he is heading home, and at the very end of the book is a calculation (possibly added by an editor) of the distance from the starting point of Naples to Jerusalem, as well as a calculation of the round-trip mileage.

Book buying might partially explain Isaac Chelo's trip in 1334. He is fascinated with interesting books and rare editions. He writes that Jerusalem has 'excellent calligraphists, and the copies are sought for by the strangers, who carry them away to their own countries. I have seen a Pentateuch written with so much art that several persons at once wanted to acquire it, and it was only for an excessively high price that the Chief of the Synagogues of Babylon carried it off with him to Baghdad.'[20]

Whatever lay behind their trips, medieval Jews had often read enough to get a good sense of what lay ahead. None of them seems to have operated like the German monk Felix Fabri, who in the fifteenth century spent a full year reading travel accounts in preparation for his second trip to the Holy Land.[21] Of course, medieval Jews did not have a genre of travel writing to read before the twelfth century. But none of the travellers went as a completely blank slate, either. Like their Christian and Muslim counterparts, the writers of Jewish travel accounts often had a relatively high level of religious and secular learning. Their information – and often their terminology – is from the Bible and sometimes the Talmud. Many were familiar with *Josippon*, the tenth-century Hebrew paraphrase of Josephus's *The Jewish Wars*, which enjoyed a relatively wide circulation in medieval Europe.

Some of the travellers clearly had historical knowledge of things outside Jewish tradition. Jacob haCohen at the end of the twelfth century expects his readers to have heard of Alexander and Aristotle. Meshullam of Volterra, three hundred years later, quotes Pliny's book on natural history as saying that crocodiles can grow as long as eighteen feet, though the longest one he himself saw was five feet long.[22]

A few travellers even had sketchy guidebooks to follow. These unknown and unnamed books, perhaps just ad hoc lists, seem to be focused entirely on the spiritual experience of visiting the holy sites. As we saw, Petahia travelled with a list of graves of holy people, and Meshullam of Volterra arrived at Jerusalem ready to recite prayers from a pamphlet (*quntres*) that he had brought.

The first Jewish travel writers show no indication of knowing that travel writing existed as a genre. Benjamin of Tudela's book is full of 'matters not previously heard of in the land of *Sepharad*',[23] – or at least not known to Jews. By the fourteenth century, travellers know that they are working in an established field. Isaac Chelo quotes and paraphrases Benjamin of Tudela, expecting his readers to have heard of him. He writes that the Western Wall is the place where Jews go to pray, 'as Rabbi Benjamin has already related'.[24]

Preparatory reading created expectations that were not always met. Genesis 19:26 tells that Lot's wife was turned into a pillar of salt for having turned back to look at the destruction of Sodom. Most of the travellers expected to see the pillar, and some did.

Benjamin of Tudela mentions rather improbably that he could see the site of the famous biblical story from the mountains around Jerusalem, and 'at a distance of two parasangs from the Sea of Sodom is the Pillar of Salt into which Lot's wife was turned; the sheep lick it continually, but afterwards it regains its original shape.'[25]

Petahia of Ratisbon actually visited Sodom but, much to the disappointment of his editor and/or copyist, did not have any exciting news. 'As to the pillar of salt, he said that he did not see it and that it no longer existed.'[26] Joshua Prawer suggests that Petahia's not seeing the pillar of salt is 'perhaps part of the original treatise of a rather critical pilgrim, which somehow escaped the scissors of the "editors"'.[27] It may, however, be a response to them. That is, the editor, or the scribe who is referred to in the text as Judah, asked Petahia if he had any information about these specific sites and Petahia responded. The dialogue itself eludes the readers; only the conclusions remain. Quite possibly there was no dialogue, only a series of sloppy editors and copyists writing down what they considered worthwhile.

Clearly Petahia's copyist and editor – or editors – imposed their own concerns on the book, making it difficult for the reader to know exactly what Petahia himself was looking at and for. It may be that Petahia dictated a more present-orientated travelogue but it was narrated and/or edited by people who preferred stories about the graves of famous men and wanted information about biblical sites. Petahia of Ratisbon was so heavily edited that his broad range of interests is narrowed down to a book that is mostly about holy graves. At one point the narrator even mentions that Petahia 'named all the cities; and stated how many days it took him to travel from city to city. However, there is no occasion to write it down.'[28]

Petahia's editor highlights an important characteristic of travel writing. Travel writers are obviously viewers. But they cannot possibly notice every single thing they see, and they cannot write down everything they notice. The very act of writing is the first step in editing. And at some time during this editing process, the writers decide whether to be a part of the story they are telling.

The level of the author's involvement generally depends on the organising principle that he chooses. Most Jewish travellers recede into the background, as they write about places and only incidentally about what they did there. These site-specific accounts rarely offer more than a glimpse of the writer. A good number of medieval pilgrimage accounts are, in fact, anonymous documents whose dates have to be guessed from internal evidence. Some longer travel accounts use the voyage itself as the organising principle. In these accounts one is most likely to see not just the pilgrimage process and holy sites, but also the return trip. Whether these accounts are in the first or the third person, they focus on the experiences of the author. Naturally enough, the first-person accounts give the closest view of the writer. But even in first-person accounts, the book is about a trip and the author is not always at the centre of the action. When the author does insert himself into the narrative, it is to bolster his reliability, to highlight some ritual activity, or to recall physical danger or discomfort.

Travellers occasionally present themselves as the bearers of proper religious teachings. Rabbi Jacob the Emissary, who never inserts himself as a character in his travel account, takes the time to express his opinion, acting as teacher and defender of religious tradition. He urges his readers to understand the Torah literally, by showing them that Hebron really is in a valley, as the Torah tells.[29] Petahia tries to teach blessings to a group of Karaites.[30] Almost all travel accounts employ the standard medieval Jewish insults against the two larger monotheistic faiths. Christian pilgrims are 'the mistaken ones', Jesus is 'that man', and Muhammad is 'the insane'. Despite these terms (written, of course, in Hebrew for a Jewish audience) there is almost no active, argumentative polemic.

The most common reason for the writer to make his way into the writing is to prove that he was diligent about gathering information from reliable sources. This is especially important when a traveller tells an unbelievable story. When Benjamin of Tudela reports that a man named Moses, a skilful archer probably belonging to an independent Jewish tribe from the mountains around Nishapur, was taken captive and ended up married to the daughter of the Chief Rabbi of Isfahan, he is careful to put himself and his source into the story. 'This same R. Moses told me all these things.'[31]

Generally, Jewish travellers do not engage in polemic or portray themselves as religious authorities. They appear as actors who show that travellers can gather information accurately under difficult circumstances without ever forgetting where they came from. One Jewish traveller takes this technique a step further than the others. Jacob ben Nathaniel haCohen tells his story in the first person. Four times in the narrative he refers to himself not as 'I' but by his full name.

The first time is to introduce himself and the difficulties of the journey. 'I, Jacob, the son of Rabbi Nathaniel haCohen, journeyed with much difficulty, but God helped me to enter the Holy Land.'[32] The last time reminds the reader of his identity. 'Here end the words of me, Jacob haCohen, of all the sights I saw in the Holy Land.'[33] The third time he is explaining to the rabbis of Jerusalem why the cisterns at the Mount of Olives do not fill up. What matters here is that he is standing 'on the grave of [that man]'.[34] The narrator mentions his name – says he is Jacob – while standing over the grave of Jesus, whom he will not name. Jacob is, in effect, saying, 'I have a name and a reality that Jesus does not. And I connect it with the Bible because that text asserts my reality over his.'

The second time Jacob mentions his name is when he has to disguise himself at Hebron to gain access to the Tomb of the Patriarchs. Here he again uses his name to assert his identity, to reclaim himself. 'In Hebron, I, Jacob, entered in the guise of a Gentile into the cave which is the cave of Machpelah. The monks have built a structure upon it and falsely deceived the world.'[35] Jacob resorts to a ruse, but he justifies his dishonesty by pointing at the dishonesty of the monks. Jacob finds his identity so threatened by the events of his journey that he needs to remind the reader who he is. None of the events surrounding his trip suggests why he would feel more alienated than other medieval Jewish travellers, yet his discomfort shows clearly. Perhaps he is uncomfortable – and needs to reassure himself – in taking on the role of writer and seeing at close range the worship of other faiths.

Jacob's case is an extreme example of a writer reaching out to his readers for reassurance. For the most part, the relationship between the traveller and his audience is weighted to the side of the writer. He is the authority, and he lets the reader know it. The author asserts his authority, but it is never absolute. If he wants the readers of his pilgrimage account to share in the experience, he must cultivate a relationship with them. Readers have to trust an author in order to let him bring a strange world home.

Meshullam of Volterra in the fifteenth century is particularly adept at bringing home a strange world. Neither a teacher nor a tour guide, he is a storyteller who combines entertainment with edification and adds practical advice. He considers the possible scepticism of his audience, assumes his readers are familiar with Italian and the large cities of Italy, and invites them to share in his thanksgiving at having been saved.

Because these are religious travels, the authority of the writers is often expressed in religious terms, pointing to the piety of the writer and of his sources. If the writer does not have all the facts, he will try to explain why.

Benjamin of Tudela implies that he would be able to give accurate information if it were not for crusader devastations. In one part of his description, Benjamin seems to be concerned about his inability to have more concrete facts about early Jewish life in Jerusalem to give his audience. He blames the problem on the crusaders.[36]

Another way of demonstrating power is to translate words. In translating, the writer mediates between the reader and the experience. Using and then translating a term from a foreign language 'certainly makes for an effect of exoticism but also creates an impression of trustworthiness'.[37] Yet the very existence of foreign words is a reminder of the division between reader and writer and of the author's attempts to heal this rupture.

Benjamin of Tudela makes sure to translate Arabic phrases into Hebrew.[38] Meshullam of Volterra uses a great number of Italian phrases either because he does not have the Hebrew vocabulary for what he wants to convey, or because the Hebrew language does not have the word he needs. Very rarely does he translate. He does, however, use Arabic place names, though sometimes he tries to explain their Hebrew origins. Also, he properly translates 'Al-Quds' as 'the holy'. On the other hand, Meshullam describes the *waqf* system of trusts without ever using the Arabic word for it.

By establishing themselves as authorities, Jewish travellers used their books to engage their readers in a direct conversation. But travellers also let the places do the talking. This is travel writing without the writer. We have already discussed the presence or absence of narrators in pilgrim accounts. Here the narrator disappears entirely. If shrines truly can express themselves, then the very text becomes unnecessary.

When shrines do speak, what do they have to say? Mostly, it seems, they say 'hands off' to those who would destroy them. Christians and Jews both tell stories of holy graves asserting their independence, as it were, from foreign rulers. Miracles prevent all kinds of desecration.

Medieval Christians often, and Jewish pilgrims always, visit their holy sites as tolerated tourists. The holy places themselves are under the physical control of another faith. No wonder that pilgrims are so often relieved to find holy sites in good condition, and no wonder that they are worried that other places will fall into ruin. Even dedicated believers assume that that relics and shrines need human tending. Places that survive without caretaking are miracles in themselves. But some miracles go beyond survival. In some cases there is a definite, active event, such as a lion protecting a grave. Such dramatic events very rarely happen at the well-established holy places in Hebron and Jerusalem.

Jews, like Christians, had their own stories of graves and relics being miraculously protected from desecration. Jewish travellers assigned almost equal importance to graves of biblical figures and graves of pious individuals from the recent past. The focus on grave sites, particularly of the post-biblical era, is probably a way of staking a claim to the land. As Joshua Prawer explains: 'This claim to the Holy Land, the belief in its inalienability, is strengthened by permanent divine intervention and the miraculous events which happen there every day. God's providence guards the tombs of the holy men from the sacrilege of being touched by the gentiles (Muslims and Christians alike). Only Jews can approach them.'[39]

Benjamin of Tudela almost never mentions miracles, but he tells one long story about a miracle at a grave, attributing the story to a Rabbi Abraham Constantini. Two labourers, working on the restoration of the Church of Mount Zion, were making up for lost time by working through their meal break when they discovered a cave. Looking for money, they stumbled upon the graves of kings David and Solomon and the other kings of Judah. 'The two men essayed to enter the chamber, when a fierce wind came forth from the entrance of the cave and smote them, and they fell to the ground like dead men, and there they lay until evening. And there came forth a wind like a man's voice, crying out: "Arise and go forth from this place!" So the men rushed forth in terror, and they came unto the Patriarch, and related these things to him.'[40] The patriarch called in Rabbi Abraham, who told the men what they had found and suggested that they go with him and the patriarch to revisit the site. The frightened men would not go back, so the patriarch had the place closed up. The story has many of the 'they appreciate it too' elements for which medieval Jewish travellers are famous. The two workers instinctively recognise the hand of God in the story, and the patriarch recognises the wisdom and authority of Rabbi Abraham Constantini.

Jacob the Emissary tells only one story about a grave's being divinely protected, presumably from a Byzantine emperor:

> On another side of Jerusalem is the Lion's cave where are the bones of the righteous who were slaughtered by the King of Greece for the sanctity of the name. He ordered that they should be burnt on the following day, but in the night the lion came and removed them one by one into the cave out of the nether pool which they had filled. And behold, in the morning the Greek King found the lion at the entrance to the cave with the slain, and then the King and all his people knew that they were saints and their bones have remained there till this day.[41]

The lion as protector of sacred bones appears as a common theme among the Christian pilgrims as well.

A century later, Isaac Chelo tells a story of Jonah's tomb influencing a Muslim who had evil designs on the Jewish population as a whole, not just against a particular holy site. 'A Mussulman lord, enemy of the Jews, formerly dwelt at Kefar Kanah. He came forth one day from his palace filled with evil designs against the sons of Israel. Passing near the tomb of the prophet, he suddenly beheld before him a man in armour of terrifying aspect.'[42] The man turned out to be none other than Jonah himself, and the Muslim noble became a good friend to the Jews.

These last anecdotes show that just as the holy sites have the power to repel evildoers, they also have the power to attract. Most travellers notice that some of their holy sites are considered holy by member of other religions as well. For Christians and Jews there is a certain amount of vindication in other faiths' attaching value to their holy places. Seeing different religions drawn to the same location somehow proves that the places have an intrinsic holiness, a holiness so strong that it can be felt by others.

Non-Jewish veneration of Jewish holy sites produces a kind of triumphalism among Jewish pilgrims. On the one hand, Muslims and Christians are destroyers of the holy sites. On the other hand, their veneration of some sites serves to reinforce, if not actually validate, Jewish belief. The unspoken but likely explanation for this appreciation of the enemy is that if a shrine affects even the unbelievers, it must be truly significant. Jewish travellers notice Muslim and Christian appropriation of their sites with a mixture of despair and satisfaction.

Benjamin of Tudela describes the tomb of Ezekiel as a library and pilgrimage site for Jews and adds that Muslims too venerate the tomb of Ezekiel. 'Distinguished Mohammedans also come hither to pray, so great is their love for Ezekiel the Prophet; and they call it *Bar [Dar] Melicha* [the Dwelling of Beauty]. All the Arabs come here to pray . . . and even at times of disturbance no man would dare touch the Mohammedan or Jewish servants who attend at the sepulchre of Ezekiel.'[43] Jacob the emissary of Rabbi Yehiel of Paris remarks in the mid-thirteenth century only that over Ezekiel's grave is a synagogue 'more beautiful than the eye of man has ever seen'[44] but does not mention any Muslim veneration of the site.

Jacob the Emissary points out a number of Jewish sites treated with respect by Muslims. At the site of Elijah's altar 'is a building where the Moslems kindle lights to the glory of that place'.[45] He may recognise that sometimes the different religions disagree about who is buried in a certain place. He writes that on the grave of Rabbi Gamliel 'there is a fine cupola and it is a prayer house for the Moslems, a fine building which they call Abuhadira'.[46] It was venerated as the grave of the early Muslim traditionalist Abu Hurayra.

The phenomenon of Muslim respect for Jewish sites is, according to Jacob the Emissary, most obvious in Jerusalem itself.

> Round the *Eben Shethia*, the Ishmaelite Kings have built a very beautiful building for a house of prayer and erected on the top a very fine cupola. The building is on the site of the Holy of Holies and the Sanctuary, and in front of the Mosque towards the Altar is a structure of pillars and the cupola is at the top of these pillars and it would seem that this was the place of the outer Altar which was in

the Court of Israel. The Moslems gather there on their holy day [he transliterates the Arabic "*id*" rather than using a Hebrew equivalent] in crowds and dance around it in procession as the Israelites used to do on the seventh day of the festivals, if we may compare holy things with profane.[47]

He is quite willing to admire the architecture, if not the ritual. There is a mosque at the grave of Samuel, and also at the graves of Jonah and Jethro, because, as Jacob explains, 'it is the custom of the Moslems to make their prayer houses upon the graves of the righteous'.[48]

Meshullam of Volterra observes in the fifteenth century that even Muslims throw stones when they pass Absalom's monument because he rebelled against his father David.[49] In fact, David receives deep respect from Muslims, who care for the key to the tomb and come to pray there. (He notices that Franciscans treat the tomb respectfully as well.) He lists a few more of the graves in the Jerusalem area – including the nearby tomb of Rachel, where 'the Moslems have placed above her grave four pillars and an arch above. They honour her and both Jews and Moslems pray there.'[50] Then he comments that 'we see that the Moslems also honour all these places and that they have the same traditions about them as we. They ask the Jews "Why do you not go to the grave of such a saint or such a prophet?"'[51] But the sense of shared patrimony remains, 'and the Moslems call the whole surroundings of Jerusalem and Mount Zion *Al-Quds*, that is, "the Holy", since they call all this region the Holy Land'.[52]

In Jerusalem and Hebron, the shared heritage of Jews, Christians and Muslims overlaps most intensely. For pilgrims, however, this does not necessarily mean that the holy sites in these cities are protected by miracles. Relatively few supernatural events are recorded by medieval travellers at the Temple Mount in Jerusalem or at the Tomb of the Patriarchs in Hebron. In fact, at the well-known shrines the pilgrims often admire the buildings and architecture of other faiths.

The city of Hebron, where Abraham was buried, was an important stop for Jewish, Christian and Muslim pilgrims. Depending on who was in control, access for pilgrims of other religions could be difficult. At the end of the fifteenth century, when the area was ruled by the Mamluks, Felix Fabri and other members of his German tour group had a difficult time persuading their guides to bring them to Hebron. When the group did arrive in Hebron, crowds came out to see them because, according to Fabri, there had not been any Latin Christian pilgrims in Hebron in years.[53]

Benjamin of Tudela in the twelfth century tells how the Christian inhabitants of Hebron have overtaken a Jewish site. 'Here there is the great church called St Abram, and this was a Jewish place of worship at the time of the Mohammedan rule, but the gentiles ['*goyim*'] have erected there six tombs, respectively called those of Abraham and Sarah, Isaac and Rebekah, Jacob and Leah.'[54] It is not clear whether Benjamin considered this a holy site for Muslims as well.

Jewish travellers were not above subterfuge when it came to visiting the holy graves at Hebron. Benjamin needed to bribe a guard to get into a subterranean chamber that he considered the real burial place of Abraham, Sarah, Isaac, Rebecca, Jacob and Leah. As he explains, most visitors are fooled into believing that the newly labelled graves at ground level are authentic. 'The custodians tell the pilgrims that these are the tombs of the Patriarchs, for which information the pilgrims give them money. If a Jew comes, however, and gives a special reward, the custodian opens unto him a gate of iron, which was constructed in the days of our forefathers, and then he is able to descend below by means of steps, holding a lighted candle in his hand.'[55] Eventually the persistent pilgrim will find the graves, with names marked in stone. Benjamin uses these engravings as proof of the authenticity of his observations. Samuel ben Samson, travelling in 1210, about thirty years after Benjamin, has a similar story. He and two fellow travellers persuaded the gatekeeper to let them sneak in during the middle of the night.[56] Jacob haCohen also visited Hebron when it was under crusader rule and, as we saw earlier, had to disguise himself as a Christian to gain access.

In the later Muslim dynasties as well, open access for Jews was not always possible. Meshullam of Volterra, who went to pray at the tomb at the end of the fifteenth century, reports that his information about the graves of Abraham and Sarah comes from Jewish women who put on veils to go unnoticed into the mosque built above the tombs. Passing as Muslims, they are able to pray at the holy graves. The men have to be content with standing outside a small window. Meshullam is impressed by the respect that Muslims show to their own holy sites and feels that they may even be outdoing the Jews at their own game. They honour the graves at Hebron greatly, having built on top of them a mosque 'as is their custom', and they give a great deal of charity in honour of those who are buried there.[57]

The medieval Jewish traveller to Hebron did not generally describe miracles, only the difficulty of access to the holy tombs. Similarly, descriptions of Jerusalem focus on the writer's grief at seeing the Temple Mount in foreign hands but not on the miraculous properties of the place itself.

Only two Jewish travellers mention any miracles associated with the Tomb of the Patriarchs. The miracle in one case seems designed to keep away Jews as well as non-Jews. Petahia of Ratisbon, travelling at about the same time as Benjamin of Tudela (while crusaders ruled Hebron), says that the Jews of Acre told him to pay to get to the lower level of the cave. But whereas Benjamin went down with a candle, Petahia could not keep a candle lighted because of a strong wind. 'Whenever he bent towards the mouth of the cave a storm-wind went forth and cast him backwards.'[58] Jacob haCohen writes that a strong wind prevents only Christians from getting to the graves. A miracle differentiating between Muslims and Christians takes place on the Temple Mount in Jerusalem, according to Petahia of Ratisbon. He repeats a common story that a Jew told the first Muslim conquerors about the exact location of the Temple Mount. He continues that the Muslims built a 'beautiful structure consisting of red, green, and variegated marble. Then came gentiles [in Hebrew, 'goyim', but clearly referring to Christians] and put images in it, but they fell down. They then fixed the images in the thickness of the wall, but in the Holy of Holies they could not place any.'[59] Petahia's story is one of the very few dealing with the Temple Mount itself and ought to be read in light of the fact that it was apparently edited to meet the tastes of a readership eager for stories of relics and miracles.

Meshullam of Volterra sees Muslim rule in Jerusalem as it affects Jewish holy sites and cemeteries. However, he does not denigrate Muslim buildings. He describes the al-Aqsa Mosque as 'beautifully gilded . . . and the Ishmaelites have covered it with lead, and they say that this is doubtless the Holy of Holies'.[60] Meshullam explains that Muslims treat it with great respect, bathing five times and abstaining from sexual relations for three days before going to the site.[61] Although the Temple Mount is in Muslim hands, it still retains its holiness and the memory of its original Jewish sanctity. Every year on the anniversary of the destruction of the Temple, 'all the lamps in the Temple Court go out of their own accord, and cannot be kindled again, and the Moslems know when it is the 9th of *Ab*, which they observe somewhat like the Jews because of this. This is clear and known to everyone without any doubt'.[62]

This is the position of the medieval Jewish traveller to Jerusalem. He remembers the glory that once was, and he is certain that even non-Jews know deep down that Jerusalem is Jewish. But until the dream of redemption is realised, he will visit the Jerusalem that he knows. Along the way, he will notice – and perhaps even admire – the beautiful structures that others have built on his sacred sites.

### NOTES

1 The subject is treated in S. D. Goitein, *A Mediterranean Society: The Jewish Communities of the Arab World as Portrayed in the Documents of the Cairo Geniza*, 5 vols (Berkeley: University of California University Press, 1969–88), and Joshua Prawer, *The History of the Jews in the Latin Kingdom of Jerusalem* (Oxford: Clarendon Press, 1988). One major collection of Jewish travel writing is J. D. Eisenstein (ed.), *Ozar Massaoth: A Collection of Itineraries by Jewish Travellers to Palestine, Syria, Egypt and Other Countries* (New York: J. D. Eisenstein, 1926, repr. Tel Aviv: J. D. Eisenstein, 1969). Excerpts from this book are translated in Elkan Natan Adler (ed.), *Jewish Travellers* (New York: Harmon Press, 2nd edn, 1966). Most quotations in this chapter are from the Adler translation with references to the original Hebrew in the Eisenstein edition.

2 A first-century BCE building in Jerusalem which might have been a synagogue with lodging quarters on the roof was inscribed 'for needy travellers from foreign lands': Robert L. Wilken, 'Christian pilgrimage to the Holy Land', in Nitza Rosovsky (ed.), *City of the Great King: Jerusalem from David to the Present* (Cambridge, MA, and London: Harvard University Press, 1996), pp. 117–35, at p. 121.

3 A'hron Oppenheimer, *'Terumot and Ma'aserot'*, in Cecil Roth (editor-in-chief), *Encyclopedia Judaica*, 16 vols (New York: Macmillan, 1972–82), xv, pp. 1075–8.

4 Bordeaux Pilgrim, *Itinerary from Bordeaux to Jerusalem*, trans. Aubrey Stewart Palestine Pilgrims' Text Society, 1 (London: Palestine Pilgrims' Text Society, 1887; repr. New York: AMS Press, 1971), p. 22.

5 Babylonian Talmud, Tractate *Moed Qatan* 26a, trans. Maurice Simon, ed. I. Epstein, 18 vols (London: Soncino Press, 1952), vol. 5, p. 52.

6 J. Mann, *Texts and Studies in Jewish History Literature*, 2 vols (Cincinnati: Hebrew Union College Press, 1931), ii, pp. 464–5.

7 M. Margolioth, *Halakhoth on the Land of Israel from the Genizah* (Jerusalem, 1974), pp. 139–41 (Hebrew), as quoted in Wilken, 'Christian pilgrimage', p. 123.

8 Mark Friedman, 'Jewish pilgrimage after the destruction of the Second Temple', in Rosovsky (ed.), *City of the Great King*, pp. 140–51. See also Moshe Gil, 'Aliya and pilgrimage in the early Arab period (634–1009)', *The Jerusalem Cathedra*, 3 (1983), 162–91.

9 Prawer, *History*, p. 173 n. 6.

10 Babylonian Talmud, Tractate *Berakhot* 54a, trans. Maurice Simon, ed. I. Epstein, 18 vols (London: Soncino Press, 1952), vol. 1, p. 108.

11 Friedman, 'Jewish pilgrimage', pp. 140–57, at p. 146.

12 Adler (ed.), *Jewish Travellers*, p. 115; Eisenstein (ed.), *Ozar Massaoth*, p. 66. The Hebrew refers to 'the Land of Israel', as do all Jewish accounts. The term 'Holy Land' is associated with Christian writings.

13 Adler (ed.), *Jewish Travellers*, pp. 73 and 78; Eisenstein (ed.), *Ozar Massaoth*, pp. 50 and 52.

14 Benjamin of Tudela, *The Itinerary of Benjamin of Tudela: Travels in the Middle Ages*, trans. Marcus Nathan Adler, 1907, with introductions by Michael A. Signer, 1983, and A. Asher, 1840 (New York: Joseph Simon, 1983), p. 61; Eisenstein (ed.), *Ozar Massaoth*, p. 19.

15 *Ibid.*, p. 21. Benjamin calls Christian pilgrims *'to'im'* – 'mistaken ones'.

16 Eisenstein (ed.), *Ozar Massaoth*, p. 39. Benjamin is one of the earliest Europeans to comment on the pearl industry in the Persian Gulf, though naturally it was well known among Arab writers. The Moroccan Ibn Battutah also visited Bahrain but may not have been there at the right time of year to observe pearl fishing. See R. A. Donkin, *Beyond price: Pearls and Pearl-Fishing: Origins to the Age of Discovery*, (Philadelphia: American Philosophical Society, 1998), pp. 123–4.

17 Signer raises most of these possibilities in the introduction to Benjamin of Tudela, *Itinerary* (1983), pp. 13–30. Jane Gerber has suggested in conversation that Benjamin may have been a textile dyer. He certainly pays close attention to different phases of the textile industry.

18 Adler (ed.), *Jewish Travellers*, p. 174; Eisenstein (ed.), *Ozar Massaoth*, p. 94. The language here may be figurative, but it may be that Meshullam had vowed to make the pilgrimage as a kind of penance.

19 Adler (ed.), *Jewish Travellers*, p. 189; Eisenstein (ed.), *Ozar Massaoth*, p. 99.

20 Adler (ed.), *Jewish Travellers*, p. 134; Eisenstein (ed.), *Ozar Massaoth*, p. 73.

21 Felix Fabri, *The Book of the Wanderings of Brother Felix Fabri*, trans. Aubrey Stewart, Palestine Pilgrims' Text Society, 2 vols (London: Palestine Pilgrims' Text Society,

1887–97; repr. New York: AMS Press, 1971), i, p. 50. On Fabri see Catherine Delano-Smith in Chapter 6 and Anne Simon in Chapter 10 below.

22 Adler (ed.), *Jewish Travellers*, p. 164; Eisenstein (ed.), *Ozar Massaoth*, p. 91.

23 Benjamin of Tudela, *Itinerary*, p. 55; Eisenstein (ed.), *Ozar Massaoth*, p. 18.

24 Adler (ed.), *Jewish Travellers*, p. 131; Eisenstein (ed.), *Ozar Massaoth*, p. 72. He is called 'Benjamin the traveller': '*ha-nose'a*'.

25 Benjamin of Tudela, *Itinerary*, p. 84; Eisenstein (ed.), *Ozar Massaoth*, p. 27.

26 Adler (ed.), *Jewish Travellers*, p. 89; Eisenstein (ed.), *Ozar Massaoth*, p. 56.

27 Prawer, *History*, p. 212.

28 Adler (ed.), *Jewish Travellers*, p. 85; Eisenstein (ed.), *Ozar Massaoth*, p. 54 has 'there is no need to write'.

29 Adler (ed.), *Jewish Travellers*, p. 120; Eisenstein (ed.), *Ozar Massaoth*, p. 68. The reference is to Genesis 37:14.

30 Adler (ed.), *Jewish Travellers*, p. 66; Eisenstein (ed.), *Ozar Massaoth*, p. 48.

31 Benjamin of Tudela, *Itinerary*, p. 118; Eisenstein (ed.), *Ozar Massaoth*, p. 39.

32 Adler (ed.), *Jewish Travellers*, p. 92; Eisenstein (ed.), *Ozar Massaoth*, p. 59.

33 Adler (ed.), *Jewish Travellers*, p. 99; Eisenstein (ed.), *Ozar Massaoth*, p. 62. The Hebrew does not emphasise the word 'me' as the English does.

34 Eisenstein (ed.), *Ozar Massaoth*, p. 61 (my trans., his brackets). Eisenstein added the phrase 'that man' to clarify; Adler has 'by the grave of Jesus'.

35 Adler (ed.), *Jewish Travellers*, p. 98; Eisenstein (ed.), *Ozar Massaoth*, p. 61.

36 Benjamin of Tudela, *Itinerary*, p. 84; Eisenstein (ed.), *Ozar Massaoth*, p. 27.

37 François Hartog, *The Mirror of Herodotus: The Representation of the Other in the Writing of History* (Berkeley: University of California Press, 1988), p. 238.

38 Benjamin must have been writing for a broad audience. Jews from Tudela retained Arabic as their spoken language even after the Christian conquest of the town in 1115, and Benjamin almost certainly knew Arabic.

39 Prawer, *History*, p. 174.

40 Benjamin of Tudela, *Itinerary*, p. 85; Eisenstein (ed.), *Ozar Massaoth*, p. 27.

41 Adler (ed.), *Jewish Travellers*, p. 119; Eisenstein (ed.), *Ozar Massaoth*, p. 67.

42 Adler (ed.), *Jewish Travellers*, p. 145; Eisenstein (ed.), *Ozar Massaoth*, p. 77.

43 Benjamin of Tudela, *Itinerary*, pp. 104–5; Eisenstein (ed.), *Ozar Massaoth*, p. 34.

44 Adler (ed.), *Jewish Travellers*, p. 128; Eisenstein (ed.), *Ozar Massaoth*, p. 71.

45 Adler (ed.), *Jewish Travellers*, p. 116; Eisenstein (ed.), *Ozar Massaoth*, p. 66 uses '*qedushat ha-maqom*' – 'the holiness of the place'.

46 Adler (ed.), *Jewish Travellers*, pp. 125–6; Eisenstein (ed.), *Ozar Massaoth*, p. 70.

47 Adler (ed.), *Jewish Travellers*, pp. 118–19; Eisenstein (ed.), *Ozar Massaoth*, p. 67.

48 Adler (ed.), *Jewish Travellers*, p. 125; Eisenstein (ed.), *Ozar Massaoth*, pp. 69–70.

49 Adler (ed.), *Jewish Travellers*, p. 192; Eisenstein (ed.), *Ozar Massaoth*, p. 100.

50 Adler (ed.), *Jewish Travellers*, pp. 188–9.

51 *Ibid.*, p. 194; Eisenstein (ed.), *Ozar Massaoth*, p. 101.

52 *Ibid.*, p. 102, my trans.

53 Fabri, *Wanderings*, i, pp. 407–16.

54 Benjamin of Tudela, *Itinerary*, p. 86; Eisenstein (ed.), *Ozar Massaoth*, p. 28.

55 Benjamin of Tudela, *Itinerary*, p. 86; Eisenstein (ed.), *Ozar Massaoth*, p. 28.

56 Adler (ed.), *Jewish Travellers*, p. 105; Eisenstein (ed.), *Ozar Massaoth*, p. 63.

57 Adler (ed.), *Jewish Travellers*, p. 185; Eisenstein (ed.), *Ozar Massaoth*, p. 98.

58 Adler (ed.), *Jewish Travellers*, p. 90; Eisenstein (ed.), *Ozar Massaoth*, p. 56.

59 Adler (ed.), *Jewish Travellers*, p. 89; Eisenstein (ed.), *Ozar Massaoth*, p. 56.

60 Adler (ed.), *Jewish Travellers*, p. 190; Eisenstein (ed.), *Ozar Massaoth*, p. 100.

61 I know of no such practice. Some Muslim pilgrims visited Jerusalem and entered the state of *ihram*, or holy readiness, there before continuing to Mecca, although this was documented well before the life of Meshullam of Volterra. See Amikam Elad, *Medieval Jerusalem and Islamic Worship: Holy Places, Ceremonies, Pilgrimage* (Leiden: Brill, 1995), pp. 62–5.

62 Adler (ed.), *Jewish Travellers*, p. 190; Eisenstein (ed.), *Ozar Massaoth*, p. 100.

# 3

## Travel in the medieval Islamic world: the importance of patronage, as illustrated by 'Abd al-Latif al-Baghdadi (d. 629/1231) (and other littérateurs)

**❰❱**

### Shawkat M. Toorawa

Shawkat M. Toorawa

INTRODUCTION: TRAVEL IN THE MEDIEVAL ISLAMIC WORLD

M ENTION travel in the medieval Islamic world to people, and they are likely to respond with 'You mean Ibn Battutah!'.[1] They may know of Ibn Fadlan (*fl.* early fourth/tenth century), especially if they have seen what is perhaps the only Hollywood adaptation (the word is loosely applied) of a medieval Arabic text other than the *Arabian nights*.[2] Scholars are just as likely to name Ibn Battutah, Ibn Fadlan and also Ibn Jubayr (d. 1217). Regrettably, the fascinating and complex subject of travel in the medieval Islamic world (here the ninth to sixteenth centuries) has received very little critical and theoretical attention indeed. Scholarship has tended to be descriptive, has focused disproportionately on a handful of travellers, and has been content with the sub-division of travel into one or more of four categories: (i) scholars' travel in search of knowledge (*al-rihlah fi talab al-'ilm* – which is understood to include the travel undertaken by individuals (*muhaddith*) in order to collect traditions (*hadith*) of the Prophet Muhammad); (ii) pilgrimage to Mecca (*hajj*); (iii) travels of adventure and exploration (*rihlah*); and (iv) mercantile travel (*li al-tijarah*). Some scholars add migration and emigration (*hijrah*). This taxonomy (which could benefit from some nuancing) is useful, but it excludes a very important, widespread and, to the best of my knowledge, unstudied form of travel: namely, journeying to, with or on account of patrons.

In the preface to their thoughtful 1990 edited volume on travel, Dale Eickelman and James Piscatori opened with the most sustained (if brief) reflection to date on what travel might be and might mean for medieval Muslims:

The subject of Muslim travel is unexpectedly complex. One might assume that religious doctrine prescribes certain kinds of travel, and that the ritual movement of Muslims leads to a heightened identification with Islam and with fellow Muslims. But the chapters of this book question that conventional wisdom. In looking for the answers to the basic questions that underlie the discussion – What does travel mean to Muslims? What are its motivations? What are its effects? – we are struck by a pervasive intricacy and even ambiguity.[3]

Eickelman and Piscatori enlarge the erstwhile narrow readings of the Arabic term *rihlah* (literally 'travel') to include 'travel for learning *or other purposes*' (emphasis mine);[4] and to pilgrimage and travel in search of knowledge they usefully add *ziyarah* (visits to shrines) and emigration (*hijrah*).[5] But, because their focus is the travel of Muslims in particular, their purview is limited and does not include the travel by non-Muslims in Islamic lands.

In the Cambridge History of Arabic Literature, medieval travel is treated principally in a volume devoted to the 'Abbasid period, which appeared in 1990.[6] But of J. F. P. Hopkins's twenty-seven pages on 'Geographical and navigational literature', only two are devoted to 'travellers' proper, perhaps because, as Hopkins claims, 'The medieval Muslim traveller travelled for trade or in search of learning, not to see the world'.[7] Hopkins does, however, specifically mention the anonymous ninth-century merchant's compilation, *Akhbar al-Sin wa al-Hind* ('Accounts of China and India'), as a work on human geography; Ibn Fadlan's tenth-century account of his embassy to the Bulghars; Buzurg ibn Shahriyar's tenth-century *mirabilia* work, *'Aja'ib al-Hind* ('Wonders of India'), 'which sometimes strains credulity to breaking point'; and the thirteenth- and fourteenth-century travels of Ibn Jubayr and Ibn Battutah respectively.[8] But he implies, by his silence about other travel and other travellers, that these are unique, and does not characterise the travels undertaken for reasons other than pilgrimage, travel in search of knowledge, and adventure.

The 1994 entry on 'Rihla' in the *Encyclopaedia of Islam* defines the term as 'a journey, voyage, travel; also a travelogue' but nevertheless focuses exclusively on travel in search of knowledge and pilgrimage, and refers only to the writings of Ibn Jubayr and Ibn Battutah.[9] No other traveller or form of travel is mentioned. This is unfortunate since the author, Ian R. Netton, as both editor of a 1993 collection and author of a 1996 volume on travel in Islam, ought to be well positioned to discuss the subject in greater depth.[10] The *Encyclopaedia of Islam* article on 'Safar', which is defined as 'journey, travel', also from 1994, is sub-divided by the author, R. Peters, into '1. In law' and '2. In Islamic life'.[11] Under the first heading is a brief discussion of the rules in Islamic law governing such issues as ritual prayer and ritual purity during a journey.[12] The second consists in nothing but the following:

2. In Islamic life. See for this, 'Funduq' [inn]; 'Khan' [hostel]; 'Rihla' [travel]; 'Tijara' [commerce]. For envoys and ambassadors, see 'Elči' [Turkish for envoy]; 'Safir [ambassador].2'. For the pilgrims to Mecca, see 'Hajj' [pilgrimage].iii.A. To the Bibls. of these articles, add I. R. Netton (ed.), Golden Roads..., London 1993.[13]

In his 1998 encyclopaedia entry on travel literature, C. E. Bosworth proves to be the scholar who has so far been the most explicit in identifying forms of travel and its motivations.[14] After mentioning the embassies of Ibn Fadlan and Abu Dulaf[15] as examples of travel outside the Islamic world, he writes:[16] 'Within the Islamic world, however, there was much travel by pilgrims, heading for Mecca and Medina or the Shi'i shrines; by scholars seeking out famous teachers or institutions of learning; by Sufi mystics attracted by a charismatic shaykh; by religious propagandists, such as the Isma'ili ones; by officials and diplomatic envoys; but above all, by traders.'

To pilgrimage (to Mecca and shrines), travel in search of knowledge, embassy, adventure and trade, Bosworth has added the travel of religious propagandists and the travel of Sufis in search of masters.

Still, neither Bosworth nor any of the other above-named scholars of travel in medieval Islam has considered patronage.

## PATRONAGE AND PATRON-MOTIVATED TRAVEL

Patronage is the support (financial and political), encouragement (moral, social and economic) and championing of an individual or group engaged in an activity without which they would otherwise have difficulty performing that activity.[17] Patronage in the classical and medieval Islamic world, though well documented, has not been studied in any detail.[18] The earliest form of patronage appears to have been that of the poets of pre-Islamic Arabia by their respective tribes. By extolling the tribe's successes in battle and the valour, virtues and virility of its heroes, living and fallen, a poet acquired prestige and often great fame. In addition, the poet was called upon to declaim satires of the tribe's enemies, often in public poetry contests. And yet it was the activities of poets who composed under quite different circumstances, the tribally unaffiliated, wandering (su'luk) poets, and those individuals attached to the north Arabian vassal courts of Byzantium and Sasanid Persia, who in fact presaged the system of patronage that would rapidly supplant the tribal one. As Islam spread, centres of cultural patronage sprang up all over the Islamic world. In addition to the court of the caliph, senior officials, regional governors and wealthy notables granted patronage. To these patrons gravitated itinerant littérateurs and scholars who composed poems and works, often for the highest bidders and often in response to the egotistic needs of a given patron. The sources describe in great detail the soirées held in the homes of these patrons; some, such as the courtier 'Ali ibn Yahya Ibn al-Munajjim (d. 889), were writers and scholars of distinction themselves.

By surrounding themselves with men of letters and learning, patrons conferred prestige on themselves and demonstrated their discernment, refinement and devotion to literature and scholarship. For patrons who were unlearned or even illiterate, patronage was a way of offsetting (or deflecting attention from) that apparent deficiency. Thus, the Turkish prince Bakjam (d. 941) patronised the courtier, anthologist and chess master Abu Bakr al-Suli (d. c. 945) when the 'Abbasid caliph al-Muttaqi (d. 944) abruptly terminated his patronage averring that the only companion he needed henceforth was the Qur'an.

Patronage could extend to entire groups, for instance, the support that the caliph al-Ma'mun (d. 833) gave to the Mu'tazili rationalists, or the support that the minister Ibn Hubayrah (d. c. 1165) gave to the entire Hanbali guild of law. The Saljuq sultan Malik Shah (d. 1092) supported astronomers, Sufi orders and colleges of law; in his patronage of the latter, he was rivalled by his own chief minister, Nizam al-Mulk (d. 1092). Patronage did not only come from officials: the bon vivants 'Abd Allah ibn Ja'far and Ibn Abi 'Atiq supported musicians in eighth-century Medina. Individuals, merchants and landowners were often the source of support for religious scholars, and in particular for mosques (especially through the institution of the eleemosynary waqf). And ordinary folk patronised prayer leaders and preachers through small gifts and stipends.

But it was the patronage of the very wealthy that motivated travel. It was the lure of someone such as Harun al-Rashid (d. 809) in Baghdad, Sayf al-Dawlah (d. 967) in Aleppo, Ibn al-'Amid (d. 990) in Shiraz, Saladin (d. 1193) in Jerusalem, that made men travel considerable distances. They not only sought out these patrons, but often also travelled with them, from one regional or seasonal court to another, on military campaigns, on diplomatic missions and in flight from enemies and aggressors.

The poet Abu Tammam (d. 845) converted, and left his Christian family in Syria for Cairo, where he studied poetry.[19] He returned to Syria around 829, a few years later, and was patronised by the caliph al-Mu'tasim (d. 842) and other senior officials in Baghdad. Abu Tammam also travelled to many regional courts including ones in Armenia and Nishapur. Unhappy with his takings (and the weather!) in Nishapur, Abu Tammam decided to return to Syria. During his journey home, he was snowed-in in Hamadhan. There, relying on the library of a friend, he composed his celebrated anthology, al-Hamasah ('Bravery') while he waited for conditions to clear. The last few years of his life Abu Tammam spent as postmaster of Mosul, a position obtained for him by the secretary al-Hasan ibn Wahb. Abu Tammam's younger Kufan contemporary Muslim ibn al-Walid (d. 823) was similarly made a postmaster in the East, in Jurjan, by a benevolent secretary of the Caliph al-Ma'mun (d. 833) after his many years at Harun al-Rashid's court in Baghdad. Another contemporary of Abu Tammam, the Baghdadi musician Ziryab (d. 845), travelled west to North Africa and was then invited to Cordoba by its ruler. During his time there he would play a major role in the articulation and elaboration of a new Andalusian culture.

The poet al-Mutanabbi (d. 965) travelled often and for many reasons. He was born in Kufa, and spent several years as a lad among the Bedouin of Lower Iraq and a few years in Baghdad before leaving for Syria in 930. He spent three years there as an itinerant panegyrist before being arrested and imprisoned for brigandage. He was released in 937 and, continuing his search for patronage, attached himself to various minor officials. When Sayf al-Dawlah took Aleppo, al-Mutanabbi fled to Damascus by way of Tripoli, but when Sayf al-Dawlah took Antioch in 948, al-Mutanabbi celebrated this in a poem, and was consequently retained by the prince at his brilliant court. This not only meant livelihood for almost a decade, but required that the poet (as was the custom) often accompany the ruler on his military campaigns.[20] Having made a number of enemies (including Sayf al-Dawlah himself), al-Mutanabbi fled in 957 to the court of Kafur in Egypt. Here too relations between poet and patron quickly soured and al-Mutanabbi fled once again, to Kufa. A year later he was in Baghdad but was forced by the situation created by his rivals to return to Kufa. He was then invited by Ibn al-'Amid to his court in Arrajan, and by 'Adud al-Dawlah (d. 983) to his court in Shiraz. A longing for Iraq and Syria saw al-Mutanabbi on the move again but he was ambushed and killed on his journey home.

The royal poet Abu Firas was a cousin of Sayf al-Dawlah's and a bitter rival of al-Mutanabbi's. He travelled to Manbij when he was appointed governor there and was also twice taken captive by the Byzantines, once in 959 when he managed to escape, and once from 962 to 966 in Byzantium itself. That stay inspired his so-called 'Rumiyyat' poems. Another companion of Sayf al-Dawlah was the author Abu Bakr al-Khwarizmi (d. 993), who was born in Khwarazm, in the extreme east of the Islamic Empire (present-day Uzbekistan), and who travelled extensively. In addition to the court in Aleppo, he attended the court of al-Sahib ibn 'Abbad (d. 995) in Rayy as well as other courts in Iran, including Nishapur, where he settled and died.

The prose stylist al-Tawhidi (d. 1023) aspired to the patronage of Ibn al-'Amid and al-Sahib ibn 'Abbad. His difficult personality ended his brief associations with them and he returned to Baghdad, but not without having acquired material for his works, including his celebrated *Akhlaq al-wazirayn* ('The faults of the two viziers'). The philosopher and historian Miskawayh (d. 1030) was tutored, and then worked as tutor, at the Buyid dynasty's courts in his native Iran – Shiraz, Rayy, Isfahan, Hamadhan. He later joined the court of 'Adud al-Dawlah in Baghdad. When the ruler died and Miskawayh's fortunes changed, he returned to Iran. Like al-Tawhidi's, his works reveal his wide travel and exposure to patrons and their courts.

Al-Biruni (d. *c.* 1050) was born in Khwarazm, where he served local rulers in the capital Kath, and also served in Jurjan, until circumstances forced him to leave. He went to the court of Mahmud of Ghazna (in south-eastern Afghanistan), where he was retained and where he earned his reputation as the one of the world's great scientists. At about the same time, al-Khatib al-Baghdadi (d. 1071), the famous historian of Baghdad, travelled extensively in search of *hadith* before returning to his home town and embarking on a very successful teaching and preaching career. But this was not the only form of travel al-Khatib al-Baghdadi was to undertake. Like so many other Muslim scholars, he went on a *rihlah*, leaving Baghdad in 1053 and travelling to Syria and Mecca, before returning in 1055. The timing of this pilgrimage may have been connected to animosity he experienced in Baghdad. That was certainly the reason for his flight in 1060 for Damascus, which he had to flee in turn eight years later. He did return to Baghdad, where he died.

The Hebrew poet Moses ibn Ezra (d. 1135) was forced to flee Granada when he found himself penniless after the fall of Islamic Spain to the North African Muslim Almoravids, who had grown impatient with their Spanish Muslim allies. He went to the Christian north, where he wrote poems to his friends complaining about his exile. Al-Mu'tamid ibn 'Abbad (d. 1095), the ruler-poet of Seville who was exiled by the Almoravids to Aghmat, also composed poetry (regarded as his finest), in which he describes his captivity and imprisonment. And the Granadan poet and jurist al-Ilbiri (d. 1067) wrote a famous lament about the destruction of a retreat near Elvira where he was exiled. The popular poet and goliard Ibn Quzman (d. 1160) was patronised by the princes of Cordoba until its fall to the Almoravids. He then travelled to Seville and Granada for supplementary patronage. Hazim al-Qartajanni (d. 1285) was a polymath who studied in Murcia, Granada and Seville before emigrating to Marrakesh when Cordoba fell in 1236 to the Christians of northern Spain during the Reconquista, and then again to Tunis in 1242.

Just as a number of poets fled the Almoravids, the blind poet al-Husri (d. 1095) fled Qayrawan to escape another group, the invading Banu Hilal.[21] In 1057 he went to Ceuta, then on to Islamic Spain, where he was poet to a number of rulers. He returned to North Africa after a series of personal tragedies, settling in Tangiers in 1090. For his part, Ibn al-'Adim (d. 1262), who served as a judge in Aleppo, was forced to flee to Cairo in 1260 when the westward-moving Mongols invaded the Levant. (Baghdad had fallen to them in 1258.)

'Umarah al-Yamani (d. 1174) was born in coastal Yemen and visited Aden as a trader. There he met travelling *da'is* or Fatimid propagandists from

Egypt. In 1155 he was made emissary to the Shi'ite Fatimids (909–1171) in Cairo. After the fall of the Fatimids to the Ayyubids (1171–1250), 'Umarah was briefly a poet to the new Ayyubid ruler, Saladin, until the latter had him executed for his alleged sympathy for the fallen Fatimids. The great sufi thinker Ibn al-'Arabi (d. 1240) was born in Murcia but left Islamic Spain in the late twelfth century and travelled widely, to regions including Syria and Anatolia, in search of teachers and knowledge, but also sometimes fleeing persecution. In Egypt, for instance, he was nearly put to death for heresy. Maimonides (Musa ibn Maymun, d. 1204) fled Cordoba for Fez with his family when the new Muslim rulers outlawed Judaism. In 1165 the family fled again, to Palestine, then to Alexandria and Cairo. After two decades in private medical practice, Maimonides became court physician to a number of Ayyubid officials and royals.

It is clear from the above sampling of travelling individuals that the world of medieval Islam occasioned and facilitated multiple forms of travel; it should be equally clear that patronage was a very significant motivator of travel. But the importance and impact of patron-motivated travel can be demonstrated by looking at the travels of the polymath 'Abd al-Latif al-Baghdadi: all his *early* travels are all in search of knowledge, instruction, teachers and books; and all his *later* travels are all motivated by, or at the behest of, patrons.

### 'ABD AL-LATIF'S EARLY SCHOLARLY TRAVEL

Most of the information we have about the life and travels of 'Abd al-Latif comes from selections of his autobiography preserved in the biographical notice devoted to him by his younger contemporary Ibn Abi Usaybi'ah (d. 1270) in his biographical dictionary of physicians, '*Uyun al-anba' fi tabaqat al-atibba'* ('Sources of information on the classes of physicians').[22]

'Abd al-Latif was raised in the company of eminent scholars in Baghdad.[23] He studied *hadith*, disputation and dialectic, grammar and calligraphy, and he memorised the Quran and key scholarly texts. When he was an adolescent his father took him to Kamal al-Din al-Anbari (d. 1181) but, 'Abd al-Latif writes, 'I couldn't understand one bit of his continuous and considerable jabbering, even though his students seemed pleased enough with it.'[24] Al-Anbari referred 'Abd al-Latif for a time to his disciple, al-Wajih al-Wasiti (d. 1215), whom he found to be kind and knowledgeable and whom he eventually 'surpassed in both memorisation and comprehension'.[25] 'Abd al-Latif memorised over 130 works with al-Wasiti and al-Anbari, often on his way home from lectures or on his way to the mosque.

After al-Anbari died in 1181, 'Abd al-Latif devoted himself to the study of the so-called foreign sciences. 'Abd al-Latif studied medicine with the son of

Ibn Tilmidh, from whom he says he learned a great deal, and alchemy with a certain 'Abd Allah Ibn Na'ili. In 1189, 'when there no longer remained in Baghdad anyone to win [his] heart or satisfy [his] desires, or to help [him] resolve what was perplexing [him]',[26] he went to Mosul, where he was to be disappointed by the paucity of scholars, but where he took up a teaching post at a *madrasah*, or college of law. Fortunately for him, he did find in al-Kamal ibn Yunus (d. 1242) an able mathematician and scholar of law also interested in alchemy. After a year of vigorous independent study supported by a teaching position at a college of law, 'Abd al-Latif read works by al-Ghazali (d. 1111), all the books of Ibn Sina (Avicenna, d. 1027), interpretations by Avicenna's disciple, Bahmanyar (d. 1067) and books by Jabir ibn Hayyan (d. *c.* 815) and Ibn Wahshiyyah (*fl.* 8th–10th century) on alchemy. 'Abd al-Latif heard about Shihab al-Din al-Suhrawardi, whom people praised very highly, and set about reading his works.

'Abd al-Latif left for Damascus in 1190, where he found a group of scholars who gathered through the patronage of Saladin. There, he debated with the grammarian al-Kindi al-Baghdadi (*fl.* late twelfth century), who was an 'intelligent, sharp-witted, and wealthy professor, with a certain amount of influence, but who was quite taken with himself and offensive to his company'.[27] 'Abd al-Latif worked on several of his own books, then came across his former teacher Ibn Na'ili again. 'Abd al-Latif describes their meetings as follows: 'I used to get together with him and he would ask me to describe certain procedures so that he could record them, procedures I thought contemptible and trivial . . . I saw through him, though.'[28] 'Abd al-Latif further reproached him for his misguided attention to alchemy and philosophy rather than to the Islamic and rational sciences but Ibn Na'ili persisted in his interests. This prompted them to part ways. Ibn Na'ili soon thereafter left for Acre to complain to Saladin about his detractors. 'Abd al-Latif made a similar trip, setting out for Jerusalem and Saladin's camp outside Acre, where he met the military judge Baha' al-Din Ibn Shaddad (d. 1234). Ibn Shaddad had heard of 'Abd al-Latif's fame and suggested that he call on the secretary 'Imad al-Din al-Katib, who in turn suggested a visit to al-Qadi al-Fadil. Al-Qadi al-Fadil urged 'Abd al-Latif to travel to Damascus, for which he would receive a retainer. 'Abd al-Latif insisted on Cairo: 'I said that I preferred Egypt, upon which he replied: "The sultan is anxious about the Franks' capture of Acre and the slaying of Muslims there . . ." "But it simply must be Egypt," I insisted, so he wrote me a short note to his agent there'.[29]

'Abd al-Latif soon found himself on his way to Cairo, with a guaranteed stipend. He writes that he went to Cairo in order to seek out three scholars: Yasin al-Simiya'i (d. early thirteenth century), Maimonides (d. 1208) and Abu al-Qasim al-Shari'i (d. 1202). The first two were a disappointment:

As it turned out, all three came to me. Yasin I found to be absurd, a liar, and a conjuring cheat . . . It was said of him that he could do things even the Prophet Moses was unable to do, that he could produce minted gold whenever he wished, of any quantity he wished, and of any minting he wished, and that he could turn the waters of the Nile into a tent in which he would then sit with his friends. He was most churlish.

When Maimonides came to see me, I found him to be tremendously learned, but overcome with the love of leadership and of service to worldy lords.[30]

In Abu al-Qasim al-Shari'i, on the other hand, 'Abd al-Latif found exactly what he was looking for and studied with him al-Farabi, the tenth-century philosopher who became known as 'the second Master' (the first being Aristotle),[31] and the second-century Alexander Aphrodisaeus, regarded as the most authoritative commentator on Aristotle of his age.

When a truce had been negotiated with the crusaders (September 1192), 'Abd al-Latif returned to Jerusalem and then, taking with him as many books as possible, sought out Saladin, in whose company he remained, and whom he describes as 'a great sovereign, generous, affectionate, and awesome to behold, who filled the hearts of those near and far with love'.[32] The thirty-dinar monthly stipend provided by Saladin was supplemented by his sons to bring the total to the extraordinary sum of 100 dinars. Makdisi writes that 'this amount, at the time, was ten times the normal monthly stipend of a college professor of law . . . Ten dinars is half the amount paid to a physician of the fourteenth century.'[33] 'Abd al-Latif then returned to Damascus, where he took up studies and teaching in the Umayyad Mosque. He also devoted himself to the study of the ancients, whom he read assiduously. He writes that he was thereby saved from two ruinous influences: 'My thanks to God were thus redoubled, for most intellectuals have followed the road to perdition simply through alchemy and the books of Avicenna.'[34] On 3 March 1193 Saladin died and Damascus came under the rule of his eldest son, al-Malik al-Afdal. Of Saladin's death, 'Abd al-Latif writes:

Saladin entered Damascus, accompanied the pilgrimage caravan out of the city to bid it farewell, returned, and contracted a fever. He was bled by a man without any skill, so his strength gave out and he died . . . I have never seen a ruler whose death so saddened the people. This was because he was loved by the pious and the profligate alike, by Muslim and non-Muslim.[35]

In an earlier article, informed by Eve Sedgwick's identification of merging patterns of male friendship, mentorship, entitlement and rivalry, I argued that the language of the medieval Arabic autobiography 'reveals the closed and male homosocially desiring structure of the relationship between men and the scholarly community'.[36] I used 'Abd al-Latif's autograph notes to show that its language, i.e. specific expressions and turns of phrase, serves to reinforce the male homosocial bond, a bond that is not one of brotherhood (as the pedagogical environment might suggest) but rather one of 'extreme, compulsory, and intensely volatile mastery and subordination'.[37]

In my reading, after 'Abd al-Latif finds Abu al-Qasim al-Shari'i, who represents the fulfilment of desire, only masters *extraordinaires* will do, hence 'Abd al-Latif's recourse to sovereigns. Whether one accepts my argument or not, the fact remains that after meeting Saladin and after al-Shari'i's death, 'Abd al-Latif is no longer guided by his need for the company of masters and peers but is at the mercy, and on the payroll, of patrons.

### 'ABD AL-LATIF'S LATER PATRON-MOTIVATED TRAVEL

'Abd al-Latif remained with al-Malik al-Afdal in Damascus until al-Malik al-'Aziz opposed al-Afdal in 1196.[38] He then joined al-Malik al-'Aziz in Cairo and was paid from the treasury. During this time 'Abd al-Latif taught Islamic sciences at the al-Azhar Mosque from dawn till four o'clock. Thereafter, he went home and taught medicine, before returning at the end of the day to teach other students at the al-Azhar. His own scholarship he accomplished at night. He followed this routine until the death of al-Malik al-'Aziz in 1198, whereupon he took up residence in town, supported by stipends from Saladin's remaining sons. It was at this time that Egypt suffered a plague, which he describes in his *Kitab al-Ifadah wa al-i'tibar* ('Book of utility and reflection').[39] The work is extant and is divided as follows:

Book I
1. General observations about Egypt
2. The flora of Egypt
3. The fauna of Egypt
4. Description of the ancient monuments of Egypt seen by the author
5. Noteworthy peculiarities concerning the buildings and the boats observed in Egypt by the author of this work
6. Foods peculiar to Egypt

Book II
1. On the Nile: the manner in which the flooding of the river takes place and the normality of this phenomenon
2. Events of the year 597 [1200–1 CE]
3. Events of the year 598 [1201–2 CE]

'Abd al-Latif's description of the plague and its horrors, including widespread cannibalism, makes grim reading indeed. In one of the less graphic passages he writes:

In the streets, wherever one stepped, there was no place one could place one's feet or direct one's gaze without encountering a corpse, or a man in the throes of agony, or even a large number of people in this state. From Cairo alone, between one hundred and five hundred dead were collected and taken to a place where the last rites could be performed. In Old Cairo, the number of dead was incalculable. They could not be not buried, but were simply thrown outside of the town. Eventually, there were no more people to carry them off so they were left where they were, in the markets, between houses and stores, even inside the houses.[40]

Saladin's brother, al-Malik al-'Adil Sayf al-Din (Latin: Saphadin, d. 1218), who had taken over the sultanate in 1200, dispersed his nephews. 'Abd al-Latif went again to Jerusalem, where he stayed for some time teaching a variety of subjects in the al-Aqsa Mosque, and where he wrote a great deal.

In 1204 he left for Damascus. He stayed in the 'Aziziyyah Mosque, where he taught law and studied independently. Many students came to him, not only to study grammar, in which he had previously distinguished himself, but also to study medicine, for which he was then renowned. He next went to Aleppo (some time after February 1212), where he composed a number of works, and thence to Anatolia (after 1220), where he stayed for many years in the service of al-Malik 'Ala' al-Din Da'ud ibn Bahram (known as Dawud Shah, d. 1237), the governor of Erzinjan, to whom he dedicated a number of works. Until his defeat at the hands of 'Ala' al-Din Kay-Qubadh (d. 1246) in 1228, Dawud Shah remained 'Abd al-Latif's patron.[41]

'Abd al-Latif travelled widely between 18 October 1228 and 31 August 1229, performing the 'Id al-Fitr prayers (marking the end of Ramadan) in Bahnasa' a few days before reaching Aleppo, then under the governorship of the Atabeg Shihab al-Din. 'Abd al-Latif wrote many works there, and taught many students medicine and the ancient sciences; he also taught *hadith* and grammar at the Friday Mosque. 'Abd al-Latif writes of his desire to perform the *Hajj* and then to go to Damascus to settle, but he became ill, put off the *Hajj*, and decided to travel to Baghdad before going to Damascus, in order to present several of his works to the 'Abbasid caliph, al-Mustansir billah (d. 1242). 'Abd al-Latif did not reach to Damascus. He died immediately after his arrival in Baghdad, on Sunday 9 November 1231, and was buried next to his father in the Wardiyyah Cemetery.

To give a better sense of the extent and the amount of travel undertaken by 'Abd al-Latif on account of his patrons and their patronage, I outline below a chronology and itinerary of his life.[42]

| | |
|---|---|
| March 1162 | 'Abd al-Latif is born in his grandfather's house on Darb al-Faludhaj, BAGHDAD, where he studies with illustrious scholars. |

| after February 1189 | 'Abd al-Latif, 27, leaves for MOSUL to find better teachers; |
| after February 1190 | disappointed, he leaves one year later for DAMASCUS. |
| after 6 April 1191 | 'Abd al-Latif, 29, goes to JERUSALEM, |
| between 4 June and 12 July 1191 | then to ACRE, to meet Saladin. Al-Qadi al-Fadil urges him to go to Damascus but he insists on Cairo to seek out three scholars. He reaches CAIRO and is supported by a stipend from al-Qadi al-Fadil. |
| after 13 September 1192 | 'Abd al-Latif, 30, goes back to JERUSALEM to see Saladin again and receives a handsome stipend from Saladin and his sons. |
| c. September 1192 | 'Abd al-Latif returns to DAMASCUS; he teaches at the Umayyad Mosque. |
| 3 March 1193 | Saladin dies. |
| | 'Abd al-Latif stays in Damascus with al-Malik al-Afdal, |
| 25 June 1196 | until the siege of Damascus by al-Malik al-'Aziz. |
| c. 13 July 1196 | 'Abd al-Latif, 34, joins al-Malik al-'Aziz at Marj al-Suffar, and accompanies him to CAIRO, where he teaches at al-Azhar and is supported by Saladin's sons. |
| 19 November 1198 | al-Malik al-'Aziz dies |
| | (Begins work on *al-Rawanid*) |
| 17 February 1200 | al-Malik al-'Adil is proclaimed. |
| 1201–2 | Plague and inflation hit Egypt. |
| | (Collects material for *Kitab al-Ifadah*) |
| 1202–3 | 'Abd al-Latif, 40, goes to JERUSALEM; he teaches at the al-Aqsa Mosque. |
| | (Composes *Fi al-Nakhl*) |
| after May 1204 | 'Abd al-Latif, 42, returns to DAMASCUS; he lives and teaches at the 'Aziziyyah. |
| | (Writes *Fi al-Jins*) |
| March 1207 | (Completes revisions on the *Kitab al-Ifadah*.) |
| 1210/11 | (Begins *Kitab al-Mudhish fi akhbar al-hayawan*) |
| February 1212 | (Completes *al-Fusul*) |
| March 1212 (?) | 'Abd al-Latif, 50 (?), leaves for ALEPPO. |
| 1218 | (Composes *Qawanin al-balaghah*) |
| August 1220 | (Edits *al-Rawanid*) |
| | (Completes *al-Radd 'ala Ibn al-Khatib fi sharhihi*) |

| | |
|---|---|
| after 1220 | 'Abd al-Latif, 58, goes to ERZINJAN, where he is in the service of its ruler, the Mengüjekid 'Ala' al-Din Dawudshah. |
| 1226 | (Composes *Kitab Tadbir al-harb*) |
| June 1228 | (Composes *Fi al-Nakhl*)<br>(Composes *Kitab al-Hikmah al-'ala'iyyah*, dedicated to Dawudshah) |
| 1228 | Dawudshah is overthrown by the Rum-Saljuq sultan Kay Qubadh I ('Ala' al-Din). |
| 18 October 1228 | 'Abd al-Latif, 66, visits ERZURUM, |
| 30 December 1228 | returns to ERZINJAN, |
| February 1229 | then goes to KAMAKH, |
| April 1229 | to DIVRIGI, |
| June 1229 | and MALATYA. |
| August 1229 | 'Abd al-Latif, 67, leaves Erzinjan for Aleppo (governed by the Atabeg Shihab al-Din), |
| 23 August 1229 | en route performing the 'Id al-Fitr prayers in BAHNASA'. |
| 31 August 1229 | 'Abd al-Latif reaches ALEPPO; he teaches medicine and other sciences there.<br>(Completes the *Kitab al-Mudhish*)<br>'Abd al-Latif intends to perform the Hajj en route to Damascus, where he intends to settle, but instead |
| before October 1231 | visits HARRAN and puts off the Hajj because of deteriorating health. |
| end of October 1231 | He makes a detour through BAGHDAD in order to present works to the Caliph al-Mustansir billah. |
| 9 November 1231 | 'Abd al-Latif, 69, dies and is buried next to his father in the Wardiyyah Cemetery. |

The foregoing makes abundantly clear the importance of travel in the medieval Islamic world, and the role also of patronage in motivating such travel. Yet not everyone travelled. There is, alas, still no study comparing the works of scholars who stayed put, the historian of Egypt al-Kindi (d. 961) for instance, and the works of those who were peripatetic, 'Abd al-Latif al-Baghdadi for instance. Might one argue that the former's *Wulat Misr wa-qudatuha* ('The governors and judges of Egypt') 'produces a jejune and repetitive literary effect'[43] whereas the latter's *Kitab al-Ifadah wa al-i'tibar* ('Book of utility and reflection') is fascinating and perceptive precisely because the latter had seen the world and the former had not?[44] If so, this calls into question Wolfhart Heinrichs's suggestion that in the case of the literary theorist 'Abd al-Qahir al-Jurjani (d. 1081), who never left his home province, 'It is not unlikely that, by foregoing the receptive mode of study with many teachers, he stimulated his own original thinking'.[45] The issue of the influence of effect of travel on literary output – both in terms of quality and in terms of quantity – as with so much else in the history of medieval Islam and medieval Arabic and Arab-Islamic literary history, remains to be investigated. We cannot properly understand a towering figure such as 'Abd al-Latif al-Baghdadi, or indeed anyone who travelled in the world of medieval Islam, without understanding the motivations for that travel.

## APPENDIX

I propose the following taxonomy as a way of thinking more accurately and critically about the travel of individuals in the medieval Islamic world.

1. Religion
   A. Pilgrimage to Mecca
      i. annual (*Hajj*)
      ii. year-round (*'umrah*)
   B. Visits to shrines (*ziyarah*)
      i. annual, on saints' birthdays (*mawlid*, *'urs*)
      ii. year-round, to get blessings (*barakah*)
   C. Collecting prophetic traditions (*hadith*)
2. Learning (religious and non-religious)
   A. Travel in search of knowledge (*al-rihlah fi talab al-'ilm*)
      i. seeking famous teachers
         a. individuals
         b. attached to institutions (see (ii) below)
      ii. travel to institutions[46]
         a. mosques (*masjid*)
         b. colleges of law (*madrasah*)
         c. sufi retreats (*ribat*)
         d. hospitals (*bimaristan*)
         e. study circles (*halqah*, *majlis*)
3. Embassy
   A. Within the Islamic world
   B. Outside the Islamic world
      i. to non-Muslim areas
      ii. from non-Muslim areas

4. Trade, commerce
   A. Over land
      i. within the Islamic world
      ii. outside the Islamic world
   B. Over sea
      i. within the Islamic world
      ii. outside the Islamic world
5. Propaganda
   A. Religious
      i. missionary
         a. Sufi
         b. Shi'ite
   B. Political
6. Government posting
7. Exploration
   A. Scientific
      i. geography
      ii. survey
   B. Adventure
8. Wanderlust/tourism
9. Marine/naval
   A. Real
   B. Imaginary
10. Forced
   A. Exile/banishment
   B. Flight (including *hijrah*)
   C. Migration
   D. Slavery
11. Warfare
12. Migration, emigration
   A. Voluntary
   [B. Forced: see (10) above]
13. Patronage
   A. Travel to patron
   B. Travel with patron

In adding to the list of forms of travel traditionally identified by scholars, I have enumerated above other forms besides patronage. I hope, however, that this article has successfully highlighted the tremendous importance of patronage in particular in motivating travel in the medieval Islamic world.

## NOTES

I am very grateful to Rosamund Allen for inviting me to contribute to this volume (and for her patience); to Roger Moss for putting us in touch; and to Manchester University Press's outside readers for their initial comments. I am grateful also to Miriam Cooke, Bruce Lawrence and Ebrahim Moosa for inviting me to share some of this material at Duke University in Durham, North Carolina, in February 2003; and to Philip Kennedy and Jonathan Rodgers for accepting a late submission based on this material at the 213th Annual Meeting of the American Oriental Society in Nashville, Tennessee, in April 2003. This article is affectionately dedicated to a great teacher and mentor, Edward Peters.

1 Ibn Battutah died in 1377. For the benefit of non-specialists: I cite (to the extent possible) primary material in English translation, and widely available English reference works, in particular Julie Scott Meisami and Paul Starkey (eds), *Encyclopedia of Arabic Literature*, 2 vols (London and New York: Routledge, 1998) and H. A. R. Gibb *et al.* (eds), *The Encyclopaedia of Islam*, 2nd edn, 11 vols and supplements (Leiden: E. J. Brill, 1954–2003); I use a simplified transliteration (see the 'Note on Arabic transliterations' on p. iv); I use only the singulars of Arabic terms; and all dates have been converted to CE.

2 *The 13th Warrior* (director, John McTiernan) is based on Michael Crichton, *Eaters of the Dead: The Manuscript of Ibn Fadlan Relating his Experiences with the Northmen in A.D. 922* (New York: Alfred A. Knopf, 1976), which is, as the subtitle reveals, based on the *Risalah* of Ibn Fadlan. Pending James Montgomery's forthcoming English translation, see *Voyage chez les Bulgares de la Volga*, trans. Marius Canard (Paris: Sindbad, 1988).

3 Dale Eickelman and James Piscatori (eds), *Muslim Travelers: Pilgrimage, Migration and the Religious Imagination* (Berkeley: University of California Press, 1990), p. xii. See also Houari Touati, *Islam et voyage au Moyen Age: Histoire et anthropologie d'une pratique lettrée* (Paris: Seuil, 2000).

4 Eickelman and Piscatori (eds), *Muslim Travelers*, p. xii.

5 Emigration is discussed only as it pertains to the colonial and post-colonial period. This explains the theoretical notion they advance that 'the very idea of travel . . . cannot be separated from the anticipation of return to home' (*ibid.*, p. xiii). The concept of diaspora intersects neatly with discussions of modern Muslim emigration.

6 J. F. P. Hopkins, 'Geographical and navigational literature', in M. J. L. Young *et al.* (eds), *Religion, Learning and Science in the 'Abbasid Period* (Cambridge: Cambridge University Press, 1990), pp. 301–27, bibliography on pp. 538–9.

7 *Ibid.*, p. 322.

8 *Ibid.*

9 Ian R. Netton, 'Rihla', in Gibb *et al.* (eds), *Encyclopaedia of Islam*, viii, p. 528.

10 Ian R. Netton, *Golden Roads: Migration, Pilgrimage, and Travel in Mediaeval and Modern Islam* (Richmond, Surrey: Curzon Press, 1993); *idem, Seek Knowledge: Thought and Travel in the House of Islam* (Richmond, Surrey: Curzon Press, 1996). Of the three articles on medieval travel in *Golden Roads*, one is on Ibn Jubayr, one on Ibn Battutah and one on the Turkish *Seyahatname* of Evliya Čelebi. In the 'travel' section *of Seek Knowledge*, all five of the articles are about Ibn Battutah and/or Ibn Jubayr.

11 R. Peters, 'Safar', in Gibb *et al.* (eds), *Encyclopaedia of Islam*, viii, p. 764.

12 Cf. Ibn al-'Arabi, *Le dévoilement des effets du voyage = Kitab al-isfar 'an nata'ij al-asfar*, ed. and trans. Denis Gril (Paris: Editions de l'Éclat, 1994).

13 Peters, 'Safar'. Bracketed translations of the Arabic terms are mine.

14 C. E. Bosworth, 'Travel literature' In Meisami and Starkey (eds), *Encyclopedia of Arabic Literature*, ii, pp. 778–80.

15 The travelling poet Abu Dulaf (*fl.* 10th century) was patronised by the rulers of Transoxania and Sistan and then those of Rayy and Shiraz. Both his surviving works describe his travels.

16 Bosworth, 'Travel literature', p. 779.

17 This section expands on Shawkat M. Toorawa, 'Patronage', in Meisami and Starkey (eds), *Encyclopedia of Arabic Literature*, ii, pp. 598–9.

18 See J. E. Bencheikh, 'Le cénacle poétique du calife al-Mutawakkil (m. 247): Contribution à l'analyse des instances de légimitation socio-littéraires', *Bulletin d'Etudes Orientales*, 29 (1977), 33–52; *idem*, 'Les secrétaires poètes et animateurs de cénacles aux IIe et IIIe siècles de l'Hégire: Contribution à l'analyse d'une production poétique', *Journal Asiatique*, 263 (1975), 265–315; and Julie Scott Meisami, *Medieval Persian Court Poetry* (Princeton: Princeton University Press, 1990).

19 For information about the figures discussed below, see Meisami and Starkey (eds), *Encyclopedia of Arabic Literature*, Gibb *et al.* (eds), *Encyclopaedia of Islam*, and also Roger Allen, *The Arabic Literary Heritage* (Cambridge: Cambridge University Press, 1998), *passim*.

20 Abu Nasr al-Farabi (Alfarabius, Avennasar, d. 950) died while accompanying his patron on a campaign. He had left Turkestan as a child, settled in Baghdad with his family and worked and taught there most of his life before accepting an invitation by Sayf al-Dawlah to join his court in Aleppo in 942.

21 The Banu Hilal were a tribe who moved from Arabia to Egypt after rebelling against the suzerainty of the 'Abbasid caliphate in Baghdad. They then moved on North Africa.

22 Ibn Abi Usaybi'ah, '*Uyun al-anba*' *fi tabaqat al-atibba*', ed. Nizar Rida (Beirut: Maktabat al-Hayat, 1965), pp. 683–96; ed. Basil 'Uyun al-Sud (Beirut: Dar al-Kutub al-'Ilmiyyah, 1998), pp. 634–48. For a résumé of the notice, see Samuel Stern, 'A collection of treatises by 'Abd al-Latif al-Baghdadi', *Islamic Studies*, 1 (1962), 53–70; for a paraphrase, see George Makdisi, *The Rise of Colleges: Institutions of Learning in Islam and the West* (Edinburgh: Edinburgh University Press, 1981), pp. 84–8; and for a translation of the autobiographical parts, see Shawkat M. Toorawa, 'Selections from the autograph notes of 'Abd al-Latif al-Baghdadi', in Dwight F. Reynolds (ed.), *Interpreting the Self: Autobiography in the Arabic Literary Tradition* (Berkeley: University of California Press, 2001), pp. 156–64.

23 On 'Abd al-Latif's teachers, see Shawkat M. Toorawa, 'The educational background of 'Abd al-Latif al-Baghdadi', *Muslim Education Quarterly*, 13:3 (1996), 35–53; revised as 'A portrait of 'Abd al-Latif al-Baghdadi through his education and instruction', in Joseph E. Lowry, Devin Stewart and Shawkat M. Toorawa (eds), *Law and Education in Medieval Islam: Studies in Memory of George Makdisi* (Oxford: Oxbow Books for the Gibb Memorial Trust, forthcoming).

24 Ibn Abi Usaybi'ah, '*Uyun al-anba*', ed. Rida, p. 684; Toorawa, 'Selections', p. 158.

25 Ibn Abi Usaybi'ah, '*Uyun al-anba*', ed. Rida, p. 684; Toorawa, 'Selections', p. 159.

26 Ibn Abi Usaybi'ah, '*Uyun al-anba*', ed. Rida, p. 686; Toorawa, 'Selections', p. 159.

27 Ibn Abi Usaybi'ah, '*Uyun al-anba*', ed. Rida, p. 686; Toorawa, 'Selections', p. 160.

28 Ibn Abi Usaybi'ah, '*Uyun al-anba*', ed. Rida, p. 687; Toorawa, 'Selections', p. 160.

29 Ibn Abi Usaybi'ah, '*Uyun al-anba*', ed. Rida, p. 687; Toorawa, 'Selections', p. 161.

30 Ibn Abi Usaybi'ah, '*Uyun al-anba*', ed. Rida, p. 687; Toorawa, 'Selections', p. 161.

31 Cf. 'Abd al-Latif al-Baghdadi, *Fi 'ilm ma ba'd al-tabi'a. Maqalat al-Lam: 'Abd al-Latif al-Bagdadis Bearbeitung von Buch Lamda der aristotelischen Metaphysik*, ed. and with commentary by A. Neuwirth (Wiesbaden: Steiner, 1976).

32  Ibn Abi Usaybi'ah, '*Uyun al-anba*', ed. Rida, p. 688; Toorawa, 'Selections', p. 162.

33  Makdisi, *The Rise of Colleges*, p. 87.

34  Ibn Abi Usaybi'ah, '*Uyun al-anba*', ed. Rida, p. 688; Toorawa, 'Selections', p. 163.

35  Ibn Abi Usaybi'ah, '*Uyun al-anba*', ed. Rida, p. 688; Toorawa, 'Selections', p. 163.

36  Shawkat M. Toorawa, 'Language and male homosocial desire in the autobiography of 'Abd al-Latif al-Baghdadi (d. 629/1231)', *Edebiyât: The Journal of Middle Eastern Literatures*, new series, 7:2 (1997), 251–65.

37  *Ibid.*, 251–2.

38  On Saladin and his family, see R. Stephen Humphreys, *From Saladin to the Mongols* (Albany: State University of New York Press, 1977).

39  *Kitab al-Ifadah wa al-i'tibar fi al-'umur al-mushahadah wa al-hawadith a1-mu'ayanah bi-ard Misr* ('Book of utility and reflection with reference to the observed conditions and the prescribed events in Egypt'): 'Abd al-Latif al-Baghdadi, *The Eastern Key: Kitab al-Ifadah wa'l-I'tibar of 'Abd al-Latif al-Baghdadi*, trans. K. F. Zand, J. A. Videan and I. E. Videan (London: George Allen and Unwin, 1964); 'Abd al-Latif al-Baghdadi, *Relation de l'Egypte par Abd-Allatif, médecin arabe de Bagdad*, trans. M. Silvestre de Sacy (Paris: Imprimerie impériale, chez Treuttel et Würtz, 1810).

40  'Abd al-Latif, *The Eastern Key*, p. 241 (= *Kitab al-Ifadah*, fol. 60$^v$; trans. mine).

41  On the Saljuqs, see Claude Cahen, *The Formation of Turkey: The Seljukid Sultanate of Rum: Eleventh to Fourteenth Century*, ed. and trans. P. M. Holt (Harlow, Essex: Pearson, 2001).

42  Dates relating to 'Abd al-Latif's life are based on the Arabic biographical notices, principally the one in Ibn Abi Usaybi'ah, '*Uyun al-anba*'. Dates relating to contact with Saladin are based on Baha' al-Din Ibn Shaddad, *The Rare and Excellent History of Saladin or al-Nawadir al-Sultaniyya wa'l-Mahasin al-Yusufiyya*, trans. D. S. Richards (Aldershot: Ashgate, 2001), and those relating to the Ayyubids on Humphreys, *From Saladin to the Mongols*. See also H. A. R. Gibb (ed.), *The Life of Saladin, from the Works of 'Imad ad-Din and Baha' ad-Din* (Oxford: The Clarendon Press, 1973). (See also Shawkat M. Toorawa, 'A detailed chronology and itinerary of 'Abd al-Latif al-Baghdadi' (in preparation), which includes Hijri dates and bibliographical data.)

43  D. S. Richards, 'al-Kindi, Abu 'Umar', in Meisami and Starkey (eds), *Encyclopedia of Arabic Literature*, ii, p. 451.

44  Abu 'Umar al-Kindi, *The Governors and Judges of Egypt*, trans. Rhuvon Guest (Leiden: Brill, 1912); 'Abd al-Latif al-Baghdadi, *The Eastern Key*.

45  Wolfhart P. Heinrichs, 'Abd al-Qahir al-Jurjani', in Meisami and Starkey (eds), *Encyclopedia of Arabic Literature*, i, p. 16.

46  Mosques (*masjid*) were, like colleges of law, eleemosynary institutions, brought into being by a *waqf* endowment. Teaching was conducted in both, as stipulated by the *waqf* deed. The *madrasah* is the precursor to the European college. Teaching was also done in hospitals, predominantly known by the Persian *bimaristan* (Arabic: *mustashfa*). The study circle, called either *halqah* ('circle') or *majlis* ('seating, session'), was held by a teacher or professor either in one of the above institutions or at his home. There is very little information on how *ribat*s first developed, but it seems likely that it was for reasons of economy of scale, and also perhaps for (fortified) protection.

# 4

## Just a bunch of dirty stories? Women in the 'memoirs' of Usamah Ibn Munqidh

❪❫

### Niall Christie

I have witnessed wonderful manifestations of women's zeal.[1]

AMONG THE MUSLIM sources for the crusades, there are few that are better known than the 'memoirs' of the *amir* Usamah ibn Murshid ibn 'Ali, better known to modern scholars as Usamah Ibn Munqidh. Usamah was originally of Bedouin origin, of the clan of Munqidh, hence the patronymic. He was born at the clan stronghold of Shayzar in north-west Syria on 4 July 1095, and lived there until about 1131, when he joined the entourage of the *atabeg* (regent) of Mosul, 'Imad al-Din Zangi (r. 1127–46). He later returned to Shayzar, but not for long. Usamah's father, Majd al-Din Murshid, was the elder brother of the head of the clan, 'Izz al-Din Sultan. Murshid had abdicated in favour of his younger sibling when the leadership of the clan passed to him in 1098, and when Murshid died in 1137 Sultan feared that Murshid's sons might try to claim the leadership, and so Sultan exiled them the following year. Usamah went to the Burid court at Damascus, where he became an associate of the *amir*, Mu'in al-Din Unur. However, by 1144 he had become embroiled in political intrigues and was soon ordered to leave by his patron. He travelled to Egypt and the Fatimid court, becoming an associate of the vizier, al-'Adil ibn al-Sallar, and remaining in the country for ten years. Once again he became embroiled in court politics, so in 1154 he returned to Damascus, where he entered the service of the Zangid sultan, Nur al-Din (r. 1146–74). Ten years later he retired to the court of the Artuqid, Qara-Arslan of Hisn Kayfa, where he collected a *diwan* (anthology of his poetry) and composed several works on poetry, rhetoric, *adab* (belles-lettres), history and religion, most of which are now lost. In the autumn of 1174 he allowed his son, Murhaf, to persuade him to join the court of Saladin (r. 1169–93), of whom Murhaf had been an associate since 1170. When Usamah joined the court, he was enthusiastically welcomed, but after two years relations between Usamah and Saladin had deteriorated, and so Usamah's last years were spent in honourable but unhappy retirement. He died on 16 November 1188, having had a great impact on both his contemporaries and later writers. He was best known for his poetry, which was quoted in his own lifetime and the century following, but his other works also had lasting fame, and were used as sources by several later writers.[2]

It is clear from this biography that Usamah himself travelled widely. Not only was he driven by necessity periodically to change patrons and countries, but he also travelled with or on the behalf of these patrons on numerous military and diplomatic missions. Towards the end of his life he composed or dictated an account of his experiences, the *Kitab al-I'tibar* ('Book of learning by example'), which has been much studied by modern historians as an account of Muslim perceptions of the Latin inhabitants of the Levant, called *ifranj* or *faranj* (Franks) by the Muslims.[3] While the work purports to be Usamah's memoirs, as Robert Irwin has shown it would be incorrect to take Usamah's work at face value. *I'tibar* means 'learning by example', and has connotations of taking heed of warnings, which resonate with passages in the Qur'an. In this way Usamah intended his work to be a lesson in good conduct for his own progeny, as a result of which it shows literary skill and care inconsistent with the nostalgic ramblings of an old man. In particular, the work is guided by a balance of likenesses and antitheses that have struck Usamah.[4] Thus while there is useful information to be drawn from its pages, such information should be treated with a certain amount of caution.

Despite the fame of his 'memoirs', one topic that has remained relatively unstudied is Usamah's presentation of women in his work. A number of scholars have examined several of Usamah's anecdotes in which both Muslim and Frankish women feature,[5] but in most of these cases they appear only as passive characters in Usamah's portrayals of various unsavoury features of the Franks. This chapter attempts to redress this imbalance somewhat by drawing attention to some of the less well-known female characters in Usamah's work, who often play very active roles in the events he witnessed in the course of his travels. It should be noted that this is merely an initial survey of the topic; space will not permit the full analysis that such a subject deserves. I will deal in turn with Usamah's family, women in combat, women as prisoners and women in politics, and then conclude with further anecdotes, all showing how Usamah's travels provided a variety of experiences of highly active Muslim and Frankish women. Before considering the less well-known female figures in Usamah's work, I will first review the more familiar anecdotes and preceding scholarship on his reactions to Frankish women.

## FRANKISH SEXUAL LAXITY

The best-known of Usamah's anecdotes are his accounts demonstrating Frankish sexual laxity. He states that 'the Franks are void of all zeal and jealousy', and then notes that a husband will happily leave his wife conversing alone with another man in the street. He also describes two occasions, the second of which he claims to have witnessed himself while visiting Tyre, when Frankish men brought their womenfolk into the public baths with them, despite that fact that according to Muslim custom, men and women used bath-houses on different days. In one of these, he also further demonstrates the Frankish lack of proper modesty when a Frankish husband has a bath attendant shave off his wife's pubes.[6] In both cases, the baths concerned were in Frankish territory.[7] It is not clear how far the Franks adopted Muslim practices concerning segregation of sexes when using bath-houses, but Usamah clearly found the presence of women in bathhouses on 'male' days remarkable.

Probably the best-known of Usamah's anecdotes on Frankish sexual laxity is this:

> Here is an illustration which I myself witnessed: when I used to visit Nablus [another town in Frankish territory], I always took lodging with a man named Mu'izz, whose home was a lodging house for the Moslems. The house had windows which opened to the road, and there stood opposite to it on the other side of the road a house belonging to a Frank who sold wine for the merchants. [ ... ] One day this Frank went home and found a man with his wife in the same bed. He asked him, 'What could have made thee enter into my wife's room?' The man replied, 'I was tired, so I went in to rest.' 'But how', asked he, 'didst thou get into my bed?' The other replied, 'I found a bed that was spread, so I slept in it.' 'But', said he, 'my wife was sleeping together with thee!' The other replied, 'Well, the bed is hers. How could I therefore have prevented her from using her own bed?' 'By the truth of my religion', said the husband, 'if thou shouldst do it again, thou and I would have a quarrel.' Such was for the Frank the entire expression of his disapproval and the limit of his jealousy.[8]

Carole Hillenbrand has described this anecdote as 'a cleverly constructed apocryphal tale', noting that it illustrates two moral failings of the Franks, their drinking of wine and lack of proper marital jealousy.[9] However, the tale may also shed a light on Usamah's lack of understanding of Frankish humour. With its three-fold questioning and punchline, the anecdote seems likely to have been a joke. Indeed, the final comment of the husband, who is clearly ignorant of the fact that he has been cuckolded, resembles the technique of the fabliaux, bawdy tales common in Europe during the period. From his own comment, it seems that Usamah, on the other hand, regards the story as genuine. He claims that he was on intimate terms with a number of Franks, and one of these might have related the story to Usamah, who did not under-stand it and took it seriously. Though Usamah claims that he witnessed the incident himself, and, by locating the house of Mu'izz opposite that of the wine seller, suggests that he heard the words of the Franks through the window, or at least saw an angry exchange taking place, this may be a narrative device to make his tale more believable.[10]

## OTHER WELL-KNOWN STORIES

While his sexual anecdotes are probably the most celebrated of his stories, Usamah recounts other well-known stories about the behaviour of Frankish women. These include the case of a Frankish woman who had been taken prisoner by his father. Usamah's father delivered the prisoner as a gift to the *amir* of Qala'at Ja'bar, Shihab al-Din, who 'took her to himself'. The woman bore Shihab al-Din a son whom he made his heir, but after her husband's death the woman escaped and married a Frankish shoemaker. Usamah clearly finds it remarkable that the woman chose life as a humble shoemaker's wife rather than among the Muslim nobility, especially when, as he notes, she was 'the real power' behind the throne.[11] As Wadi' Haddad notes, this is one of a number of occasions when Usamah demonstrates his belief that even if they are fully acculturated into Muslim society, Franks will still revert to their true nature eventually.[12] Another similar anecdote follows, although in this case it is a male Frank who, despite having converted to Islam, marrying a Muslim wife and having two children, eventually takes his family and returns to the Franks. Usamah then comments, 'May Allah, therefore, purify the world from such people!'[13]

In another anecdote, Usamah describes a race between two old women that he claims to have witnessed during a Frankish festival at Tiberias. The women race each other, falling and rising with every step, while being urged on by detachments of horsemen. As Hillenbrand notes, the story is a caricature, particularly when one of them eventually finishes the course and wins the prize, a scalded pig, a characteristic symbol for the Muslims of Christian impurity.[14]

One final instance of Usamah's well-known anecdotes about women bears mentioning. This occurs in his accounts of Frankish medicine. As Irwin has shown, these are symptomatic of Usamah's use of balance in that he gives accounts of both good and bad Frankish medicine.[15] In the most gruesome of these, a Frankish woman dies when a Frankish physician attempts to cure her consumption by cutting a cruciform incision into her head and rubbing salt in, in order to remove a devil that he believes has possessed her. The woman here occupies only a passive role in the anecdote, which, as Hillenbrand has noted, is a comment on the superiority of Middle Eastern medicine;[16] indeed, a Syrian Christian physician has previously, and more sensibly, attempted to cure the illness by changing the patient's diet and making 'her humour wet'. Given that he has immediately beforehand noted the fact that the same Frankish physician had indirectly killed a knight, in whose leg an abscess had opened, by having the leg amputated (the knight bled to death), he may well be emphasizing the assertion that Frankish doctors are equally barbaric towards their male and female patients.[17]

### USAMAH'S FAMILY

Irwin has stated that Usamah has 'the traditional Arab compunction against talking about love, women or even children'.[18] While it is true that Usamah does not give much discussion of these topics in themselves, his family is very present in his work, and he shows what seems to be serious concern for their welfare. When the Franks and Byzantines besiege Shayzar in 1138, Usamah insists on returning there from the court of one of Zangi's *amir*s, Salah al-Din Muhammad (not the famous Ayyubid sultan), to see to his family's safety.[19] He also describes how he twice had to extract his family from the hands of Egyptian viziers, the implication being that they were held as hostages to ensure his loyalty.[20] Usamah also describes how when his family was eventually able to travel from Egypt to Syria, the result of negotiations between Nur al-Din and the Egyptian vizier, their boat was wrecked by Franks under the command of Baldwin III (r. 1143–63), despite the fact that Nur al-Din had also secured a safe conduct for Usamah's family from that same monarch. After most of their belongings were confiscated, Usamah's family were allowed to go on their way to Damascus, and he comments that 'The safety of my children, my brother's children, and our harem made the loss of money which we suffered a comparatively easy matter to endure – with the exception of the books, which were four thousand volumes, all of the most valuable kind. Their loss has left a heartsore that will stay with me to the last day of my life.'[21] Although Usamah is clearly pleased that his family is safe, it seems that their primacy in his affections is not entirely secure!

A number of women had an impact on Usamah's life. Of these it seems that perhaps the most influential was his grandmother. He describes how in his youth, after he returned from a hunting expedition with his father conducted near Shayzar, she warned him to be careful of upsetting his uncle – wisdom that would later prove to be justified when 'Izz al-Din Sultan expelled Usamah and his brothers from Shayzar in 1138, to prevent them from claiming leadership of the clan:

> She said to me with anger and with irritation, 'O my boy, what makes thee face these adventures in which thou riskest thine own life and the life of thy horse,

breaking thy weapons[,] and increasest the antipathy and ill feeling which thine uncle cherishes in his heart against thee?' I replied, 'O my grandmother, the only thing that makes me expose myself to danger in this and similar cases is to endear myself to the heart of my uncle.' She said, 'No, by Allah! This does not bring thee nearer to thine uncle, but, on the contrary, it alienates thee from him and makes him feel more antipathy and ill will towards thee.' I then realized that my grandmother (may Allah's mercy rest upon her soul!) was giving me wise counsel and was telling me the truth. By my life, such are the mothers of men!'[22]

Usamah's grandmother may well have been aware of the possible tensions between Usamah and his uncle before he was. He then continues his work with an account of her piety, stating that even at the age of one hundred she refused to sit to perform her prayers.[23] Usamah's grandmother seems to have been a formidable woman.

Usamah's mother also seems to have been a strong figure. He describes how when Shayzar was attacked by Isma'ilis in April 1109, his mother distributed his weapons and armour to the defenders of the fortress, and then led his sister out onto the balcony of his house. Usamah came into the room, looking for weapons, and remarked on the fact that his mother and sister were on the balcony. His mother replied:

'O my dear son, I have given her a seat at the balcony and sat behind her so that in case I found that the Batinites[24] had reached us, I could push her and throw her into the valley, preferring to see her dead rather than to see her captive in the hands of peasants and ravishers.' I thanked my mother for her deed, and so did my sister, who prayed that mother be rewarded [by Allah] in her behalf. Such solicitude for honor is indeed stronger than the solicitude of men.[25]

Usamah's mother makes her presence felt a second time in his work in another story about the Franks, used to illustrate their lack of sense. He mentions a knight in the army of the King of Jerusalem, Fulk of Anjou (r. 1131–43), with whom he claims to have had 'bonds of amity and friendship'. He states that the knight suggested that Usamah's son should go with back to Europe with him to learn the ways of Frankish knights. Usamah was horrified, seeing such a fate as being worse than captivity in Frankish hands; indeed, he claims that the knight said to him 'words which would never come out of the head of a sensible man'. However, rather than state this outright, Usamah dissembled, claiming that the only objection was that '"His grandmother, my mother, is so fond of him and did not this time let him come out with me until she exacted an oath from me to the effect that I would return him to her." Thereupon he [the Frankish knight] asked me, "Is thy mother still alive?" "Yes." I replied. "Well," said he, "disobey her not."'[26]

Usamah is clearly unaware of the European practice of fostering the sons of nobles out to other households for education in the knightly arts, but at the same time his Frankish friend also seems to give little thought to the potential fate of a Muslim in Europe during a period when Muslims and Christians were at war. It is impossible to say whether or not this event ever happened, or even if it did, whether or not Usamah had honestly made this promise to his mother; however, she was clearly a strong woman who exerted a great influence on her children, and so it is entirely possible that she extracted such a promise from him.

A third female figure who seems to have had some influence on Usamah is his nurse, Lu'lu'ah, although his attitude towards her seems to have been somewhat ambivalent. He describes her as a pious woman, sincerely devoted to fasting and prayer. He also gives an account of a vision she experienced, saying:

> From time to time Lu'lu'ah suffered from colic. One day she had such a violent attack that she became unconscious and was given up for lost. For two days and nights she remained in that condition; then she awoke and said, 'There is no God but Allah! How marvelous is the state through which I have just passed! I met all our dead ones and they related to me extraordinary things. Among other things they said to me, 'This colic shall never again come back to thee.' In fact, she lived after that for a long time and the colic never attacked her. She lived until she was almost a hundred years old, observing regularly her prayers – may Allah's mercy rest on her soul![27]

However, while Usamah is clearly impressed by his nurse's vision, he also describes a mistake she made in her old age, when he found her washing a cloth with some cheese, having mistaken the latter for soap. He does not say whether he thought this mistake was a result of galloping senility or failing eyesight. He closes this account with a Qur'anic quotation, which Philip Hitti translates as 'Blessed be Allah the most truthful of sayers, who says: "Him whose days we lengthen, we reverse his exterior form." '[28] However, if one translates the Arabic verb *nakasa* slightly differently, the quotation can read: 'Him whose days we lengthen, we make lower in exterior form.' What Usamah seems to be saying here is that while God lengthened his nurse's life, at the same time He reduced her physique and capabilities. This is a particularly sad remembrance for Usamah, as he is writing towards the end of his life when his own capabilities have also deteriorated, something that he bemoans with some bitterness in his work.[29]

## WOMEN IN COMBAT

Mention has already been made of the measures Usamah's mother took when Shayzar was attacked by Isma'ilis in April 1109. This is but one of several anecdotes Usamah gives of women becoming involved either directly or indirectly in conflicts taking place in various parts of the Levant. In a number of these women themselves fight. Usamah describes several occasions when he witnessed or heard of Muslim or Frankish women fighting. After the assassination in 1154 of the Fatimid caliph al-Zafir (r. 1149–54), the assassin's father, the vizier 'Abbas, had a number of other members of the royal family put to death, reserving as nominal caliph the infant al-Fa'iz (r. 1154–60).[30] This provoked a revolt in Cairo, against which Usamah was required to fight in the army of 'Abbas. Usamah mentions that the rebels included women and children who pelted 'Abbas's army with stones.[31] He also notes that an old woman named Funun fought with a sword against the Isma'ili attack on Shayzar in 1109,[32] and gives accounts of a Frankish woman who wounded a Muslim with a jar and a Muslim woman from Shayzar who captured three Franks during an attack on the town.[33] As Helen Nicholson has noted, while it was unusual for women to take part in battle, it was not unheard of, particularly in cases of dire necessity.[34] Most of the instances given by Usamah fall under this heading. Moving away from less classic models of combat, Usamah also describes one occasion when a Muslim woman, incensed at her husband's collaboration with the Franks of Kafartab, killed him with the help of her brother.[35] Another case of Muslim subterfuge against the Frankish enemy occurs in an account Usamah heard at Nablus of a Frankish trial in which ordeal by water was employed as the means of determining the truth. While this account is actually more directly concerned with displaying the barbarity of Frankish justice, Usamah notes that the accused was tried for aiding his mother, who had been married to a Frank but had murdered her husband, in the killing of Frankish pilgrims.[36] So it seems from Usamah's memoirs that women did engage in combat, on both sides and in a wide variety of locations, during the period.

In addition to fighting, Usamah notes a number of instances when women became less directly involved in combat, in varying ways. Another common role of women in military conflicts was as support staff to the troops, supplying food and water, running errands and the like.[37] Usamah gives us one account of this sort, noting that during an encounter in the late 1120s between Bohemond II of Antioch (r. 1126–30) and the Muslims of Shayzar, an aged slave named Buraykah supplied water to the Muslim troops, and refused to run away even when most of them fled in the face of the Frankish advance.[38] More will be said about Buraykah below. On a smaller scale, Usamah notes another instance when a Muslim woman was an effective support in combat. He cites a story that he claims to have heard in Mosul, from a Baghdadi poet named al-Mu'ayyad, in 1169–70. The poet informed him that his father held as an *iqta'* (fief) a village that was infested with vagabonds. One day a Turk, accompanied by a maiden on a mule and carrying a saddlebag full of money and jewellery, arrived in the village. Against the advice of the poet's father, the Turk set out from the village on a road frequented by the vagabonds who, having been informed by al-Mu'ayyad's father of what the Turk was carrying, intercepted him. The Turk nocked an arrow to his bow to shoot at the vagabonds, but his string broke, and he was forced to flee, leaving the maiden and riches behind. It was at this point that the maiden's intelligence saved them and their wealth. Usamah, citing al-Mu'ayyad, states:

> The maiden said, 'O young men, by Allah, dishonor me not. Rather let me buy myself and the mule also for a necklace of gems which is with the Turk and the value of which is five hundred dinars. Then take ye the saddlebag and all that is in it.' 'We accept', they replied. She said, 'Send with me someone from among you so that I may speak with the Turk and take the necklace.' Accordingly they sent with her someone to guard her until she came near the Turk and said to him, 'I have bought myself and the mule for the necklace which is in the leg of thy left boot, thy shoe. Deliver it to me.' 'All right', said he. Presently he went aside, took off his boot and lo! there was in it a bowstring, which he immediately fixed on his bow and turned back on them. They kept on fighting him while he was killing one after the other until he had killed forty-three men of their number. [ . . . ] [After the battle was over] the Turk drove his mule with all that was on it and continued his march. Thus Allah (exalted is he!) sent through him upon the vagabonds a calamity and great wrath.[39]

It is likely that this story is at least partially untrue, being more reminiscent of the *Arabian nights* than a historical account. However, it is impossible to tell whether it was al-Mu'ayyad or Usamah who fabricated or exaggerated the account. A clue may lie in the last sentence of the quotation. As Irwin has shown, the main lesson of Usamah's work is that God, rather than man, determines all things, and the decrees of fate cannot be denied.[40] This anecdote is entirely in keeping with Usamah's purpose; the Turk kills an astonishing number of the enemy single-handed, clearly asserting the fact that God's will cannot be opposed. This makes one think that Usamah may be the one fabricating the story as part of his moralistic account of his travels and adventures. However, given that I have already shown Usamah's powers of discernment to be questionable, one cannot be sure.

To return to accounts that are probably more factually accurate, Usamah gives tales of a number of other instances when women were indirectly involved in combat. One of his better-known anecdotes concerns an incident that took place during the attack by Isma'ilis on Shayzar mentioned above. He states that a cousin of his named Shabib, who was inexperienced in combat, feared that Shayzar was lost, and so he attempted to muster his household to escape. However, while he was doing this, an armoured figure entered the room:

As soon as Shabib saw the person, he felt certain of death. The person laid down the helmet and behold! It was none other than the mother of his cousin, Layth-al-Dawla Yahya (may Allah's mercy rest upon his soul!). She said to him, 'What dost thou want to do?' He replied, 'Take whatever I can, descend from the castle by means of a rope and live in the world.' To this she replied,'What a wretched thing thou doest! Thou leavest thy uncle's daughters and the women of thy family to the ravishers and thou goest away! What kind of life will thine be when thou art dishonoured by thy family and when thou fleest away, leaving them? Get out, fight in behalf of thy family until thou art killed in their midst! May Allah do this and that with thee![41]

Shamed by his kinswoman, Shabib abandoned his plans for flight, and Usamah comments that he later became a famous cavalier.

Another instance of a woman's indirect involvement in combat is noted in Usamah's description of the assassination of the Egyptian vizier al-'Adil ibn al-Sallar in 1153. He notes that the conspirators were able to attack al-'Adil in his harem at home, for al-'Adil's wife was the grandmother of their leader, Ibn 'Abbas, and so 'the latter could be admitted without special permission'.[42] Usamah, rather unhelpfully, does not make it clear whether al-'Adil's wife knew of the plot. It has been suggested that Usamah himself was involved in the assassination of al-'Adil,[43] which makes us treat his account with some caution. After all, by this time Usamah had already been forced to leave both Shayzar (in 1138) and Damascus (in 1144) as a result of political intrigues, so his involvement in such affairs would not be unprecedented.

Usamah describes another instance of a woman's involvement in war. In 1133, after taking part in a battle between Zangi and the Caliph al-Mustarshid (r. 1118–35) at Baghdad, Usamah accompanied Salah al-Din Muhammad when he besieged a castle named Masurra, about six days' march from Mosul. Usamah states: 'Presently a woman appeared on the castle and said, "Have ye calico?" We replied, "What a fine time is this for selling and buying!" She said, "We need the calico so that we may shroud you with it in your coffins. In five days at most ye'll all be dead." She meant by that that the place was infested with disease.'[44] There are two ways of reading this. The woman's warning may be an attempt to break the siege by scaring the besieging force away. On the other hand, she does not actually say that the town is infested with disease, and as Usamah makes no further mention of disease in his account, the woman's words may be a veiled threat made to the besieging force, essentially implying that if they do not leave the inhabitants of the town will fight and defeat them. Whatever the truth of the matter, the town capitulated a short time later, after Salah al-Din Muhammad had a prisoner cut in half. In his account Usamah presents us with a woman who was in some serious way involved in the defence of the castle, although her methods were more subtle than swinging a sword or throwing rocks.

## WOMEN PRISONERS

Usamah expresses his and others' views on the disturbing topic of women in captivity, both those taken captive and those for whom captivity was a fear. As Hadiah Dajani-Shakeel notes, the possibility of women being taken captive deeply troubled some Muslims.[45] Usamah tells the tale of a Kurd named Abu'l-Jaysh, whose daughter, Rafful, was captured by the Franks in 1122–23. Abu'l-Jaysh became obsessed, walking around the town telling people that Rafful had been captured. Shortly afterwards, Rafful's body was found in the river near Shayzar. Rather than remain the captive of a Frank, she had thrown herself from his horse and drowned herself. When he learned of this, Abu'l-Jaysh's anguish was abated, according to Usamah.[46] In similar vein, Usamah describes how his uncle was unwilling to allow a woman whom he had previously married, then divorced, to remain a captive of the Franks, even though it cost him five hundred dinars to secure her release.[47] Usamah himself also mentions that he often used to ransom Muslim captives, including female captives, from the Franks.[48]

Usamah gives one more example of a story involving a Muslim captive. He describes how the home and harem of al-Afdal Ridwan, a vizier of one of the previous Fatimid caliphs, al-Hafiz (r. 1131–49), was pillaged when he fell out of favour with his master and was driven out of Egypt. Apparently shortly after the event a leader in the Egyptian forces bought a maiden from the Sudanese troops, only to discover that she was Qatr al-Nada,[49] al-Afdal's daughter. He informed the caliph of this, and the latter sent for her and took her back into the palace.[50] The generous view is that even though her father had fallen from favour, al-Hafiz was still concerned that al-Afdal's daughter should be treated well. In this way we see a general concern for the welfare of female prisoners, even if they might be the children of enemies. The less generous view is that al-Hafiz recognised her value as a hostage, and that is why she was brought back to his palace.

## WOMEN IN POLITICS

Usamah's work also includes two anecdotes that give us depictions of women's involvement in politics in the twelfth century. The first is from his time at the Egyptian court. During the revolt mentioned above, following the assassination of the Fatimid caliph, al-Zafir, the daughters of al-Zafir's predecessor al-Hafiz summoned the governor of Middle Egypt, Tala'i' ibn Ruzzik, to help them. 'Abbas fled in the face of ibn Ruzzik's advance and was subsequently killed, while ibn Ruzzik became the new vizier. Usamah only makes a passing reference to al-Hafiz's daughters' appeal to ibn Ruzzik, but it is interesting nonetheless to note that he was aware of their involvement in these affairs.[51]

Another instance of women's involvement in politics noted by Usamah is that of a dispute between Zangi and the *amir* of Badlis over the hand of the heiress to the Armenian capital of Khilat, which took place in 1134. The father of the heiress was dead, and Usamah notes that Khilat was ruled by her mother, acting as regent. The matter was eventually resolved when Zangi marched with an army (of which Usamah was a member) to Khilat, entered its castle and wrote a marriage contract between himself and the heiress.[52]

In both of these accounts, Usamah does not give significant details about the influential women concerned. However, the fact that he mentions them at all indicates that he regards them as being worthy of note; it was not common for women in medieval Muslim societies to have such public political power. In the second case in particular, a woman is noted as being in charge of an important city, over a hundred years before the Mamluk takeover of Cairo and the celebrated reign of Shajar al-Durr as Sultana of Egypt (r. 1250). However, while political power was normally expected to rest in the hands of men, it is clear that the reality on the ground did not always reflect these expectations. The involvement of women in Muslim politics was not unprecedented,[53] but it was sufficiently rare to make these instances remarkable.

### OTHER WOMEN IN USAMAH'S WORK

So far I have looked at women in Usamah's work who take active roles in a number of different spheres of life. However, he also recounts a number of other stories that do not fall neatly into these categories and in which women assert themselves. In late 1150 or early 1151 Usamah travelled from Egypt to Syria on a diplomatic mission for al-ʿAdil ibn al-Sallar, who was attempting to negotiate an alliance with Nur al-Din against the Franks. When he arrived at the oasis of al-Jafr, in the desert between Egypt and the Holy Land, Usamah was approached by a woman who sought his aid to obtain the return of goods and livestock stolen from her. He made enquiries, and soon the stolen items and livestock were recovered.[54] Another example of a woman taking action in a legal matter occurs in a story cited by Usamah about the clairvoyance of the *shaykh*, Muhammad al-Basri. According to Usamah, who heard the story from a *shaykh* named Siraj al-Din (who himself heard it from the historian, Ibn al-Jawzi (d. 1201), so the story was third-hand) while visiting Isʿird in Diyar-Bakr, the *shaykh* was approached by a woman who had lost her dowry certificate. As al-Basri had been one of the witnesses to the writing of the document, she asked him to testify on her behalf at an upcoming tribunal. He replied, 'I shall not do so unless thou bringest me first some sweets.' After some confusion, the woman eventually brought some sweets wrapped in a piece of paper, which turned out to be the missing document.[55]

While this anecdote clearly has hagiographical overtones, and the woman herself is made to look somewhat silly, it nonetheless presents another instance of a woman asserting herself in legal matters, for she is apparently fighting for her rights regarding her dowry.

In the wake of the conquest of Masurra, described above, which Usamah had attended as a member of Salah al-Din Muhammad's army, the latter had the watchmen of the castle and the Christian and Jewish prisoners brought to him:

> An aged Kurdish woman presented herself and said to the watchman, 'Hast thou seen my son, so and so?' The watchman replied, 'He was killed. An arrow hit him.' She then said, 'And my son, so and so?' The watchman replied, 'The *amir* has cut him in two.' The woman shrieked and uncovered her head, the hair of which was like carded cotton. The watchman said to her, 'Be still, because of the *amir*.' She replied, 'And what thing is left that the *amir* can do with me? I had two sons, both of whom he has killed.' They pushed her away.[56]

The bystanders may have felt that the woman was lucky to escape with her life, but she clearly had no reticence about behaving in an impudent and indecorous fashion in the presence of an *amir*, even one who had proved to be as intimidating as Salah al-Din Muhammad. Whether this was the result of great bravery or overwhelming distress is impossible to tell, but Usamah seems to have regarded her behaviour as being of enough interest to mention in his narrative. No doubt this woman was not the only one grieving at the end of the siege, but she is the only one he describes in his account of the events.

A final anecdote that also demonstrates Usamah's recourse to women as both exemplary and admonitory figures concerns Buraykah, who was last seen giving water to Muslim troops fighting the forces of Bohemond II of Antioch. Usamah was told another story about Buraykah by one of his father's lieutenants named Baqiyyah ibn al-Usayfir. Baqiyyah stated that one night he had travelled home to deal with some personal business when he observed a strange, unidentified creature among the tombs in the town grave-yard. He was initially frightened by the apparition, but took a tighter grip on his nerves and investigated it more closely. Baqiyyah told Usamah:

> 'Taking up my sword, my leather shield and my javelin, which were with me, I advanced step by step, while I could hear some singing and a voice coming out of that object. When I was close by it, I jumped over it, holding my dagger in my hand, and got hold of it and behold! it was Buraykah with her hair spread all over, riding on a reed and neighing and roaming among the tombs. "Woe unto thee," said I, "what dost thou at this hour here?" "I am exercising sorcery," she replied. I said, "May Allah abominate thee, abominate thy sorcery and thy art from among all arts!"'[57]

While magic is tolerated in Islam as long as it does no harm to others, harmful magic, including magic conducted through recourse to demonic inspiration, is prohibited on pain of death. It is this malevolent form of magic that Buraykah implies when she states 'asharu' (translated by Hitti as 'I am exercising sorcery').[58] Hence Baqiyyah's reaction is understandable. In addition, Buraykah is roaming the graveyard, dishevelled, in an immodest manner, and behaving in a way that is, in the Muslim view, entirely unbecoming to her sex. In this way, although a strong woman, she forms a contrast to the strong women of Usamah's family, discussed earlier, who while also asserting themselves are careful to stay within the bounds of Muslim propriety and decorum. So this tale, like so many others given by Usamah, forms part of his wider, balanced work.

## CONCLUSION

It is clear from Usamah's work that he travelled widely; he not only emigrated periodically as the result of political mis-steps, but also took part in a large number of military expeditions and political missions that led him to visit a large number of cities, towns and fortresses in Iraq, Syria, the Holy Land and Egypt. While on these travels he encountered or heard stories about many strong, active women, who asserted themselves in a variety of ways. The women he describes in his work are not merely the passive figures of deprecatory stories about the Franks; they fill a variety of roles, and even if one assumes that some of Usamah's anecdotes are dubious, it is still clear that there were many women who made a lasting impression on the author and others he knew. Medieval history, and medieval Islamic history in particular, is often regarded as being mostly about men of the educated upper classes, who wrote the chronicles and fought the battles, with women and the lower classes usually occupying a passive role and being largely silent. The women in Usamah's work form a stark contrast to this view. They assert themselves in society, often exerting influence on the men, and even periodically taking over traditionally male roles. It is also important to note how widespread they are. As has been noted, Usamah travelled all over the Levant, and wherever he went he encountered these strong female figures.

This chapter has attempted to counter the excessive concentration of modern scholarship on a small number of Usamah's stories about women by drawing attention to these other female characters. This has been merely a preliminary enquiry; the subject of women in Usamah's work awaits greater consideration. Only with further investigation will it be possible, as Usamah intended, to preserve a sense of balance with regard to his Kitab al-I'tibar.

## NOTES

1 Usamah Ibn Munqidh, *An Arab-Syrian Gentleman & Warrior in the Period of the Crusades*, trans. P. K. Hitti (New York: Columbia University Press, 2000), p. 156; *idem*, *Usamah's Memoirs Entitled Kitab al-I'tibar*, ed. P. K. Hitti, (Princeton: Princeton University Press, 1930, repr. Beirut: United Publishers, 1981), p. 163. Quotations are from the 2000 edition, by permission of Columbia University Press.

2 Usamah, *Arab-Syrian Gentleman*, pp. 3–21; R. S. Humphreys, 'Munki<u>dh</u>', in H. A. R. Gibb *et al.* (eds), *The Encyclopaedia of Islam*, 2nd edn, 11 vols and supplements (Leiden: E. J. Brill, 1954–2003), vii, pp. 557–80.

3 For example by Carole Hillenbrand, in *The Crusades: Islamic Perspectives* (Edinburgh: Edinburgh University Press, 1999) and Robert Irwin, in 'Usamah ibn Munqidh: An Arab-Syrian gentleman at the time of the crusades reconsidered', in J. France and W. G. Zajac (eds), *The Crusades and their Sources: Essays Presented to Bernard Hamilton* (Aldershot: Ashgate, 1998), pp. 71–87.

4 See Irwin, 'Usamah', pp. 72–5.

5 Including the works of Hillenbrand and Irwin, cited in n. 3 above. Other works that address this aspect of Usamah's work include Wadi' Z. Haddad, 'The crusaders through Muslim eyes', *The Muslim World*, 73 (1983), 234–52; Hadiah Dajani-Shakeel, 'Some aspects of Muslim–Frankish Christian relations in the Sham region in the twelfth century', in Yvonne Yazbeck Haddad and Wadi' Z. Haddad (eds), *Christian–Muslim Encounters* (Gainesville, FL: University Press of Florida, 1995), pp. 193–209; and David W. Morray, *The Genius of Usamah ibn Munqidh: Aspects of* Kitab al-I'tibar *by Usamah ibn Munqidh* (Durham: Centre for Middle Eastern and Islamic Studies, University of Durham, 1987).

6 Usamah, *Arab-Syrian Gentleman*, pp. 164–6; *Usamah's Memoirs*, pp. 174–5. On this aspect of Usamah's work, see Hillenbrand, *Crusades*, pp. 276–81 and 347–8 and Haddad, 'The crusaders through Muslim eyes', 240–1.

7 Usamah states that the bath-house keeper who told him the first story was from Ma'arrat al-Nu'man.

8 Usamah, *Arab-Syrian Gentleman*, pp. 164–5; *Usamah's Memoirs*, p. 174.

9 Hillenbrand, *Crusades*, p. 348.

10 The author is indebted to John Mattock, Michael Brett, Richard Kimber and Ionut Epurescu-Pascovici for their thoughts on this matter.

11 Usamah, *Arab-Syrian Gentleman*, pp. 159–60; *Usamah's Memoirs*, pp. 166–7.

12 Haddad, 'The crusaders through Muslim eyes', p. 241.

13 Usamah, *Arab-Syrian Gentleman*, p. 160; *Usamah's Memoirs*, pp. 167–8.

14 Usamah, *Arab-Syrian Gentleman*, p. 167; *Usamah's Memoirs*, p. 177; Hillenbrand, *Crusades*, p. 350.

15 Irwin, 'Usamah', p. 74.

16 Hillenbrand, *Crusades*, pp. 352–3.

17 Usamah, *Arab-Syrian Gentleman*, p. 162; *Usamah's Memoirs*, pp. 170–1.

18 Irwin, 'Usamah', p. 77.

19 Usamah, *Arab-Syrian Gentleman*, p. 26; *Usamah's Memoirs*, p. 3.

20 Usamah, *Arab-Syrian Gentleman*, pp. 49–52 and 60; *Usamah's Memoirs*, pp. 29–34 and 43.

21 Usamah, *Arab-Syrian Gentleman*, p. 61; *Usamah's Memoirs*, pp. 44–5.

22 Usamah, *Arab-Syrian Gentleman*, p. 156; *Usamah's Memoirs*, p. 162.

23 Usamah, *Arab-Syrian Gentleman*, p. 156; *Usamah's Memoirs*, pp. 162–3. Muslim ritual prayers normally involve a number of changes between standing, kneeling and prostration.

24 Another term used to refer to the Isma'ilis, for their pursuit of the *batin*, the inner holy truths of religious texts and formulations. This doctrine was considered heretical by most mainstream (Sunni) Muslims.

25 Usamah, *Arab-Syrian Gentleman*, p. 154; *Usamah's Memoirs*, pp. 159–60.

26 Usamah, *Arab-Syrian Gentleman*, p. 161; *Usamah's Memoirs*, pp. 169–70.

27 Usamah, *Arab-Syrian Gentleman*, p. 218; *Usamah's Memoirs*, pp. 241–2.

28 Usamah, *Arab-Syrian Gentleman*, p. 218; *Usamah's Memoirs*, p. 242. The quotation is from Qur'an, 36:68.

29 Usamah, *Arab-Syrian Gentleman*, pp. 190–2 and 194–5; *Usamah's Memoirs*, pp. 207–9 and 211–13. On this theme, see also Irwin, 'Usamah', p. 76.

30 'Abbas was the vizier of the Fatimid caliph from 1153 to 1154. He had obtained this position after arranging the murder of the previous vizier, al-'Adil ibn al-Sallar. 'Abbas's son (ibn 'Abbas) then murdered the Fatimid caliph al-Zafir (r. 1149–54), while 'Abbas himself massacred most of the rest of the Fatimid princes, leaving only the infant al-Fa'iz (r. 1154–60), thus ensuring his control of Egypt. However, this provoked a revolt. The Armenian governor of Upper Egypt, Tala'i' ibn Ruzzik, then moved on Cairo. 'Abbas fled and was subsequently killed, while ibn Ruzzik became the new vizier. Usamah gives us his own version of events, in which he claims no involvement, while others claimed Usamah was involved in the plot against al-'Adil.

31 Usamah, *Arab-Syrian Gentleman*, p. 48; *Usamah's Memoirs*, p. 27.

32 Usamah, *Arab-Syrian Gentleman*, p. 154; *Usamah's Memoirs*, p. 160.

33 Usamah, *Arab-Syrian Gentleman*, pp. 158–9; *Usamah's Memoirs*, pp. 165–6.

34 Helen Nicholson, 'Women on the Third Crusade', *Journal of Medieval History*, 23 (1997), 335–49.

35 Usamah, *Arab-Syrian Gentleman*, pp. 157–8; *Usamah's Memoirs*, pp. 163–4.

36 Usamah, *Arab-Syrian Gentleman*, p. 168; *Usamah's Memoirs*, p. 179.

37 Niall Christie, 'Crusade literature', in Suad Joseph *et al.* (eds), *The Encyclopedia of Women and Islamic Cultures* (Leiden: E. J. Brill, 2003), i, pp. 16–21.

38 Usamah, *Arab-Syrian Gentleman*, p. 152; *Usamah's Memoirs*, p. 157.

39 Usamah, *Arab-Syrian Gentleman*, p. 101; *Usamah's Memoirs*, pp. 92–4.

40 Irwin, 'Usamah', p. 75.

41 Usamah, *Arab-Syrian Gentleman*, p. 153; *Usamah's Memoirs*, pp. 158–9.

42 Usamah, *Arab-Syrian Gentleman*, p. 43; *Usamah's Memoirs*, p. 22.

43 The best-known proponent of this claim is the Mosuli chronicler Ibn al-Athir (d. 1233). Hitti, on the other hand, refutes this claim. For more details, see Usamah, *Arab-Syrian Gentleman*, p. 12.

44 *Ibid.*, p. 188; Usamah, *Usamah's Memoirs*, p. 203.

45 Hadiah Dajani-Shakeel, 'Aspects', p. 206.

46 Usamah, *Arab-Syrian Gentleman*, p. 179; *Usamah's Memoirs*, pp. 192–3.

47 Usamah, *Arab-Syrian Gentleman*, p. 100; *Usamah's Memoirs*, p. 92.

48 Usamah, *Arab-Syrian Gentleman*, pp. 110–12; *Usamah's Memoirs*, pp. 105–7. Usamah is by no means the only source from this period for whom the treatment of both male and female captives is a concern. For more on this topic, see Shakeel, 'Aspects', pp. 205–7 and Hillenbrand, *Crusades*, pp. 549–52.

49 A name that picturesquely translates as 'Dewdrop'.

50 Usamah, *Arab-Syrian Gentleman*, p. 55; *Usamah's Memoirs*, pp. 37–8.

51 Usamah, *Arab-Syrian Gentleman*, pp. 47–8; *Usamah's Memoirs*, pp. 27–8.

52 Usamah, *Arab-Syrian Gentleman*, pp. 118–19; *Usamah's Memoirs*, pp. 114–15.

53 An earlier example is Khayzuran, the mother of the 'Abbasid caliph Harun al-Rashid (r. 786–809).

54 Usamah, *Arab-Syrian Gentleman*, p. 36; *Usamah's Memoirs*, pp. 13–14.
55 Usamah, *Arab-Syrian Gentleman*, p. 202; *Usamah's Memoirs*, pp. 221–2.
56 Usamah, *Arab-Syrian Gentleman*, p. 189; *Usamah's Memoirs*, p. 204.
57 Usamah, *Arab-Syrian Gentleman*, p. 152; *Usamah's Memoirs*, pp. 157–8.
58 For more information on magic in Islam see T. Fahd, 'Sihr', in Gibb *et al.* (eds), *Encyclopaedia of Islam*, ix, pp. 567–71.

# 5

## The Mendicants as missionaries and travellers in the Near East in the thirteenth and fourteenth centuries

**( )**

### Andrew Jotischky

A T THE PAPAL consistory in 1322, Franciscan and Dominican prelates who were debating the question of apostolic poverty found themselves arguing over which Order had the more profound experience of the East. Jerome of Catalonia, the Franciscan Bishop of Caffa (Crimea), declared that the Minors had, in the course of eighty years of preaching among the Tartars, founded forty churches there and seen nine new martyrs crowned for their faith; he himself had spent twenty-two years preaching the Gospel to the Tartars and the Greeks. 'It is scarcely possible', he asserted, 'that such an Order, which has sent missionaries throughout the whole world, from the borders of Morocco to the Indies, could be corrupt . . . Nobody in the whole Church has been quicker or shown greater readiness to consecrate their lives [for the faith] than the Order of Minors'.[1] The defence of the Franciscan teaching on poverty – and thus on its orthodoxy – rested, for Jerome, on its record as a missionary Order.

By the 1320s, a century or so after the deaths of their founders, the Franciscans and Dominicans had assumed total responsibility for missionary work within the Church. Like the Franciscans and Dominicans, the Carmelites maintained priories in the Crusader States until 1291, and subsequently in Cyprus. But, perhaps surprisingly for an order whose origins lay in the Holy Land, the Carmelites established no eastern missions in this period, and generally speaking showed little interest in pilgrimage or the crusade.[2] The Dominican Society of Pilgrim Friars had founded convents throughout the Near East, the Caucasus and Persia; the Franciscans had penetrated into Transcaspia and even founded a Latin bishopric in China. No class of people in Europe, other than exceptional merchants such as the Polos of Venice, had travelled so widely in the East, or encountered so much of eastern society, as the friars. The number of friars engaged in such exotic activities was small, compared with those whose ministry lay within the Catholic West, yet these few have left a disproportionate body of contemporary records, mostly in the form of personal travel accounts and descriptions of the peoples and lands they encountered. For this reason, the modern literature on the friars as missionaries is extensive, and the most exotic and far-flung missions have attracted particular attention.[3] The purpose of this chapter is not to add to this literature, but instead to examine more closely some aspects of the friars' experiences in the most familiar of the eastern regions: the Holy Land. I shall pay particular attention to Mendicants' attitudes to the indigenous Christians, and examine these in the context of a developing ideology of mission to non-Catholic Christians in the papacy.

The Franciscan mission in the East began with the example of the founder himself. Francis's attempt to convert the Sultan of Egypt, al-Kamil, during the Fifth Crusade (1219) was his third attempt at preaching to the infidel: earlier attempts in 1212 and 1213 had both ended in disappointment. Later Franciscan writers extended Francis' activities to include preaching to Muslims in the Holy Land, and even, in one anecdote, succeeding in secretly convert-ing al-Kamil to Christianity.[4] For Francis himself, preaching to the infidel was the logical corollary of the attempt to regenerate Christian society. The Crusader States, where Christians of different traditions lived in close proximity to Muslims, offered a field of activity in which both could be accomplished side by side. Moreover, the presence of large numbers of eastern Christians gave new scope to reforming ideals. The Holy Land was a frontier not only in political terms between Islamic and Christian territories, but also between 'correct' and 'deviant' Christian practice. The indigenous Christians, most of whom were Greek Orthodox in religious tradition (the *Suriani*, as most western writers called them), were brought up among Muslims, spoke Arabic and copied Muslim social and religious customs. They occupied a conceptual frontier between Catholicism and Islam. They did not stand in need of conversion in the same sense as non-Christians, but both their allegiance to Rome and their understanding of the sacraments of the Church was, from the papacy's point of view, questionable. A contem-porary admirer of Francis, Jacques de Vitry, Bishop of Acre, was shocked by the freedom given to indigenous Christians to practise observances contrary to Roman custom, even though they were supposed to be under the authority of Latin bishops. But this was perhaps to be expected when the example they had from Europeans was so poor: Jacques himself had to go into the streets of the Italian quarter of Acre to exhort its residents to attend Mass.[5]

As Jerome of Catalonia was to confirm, martyrdom was one of the dangers inherent in the mission to the Holy Land. According to his biographer, Thomas of Celano, Francis specifically desired martyrdom as the outcome of preaching to the Muslims, and his *Regula non bullata* specified martyrdom as a possible outcome of the mission.[6] When the Master of the Dominican Order, Jordan of Saxony, asked for volunteers at the chapter-general of 1230, nobody came forward until eventually Peter of Rheims, the provincial of France, announced that he was prepared to go to his death in 'the land consecrated by Saviour's blood'.[7] In 1256 the Dominican chapter-general received reports of two martyrs in the Holy Land.[8] In 1266 The Templar Grand Master asked the Franciscan provincial of the Holy Land to send friars to give spiritual aid to the Templars besieged in Safed. James of Podio and his three companions persuaded the Templars to accept martyrdom rather than conversion to Islam, a fate in which the friars shared.[9] Seven Franciscans were killed in 1269, and a further seven in the sack of Tripoli in 1289, while the fall of Acre in 1291 resulted in the deaths of fourteen Franciscans and some Claresses. Sporadic outbreaks of anti-Christian violence resulted in further suffering in the fourteenth century: usually, as in 1365, when sixteen Franciscans from Jerusalem were imprisoned and tortured in Damascus, following a western attack on Muslim territory.[10] Four Aragonese friars who had been imprisoned in Egypt, presumably captives from the fall of Acre, were released in 1303.[11]

These examples apart, the friars had remarkable ease of access throughout Muslim territories. From the 1230s onward they were encouraged to develop the ministry of visiting Christian prisoners of war. A surviving *firman* ('letter of authority') of 1254 from the Sultan of Homs, al-Mansur, allows Franciscans to exercise ministry to all Christians in his territories, though friars presumably required a corresponding document from the Christian authorities, such as the letter provided by Gregory IX for the Franciscan Manasses in 1238, authorising him to visit Christian prisoners.[12] The cordial relations established by James II of Aragon with the Sultan an-Nasir of Egypt allowed a group of Franciscans led by Angelo da Spoleto to visit prisoners in Cairo in 1303–4. The friars stayed in Cairo for three weeks, visiting them daily, hearing their confessions and giving them communion from a portable altar.[13]

After the loss of the Holy Land in 1291, friars, like any other travellers, needed formal permission from Muslim authorities to make pilgrimages to the Holy Land. Perhaps because Muslim rulers had become used to them in their capacity as envoys of popes and kings, such permission seems to have been granted readily, though of course it is in the nature of the surviving evidence that we know only those cases where permission was granted. Angelo da Spoleto and his companions asked to go to the Holy Land after visiting the Christian prisoners in Cairo.[14] The Irish Franciscan Symon Semeonis (1322) did not visit prisoners (though there were still apparently westerners in captivity as late as 1327),[15] but applied for authorisation to visit the holy places from the sultan's officials in Cairo. This was a special passport issued on request to Mendicants, who could claim exemption from the normal dues payable by pilgrims. According to Symon's description, it consisted of an image of the sultan's fingers in ink – an early form of fingerprint, evidently.[16] To judge from the thorough examination of Symon's belongings on entry into Alexandria, claims of poverty were assessed carefully before exemption was granted. Even so, Symon and his companion were kept waiting for five days before being granted a permit to proceed to Cairo – as the friar explained, the sultan did not welcome those from whom he could make no money.[17]

Payment of tribute was resented by the Franciscan Niccolo da Poggibonsi, whose *Libro d'Oltramare* (1346) is one of the most vivid travel accounts of the period. In addition to the tax levied at the port of entry, extra tolls were constantly demanded. In Jerusalem, having already paid a 'fat tribute', he resorted to the dodge of changing places with one of the resident Franciscans of the convent in Jerusalem in order to be able to spend more than a single day in the city.[18] But there was no escaping the tribute of twelve denarii to the gatekeeper at the tomb of St Mary of Egypt on the Mount of Olives, or the entrance fee at the tomb of the Blessed Virgin.[19] The tribute for passage through Samaria was four florins (but very few pilgrims took this dangerous route and presumably the local authorities could charge whatever they wanted); to enter Acre Niccolo paid seven dirhems; to enter Bethany, twelve denarii; while at Bethgala by the Jordan, the traditional site of the baptism of Christ, he had to pay four and a half dirhems. The toll to enter a city like Acre, or to go a longer distance, such as from Jericho to Damascus, was more substantial than the tribute for individual shrines. The total tribute for the journey from Jericho to Damascus, paid in stages along the way, was thirteen dirhems.[20] This was heavy on the pocket, particularly for a Mendicant. The fact that Niccolo specifies amounts in different currencies suggests that tolls were collected by different agencies. The English Franciscan whose pilgrimage took place a year before Niccolo's paid his toll to enter Bethany not to the Muslims but to the Greek Orthodox monks who occupied the village.[21] Moreover, the tolls paid en route to Damascus were sometimes taxes levied by municipalities, sometimes tolls charged by families who had been given the right to farm them.[22]

Tolls and taxes were only one hazard of travel in the Holy Land in the fourteenth century. Pilgrimage had always been a physically demanding, even on occasion a dangerous pursuit. Some regions of the Holy Land had a reputation for brigandage. Even after the crusader conquest of 1099 the safety of pilgrims in the hinterland could not be guaranteed; thus in 1106–7 the Russian pilgrim Daniel was advised to travel north only with an armed escort from Jerusalem through Samaria.[23] Two hundred and forty years later, Niccolo da Poggibonsi reported that most pilgrims avoided Samaria, even though it was a quicker and cheaper way to get to Galilee, because of the danger of being attacked by the villagers.[24] Brigandage was a perennial danger, regardless of changes in government. Anthony de Reboldis, a Franciscan from Cremona who travelled from Egypt to the Holy Land in 1331, fell foul of the Bedouin of the Sinai. It was necessary, he explained, to hire Bedouin guides in order to go to St Catherine's on Mount Sinai, but it was also inherently risky, because once in the desert the guides were likely to turn on their employers. The passport with which Anthony and his party had been provided by the sultan was of little use, because in the desert the Bedouin recognised no authority. Three days before they reached Gaza, the party of nine pilgrims was attacked by Bedouin, whom they managed to fend off with sticks and stones and a bow and arrow that one pilgrim was apparently carrying.[25] Niccolo da Poggibonsi suffered a more frightening experience still in the Sinai, when the interpreter he had brought with him from Egypt was kidnapped by Bedouin, and he was temporarily stranded in the desert.[26] Perhaps more worrying even than the threat of assault was the Bedouins' predilection for leading pilgrims astray in the desert. Angelo da Spoleto describes how only experienced guides, who could navigate by the stars, could find their way through the sand-covered landscape between Alexandria and Cairo, in which no plants grew and no humans could live.[27] Nature, too, provided its own dangers. Niccolo was almost shipwrecked during a storm on the sea route from Beirut to Egypt, and his companion nearly drowned when he fell down the steep bank into the Jordan at the place of Christ's baptism.[28] Aside from describing life-threatening dangers, Mendicant travellers remarked on the physical discomforts to be expected in the Near East. James of Verona (1335) found that Christians were not allowed to ride horses in the Holy Land, while Niccolo da Poggibonsi complained that the inns in which pilgrims were expected to stay provided neither food nor beds, but only an enclosure in which to rest.[29]

The need to employ guides or dragomans as interpreters and to arrange for fees to be paid or passes obtained drew western friars into temporary relationships with a 'subculture' of people whose religious affiliation and ethnic origin defined them as marginal to the societies in which they lived. The four dragomans mentioned by Symon Semeonis, all westerners in captivity in Egypt, consisted of a friar known only by the Latinised form of what was evidently his Arab name, Assedinus; Peter, a Templar who had married a Muslim woman; and two Italians whom Symon describes as Jacobites (the usual term for Syrian Orthodox; in this case, probably Egyptian Copts). Symon refers to all these as 'renegati', meaning that they had formally accepted conversion to Islam; the friar, however, told Symon that he was still a practising Christian in secret.[30]

The attitudes expressed by friars toward the Christians whom they encountered in the Near East are complex. Three fourteenth-century friars were particularly interested in the eastern Christians: the Franciscans Symon Semeonis and Niccolo da Poggibonsi and the Augustinian hermit James of Verona. They were confronting a phenomenon new to them – the existence of Christians whose beliefs differed in few essentials from their own, but whose religious customs and appearance were alien. The most immediate problem was that it was as difficult to distinguish between different Christian traditions as it was to tell eastern Christians from Muslims. Niccolo da Poggibonsi could tell the difference between Greeks, Georgians, Copts, Armenians, Muslims and even Ethiopians in Cairo only by their dress: some wore linen, some camel skins, others silk.[31] This last sounds like exaggeration, for Niccolo was only too aware of different skin colours: on his first sighting of black men, in a Muslim ship off Alexandria, he professed himself terrified by the appearance of creatures who resembled demons; and in the desert, he described the dark skin of the 'savage Arabs', who were naked save for a camel skin around their private parts.[32] Symon Semeonis found the colour of the turban a useful clue to identifying the wearer's race.[33] Symon was a close observer of costume, for in the Balkans, noting that the Albanians dressed like Greeks, he discoursed on various styles of headgear: for example, the Greek flat hat designed to show off the hair, and the Slavic oblong hat in which a feather might be worn.[34] In Crete he remarked that the women, both Greeks and Jews, wore a sacerdotal costume embroidered with gold.[35]

Some indigenous Christians, whom Symon identifies as Greeks and Jacobites, were known as 'Christians of the girdle' (*Christiani de cinctura*) by the belts they wore around their outer robes. Most Muslims, in contrast, never wore belts, but instead a cloth or towel bound around the waist.[36] The term 'Christians of the girdle' seems to have become widespread in the fourteenth century. It is not always clear, however, exactly what group of people is being referred to by the term. Symon means Copts when he speaks of Jacobites, and Niccolo da Poggibonsi likewise uses the term for Greek Orthodox and Copts.[37] James of Verona seems to reserve the term for Jacobites, although he mistakenly says that their offices resemble those of the Greeks.[38] Angelo da Spoleto, however, distinguishes between the 'Christians of the girdle' and the Jacobites. Both are found throughout Egypt, but the Jacobites, he says (meaning the Copts), are descended from the original pre-Muslim inhabitants of Egypt, and form a distinct Church. The 'Christians of the girdle' with whom Angelo came into contact were serving in the sultan's bodyguard, so he must be referring to an enslaved population of Christians, mostly from the Orthodox world.[39] At any rate, the term is used primarily in Egypt, and probably therefore derives from local Egyptian usage.[40]

It is striking that Mendicants who encountered eastern Christians while on pilgrimage seem to have been relatively untroubled by such variations of religious custom and observance as they noticed. Symon Semeonis noted that the ceremonies of the Jacobites (he means Copts) differed from Roman custom, but declared that 'in all other essential articles of faith, they err only a little, and are faithful believers'.[41] Their scepticism regarding infant baptism, their practice of signing the cross with one finger only, the lack of clerical celibacy, their relaxed attitude toward consanguinity in marriage, and their failure to practise auricular confession are duly recorded, but with the exception of the latter, Symon draws no adverse conclusions.[42] The only note of disapproval, indeed, concerns Jacobite monasticism, which Symon describes as 'restricted and almost inhuman' – a revealing comment from a Franciscan in the 1320s, when his Order was itself divided over the question of observance.

Niccolo da Poggibonsi's favourable opinion of the Jacobites in Egypt was doubtless encouraged by the generous hospitality he and his companions enjoyed from them. Although the Franciscans and their hosts could not understand each other, 'by hints and hand signs, we got on'. One wealthy Jacobite layman tried to make them a present of money so as to enable the Franciscans to travel home in comfort, but was astonished to learn that their Rule prohibited the carrying of money; nevertheless, the friars accepted a compromise whereby he paid for their passage. Niccolo's observations mostly concern the Mass. He found it strange that the priests sat on the ground, 'like women', to sing the Mass, while the deacons and subdeacons, their heads covered with a cloth, read the lessons and Gospel from the altar.[43]

In the Holy Land, Niccolo also attended Greek Orthodox services, and noted differences in ceremonial from Roman custom. He observed Orthodox services at Christmas in Bethlehem and at Epiphany by the Jordan; he visited the Orthodox monasteries of St John the Baptist by the Jordan, and knew of other Orthodox monasteries on Mount Quarantana (near Jericho), in Sebaste and by the Dead Sea.[44] Niccolo was interested in the use of wooden clappers rather than bells to announce the Mass: the priests struck a wooden plank with two mallets to produce a sound that could be heard all over the city. He remarks on the priests' use of their hands to signify musical notation: presumably he means that the priest conducted while the congregation sang. Although he notes the different custom entailed in the Eucharist, he offers no comment on the Orthodox use of leavened bread, even though this was one of the most bitter grievances in Greek/Latin polemic.[45] As Niccolo remarks, 'the Greeks hold the Latins in greater hatred than the Saracens, and on account of this hatred are separated from Rome'. For Niccolo, however, the problem is one of authority – the Orthodox 'make as vicar over them the patriarch of Constantinople instead of the pope'. Yet this authority is useless, for the Orthodox clergy in the East cannot prevent their own flock from being sold as slaves in the markets: 'O Greeks, who were once masters of the world, and are now enslaved, and priced up to be sold like animals!'[46]

Although his remarks are based on personal observation rather than ideology, Niccolo's view of the native Orthodox is a traditional one based on an ethnographical genre first found in the late twelfth century, most fully articulated by Jacques de Vitry in the 1220s, and followed by pilgrims and crusading theorists of the late thirteenth and early fourteenth centuries. The Orthodox are contemptible, in the final analysis, because they are too weak to protect themselves against domination by whomever happens to be the strongest power in the region at the time, whether Muslim or Frankish Christian: as Jacques de Vitry had said, 'everywhere they are servile, and always pay tribute [to others]'.[47]

James of Verona's pilgrimage account was also influenced by the model of ethnographic descriptions of the people of the East. He lists the different Christian traditions in two places: first, while he was in Cyprus before embarking for the Holy Land, and later, as a preliminary to his account of the feast of the Assumption, which he celebrated with 'all the Christians of the Holy Land and from other parts of Syria, Egypt and Palestine' at Bethlehem.[48] As a rule, doctrinal differences are less important to him than observable customs. The Georgians, for example, are distinguishable from Greeks for using unleavened bread in the Eucharist, like Latins, but are like Greeks in not elevating the host. They are, however, 'devoti Christiani'. The Jacobites practise circumcision, but otherwise use Greek custom. The Armenians, in contrast, have an office 'like true Christians'. Maronites and Georgians baptise 'in the manner of Christians', but use a Greek office. Sometimes, however, doctrine is an index of difference. The Greeks of Cyprus he describes as using fermented bread in the Eucharist, not elevating the host, and not believing that the Holy Spirit proceeds through the Son.[49]

The two lists betray slight but significant contradictions and differences. On his first encounter with Nestorians (or the Church of the East) in Cyprus, James identifies them as followers of the 'perfidious heretic' Nestorius, who taught that Christ was wholly human. Although they used Greek in their office, he considered their customs unique to them.[50] However, when he lists the different traditions at Bethlehem, James says that the Nestorians use largely Greek ceremonial and remarks that they do not practise circumcision – thus distinguishing them from the Syrian Orthodox. Moreover, he now concedes that they do not follow the teaching of Nestorius in most respects.[51] Either James had encountered two divergent groups within the Church of the East, or, more likely, he had changed his mind on closer observation of their offices. The office of the Assumption may anyway have differed little from one tradition to another. In Jerusalem, James also encountered the Ethiopian monks who maintained a chapel to one side of the Holy Sepulchre. Like the Greeks, they used leavened bread, and did not practise elevation of the host; like the Jacobites, they practised circumcision and branding as well as baptism by water; they sang both day and night.[52] Despite the formulaic elements in James's account of the indigenous Christians, it is clear that he was, like Niccolo, a close observer of local religious traditions. Like Niccolo, he visited Orthodox monasteries in the Holy Land: the monastery of St Gerasimus, between Jericho and the Jordan, where he was warmly welcomed by the monks; St John the Baptist, by the Jordan; Mount Quarantana, where two Greek monks lived; and St Catherine's on Mount Sinai.[53] His choice of words is sometimes revealing: for example, listing the order in which the different Christian clergy said Mass at the Tomb of the Virgin, he begins with 'we, the true Christians', followed by all the other confessions in turn.[54] The eastern Christians were categorised according to how far they strayed from the Roman norm in observance of ecclesiastical custom.

The pilgrimages of Symon Semeonis, James of Verona and Niccolo da Poggibonsi, which spanned the years from 1323 to 1346, took place at a critical time in the history of the Latin Church in the Holy Land. Crusades for the recovery of the Holy Land were still being planned, although such expeditions as did leave the West had in practice more limited aims.[55] Of more lasting significance was the establishment of the Franciscan custody in the Holy Land. The custody was negotiated between James II of Aragon and Sultan an-Nasir, initially in 1322 on behalf of the Dominicans, then, after the failure of the Dominican mission in 1323, on behalf of the Franciscans. When James II died in 1327, negotiations were completed by Robert the Wise and Sancia of Naples. In 1333 a group of Franciscans settled near the Holy Sepulchre, and by 1336 they had also gained some rights over the Cenacle on Mount Sion, the Tomb of the Virgin in the Kidron Valley outside the eastern wall of Jerusalem, and parts of the Church of the Nativity in Bethlehem.[56]

The evidence for the rights and status of the Franciscans in the Holy Land in the 1330s and 1340s, and for the practical implications of the sultan's concessions, comes largely from pilgrimage evidence, including that of James of Verona and Niccolo da Poggibonsi. It is clear from both of these sources that the Franciscans were not given absolute ownership of the sites, but had to share rights of occupation with the eastern Christians; hence James's list of Christians celebrating at Bethlehem on the feast of the Assumption, and the order of services at the Tomb of the Virgin. Nevertheless, it is striking that the Franciscans were given priority where restrictions of space did not allow all clergy to celebrate together. Even more suggestive is the coincidence of clergy of all confessions celebrating the feasts on the same day, for in most years the Orthodox calendar, which eastern Christians followed, designated different days for these feasts. No western pilgrim remarks on this phenomenon, which probably arose because the Muslim authorities were reluctant to allow celebrations to take place over a long period. That the eastern Christians were required to fall into line with western practice indicates the privileged position that had been negotiated on their behalf by the western monarchs.

Alongside these travellers' reports must be read the contemporary treatment of the eastern Christians in papal sources, and in the treatises on the recovery of the Holy Land by friars, such as the Dominicans William Adam and Ricoldo da Monte Crucis, who had travelled extensively as missionaries, or the Franciscan Fidenzo of Padua, who as provincial of the Holy Land was resident in Acre. All these sources, however, were informed to varying degrees by received traditions regarding the customs, beliefs and morality of the eastern Christians. The genre of listing and describing the eastern peoples resident in the Crusader States according to customs, religious affiliation and ethnic characteristics began in the last quarter of the twelfth century, with the anonymous treatise known as the *Tractatus de locis et statu Sancte Terre*.[57] The peoples listed are Greeks, Syrians, Jacobites, Armenians, Maronites, Georgians, Copts and Nestorians. Jacques de Vitry developed a fuller and more sophisticated version of this taxonomy in his *Historia Orientalis*, and dozens of variant readings of this original list found their way into thirteenth-century pilgrimage accounts.[58] The Dominicans Burchard of Mount Sion and Ricoldo da Monte Crucis have slightly different versions,[59] but elements of the original can be found in a variety of sources – narrative chronicles, letters, papal bulls – from throughout the thirteenth century and beyond.[60] In order to understand the ideological context in which Mendicant travellers of the fourteenth century recorded their observations of the Christians of the East, a brief survey of the attitudes revealed in some of these sources is necessary.

A coherent papal ideology regarding eastern Christians began to emerge from the 1230s onward. Honorius III had declared that the Syrians, Greeks and Armenians all bore a mutual witness to the faith with the Latins in the East, but there was no systematic attempt to theorise the relationship of the Roman Church with the different Christian traditions before Gregory IX's Decretals (1234), in which separate chapters dealt with Muslims, Jews and schismatics.[61] Gregory's successor, Innocent IV, was primarily interested in relationships with non-western societies in the context of furthering the crusade, but in the course of developing a legal basis for such relationships he touched by implication on the status of the eastern Christians. The starting point for any justification of crusading, in Pope Innocent's view, was the Christian right of ownership to the Holy Land.[62] But this left open the question of the relationship between different groups of Christians. Did Innocent IV think that the indigenous Christians of the East enjoyed the same legal rights of self-determination as the western Church? Papal bulls give a partial answer. Popes distinguished between Catholics and 'schismatics'; indeed, they tended to identify eastern Christians with Muslims rather than Catholics. In

1235, Gregory IX's bull *Cum hora undecima* licensed the Dominican missionary William of Montferrat to dispense the sacraments, to excommunicate and to give absolution in the lands of 'schismatics and heretics'.[63] That Gregory was associating eastern Christians with Muslims is implied in a letter of 1238 to the Franciscans and Dominicans in the east, speaking of the conversion of 'infidels and others'.[64] Innocent IV's reissue of *Cum hora undecima* in 1254 lists as peoples to whom friars should preach, in addition to Muslims and pagans, Greeks, Syrians, Armenians, Georgians, Copts, Maronites, Nestorians and others.[65] Innocent IV, however, was primarily concerned with the legalistic issue of irregularities arising from the acceptance of eastern Christians into the Roman Church, such as arose over ordination or marriage. On this question, he recommended that canon law be relaxed, on the grounds that one could not expect schismatics to be subject to any law other than natural law.[66] How far this tolerant legal attitude was reflected in realities in the Holy Land can be seen from some developments in the 1230s and 1240s.

*Cum hora undecima* seems to have had startling results. In 1237, the Dominican provincial in the Holy Land, Philip, announced the conversion of the Syrian Orthodox Patriarch of Antioch, Ignatius II, and the imminent conversion of the Nestorian *catholicos* of Baghdad.[67] This unexpected development arose during the patriarch's visit to Jerusalem, where the Dominicans were the main representatives of the Roman Church. Moreover, Philip reported that Arabic was being studied in Dominican houses in the Holy Land, and that some friars were already able to preach in the language.[68] At the same time, approaches were made to the Coptic patriarch in Alexandria, though nothing resulted from this.[69] Although these personal conversions did not effect the reconciliation of the separated eastern Churches to Rome, they did lead to remarkable concessions in practical matters of ministry. Thus, for example, Gregory IX allowed Templar prisoners in Aleppo to receive the sacraments of Eucharist and confession from Syrian Orthodox priests, if Franciscans were unable to visit them.[70] The conversion of their patriarch left the Syrian Orthodox clergy in an anomalous position, which Innocent IV sought to resolve in 1244, when he instructed the Dominicans of the Holy Land to ensure that Syrian priests who had followed their patriarch's example should be allowed to continue living among their own flocks, and to remain in communion with them.[71] Their situation was thus brought into line with that of Greek Orthodox clergy ministering under Latin bishops in the east.

In 1246, Innocent IV sought to clarify the position of the Greek Orthodox themselves. Unlike the Syrian Orthodox, the Arabic-speaking Greek Orthodox, who constituted the largest body of indigenous Christians under crusader rule, were not officially separated from Rome, and thus fell under the jurisdiction of Latin bishops. The Franciscan Lorenzo da Orte was appointed

papal legate in the east in 1246, with responsibility for Christians of all traditions. He was specifically requested, however, to protect the Greek Orthodox
in the patriarchates of Jerusalem and Antioch, and allusion was made in the
Pope's letter to injuries suffered by the Orthodox at the hands of Latins.[72]
Bernard Hamilton has pointed out that an accompanying letter from Innocent
IV to the Greek patriarch of Antioch marks the first time since 1100 that
the papacy had admitted the existence of such an office. Furthermore, he
argues, Innocent IV's design was the creation of a uniate Orthodox Church
at Antioch, in which Orthodox clergy would be ultimately responsible to the
Pope himself.[73]

Such highly practical solutions to theoretical questions make the attitudes
that prevail in descriptive sources, and which can to some extent be discerned
in the pilgrims we have considered, all the more puzzling. Although some
pilgrim guides commended the unquestionable piety of eastern Christians,[74]
the overall impression from written sources remains one of distrust of the
'otherness' revealed in their practices. Bernard Hamilton argues that attitudes
towards the separated Christians became friendlier than those towards the
Greek Orthodox, as it emerged that the Jacobites and Nestorians either no
longer subscribed to the original beliefs of their heterodox founders, or were
too ignorant of theology to know what they were supposed to believe.[75] To
some extent this is borne out by the Mendicants' observations. James of
Verona remarked in 1335 that the Nestorians no longer followed Nestorius's
teaching in many particulars, but seemed in their practices to be indistinguishable from the Greek Orthodox.[76] But, as Oliver of Paderborn had
remarked of the Jacobites, 'whether they really believe in their hearts what
they say they believe, God only knows'.[77] The Dominican Ricoldo of Monte
Crucis, who had spent far longer in the east, was less tolerant of Jacobite and
Nestorian errors: to him, devoutness in error was worthless.[78] Moreover,
even if western critics were prepared to forgive their dubious theology, many
of the customs practised by the Jacobites remained deeply problematic
for western observers. Jacques de Vitry was suspicious of their custom of
circumcision, which smacked of Judaism and Islam, and even of making the
sign of the cross with a single finger. He also disapproved of the Jacobite
custom of confessing secretly to God rather than to a priest. More horrifying
was the practice of branding the sign of the cross on to their children's
bodies, known as the baptism by fire.[79]

It is true that crusade theorists of the late thirteenth and early fourteenth
centuries sometimes express grief for the plight of the eastern Christians. The
Dominican William Adam, writing in 1316–18, drew attention to the 'weeping
voice of the oppressed Christian people': similar sentiments to those expressed
by his provincial, Ricoldo of Monte Crucis, in 1291.[80] But these occur in the
context of rhetorical pleas for new crusades, and are probably closer to the

formulas of crusade preachers than to the genuine sympathy of James of Verona for the Armenian refugees he saw at Famagusta in 1335.[81] More typical was probably the attitude of Marino Sanudo, who argued that the disaster of 1187 was partly due to the presence in the Crusader States of heretical Jacobites, Greek Orthodox and Nestorians.[82] Fidenzo of Padua, the Franciscan provincial of the Holy Land (r. 1266–91), argued that unity among Christians was essential if the Holy Land was to be recovered, but, paradoxically, that the presence of the Greek and Syrian Orthodox was harmful to such prospects.[83]

The deepest scorn was reserved for the *Suriani*, or Arabic-speaking Greek Orthodox. Although they were not in fact schismatics, as were the separated Christians, the fact that they were culturally indistinguishable from the Muslims and spoke Arabic made them targets for western opprobrium. Jacques de Vitry accused them of vacillating, of being halfway between the Roman and Greek churches, and thus of being duplicitous: 'they say one thing, but in their hearts think another'.[84] Moreover, they were servile, cunning, and poor fighters and lacked charity.[85] Fidenzo of Padua copied the passage about the indigenous Orthodox from the *Tractatus*, concluding that their lack of warlike experience rendered them of little use in the defence of the Holy Land.[86]

The author of the *Directorium ad passagium faciendum* (1332), who was probably William Adam himself, but certainly a Dominican friar with long experience of the east, adopted the same attitudes as Jacques de Vitry.[87] The *Suriani*, he declares, 'were expelled from their homeland, because they were unable either to fight for their freedom or to defend their country, and therefore they wander as refugees in different lands, without enjoying their own territory'. They were, moreover, untrustworthy: they broke their word easily, feigned grief and were inclined to plot against their rulers. They hid evil deeds under the guise of good.[88] Worse still were the *Gasmuli* – those who had a Greek father and Latin mother. These were unstable in faith, serial liars, treacherous, cruel, incontinent and gluttonous. 'With Greeks they pretend to be Greeks, with Latins, to be Latin'.[89] Similarly, the children of one Muslim and one Greek parent, the product of two bad blood lines, cared only for theft, booty and rape.[90] Racial slurs such as these demonstrate the longevity of the ethnographic tradition first noted in the last quarter of the twelfth century. This tradition informed all the sources discussed here, to the extent that categorization of peoples by religious practice became the standard means of understanding the diverse society of the Near East. Friars, whether as pastors of a resident population, ministers to captives, or pilgrims to the Holy Land, were heirs to this tradition.

Yet despite the negative attitudes to eastern Christians that prevail in many of the examples discussed here, the tone of the reportage by Mendicant travellers is largely one of polite curiosity rather than hostility. Some friars positively welcomed the diversity of peoples, and thus of religious practice, to be found in the Holy Land. The Dominican Burchard of Mount Sion rejoiced in the monks and nuns from Georgia, Armenia, Chaldea, Syria, Persia, India and Ethiopia who showed such devotion to the land of the Saviour's birth.[91] The Augustinian hermit James of Verona, a sympathetic and thoughtful observer of customs and peoples, found the experience of celebrating Mass in Bethlehem on 15 August 1335, amid a host of Christians from all parts of the known world, intensely moving. Five thousand were present, he estimated, of whom over a hundred were Franks. He recalls:

> O God, what joy it was to hear so much noise in praise of God and the glorious Virgin. The whole church was full of people, and there we stayed until almost Vespers, before going to Mount Sion. There too I celebrated Mass on the vigil of the glorious Virgin, in the place where she ascended [to Heaven]. Later in the evening everyone went to the Tomb of the Virgin in the valley of Josaphat, and there I sang a solemn Mass on the feast of the Assumption, along with people of all other nations. Never have I known such joy as in those three days, God be blessed![92]

### NOTES

1 G. Golubovich (ed.), *Biblioteca bio-bibliografica della Terra Santa e dell' Oriente francescano*, 5 vols (Florence: Quaracchi, 1906–27) iii, p. 48.

2 See Andrew Jotischky, *The Carmelites and Antiquity: Mendicants and their Pasts in the Middle Ages* (Oxford: Oxford University Press, 2002), pp. 36–7.

3 The major studies are L. Lemmens, *Geschichte der Franziskanermissionen* (Münster: Aschendorff, 1929); B. Altaner, *Die Dominikanermissionen des 13 Jahrhunderts* (Habelschwerdt: Frankesbuchhandlung, 1924); R.-J. Loenertz, 'Les missions dominicains en Orient au XIVe siècle', *AFP*, 2 (1932), 1–83; *idem*, 'La societé des Frères Pérégrinants: Étude sur l'Orient dominicain', *AFP*, 45 (1975), 107–45; C. H. Dawson (ed.), *The Mongol Mission: Narratives and Letters of the Franciscan Missionaries in Mongolia and China in the Thirteenth and Fourteenth Centuries* (London: Sheed and Ward, 1955); O. van der Vat, *Die Anfänge der Franziskanermissionen und ihre Weiterentwicklung im Näher Orient und in den mohammedanischen Ländern während des 13 Jahrhunderts* (Werl im Westfalen: Franziskus-Druckerei, 1934); M. W. Baldwin, 'Missions to the East in the thirteenth and fourteenth centuries', in N. P. Zacour and H. W. Hazard (eds), *The Impact of the Crusades on the Near East*: K. Setton (gen. ed.), *A History of the Crusades*, 6 vols, 2nd edn, v (Madison, WI: University of Wisconsin Press, 1985), pp. 452–518; J. Richard, 'Les missions chez les Mongoles aux XIIIe et XIVe siècles', in Simon Delacroix (gen. ed.), *Histoire universelle des missions catholiques*, 4 vols (1956–59), i: pp. 173–95 *Les missions des origines au XVIe siècle* (Paris: Grund, 1956); J. Richard, *La papauté et les missions*; d'Orient au Hoyen Age (XIII<sup>e</sup>–XV<sup>e</sup> siècles), Collection de l'École Française de Rome, 33 (Rome, 1977). E. R. Daniel, *The Franciscan Concept of Mission in the High Middle Ages* (Lexington: University Press of Kentucky, 1975); C. Delacroix-Besnier, *Les Dominicains et la chrétienté grecque aux XIVe et XVe siècles*, Collection de l'École Française de Rome, 237 (Rome: École Française de Rome, 1997); see also the papers in *Espansione del Francescanesimo tra Occidente e Oriente nel secolo XIII: Atti del VI Convegno Internazionale* (Assisi: Società Internazionale di Studi Francescani, 1979).

4 There is no evidence that Francis ever went to the Holy Land, though it is implied in much of the thirteenth- and fourteenth-century literature on his life. The secret conversion story occurs in the fourteenth-century legendary *Actus beati Francisci et sociorum eius*, XXVII; ed. P. Sabatier (Paris: Fischbacher, 1902), pp. 20–21. For extracts from relevant sources see Golubovich (ed.), *Biblioteca*, i, pp. 19–57.

5 Jacques de Vitry, *Historia Orientalis*, LXXIII–LXXIV; ed. F. Moschus as (*Jacobi de Vitriaco libri duo quorum prior Orientalis, sive Hierosolymitanae, alter, Occidentalis historiae*) (Douai: Balthazar Bellerus, 1597; repr. Farnborough: Gregg International Publishers, 1971), pp. 133–6; *idem, Lettres de Jacques de Vitry*, II, ed. R. B. C. Huygens (Leiden: Brill, 1960), p. 86.

6 Thomas of Celano, *Vita prima*, XX; in E. Alençon (ed.), *S. Francisci vita et miracula* (Rome: Deschée, Lefebvre, 1906), pp. 57–60. See also Ernoul, *La chronique d'Ernoul*, ed. L. de Mas Latrie (Paris: Societé de l'Histoire de France, 1871), pp. 431–5; Bernard the Treasurer, *Liber de acquisitione Terrae Sanctae*, in Golubovich (ed.), *Biblioteca*, i, pp. 13–14. *Regula non bullata*, I, 16; in H. Boehmer (ed.), *Analekten zur Geschichte des Franciskus von Assisi*, 6 vols (Tübingen and Leipzig: J. C. B. Mohr, 1904), i, pp. 14–15.

7 Gerard de Frachet, *Vitae fratrum ordinis Praedicatorum*, IV, 1; ed. B. Reichert, MOPH, 1 (Rome: Institutum Historicum Fratrum Praedicatorum Romae, 1897), pp. 150–1. See also R.-J. Loenertz, 'Frère Jacques de Milan, missionaire en Orient au XIIIe siècle', *AFP*, 8 (1938), 274–84.

8 *Litterae encyclicae magistrum generalium ordinis Praedicatorum 1233–1376*, ed. B. M. Reichert, MOPH, 5 (Rome: Institutum Historicum Fratrum Praedicatorum Romae, 1900), p. 42.

9 Gaston Raynaud (ed.), *Les gestes des Chiprois*, RHC Docs Arms, 2 vols (Paris: Société de l'Orient Latin, 1869–1906), ii, p. 765.

10 *Chronicon XXIV generalium*, 416; in Golubovich (ed.), *Biblioteca*, ii, pp. 61–2, 108–9; *Chronicon de Lanercost*, ed. J. Stevenson (Edinburgh: Maitland Club, 1839), p. 129.

11 A. Atiya, *Egypt and Aragon: Embassies and Diplomatic Correspondence between 1300 and 1330 AD* (Leipzig: F. A. Brockhaus, 1938); repr. in *Abhandlungen für die Kunde des Morgenlands*, 23 (Kraus reprint, 1966), pp. 20–1 (original pagination). Golubovich (*Biblioteca*, iii, p. 76 n.1) thought the prisoners were Templars or Hospitallers, but members of the military Orders were usually executed.

12 Golubovich (ed.), *Biblioteca*, i, pp. 180–1, ii, pp. 297–8, 338.

13 Angelo de Spoleto, *De fratribus Minoribus visitantibus captivos in Babilonia*, in Golubovich (ed.), *Biblioteca*, iii, pp. 68–72.

14 *Ibid.*, p. 70.

15 Atiya, *Egypt and Aragon*, pp. 52–3.

16 Symon Semeonis, *Itinerarium Symonis Semeonis ab Hybernia ad Terram Sanctam*, LXXVIII; ed. M. Esposito, Scriptores Latini Hiberniae, 4 (Dublin: Dublin Institute for Advanced Studies, 1960), p. 96. An English Franciscan in 1345 successfully obtained the same passport (Golubovich (ed.), *Biblioteca*, iv, p. 450), while Anthony de Reboldis had a similar passport in 1331, which he refers to simply as a letter (*Itinerarium*, in Golubovich (ed.), *Biblioteca*, iii, p. 337). The Dominican Humbert de Dijon, who was given permission to visit the Holy Land in 1330 by the sultan at the end of his diplomatic mission to Egypt, sailed first to Acre, where he awaited a safe-conduct, then travelled overland down the coast and across Sinai to Cairo (T. Kaeppeli and P. Benoit, 'Un pèlerinage dominicain inédit du XIVe siècle: Le *Liber de locis et conditionibus Terrae Sanctae et sepulcro* d'Humbert de Dijon OP (1332)', *Revue Biblique*, 62 (1955), 513–40, at 518). William Adam reports the cost of a regular permit to visit the holy places, which could be purchased on arrival in the Holy Land, as 35 *tournois grossi* in 1317–18: *De*

*modo Sarracenos extirpandi*, II; ed. C. Kohler, RHC Docs Arms, 2, (Paris: Imprimerie Nationale, 1906) p. 528.

17 Symon, *Itinerarium Symonis Semeonis*, XXVI–XXVII; ed. Esposito, pp. 46–8.

18 Niccolo da Poggibonsi, *Libro d'Oltramare*, XXXIII; ed. B. Bagatti (Jerusalem: Tipografia dei Francescani, 1945), p. 26.

19 *Ibid.*, LXXIV, LXXXII; ed. Bagatti, pp. 47, 50–1. Although custody of the tomb itself was granted to the Franciscans in 1333/34, the Muslim government retained rights of entry to the church itself.

20 *Ibid.*, CXCI, CXXXVIII, CXL, CXLV, CLII; ed. Bagatti, pp. 70, 80, 81, 83, 88–9. It is difficult to estimate what these charges amounted to. Even in Europe silver fluctuated considerably in its rate of exchange to gold, and there was no consistent or fixed rate of exchange in a 'frontier territory' such as the Near East. In the thirteenth century, the florin (a Florentine gold coin) was worth about 240 denarii (pennies with a small silver content); a dirhem (a local coin minted in the Holy Land, also called 'dragma') was roughly equivalent to a silver grosso in the West, and worth about twelve denarii. There seems to be no comparable evidence for the mid-fourteenth century.

21 *Itinerarium cuiusdam Anglici*, in Golubovich (ed.), *Biblioteca*, iv, pp. 426–60, p. 458.

22 Niccolo, *Libro d'Oltramare*, CLII; ed. Bagatti, pp. 88–9.

23 Abbot Daniel, *The Life and Journey of Daniel Abbot of the Russian Land*, trans W. F. Ryan, in J. Wilkinson, with J. Hill and W. F. Ryan (eds), *Jerusalem Pilgrimage 1099–1185*, Hakluyt Society, 2nd series, 167 (London: Hakluyt Society, 1988), p. 154. The Templars were founded in 1119 to provide armed escorts for pilgrims travelling from Jerusalem to Jericho; see M. Barber, *The New Knighthood: A History of the Order of the Temple* (Cambridge: Cambridge University Press, 1994), pp. 3–6.

24 Niccolo, *Libro d'Oltramare*, CXIX; ed. Bagatti, p. 70.

25 Anthony de Reboldis, *Itinerarium*, p. 337.

26 Niccolo, *Libro d'Oltramare*, CCII–CCIII; ed. Bagatti, pp. 119–21.

27 Angelo, *De fratribus Minoribus visitantibus*, p. 69.

28 Niccolo, CLXIII, *Libro d'Oltramare*, CXLVIII; ed. Bagatti, pp. 97–8, 84.

29 James of Verona, *Liber peregrinationis Fratris Jacobi da Verona*, ed. R. Röhricht in *Revue de l'Orient Latin*, 3 (1895), 155–303, at 182; Niccolo, *Libro d'Oltramare*, CL; ed. Bagatti, pp. 86–7.

30 Symon, *Itinerarium Symonis Semeonis*, LXXIX; ed. Esposito, pp. 96–8.

31 Niccolo, *Libro d'Oltramare*, CLXXVII; ed. Bagatti, p. 105.

32 *Ibid.*, CLXIV, CCIV; ed. Bagatti, pp. 99, 121.

33 Symon, *Itinerarium Symonis Semeonis*, XXXIV; ed. Esposito, 58.

34 *Ibid.*, XVII; ed. Esposito, p. 38.

35 *Ibid.*, XXI; ed. Esposito, p. 42.

36 *Ibid.*, XXXIV–XXXV; ed. Esposito, p. 58. The dress worn by ordinary Muslims appeared to Symon very similar to the Franciscan habit, save for the absence of a cowl.

37 Niccolo, *Libro d'Oltramare*, CIX, CXCI; ed. Bagatti, pp. 65, 113.

38 James of Verona, *Liber peregrinationis*, 217.

39 Angelo, *De fratribus Minoribus visitantibus*, pp. 69–70. Probably most of them were enslaved as a result of piracy.

40 Niccolo da Poggibonsi, however, describes a cemetery of the 'Christians of the girdle' beneath the Franciscan church on Mount Sion: *Libro d'Oltramare*, XLIV; ed. Bagatti, p. 73.

41 Symon, *Itinerarium Symonis Semeonis*, XXXII; ed. Esposito, 54–6.

42 *Ibid.*, XXXII; ed. Esposito, 56.

43 Niccolo, *Libro d'Oltramare*, CCLVI; ed. Bagatti, 148.

44 *Ibid.*, CIV, CXVIII, CXXII, CXLVI, CXLVIII, CLI; ed. Bagatti, pp. 62, 69, 71, 81, 85, 87–8. Mount Quarantana, a fifth-century foundation, had been occupied by Frankish monks in the twelfth century. The monastery by the Dead Sea must have been St Chariton.

45 *Ibid.*, CCLII; ed. Bagatti, p. 146. Mendicants had debated the question of the Eucharist with Orthodox clergy in 1232 (G. Golubovich, 'Disputatio Latinorum et Graecorum seu relatio Apocrisariorum Gregorii IX de gestis Nicaea in Bithynia et Nymphaeae in Lydia', *Archivum Franciscanum Historicum*, 12 (1919), 418–70), and in the negotiations with Michael VIII in 1272 (Martiniano Roncaglia, *I Francesci in Oriente durante la crociate (sec XIII): Storia della provincia di Terra Santa* (Cairo: Centro di Studi Orientali, 1954), pp. 156–7).

46 Niccolo, *Libro d'Oltramare*, CCLII; ed. Bagatti, 146.

47 Jacques de Vitry, *Historia Orientalis*, LXXV; ed. Moschus, p. 137.

48 James of Verona, *Liber peregrinationis*, pp. 178, 219.

49 *Ibid.*, p. 178. Niccolo da Poggibonsi, however, reported that the Orthodox did elevate the host: *Libro d'Oltramare*, CCLII; ed. Bagatti, p. 146.

50 James of Verona, *Liber peregrinationis*, p. 178.

51 *Ibid.*, p. 217.

52 *Ibid.*, pp. 190–1.

53 *Ibid.*, pp. 210–11, 214–15, 228–34. James also mentions an Armenian monastery at Beth Zechariah and the Georgian monastery of Holy Cross, which both lie west of Jerusalem (*ibid.*, p. 222).

54 *Ibid.*, pp. 197–8. It is noteworthy that on two occasions, in his account of the Armenian monastery of St James in Jerusalem, and in his list of eastern Christians at Bethlehem, he describes the Armenians as 'veri christiani', and does not list them separately in the schedule of services at the Tomb of the Virgin.

55 James of Verona found that rumours of the crusade made it politic for him to leave Egypt hurriedly in 1335; see *Liber peregrinationis*, p. 244. On crusading plans, see N. Housley, *The Avignon Papacy and the Crusades* (Oxford: Clarendon Press, 1986), pp. 26–8, 172–3.

56 See Golubovich (ed.), *Biblioteca*, iv, pp. 52–6 for the bulls of Clement VI confirming their rights; L. Lemmens, *Die Franziskaner im Heiligen Lande* (Münster: [s.n.], 1919); M. Piccirillo, *La custodia di Terra Santa e l'Europa: I rapporti politici e l'attivita culturale dei Francescani in Medio Oriente* (Rome: IL Veltro Editrice, 1983), pp. 95–116; H. Fürst, *Die Custodie des Heiligen Landes: Die Mission der Franziskaner im Heiligen Land und im Vorderen Orient* (Munich: Kommissariat für das Heilige Land, 1981). S. de Sandoli, *The Peaceful Liberation of the Holy Places in the Fourteenth Century*, Studia Orientalia Christiana Monographiae, 3 (Cairo: Franciscan Center for Oriental Studies, 1990), is unsubstantiated in places.

57 B. Z. Kedar, 'The *Tractatus de locis et statu sancte terre Ierosolimitane*', in J. France and W. G. Zajac (eds), *The Crusades and their Sources: Essays Presented to Bernard Hamilton* (Aldershot: Ashgate, 1998), pp. 111–33, with edition of the treatise at pp. 123–31.

58 Jacques de Vitry, *Historia Orientalis*, LXXIII–LXXXII; ed. Moschus, pp. 133–62. Kedar, 'The *Tractatus*', pp. 111–22, argues that the anonymous accounts in which the lists are found are variants of the original, which he dates to 1168/87.

59 Burchard of Mount Sion, *Descriptio Terrae Sanctae*, XII; in J. C. M. Laurent (ed.), *Peregrinatores medii aevi quatuor* (Leipzig: J. C. Hinrichs, 1864, 3rd edn 1873), pp. 89–94; Ricoldo da Monte Crucis, *Liber peregrinacionis*, XVII–XXI, in Laurent (ed.), *Peregrinatores*, pp. 124–31.

60 A.-D. von den Brincken, *Die 'Nationes Christianorum Orientalium' im Verständnis der lateinischen Historiographie*, Kölner Historische Abhandlungen, 22 (Cologne: Böhlau, 1973), pp. 76–152, 164–327.

61 *Acta Honorii III et Gregorii IX (1216–41)*, ed. A. L. Tautu, CICO, 3 (Vatican: Typis Polyglottis Vaticanis, 1950), pp. 108, 139; E. Friedberg (ed.), *Corpus iuris canonici*, 2 vols (Leipzig: Tauchnitz, 1879–81; repr. Union, NJ: Lawbook Exchange, 2000), Decretal. Greg. IX, V, 6–8, II, cols 771–90.

62 J. Muldoon, *Popes, Lawyers and Infidels: The Church and the Non-Christian World 1250–1550* (Liverpool: Liverpool University Press, 1979), pp. 6–7.

63 *Acta Innocentii papae IV (1243–54)*, ed. T. Haluscynskyj and M. Wojnar, CICO, 4 (1) (Rome: Pontifica Commissio ad Redigendum Codicem Iuris Canonici Orientalis, 1966), pp. 286–7 (the reissue by Innocent IV).

64 *Registres de Grégoire IX*, ed. L. Auvray, BEFAR, series 2:9, 4 vols (Rome: E. de Bocard, vice A. Fontemoing, 1896–1955), ii, no. 4400.

65 *Acta Innocentii Papae IV*, CICO, 4 (2), p. 38.

66 Muldoon, *Popes, Lawyers and Infidels*, pp. 37–8.

67 Matthew Paris, *Chronica majora*, ed. H. R. Luard, Rolls Series, 7 vols (London: Longman & Co., 1872–83), iii, pp. 396–9; Alberic of Trois Fontaines, *Chronica*, ed. F. Schaffer-Boichorst, MGHSS, 35 (Munich, 1874), pp. 941–2.

68 Matthew Paris, *Chronica majora*, iii, p. 398.

69 *Ibid.*

70 *Registres de Grégoire IX*, ii, no. 4404.

71 *Registres d'Innocent IV*, ed. E. Berger, BEFAR, series 2:1, 4 vols (Paris: Thorin, 1884–1921), i, no. 573; Bernard Hamilton, *The Latin Church in the Crusader States: The Secular Church* (London: Variorum, 1980), pp. 351–2.

72 *Bullarium Franciscanum*, ed. J. H. Sbaralea, 5 vols (Rome: Typis Sacrae Congregationis de Propaganda Fide, 1898), i, pp. 421–2.

73 Hamilton, *Latin Church*, pp. 322–3.

74 Burchard, *Descriptio*, XIII; in Laurent (ed.), *Peregrinatores*, pp. 91–2. Here he praises the devoutness of the Armenian *catholicos*.

75 Hamilton, *Latin Church*, p. 358.

76 James of Verona, *Liber peregrinationis*, p. 217.

77 Oliver of Paderborn, *Historia Damiatana*, LXVI; in *Die Schriften des Kölner Domscholmasters, Späteren Bischofs von Paderborn und Kardinal-Bischofs von S. Sabina Oliveus*, ed. O. Hoogeweg, Bibliothek des Litterarischen Vereins Stuttgart, 202 (Tübingen: Litterarischer Verein Stuttgart, 1894), p. 266.

78 Ricoldo of Monte Crucis, *Liber peregrinacionis*, XVII, XX; in Laurent (ed.), *Peregrinatores*, pp. 124–6, 127–31.

79 Jacques de Vitry, *Historia Orientalis*, LXXVI; ed. Moschus, pp. 146–7; *idem, Lettres*, II, p. 83. The chapter on the Jacobites was copied by Matthew Paris into his *Chronica majora*, iii, pp. 400–1.

80 William Adam, *De modo*, pp. 522, 543–4; Ricoldo of Monte Crucis, 'Epistolae V commentatoriae de perditione Acconis 1291', ed. R. Röhricht, *Archives d'Orient Latin*, 2 (1884), 264–96.

81 James of Verona, *Liber peregrinationis*, p. 177.

82 Marino Sanudo Torsello, *Marino Sanudo dictus Torsellus: Liber secretorum fidelium crucis*, in J. Bongars (ed.), *Gesta Dei per Francos*, 2 vols (Hanover: heredes Johannis Aubrii, 1611), pp. 231–2.

83 Fidenzo of Padua, *Liber recuperationis Terrae Sanctae*, VII, XLII; in Golubovich (ed.), *Bibliotheca*, i, pp. 13, 37.

84  Jacques de Vitry, *Historia Orientalis*, LXXV; ed. Moschus, p. 137; *idem, Lettres,* II, p. 84; cf. Burchard, *Descriptio*, XIII; in Laurent (ed.), *Peregrinatores*, p. 89.

85  Jacques de Vitry, *Historia Orientalis*, LXXV; ed. Maschus, pp. 137–8.

86  Fidenzo, *Liber recuperationis Terrae Sanctae*, VII; in Golubovich (ed.), *Biblioteca*, i, p. 13.

87  See pseudo-Brocardus, *Directorium ad passagium faciendum*, ed. C. Kohler, RHC Docs Arms, 2 (Paris: Académie des Inscriptions et Belles Lettres, 1967), pp. 367–517, and pp. cliv–clx for C. Kohler's arguments about authorship. Kohler's identification with Adam is accepted by Brincken, *Die 'Nationes Christianorum Orientalium'*, p. 64, but Loenertz, 'La societé', prefers the Dominican missionary Raymond Etienne, and is followed by Delacroix-Besnier, *Les Dominicains*, p. 18.

88  Pseudo-Brocardus, *Directorium*, pp. 491–2.

89  *Ibid.*, p. 490.

89  *Ibid.*

90  *Ibid.*, p. 493.

91  Burchard, *Descriptio*, 'Prologus'; in Laurent (ed.), *Peregrinatores*, p. 20.

92  James of Verona, *Liber peregrinationis*, p. 219.

# 6

## The intelligent pilgrim: maps and medieval pilgrimage to the Holy Land

❮❯

### Catherine Delano-Smith

IN 1480, the monk Felix Fabri returned to Ulm from his Jerusalem
pilgrimage dissatisfied. Far from being able to speak with authority on the
holy places, he felt as though he had hardly seen them, so hurried and above
all so ill-prepared had the visit been. He resolved to make a second journey,
this time fully prepared. He read everything he could find on Jerusalem,
'stories of the pilgrimages of the Crusaders, the tracts written by pilgrims,
and descriptions of the Holy Land'.[1] He studied 'nearly all the Canonical and
Catholic Scriptures, reading books, texts, glosses', working harder, he tells us
'in running from book to book, in copying, correcting, collating what I had
written, than I did in journeying from place to place on my pilgrimage'.[2] And
he evidently sought out maps, managing to see those currently being prepared in his home town for the first printing north of the Alps of Ptolemy's
Geography.[3] He may also have seen other maps of the world, for he realised
that only these showed 'regions of the East so far distant from us that . . . the
ancients, such as Aristotle, Ptolemy, and Augustine could not admit' that
they existed.[4]

Felix Fabri was sharp-witted, intelligent and scholarly. He also had time
for research, access to libraries, and a web of contacts to tell him about or
supply him with material. Not many amongst the many thousands who,
between 1050 and 1500, journeyed in the eastern Mediterranean for one
reason or another would have been as privileged or as assiduous as Fabri.
Indeed, very few would have even seen a map, partly because maps were the
last thing needed in the actual process of travelling, and partly because maps
were comparatively rare – although much less so than is generally supposed
– and restricted to specific contexts or user groups. Amongst the different
types of maps available, several would have been of particular interest to a
well-read Christian about to set out for the Holy Land. In this chapter, we
invoke an imaginary, timeless, placeless, learned and pious pilgrim as our

hero to help us sample a selection of the types of maps that would have been found in Europe at some time between 1050 and 1500.

Our pilgrim's starting point, it is safe to assume, would have been the Bible, with which he would have been intimately familiar. He would probably also have read at least some of the theological treatises and biblical commentaries piled on the shelves in monastic and ecclesiastical libraries, many of which contain maps and diagrams.[5] Looking through these for descriptions of the territory he was soon to be treading and the places he would be visiting, our pilgrim's attention would have been focused on two Old Testament subjects, the division of Canaan into twelve tribal territories (Joshua 15) and the temple in Jerusalem with its Tabernacle (Exodus 12, I Kings 1), both of which had been illustrated with maps since late antiquity.[6] In the preface to his translation of Eusebius's Onomasticon (c. 303), Jerome notes that Eusebius had supplied a 'chorography of the land of Judea and the separate tribal lots' and a 'brief pictorial exposition of the Temple in Jerusalem', neither of which has survived.[7]

Medieval exegetical maps are unlikely to look very different from Eusebius's since they observed the same graphic principles (visual simplicity and topological structure) and illustrated the same textual passages. Thus, for example, the map glossed into an early thirteenth century students' Bible now in Oxford, showing a rectangular Canaan ruled into twelve long strips, may be taken as an echo of what Eusebius would have sketched out at the beginning of the fourth century to show the historical division of the land of Canaan.[8] A second map of similar appearance in the volume, illustrating an imaginary land (Ezekiel's vision of Canaan restored) and deriving from a diagram in Richard of St Victor's commentary on the Book of the Prophet Ezekiel (for Chapters 47–8), would have been probably only of passing interest to our pilgrim, although it was this rather than the historical version of the division of Canaan that Nicholas of Lyra chose to illustrate in his Postillae (1321–32).[9] The third map in the Oxford Bible, a plan of Solomon's temple in Jerusalem, reflects the continuing preoccupation of medieval theologians with the arrangement of the Tabernacle and its furnishing in the historical edifice and the popularity of, in particular, Bede's commentaries (De tabernaculo, 721–2; De templo, 729–31).[10] Bede tells us that he had studied Cassiodorus's Bible, with its magnificent double-folio plan of temple and Tabernacle, when it was in his monastery at Jarrow early in the eighth century, but he evidently preferred not to provide his treatises with diagrams and it was left to later copyists and writers to add the relevant visual aid (Figure 3).[11] Medieval interest

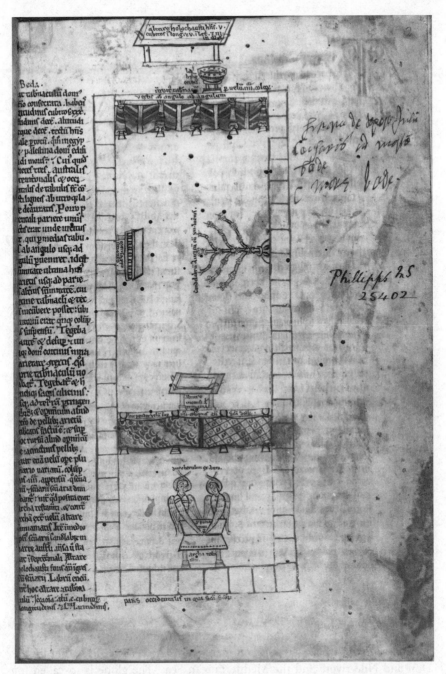

3 An exegetical plan of the Tabernacle, showing the layout in the ancient temple in Jerusalem and the position of the furnishings described in Exodus, Chapter 40, drawn at Kirkham Abbey, Lincolnshire, in the thirteenth century. The plan illustrates an extract from Bede's treatise on the Tabernacle.

in the Temple was not solely historical. The twelfth century saw a rise in expositions in which the structure was explained as an allegory of Christ and the Church.[12]

A rather different theme, that of apocalypse, linked maps with the Book of the Revelation of John the Divine. A sense of apocalypse was never far from the medieval mind, especially as millennial and other holy years approached, and was reflected in contemporary maps as well as writing. In the eighth century, for example, Beatus of Liébana included two plans in his commentary on the Apocalypse, not only the usual plan of the Heavenly Jerusalem (for Revelation 21), but also a map of the world.[13] The latter map, depicting time as well as space, was an important visual accompaniment to Beatus's text. It portrays the Earthly Paradise in the extreme east (signifying the beginning of time and of world history) and Jerusalem of Judea (signifying also the Heavenly Jerusalem and the end of time), and illustrates the establishment on earth of the Christian Church through the work of the apostles.[14]

## MAPS OF THE WORLD

Having re-read his Bible for the relevant geographical descriptions, the next step for our studious pilgrim would have been to locate Palestine in his mental map of the world. The fragmented politics of medieval Europe did not encourage scientific world-scale surveys similar to the one organised by Julius Caesar in the last century BCE, and until Ptolemy's Geography became available (in Constantinople after 1295, in the Latin West after 1409) our pilgrim might have had difficulty in getting hold of such a map. Few if any Roman world maps would have been extant as late as 1050, although there were almost certainly copies and derivatives. Classical geographical knowledge was more securely preserved in text books, and the diagrams in many of these afforded a second line of transmission. The two traditions, that of mapping the (known) world and the textbook diagram of world geography, eventually came together in a third type of world map, the exclusively medieval, and overwhelmingly belief-driven, *mappamundi*.

One of the most widely read descriptions of the world in the Middle Ages is found in the *Etymologiae*, Isidore of Seville's encyclopaedia of Roman knowledge, compiled between 622 and 633. In book 14, Chapter 2, Isidore repeats the standard classical account of the earth surrounded by an Outer Ocean and containing three inhabited continents separated from each other by the Don and Nile rivers and the Mediterranean Sea: 'The globe is so-called for its roundness . . . It is divided into three parts, which are called Asia, Europa, Africa'. In most manuscripts, a simple diagram (usually not much more than three lines within a circle) summarises the textual description. Given that the east (the direction of the rising sun) was placed at the top, the lines of the two rivers and the Mediterranean Sea inevitably form a T. Already before the eleventh century, the diagram had been invested with Christian symbolism, the T standing for the Cross, and individual scribes had long been inserting a biblical feature or two as they penned the diagrams; the names of Noah's sons (Sem, Cham and Japhet) on the three continents, Mount Sinai, the Red Sea crossing and, of course, Jerusalem, for instance.[15] Diagrams in Isidore's *De natura rerum* illustrate other aspects of world geography, such as the climatic zones and the path of the zodiac.[16]

From such textbook diagrams, our pilgrim could have situated Palestine in global terms, but to see Palestine in the context of the geography of the Eastern Mediterranean basin, a map showing the world on a larger scale and with more detail was needed. Did such a map exist, and would it have been derived from something produced by the Romans? Not all modern scholars are willing to admit that a relatively detailed map of the inhabited world was ever produced in Roman times, let alone that copies or derivatives could have reached the Middle Ages. They cite Pliny's criticism of Agrippa's map – 'who would believe that Agrippa, who was very careful and took great pains over his work, should, when he was going to set up the map to be looked at by the citizens of Rome, have made this mistake . . . ?' – and suggest that what was displayed in the colonnade of the Portus Vipsania in the last years BCE was not a map but a written description.[17] The issue, however, is not about maps for 'practical' or administrative purposes (still less about maps to scale) but about topographical representation for didactic reasons. It is difficult seriously to doubt that topographical maps were drawn in Roman times. Apart from Ptolemy's regional maps from the mid-second century CE, and putting aside the suspicion aroused by some medieval maps that some geographical details are simply too good to have come from medieval local knowledge, the discovery in 1997 of a topographical map drawn early in the first century BCE must put the question beyond dispute.[18]

In the second century CE Claudius Ptolemy compiled, amongst other works, two texts of paramount importance (in the longer term), the Almagest and the Geography. The Almagest deals with the astronomical determination of the co-ordinates needed for the construction of a mathematically accurate maps, and the Geography provides the theoretical principles for the construction of graticules to create an illusion of a flattened globe on a map.[19] It also lists some eight thousand co-ordinates for the plotting of topographical features on maps. Whether any maps were actually drawn in Ptolemy's day, by Ptolemy himself or by somebody else, has not been determined, although it does seem that Ptolemy's map of the world had a separate history from that of the regional maps.[20] Maps and text alike apparently remained in the Islamic world until the end of the thirteenth century and in the Byzantine Empire until the early fifteenth century.

This is not to say, however, that no mathematically constructed world maps could have been compiled in the West before 1400. In close-knit scholarly communities, especially perhaps in southern Europe, an awareness of Ptolemy's astronomical work may never have been completely lost, although it was not until the eleventh and twelfth centuries that circumstances encouraged the necessary revival of learning and renewal of intellectual contacts with the Islamic world. 'Lost' texts from antiquity were now reaching medieval scholars in western Europe, together with Arab writings on medicine, mathematics, astronomy and, more specifically, tables of latitude and longitude.[21] In the new climate, at least one map of the world appears to have been constructed from such co-ordinates: in England, about 1262, by Roger Bacon, a scholar said to have been unparalleled in his knowledge of Arabic texts by anyone outside Spain. Bacon's map has not survived, but from what he wrote it would seem that it had a graticule, was orientated to the north, and included, in his words, 'cities . . . shown by little red circles'.[22] Bacon's example does not seem to have been followed, possibly because the challenging mathematics involved deterred many from even trying. The usefulness of maps was widely recognised. Sacrobosco and Robert Grosseteste both wrote treatises entitled *De sphera* (probably in the 1220s or 1230s), Jacques de Vitry, Bishop of Acre, wrote in 1218 of the usefulness of a *mappamundi*, and in the early fourteenth century Paolino Veneto commented that 'without [maps] I would say it would not so much be difficult as impossible to imagine or conceive in the mind the dispersal of the sons of Noah and the four great kingdoms'.[23] Notwithstanding, no other maps of the world based on a graticule are known in Europe until the reappearance of Ptolemy's Geography. Instead, there were circular world maps like the one Petrus Vesconte had drawn for Marino Sanudo's *Liber secretorum* by or around 1321.[24]

The vacuum left by scientific classical geography after the fall of the empire was in the Middle Ages taken over by overtly Christian descriptions of world geography. One of the most revealing maps of the period, the Anglo-Saxon (or Cotton Tiberius) map of about 1050, shows how the two strands of classical geography and early medieval theology came together in a precursor of the later *mappaemundi* proper (see Frontispiece).[25] Underpinning the east-orientated rectangular-shaped map, however distantly, is an unknown Roman map of the world from which the compiler of the Anglo-Saxon map took the basic structure of his map, its continental outlines (often remarkably detailed and realistic; the British Isles are especially well represented, for example), its rivers, mountains, islands, seas, towns and cities, and its political boundaries, which are those of Roman provinces. The Anglo-Saxon map is found in an codex containing Priscian's sixth-century translation of Dionysius's verse description of the world.[26] Superimposed on the basic world geography is a quantity of biblical and other material. Places in which a pagan Roman like Dionysius would have had no interest (e.g. Bethlehem) and Old Testament features (such as the mountains of Pisgah and Sinai, and the territories of the Twelve Tribes of Israel) are marked. There are other Old Testament references; to the Red Sea crossing, Gog and Magog, Noah's Ark, Babylon, the Tower of Babel and the lands of the Philistines, Moabites and Amonites, for example. The four empires of human history (Persia, *Media*, Macedonia and Rome) are mentioned, and mythico-historical features such as the burning mountain in Asia and other marvels derived from Pliny's Natural History are portrayed. The Anglo-Saxon map is a hybrid *par excellence*, incorporating pagan as well as Christian source material and blending classical scientific geography with an increasingly pervasive and dominating pan-European Christianity.

## MAPPAEMUNDI

*Mappaemundi* are more than merely schematic maps of the world with a vast quantity of adventitious material. They stand on their own as integral and profound cartographical conceptions in an age when symbolism was 'very nearly the breath of life', as Johan Huizinga has put it.[27] One of the difficulties encountered by the modern scholar is terminological ambiguity, both in Latin and English, and it is perhaps worth trying to make a distinction between a *mappa mundi* and a *mappamundi* to eliminate confusion in our own writing. A *mappa mundi* translated literally means a 'map of the world', that is, a geographical world map, but it can also indicate a cosmological map, for which I reserve the term *mappamundi*. The distinction was clear enough in 1449, to Jean Germain when he distinguished 'mappemondes temporelles' [i.e., 'of the present'] with their 'provinces, pays, aucunes citez, villes, chasteaulx, meres, rivieres, ysles' and so on, and the other 'mappemondes', 'appelée spirituelle' [*sic*].[28] *Mappaemundi* are maps entirely subordinated to religious belief and theological doctrine, and an indication of the Earthly Paradise (not itself shown on the Anglo-Saxon map, but alluded to in the name of the Paradisical river Pison) could almost be used as a convenient diagnostic.[29] On a *mappamundi*, eschatological time – the Christian's history of humankind from the creation of the world and the Garden of Eden (the Earthly Paradise) to the Heavenly Jerusalem, and spiritual itinerary from sin through repentance to redemption – is as important as space, and as relevant as time (and places) present and time (and places) past (Figure 4).[30] Geographical realism was neither irrelevant nor ignored, but the encyclopaedic tendencies of medieval theology meant that so much information had to be packed into a *mappamundi* that structural flexibility was essential. Not surprisingly, *mappaemundi* tend to be large. Some were painted directly on to a wall or on several parchments that were then fixed together for hanging

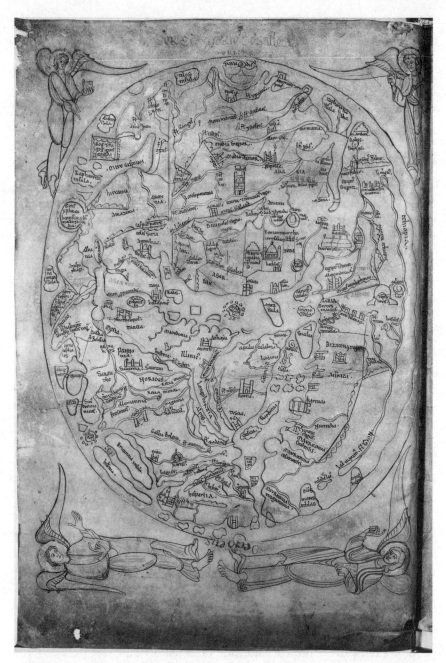

4 The Sawley Abbey *mappamundi*. Compiled at Durham as a frontispiece in a copy of Henry of Autun's *Imago mundi* and presented to the Yorkshire monastery about 1200. The Earthly Paradise is depicted in the east, at the top of the map, and the ancient Greek religious sanctuary of Delos is at the centre. 29.5 × 20.5 cm.

in a monastery or palace.[31] Felix Fabri reported how he saw 'a very fine [painted] map of the world' – in fact, Fra Mauro's recently completed map – in a monastic church on one of the islands in the Venetian lagoon.[32] Smaller versions may sometimes represent drafts or copies. A few, like the tiny 'Psalter Map' of about 1265 (9 cm), were reduced for use privately by a privileged individual, possibly a pious high-born lady who conducted her meditations in her own chamber.[33]

The heyday of the great *mappaemundi* was relatively short, lasting two and a half centuries or so, from about 1100 to about 1350. It was preceded by a period in which, as we have seen, T-O diagrams and geographical maps of the world were gradually 'Christianised', and it was followed by a period of quantitative and qualitative change. Few new *mappaemundi* were made after the middle of the fourteenth century, and those that were either are unimpressive (like the Aslake map of *c.* 1350) or are copies of existing maps (like those in Ranulf Higden's immensely popular *Polychronicon* of 1342).[34] At their peak, though, the *mappaemundi* of western Europe were arguably amongst the most remarkable and profoundly learned maps ever produced.

Explanations of the rise of *mappaemundi* must lie in the cultural and theological context, as yet little studied in connection with the maps. An important factor was the change in attitude towards pilgrimage to the Holy Land in the ninth and tenth centuries, which was associated with the increased emphasis on personal salvation and on the personal in Christian devotion.[35] A second factor was the crusades, first called in 1095. Events in Syria and the Levant heightened awareness at home of the places involved in the origins of Christianity, a grounding which was reflected in liturgical re-enactments of geographical reality (as in the ritual of the Stations of the Cross) and in the need to accommodate the flood of new relics being brought back by pilgrims.[36] Millennialism was another factor. The years of 1000 and 1033 created a new collective consciousness of pilgrimage as the numbers of those making the journey to the Holy Land vastly increased and as the pilgrims were organised for the journey into large groups under designated leaders.[37] As apocalypse approached, minds became fixed on the earthly Jerusalem, symbol of the heavenly city which was shortly to replace it as human time came to an end, and on the site of Christ's crucifixion, increasingly conflated with the idea of imminent universal resurrection.[38] For those unable to travel, the journey to Jerusalem had to be made 'in the heart, not with the feet', aided – for those with access to a *mappamundi* – by contemplation of the site of Jerusalem on the map.[39]

As he stood in front of a *mappamundi*, our pilgrim's eye would have been drawn towards the central part of the map, seeking Jerusalem.[40] Then he would have located himself, trying not to be dismayed by the distance between him and his destination.[41] As he let his eye return to the Holy Land, our pilgrim's spirits should have risen to find so many familiar biblical names and features. Palestine occupies too small a space on a *mappamundi*, though, to allow much local detail to be shown, and the compiler of the map had to select. Given the eschatological theme of the genre, Old Testament events associated with the wider region tend to outnumber those from the New Testament within Palestine.[42] On the Hereford map, for example, we can see the Red Sea crossing, Joseph's Granaries, Mount Horeb, Hebron, Jericho (to which Moses led the Israelites), Dan and Bersheeba, and – toponym for the future – the Valley of Jehosophat, amongst others, are depicted, together with Bethlehem (with a vignette of the manger), Nazareth, Cana (site of Christ's first miracle), and the mounts of Olives and Calvary.[43] Dominating all is Jerusalem, depicted symbolically in plan as a circular walled city, surmounted by the Crucifixion, by now a symbol less of Christ glorified than of his sufferings on earth.[44]

By the second half of the fifteenth century it had become difficult to find intellectual justification for many of the characteristic features of a *mappamundi*. The circular frame was constraining as distant parts of the Old World were becoming better known, and on Andrea Bianco's map of 1436 eastern Asia breaches the circle frame. Jerusalem's 'centrality' was neatly disposed of by Fra Mauro, who explained on his map of 1459 that he had placed the holy city further west so that it would be in the middle of the inhabited world (allowing for the greater population density of the western part of the world) rather than at the geographical centre of the earth.[45] Mauro also found a solution for the increasingly challenging question of the location of the Earthly Paradise, evidence for which a growing number of travellers returning from the Far East were failing to report. Reinforcing visually the belief that the Earthly Paradise is of the world but not in it, he portrayed it in a corner between the circular map and its square frame. Not all his contemporaries were as critical as Mauro. In 1452, in Italy, Giovanni Leardo had created a *mappamundi* in traditional style, enclosing it in concentric rings constituting an elaborate calendar for computing the date of Easter.

### REGIONAL MAPS OF THE HOLY LAND

Unlike Ptolemy's map of the region, surviving medieval topographical maps of the Palestinian region relate almost exclusively to Christianity. Some are known to have been made by returning pilgrims to illustrate written accounts of their travels. The others have various origins. Most were made in (or have survived from) the thirteenth and early fourteenth centuries. One of the earliest of the regional maps is the so-called Jerome map, one of two in the same hand compiled at Tournai, France, probably in the late twelfth century, as a general illustration in a codex of Jerome's etymological works.[46] Although it contains some biblical material, and is characterised by an excessively large sign for Jerusalem, the map of Palestine is unlikely to be connected with anything Jerome (or, more likely, Eusebius) might have created in the fourth century, but rather was put together from whatever sources the artist had to hand. Paul Harvey has concluded that both the map of Palestine and the map of Asia on the other side of the folio are palimpsests, and that the scribe had made two previous attempts before being leaving the Palestine map as we find it.[47] Even so, his map is rich in names for the area shown. Only the Ebstorf *mappamundi*, with seventy-four names in the corresponding area, as opposed to sixty-nine on the Jerome map, is more detailed.[48]

In contrast, Matthew Paris's two maps focus specifically on Palestine. One is drawn separately on the back of a discarded and folded bifolium and appears to be a copy, or a note, of something Paris was shown or was being told about.[49] It has north at the top and shows the area between Antioch and Cairo. It shows places likely to interest a crusader – fortresses (including some thirty crusader castles), monasteries, roads, ports, bishop's seats – as well as the holy places our pilgrim would have looked for. Bethlehem has a star, and two pitchers mark Cana. The relevance of contemporary politics is also underlined by references to modern boundaries, such as those to the small torrent which 'divides Syria from Palestine', the river between Arabia and Syria, and the 'Land inhabited by pagans and Saracens, whose lord is the Sultan of Damascus'.[50] Paris's second map of Palestine exists in three versions, all dating from the 1250s and all sufficiently different to suggest a constant process of revision and updating.[51] The position of the map, immediately following Paris's graphic itinerary in the *Chronica maiora*, is significant and the two maps would seem to be related, which explains the map's focus on the towns of Acre and Jerusalem rather than the region as a whole.[52] Outside the towns, topographical and other details are described mostly in writing. There are, again, references to contemporary politics ('Armenia is Christian', for example), routes leading inland are marked, the Jordan flows from its two sources straight into the Dead Sea, a star hangs over Bethlehem and a line from the birthplace of Christ to Nazareth gives the distance in units of time ('three days').[53]

The maps in the *Chronica maiora* remained at St Albans, to be studied in the library. In contrast, Marino Sanudo's recovery treatise, the *Liber secretorum*, with its many maps, was produced in multiple copies (at least two of which were by Sanudo himself) in the fourteenth century.[54] Included are two maps showing Palestine, one a general map of the Eastern Mediterranean, the other an east-orientated delineation of Palestine itself with an overlying reference grid by which places described in the text are easily located on the map.[55] Vesconte's authorship of the maps in Sanudo's treatise is still not universally accepted.[56] However, it is arguable that Sanudo had a not inconsiderable input into the grid map of Palestine and that it is not unreasonable to persist in referring to this particular map as Sanudo's rather than Vesconte's (see Figure 10). Harvey suggests that Sanudo took the idea of a reference grid from an Arab source, but it is arguable that Sanudo was provoked into thinking of a way of improving on Burchard of Mount Sion's confusing written description of the country, a work from which Sanudo (and others) borrowed heavily.[57] Burchard was a German Dominican friar who spent ten years around 1283 in the Holy Land and who sent a detailed description of Palestine home to Germany with a letter and, it is said, enclosing a map 'on a separate sheet'.[58] Only one manuscript of the later, much expanded, version of Burchard's text is known to have a map.[59] The surviving map seems not to have been a early or even necessarily a close copy of anything Burchard might have produced and is thought to date from the fourteenth-century copy.[60] It is a densely packed map, giving the impression of boxes and writing, and there is little pictorial representation. Boxed names indicate the location of the Tribal Territories, the names of some routes are written at an angle corresponding to the direction of the road, towns are indicated by turreted place signs (in Byzantine style), and villages and biblical sites by a line encircling their name. Red lines separate the provinces of Galilee, Samaria and Judea. There is no trace, however, of any of the twelve lines, centred on Acre, by which Burchard divided the country in order to list in his text 'the cities and places mentioned in Scripture [so] that it may be easy to find the situation of each place and the part of the world wherein it lies'.[61] Despite his remarkable attempt at systematic description, Burchard's text is frustratingly difficult to follow, and it is not beyond the bounds of imagination to see impatience with Burchard's text (? and map) as the germ of Sanudo's and Vesconte's reference grid.

In the fifteenth century Sanudo's map was inserted into copies of Ptolemy's Geography as a 'modern' map complementing the second-century 'Fourth Map of Asia'. Ptolemy's map of Palestine and surrounding lands is an uncompromisingly geographical map of a part of the later Roman Empire, correctly showing the Jordan river with a single source, although with an error (possibly due to later copying of the co-ordinates) in the coastline south of Apollonia. Yet some of the Palestinian names would have been familiar to medieval readers from the Bible, towns such as Ascalon, Lydd and Jerusalem, and provinces such as Judea, Samaria and Galilaea, although they would have missed places such as Bethlehem, Cana and Nazareth, which had significance for Christians but which would have been considered of no importance to the Roman administration.

## PLANS OF JERUSALEM AND THE HOLY SITES

Finally, our pilgrim would have come to the study of local plans. Towns were rarely shown in plan in the Middle Ages, but Jerusalem was the outstanding exception. Acre had been represented by both Matthew Paris and Vesconte (see Figure 7). Paris's generously large outline of the port city allowed him space to show the major features a pilgrim would have needed to know about or to be able to recognise and locate. Paolino Veneto showed Antioch in plan as a square walled city with prominent gates, some of which led to bridges over the streams watering the city, and also copied the plan of Jerusalem in Sanudo's *Liber secretorum*.[62]

Jerusalem had a place of triple importance in medieval exegesis: as a historical city, as a symbol of the heavenly city, and for its allegorical significance.[63] Pilgrims passing through Rome would have seen the mosaic on the tympanum in the sixth-century Church of Santa Maria Maggiore portraying the faithful as a flock of sheep waiting patiently at the single gate of the high-walled city signifying the Christian church.[64] At least fifteen plans of Jerusalem are known from the crusader period, most of them found in codices. Some represent the city geographically. Others are so stylised as to be largely symbolical. Of the first group, the plan from Cambrai, dating from the 1140s and displaying a schematic rhumboidal city, betrays personal local knowledge.[65] In contrast, Sanudo's plan presents a more realistic appearance, although the extent to which he was recording anything he had actually seen is debatable, while the lozenge-shaped plan attributed to Burchard is plainly imaginary.[66] By the fifteenth century there were other representations of the city of Jerusalem in realistic style, like the manuscript plan attributed to Sebald Rieter (*c.* 1475) and the detailed representations of the city on printed regional maps such as Lucas Brandis's (1475, said to be based on Burchard's) and Bernhard von Breitenbach's and Erhard Reuwich's scenic map (1486).[67]

Some of the stylised plans of Jerusalem are rectangular (Figure 5), but most represent a circular city divided into quadrants by four streets.[68] Some presentations are more ornate, some show additional streets, but in all of them geographical reality is subordinate to symmetry. One result is that occasionally individual buildings, like the Church of the Knights of St John, are portrayed on the wrong side of the street and thus in the wrong quarter, as on the map in Figure 5. Despite the stylisation, the key structures and sites are pictured in considerable detail, usually from a horizontal viewpoint, sometimes in plan. Our pilgrim would have been able without difficulty to pick out, for example, the main city gates, the churches on Temple Mount (the Dome of the Rock and the al-Aqsa Mosque which occupied the site of Solomon's Temple) and the Church of the Holy Sepulchre. On some plans, holy sites beyond the city walls are also represented, such as the Mount of

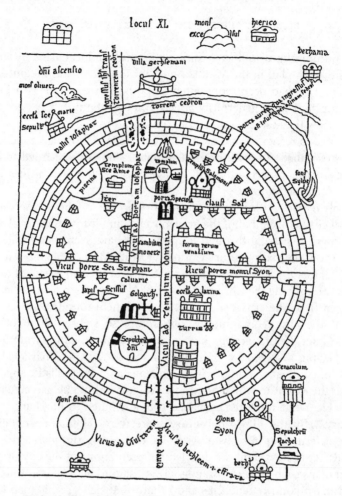

5 Stylised plan of the city of Jerusalem from a twelfth-century manuscript of the 'Gesta' in the St Omer codex. Symmetry and realism have been combined to convey the impression of a densely packed urban centre at the same time as portraying the most important individual structures a Christian visitor would want to see. The Hospitallers' *Ecclesia latina* has been misplaced in the south-western (instead of the south-eastern) quarter.

Olives with Gethsamene, the river Jordan (with twin sources), Lazarus's house at Bethany and, further away, the Old Testament city of Jericho.

For a plan of a particular holy site, our pilgrim would have had to go back to the exegetical treatises for Bede's *De locis sanctis* (*c.* 709) or, better still, Bede's source, Adomnán's account of the holy places (*c.* 680). Adomnán's drawings of the churches in Jerusalem were based on diagrams made on wax tablets while Arculf, it seems, was relating his travels in the Holy Land. Adomnán's plans survive in four ninth-century manuscripts, Bede's versions in five manuscripts (dating from the ninth, tenth and eleventh centuries).[69] All have north at the top. The simplest of the four shows the church at Jacob's Well, a cruciform structure with a square-walled well in the centre of the transept. In the plan of the 'great round church' of the Ascension, where the exact site of the Ascension is marked by a pair of footprints, the three circular roofed porticos are represented as concentric circles with breaks for doors and marks for the eight lamps which shone thought the western window. In the plan of the Great Basilica on Mount Sion, internal features are described in writing instead of graphically, except in one manuscript where the column of the flagellation is depicted.[70] Adomnán's most complicated plan shows the various buildings on Golgotha: the three churches (the Round Church and the churches of St Mary the Virgin and Golgotha), a courtyard, Constantine's basilica, and Christ's Tomb (Figure 6). In the Round Church, Arculf measured the sepulchre 'with his hand, and found it to be seven feet long'.[71]

Bishop Arculf was not unique amongst medieval pilgrims to the Holy Land in taking measurements. In 1106 or 1107 Daniel, the abbot from Russia, had taken advantage of being left alone in the Round Church to measure the sepulchre.[72] Muslim pilgrims were also interested in precision. Nasir-i-Khusra was probably not the first and was certainly not the last, in 1047, to take measurements in the vicinity of the al-Aqsa Mosque; in 1154, Muhammad al-Idrisi found that the length of the court around the mosque 'measures 200 fathoms, and its breadth is 180 fathoms'.[73] Nor, as we have seen, was Arculf the only pilgrim or traveller to have left maps, even if these were actually penned by Adomnán, his mouthpiece. John Poloner's written description of the Holy Land was originally accompanied by a map which is now lost, but which Poloner himself described, telling us which colours were used for different territories and explaining the 'marks' he invented to indicate sites of special interest: an inverted V with an asterisk, for example, indicated 'the place where the Lord satisfied four thousand people with seven loaves'.[74] The maps of Gabrielle Capodilista and the Eton schoolmaster William Wey, who travelled together in 1458, have survived, together with their journals.[75] Not every geographically-minded pilgrim, though, chose to express his observations cartographically. In 1158 John Phocas saw it as his duty to 'attempt to depict the country by words as though by a map'.[76] Where Adomnán, at least, differed from his successors was in the ambition of his text on the holy places. This should be seen, O'Loughlin points out, more as a specific type of exegetical manual than as a simple travelogue.[77] Other pilgrimages were written down for those who could not themselves go to Jerusalem, like those of John of Würtzburg (c. 1130) and Theodoric (1169–74), or to aid future

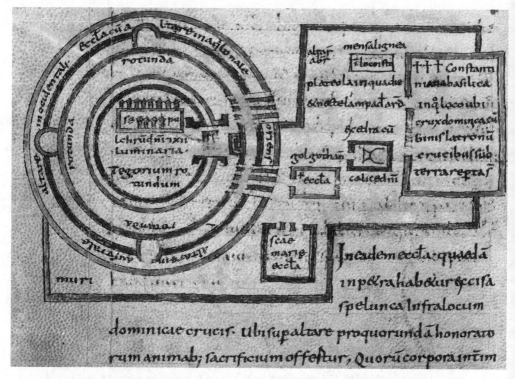

**6** Plan of the holy places on Golgotha. Adomnán's drawing, from Arculf's recollections and measurements, shows the Round Church, with the Sepulchre, to the west and the other churches and buildings grouped around a courtyard to the east. Adomnán's plans illustrate his *De locis sanctis* (c. 680) and were copied with only minor modification by Bede for his own treatise on the holy places, thus ensuring for them wide circulation later in the Middle Ages. 9.5 × 16 cm.

pilgrims, like William Wey's 'Information for pilgrims unto the Holy Land' (1462), and not only to record the high point of a person's life.

By now, our hypothetical pilgrim was ready to see Palestine and its holy places for himself. Ready to set out, he needed no more maps. He scarcely needed even an itinerary – the usual travel aid – for he would not go far on his own before meeting up with other eastward-bound travellers, merchants and pilgrims.[78] Routes to the Mediterranean, either direct to Marseilles or over the Alps to the Ligurian or Adriatic ports of Italy, were well defined. From 1026, a new continental route down the Balkan peninsula had been opened up.[79] While looking at a map of the world or at a *mappamundi*, our pilgrim would perhaps have fingered a route across Europe, as invited by the compiler of the Ebstorf map, who pointed out that readers of the map might find it 'of no small usefulness . . . to see the direction to be taken . . . and chose for themselves which monuments they will contemplate and which routes to travel'.[80] Or he would have read one of the many guides left by earlier pilgrims, or found an itinerary in some other text, often in an unexpected place. One mid-fifteenth-century English account detailing the steps to be taken for a pilgrimage from London to Jerusalem, and giving a village by village itinerary, came to light in 1999 in a physician's handbook.[81] At sea, way-finding was in the hands of the ship's master. Even here, charts – as opposed to maritime itineraries – are not thought to have been used in the Mediterranean until the late thirteenth century.[82] So it is unlikely to have been a chart that Daniel the Abbot saw in 1106 as he sailed from Constantinople 'along the curve of the coast' and through the Sea of Marmora, although Daniel does make it sound as if he were describing a coastline seen on a map as well as from the deck of a ship.[83] It is not impossible that there were marine maps of some sort by the early twelfth century, if not fully fledged portolan charts drawn onto a network of rhumb lines, for in the year after Daniel made his journey, the Byzantine emperor Alexius is reported as having drawn 'a map of the coasts of Lombardy and Illyricum, with the harbours on either side' which he sent, with 'written instructions', to Contostephanus with further advice as to where to moor his ships.[84] In 1483, though, Felix Fabri was able to marvel at the portolan chart he saw on his ship, which he described as 'a chart all of an ell long and an ell broad, whereon the whole sea is drawn with thousands and thousands of lines, and countries are marked with dots and miles by figures'.[85] Our pilgrim, by now safely sailing eastwards, could afford to relax in the knowledge that he had already done all he could to see examples of every kind of map that would enhance his understanding of the places he was about to see; others would get him there.

### NOTES

1 Felix Fabri, *The Book of the Wanderings of Brother Felix Fabri*, trans. Aubrey Stewart, Palestine Pilgrims' Text Society, 2 vols (London: Palestine Pilgrims' Text Society, 1887–97; repr. New York: AMS Press, 1971), i, p. 50.

2 Felix Fabri, *Fabri evagatorium in Terra Sanctae, Arabiae et Egypti peregrinationem*, ed. Conrad Dieter Hassler, 3 vols (Stuttgart: Societas Literaria Stuttgardiensis, 1843–49), i, p. 2 ('Epistola'). See also F. M. Prestcott, *Jerusalem Journey: Pilgrimage to the Holy Land in the Fifteenth Century* (London: Eyre & Spottiswoode, 1954), pp. 59–76.

3 Fabri had evidently studied the maps in the Geography closely, for he refers to several by title when discussing the centrality of Jerusalem: *Wanderings*, i, p. 376.

4 Fabri, *Fabri evagatorium*, i, p. 3. The translation is Prescott's: *Jerusalem Journey*, p. 73.

5 Our imaginary pilgrim is male. The presence of women in group pilgrimage on the grounds of distraction, always a delicate question, would have been exacerbated when some came to treat the event as a social occasion, as noted by Johan Huizinga, *The*

*Autumn of the Middle Ages*, trans. Rodney J. Payton and Ulrich Mammitzsch (Chicago: University of Chicago Press, 1966; first published in Dutch in 1921), p. 185.

6  I Kings (A.V.) equates to III Kings in the Vulgate Bible.

7  Eusebius's works continued to be studied in the Reformation, when maps of the division of Canaan, and the Temple, were still being included in biblical commentary: see Catherine Delano-Smith, 'Maps as science *and* art: Maps in sixteenth-century Bibles', *Imago Mundi*, 42 (1990), 65–83, and Elizabeth M. Ingram, 'Maps as readers' aids: Maps and plans in Geneva Bibles', *Imago Mundi*, 45 (1993), 29–44.

8  Oxford, Bodleian Library, B.N.C. 5, fol. 32. The map was redrawn on a blank folio (442) at the end of the volume.

9  *Ibid.*, fol. 281 and again, at the end of the volume, fol. 442ᵛ. Richard of St Victor of Paris died in 1173. The map on fol. 218 is reproduced (with an incorrect press-mark) in Catherine Delano-Smith and Roger J. P. Kain, *English Maps: A History* (London: The British Library, 1999), p. 18. Nicholas of Lyra provided his commentary with thirty-eight drawings (many comparing Jewish and Christian interpretations), seventeen of which are plans. Paul of Burgos later added three illustrations, including one in plan. In the first printed edition of the *Postillae* (Rome, 1471–72) the spaces left for illustrations remain empty, and it was 1481 before these first appeared in print in the Nuremberg edition.

10  See Jennifer O'Reilly, introduction to Bede, *Bede: On the Temple*, ed. and trans. with notes by Seán Connolly, Translated Texts for Historians, 21 (Liverpool: Liverpool University Press, 1995), pp. lii–lv and frontispiece; and Bede, *Bede: On the Tabernacle*, ed. and trans. Arthur G. Holder, Translated Texts for Historians, 18 (Liverpool: Liverpool University Press, 1994), frontispiece.

11  Three copies of Cassiodorosus's Great Pandect were made at Jarrow, but both the original and two of the copies are now lost. The surviving copy, the Codex Amiatinus, is in Florence, Biblioteca Laurenziana, I.c.II. The plan occupies fols 2ᵛ–3ʳ and is reproduced in colour in Delano-Smith and Kain, *English Maps*, plate 1. See also R. L. S. Bruce Mitford, 'The art of the Codex Amiatinus', Jarrow Lecture, 1967, rep. in *Journal of the British Archaeological Association*, 3rd series, 32 (1969), 1–25, and J. J. G. Alexander, *A Survey of Manuscripts Illustrated in the British Isles*, 1, *Insular Manuscripts 6th to 9th Century* (London: Harvey Miller, 1978).

12  Exponents of the allegorical interpretation included Peter of Celle (*c.* 1115–1183), Peter of Poitiers (1193–1205) and, perhaps most influentially, Joachim of Fiore (d. 1202).

13  Like earlier comentators (Cosmas Indicopleustes, for example), Beatus depicted a square walled city with gates and the Archangel. The New Jerusalem was another long-lasting exegetical plan: see Delano-Smith, 'Maps as science *and* art', 69 and fig. 5. For a ninth-century example from Ireland, see Thomas O'Loughlin, 'The plan of the New Jerusalem in the Book of Armagh', *Cambrian Medieval Celtic Studies*, 39 (2000), 23–38. The interpretation of Revelation as a spiritual allegory goes back to St Augustine.

14  Alessandro Scafi, *Mapping Paradise: A History of Heaven on Earth* (London: The British Library, forthcoming), Chap. 5. I am grateful to Dr Scafi for sight of this chapter prior to publication.

15  The informal process of 'Christianisation' of the traditional T-O diagram is well illustrated in the selection of diagrams from Sallust's History of the Jugurthine war illustrated in Konrad Miller, *Mappaemundi: Die ältesten Weltkarten*, 6 vols (Stuttgart: J. Roth, 1895–98), iii, pp. 110–15.

16  On exegetical geography and Isidore's influence on medieval geographical texts, see Natalia Lozovsky, *The Earth is our Book: Geographical Knowledge in the Latin West ca. 400–1000* (Ann Arbor: Michigan University Press, 2000).

17  Quotation from O. A. W. Dilke, 'Maps in the service of the state: Roman cartography to the end of the Augustan era', in J. B. Harley and David Woodward (eds), *Cartography in Prehistoric, Ancient, and Medieval Europe and the Mediterranean: The History of Cartography* (in progress), i (Chicago: Chicago University Press, 1987), pp. 201–11, esp. p. 208. Dilke also refers to a map of the *oikumine* said to have been displayed in a portico in Autun, France, in 300 CE: O. A. W. Dilke, *Greek and Roman Maps* (London: Thames and Hudson, 1985), pp. 41–54. See also Peter Wiseman, 'Julius Caesar and the Hereford world map', *History Today*, 37 (1987), 53–7. The strongest expression of doubt about Roman mapmaking comes from Kai Brodersen, *Terra cognita: Studien zür römischen Raumerfassung* (Hildesheim: Olms, 1995), pp. 269–72, and 'The presentation of geographical knowledge for travel and transport in the Roman world', in Colin Adams and Ray Laurence (eds), *Travel and Geography in the Roman Empire* (London: Routledge, 2001), pp. 7–21. Agrippa's map (or description) was the outcome of Julius Caesar's initiative three decades earlier, when Caesar had given orders for measurements and observations to be made of the whole of the known world, an episode alluded to on both the Hereford and the Ebstorf *mappaemundi*.

18  Barbel Kramer, 'The earliest known map of Spain (?) and the Geography of Artemidorus of Ephesus on papyrus', *Imago Mundi*, 53 (2001), 115–20.

19  For the difference between linear perspective and true geometric projection, see *Ptolemy's Geography: An Annotated Translation of the Theoretical Chapters*, ed. and trans. J. Lennart Berggren and Alexander Jones (Princeton and Oxford: Princeton University Press, 2000), pp. 31–40, and David Woodward, 'The image of the world in the Renaissance', in David Woodward, Catherine Delano-Smith and Cordell Yee, *Plantajements i objectivos d'una història universal de la cartografia: Approaches and Challenges in a Worldwide History of Cartography* (Barcelona: Institut Cartogràfic de Catalunya, 2001), pp. 133–52.

20  Berggren and Jones, *Ptolemy's Geography*, esp. pp. 45–50, suggest the map may have been made in the sixth century in Alexandria. See also Tony Campbell, *The Earliest Printed Maps 1472–1500* (London: The British Library, 1987), p. 122.

21  The Alphonsine Tables, compiled in Spain in 1080, were updated about 1272 as the Toledan Tables. Adelard of Bath translated the Khorazmian Table in 1162: see J. K. Wright, *The Geographical Lore of the Time of the Crusades: A Study in the History of Medieval Science and Tradition in Western Europe*, American Geographical Society Research Series, 15 (New York: American Geographical Society, 1925); republished with additions (New York: Dover Publications, 1965), pp. 95–6, 86–7. On the reception of Arab scholarship in general, see Charles Burnett, *The Introduction of Arabic Learning into England*, Panizzi Lectures 1996 (London: The British Library, 1997).

22  Quoted by David Woodward, 'Roger Bacon on geography and cartography', in Jeremiah Hackett (ed.), *Roger Bacon and the Sciences: Commemorative Essays* (Leiden, New York and Cologne: Brill, 1997), pp. 199–222, esp. p. 210. See also David Woodward, 'Roger Bacon's terrestrial co-ordinate system', *Annals of the Association of American Geographers*, 80:1 (1990), 109–22; O. A. W. Dilke, 'Cartography in the Byzantine Empire', in Harley and Woodward (eds), *History of Cartography*, i, pp. 258–75, esp. p. 268 n. 51; and Patrick Gautier Dalché, 'Connaissance et usages géographiques des coordonnées dans le Moyen Âge latin (du Vénérable Bède à Roger Bacon)', in Louis Callebat and Olivier Desbordes (eds), *Science antique, science médiévale (autour d'Avranches 235): Actes du colloque internationale (Mont-Saint-Michel, 4–7 septembre 1998)* (Hildesheim, Zürich and New York: Olms-Weidmann, 2000), pp. 401–36. Bacon had already sent the text of his *Opus maius* to Pope Clement and the map was supposed to have followed, but nothing more has been heard of it.

23 Woodward, 'Roger Bacon on geography and cartography', pp. 213 and 219.

24 On which see Evelyn Edson in Chapter 7 below, pp. 138–9.

25 London, British Library, MS Cotton Tiberius B.V., fol. 56ᵛ. For line drawings of the map and transcriptions of place names, see Miller, *Mappaemundi*, i. For reproductions in colour, see P. D. A. Harvey, *Medieval Maps* (London: The British Library and Toronto: University of Toronto Press, 1991), fig. 19, p. 26; *idem, Mappa Mundi: The Hereford World Map* (London: Hereford Cathedral and The British Library, 1996), p. 28; and Edson, *Mapping Time and Space*, fig. 1.5 and pp. 8–9 and 74–80.

26 Dionysius's *Periegesis* was composed in the second century CE.

27 Huizinga, *The Autumn of the Middle Ages*, p. 249.

28 Quoted by Jacques Paviot, 'La mappemonde attribuée à Jan van Eyck par Fàcio: Une pièce à retirer du catalogue de son oeuvre', *Revue des Archéologues et Historiens d'Art de Louvain*, 24 (1991), 57–62. Moreover, either term may indicate a written description of the geographical world and not a map at all: see David Woodward, 'Medieval *mappaemundi*', in Harley and Woodward (eds), *History of Cartography*, i, pp. 286–370, at pp. 287–8; and Marcia Kupfer, 'The lost wheel map of Ambrogio Lorenzetti', *Art Bulletin*, 78:2 (1996), 286–310, esp. 291. The different senses are not always made clear in the modern literature.

29 Alessandro Scafi, 'Paradise: The essence of a *mappamundi*', in P. D. A. Harvey (ed.), *The Hereford World Map: Medieval World Maps and their Context* (London: The British Library, forthcoming). I am again indebted to Alessandro Scafi for drawing my attention to the naming of the river Pison: see Scafi, *Mapping Paradise*.

30 The literature on *mappaemundi* is vast. For the recent focus on the theological dimensions, see Marcia Kupfer, 'The lost *mappamundi* at Chalivoy-Milon', *Speculum*, 66 (1991), 540–71; Alessandro Scafi, 'Mapping Eden: Cartographies of the Earthly Paradise', in Denis Cosgrove (ed.), *Mappings* (London: Reaktion, 1999), pp. 50–70, and *idem, Mapping Paradise*.

31 One of the largest known *mappaemundi*, lost in the bombing of Hanover in 1943, was made at Ebstorf in about 1239 and measured over 3.5 metres (12 feet) in diameter. It was drawn on thirty goat skins sewn together: see Armin Wolf, 'News on the Ebstorf world map: Date, origin, authorship', in Monique Pelletier (ed.), *La géographie du monde au Moyen Age et à la Renaissance* (Paris: Editions du Comité des Travaux Historiques et Scientifiques, 1989), pp. 51–68. The largest extant *mappamundi*, the Hereford map, was drawn on a single parchment measuring 158 × 113 cm: see Harvey, *Mappa Mundi*, p. 1.

32 Fabri, *Wanderings*, i, p. 110. Although Fabri described the wrong convent and the wrong island, what he saw was Fra Mauro's map, completed only twenty-four years previously. I am grateful to Piero Falcetta, of the Biblioteca Marciana, Venice, for confirmation of the identity of the map seen by Fabri.

33 It would be worth considering the role of the Psalter *mappamundi* (c. 1260) in the context of the production and use of private devotional books. On these books, see Michael Clanchy, 'Images of ladies with prayer books: What do they signify?', in R. N. Swanson, *The Church and the Book* (Woodbridge: The Boydell Press for The Ecclesiastical History Society, 2004), pp. 106–22.

34 Peter Barber, 'The Evesham world map: A late medieval English view of God and the world', *Imago Mundi*, 47 (1995), 13–33, esp. 13–17.

35 Colin Morris, 'Memorials of the holy places and blessings from the East: Devotion to Jerusalem before the crusades', in R. N. Swanson (ed.), *The Holy Land, Holy Lands, and Christian History*, Studies in Church History, 36 (Woodbridge: The Boydell Press for The Ecclesiastical History Society, 2000), pp. 90–109.

36 Morris, 'Introduction', in Swanson (ed.), *Holy Land, Holy Lands*, pp. xxi–ii, and 'Memorials', esp. pp. 94–9.

37 Norman Cohn, *The Pursuit of the Millennium: Revolutionary Millenarism and Mystical Anarchists of the Middle Ages* (London: Paladin, 1970), p. 63; Morris, 'Memorials', p. 98.

38 Cohn, *Pursuit of the Millennium*, pp. 64–5; Morris, 'Memorials', p. 109; Stephen Wessley, 'The role of the Holy Land for the early followers of Joachim of Fiore', in Swanson (ed.), *Holy Land, Holy Lands*, pp. 181–91.

39 A point made cogently by Daniel Connolly in connection with Matthew Paris's graphic itinerary (1250s). The quotation originated with Bernard of St Clairvaux: see Daniel Connolly, 'Imagined pilgrimage in the itinerary maps of Matthew Paris', *Art Bulletin*, 81 (1999), 598–622, esp. 598 and n. 9. In similar vein, Morris, 'Memorials', p. 98, notes the role of crucifixes 'as a substitute for holy places in Palestine' in the tenth century. See also Kathleen Margaret Rudy, 'North European responses to Holy Land pilgrimage, 1453–1550', unpublished PhD dissertation, Columbia University, 2000 (AAT 3005788), www.lib.umich.com/dissertations/fullcit/3005788.

40 Contrary to popular belief, Jerusalem is found at the centre only on some of the later *mappaemundi*. David Woodward explains 'the strengthening of the idea of Jerusalem as the spiritual center' as 'a natural outcome of the Crusades': 'Reality, symbolism, time and space in medieval world maps', *Annals of the Association of American Geographers*, 75:4 (1985), 510–21, esp. 515–17. See also Woodward, 'Medieval *mappaemundi*', pp. 340–1.

41 On the perception of distance in this context, see Thomas O'Loughlin, 'The view from Iona: Adomnán's mental maps', *Peritia: The Journal of the Medieval Academy of Ireland*, 10 (1996), 98–122, and *idem*, 'Living in the ocean', in Cormac Bourke (ed.), *Studies in the Cult of Saint Columba* (Dublin: Four Courts Press, 1997), pp. 11–23.

42 Scott D. Westrem cautions against exaggerating the importance of biblical material, especially for parts of the map well away from the Bible lands: *The Hereford Map* (Turnhout: Brepols, 2001), p. xxviii.

43 Westrem, *ibid.*, pp. 157–73, identifies and comments on each place on his reproduction of this part of the Hereford map (section 6).

44 Morris, 'Memorials', p. 98.

45 The quotation is given in full in Alessandro Scafi, 'Il Paradiso Terrestre di Fra Mauro', *Storia dell'Arte*, 93–4 (May–December 1998), 411–19.

46 London, British Library, Additional MS 10049, fol. 64$^{r-v}$. The works by Jerome are *Hebraicorum quaestionum*, *Liber nominum* and his version of Eusebius's *De situ et nominibus locorum Hebraicorum*.

47 P. D. A. Harvey, 'The twelfth-century Jerome maps of Asia and Palestine', paper presented to the Seventeenth International Conference on the History of Cartography, Lisbon, 6–10 July 1997, and personal communication.

48 Paul D. A. Harvey, 'The biblical content of medieval maps of the Holy Land', in Dagmar Unverhau (ed.), *Geschichtsdeutung auf alten Kartens: Archäologie und Geschichte*, Wolfenbütteler Forschungen, 101 (Wiesbaden: Harrassowitz, 2003), pp. 56–63. Both Jerome maps are illustrated in Edson, *Mapping Time and Space*, pp. 28–9.

49 Oxford, Corpus Christi College, MS 2*. See Evelyn Edson, 'Matthew Paris's "other" map of Palestine', *Map Collector*, 66:1 (1994), 18–22; P. D. A. Harvey, 'Matthew Paris's maps of Palestine', in Michael Prestwich, Richard Britnell and Robin Frame (eds), *Thirteenth Century England*, 8 (Woodbridge: Boydell and Brewer, 2001), pp. 165–77; and Harvey, 'Biblical content'. Richard Vaughan, *Matthew Paris* (Cambridge: Cambridge University Press, 1958), pp. 13–18, lists Paris's known friends and informants.

50  'Iste torrens qui parvus est dividit Siriam a Palestina; Iste fluvius dividit Arabiam . . . a Siria . . . ; Terra a paganis et Saracenis inhabitata, cuis dominus Soldanus Damasci': Reinhold Röhricht, 'Karten und Pläne zur Palästinakunde aus dem 7. bis 16. Jahrhundert', *Zeitschrift des Deutschen Palästina-Vereins*, 18 (1895), 177–8, plate VI.

51  London, British Library, Royal MS 14 C vii, fols 4ᵛ–5ʳ; Cambridge, Corpus Christi College, MS 16, fols iiᵛ and vʳ, and MS 26, fols iiiʳ–ivᵛ. On Paris's Palestine maps in general, see: Miller, *Mappaemundi*, iii, pp. 83–94; Vaughan, *Matthew Paris*, pp. 244–5; and Paul Harvey, 'Matthew Paris's maps of Palestine'.

52  On one version of the itinerary (Cambridge, Corpus Christi College, MS 26), a special sign identifies the Apulian port of Otranto as 'The way to Acre via Apulia': Suzanne Lewis, *The Art of Matthew Paris in the Chronica Majora* (Aldershot: Scolar Press with Corpus Christi College, Cambridge, 1987), p. 325. On the connection between the itinerary and the map of Palestine, see Connolly, 'Imagined pilgrimage'.

53  Paris manipulated spatial relationships so that he could exaggerate what he wanted the reader to focus on and still have room for everything else. The contiguity of Nazareth, Babylon and Cairo in the top right corner is thus less perplexing than it has seemed to some modern commentators.

54  Sanudo's work is discussed by Evelyn Edson in Chapter 7 below, pp. 138–49.

55  Paul Harvey analysed all the medieval manuscript versions of Sanudo's grid map and presented his initial findings in a paper 'The medieval grid maps of Palestine', at the Nineteenth International Conference on the History of Cartography, Madrid, 1–6 July 2001. Pending further publication, see his 'Biblical content'.

56  See Evelyn Edson on Sanudo's authorship in Chapter 7 below, pp. 137–8.

57  Harvey, 'Biblical content'.

58  The reference to the map is cited by J. C. M. Laurent (ed.), *Peregrinatores medii aevi quatuor*, 2nd edn (Leipzig, 1873), p. 23, who omits to identify which of the twenty-six, or more, extant copies of Burchard's letter (all lacking any map) contains the crucial phrase.

59  Florence, Biblioteca Laurenziana, MS Plut. LXXVI, sui. 56, fols 97–8. I am indebted to Paul Harvey for sight of a colour photograph of the map.

60  Harvey, 'Biblical content'. The place names were transcribed by Reinhold Röhricht, 'Marino Sanudo sen als Kartograph Palästinas', *Zeitschrift des Deutschen Palästina-Vereins*, 21 (1898), 84–128, plate 5.

61  Burchard of Mount Sion, *Burchard of Mount Sion: A Description of the Holy Land*, trans. Aubrey Stewart, annotated by C. R. Conder, Palestine Pilgrims' Text Society, 12 (London: Palestine Pilgrims' Text Society, 1897; repr. New York: AMS Press, 1971), p. 4.

62  London, British Library, MS Egerton 1500, fol. 47ᵛ. The manuscript contains the 'Abbreviamen de las historias', an incomplete fourteenth-century Provençal translation of Paolino's 'Chronologia magna'. For a description of Sanudo-Vesconte's map of Jerusalem, see Evelyn Edson in Chapter 7 below, p. 148.

63  Adriaan H. Bredero, 'Jérusalem dans l'occident médiéval', in Pierre Gallois and Yves-Jean Riou (eds), *Mélanges offerts à René Crozet*, Cahiers de civilisation médiévale, supplement (Poitiers: Université de Poitiers, Centre d'études supérieures de Civilisation Médiéval, 1996), pp. 259–71.

64  The mosaic is reproduced in Rehav Rubin, *Image and Reality: Jerusalem in Maps and Views* (Jerusalem: The Hebrew University Magnes Press, 1999), p. 20.

65  Cambrai, Bibliothèque Municipale, MS 466, fol. 1ʳ. See P. D. A. Harvey, 'Local and regional cartography in medieval Europe', in Harley and Woodward (eds), *History of Cartography*, i, pp. 464–501, esp. p. 473, and Rubin, *Image and Reality*, p. 32, fig. 12. The map was placed in the front of a miscellany of treatises relating to counts and

bishops in France and Flanders. I am grateful to Rehav and Milka Rubin for additional details about the context of several of plans of Jerusalem.

66  Florence, Biblioteca Laurenziana, MS Plut. LXXVI, sui. 56, fol. 97. Reproduced in Rubin, *Image and Reality*, pp. 34–6 and figs 13 and 14.

67  Rieter's map is reproduced in Rubin, *Image and Reality*, fig. 15, the other two in Kenneth Nebenzahl, *Maps of the Bible Lands: Images of Terra Sancta through Two Millennia* (London: Times Books, 1986), plates 20 and 21. This book is also published as *Maps of the Holy Land: Images of Terra Sancta through Two Millennia* (New York: Abbeville, 1986).

68  About a dozen examples of plans of Jerusalem of this type are known, dating from the period of Christian control (1099–1187). For reproductions see Röhricht, 'Karten und Pläne (1892), 34–9, figs i–v; S. de Sandoli, *Itineraria Hierosolymitana crucesignatorum (saec. xii–xiii)*, 4 vols (Jerusalem: Studium Biblicum Franciscanum, 1978–84), i and ii; and Rubin, *Image and Reality*, pp. 25–31 and figs 7–10. Rubin interprets the internal divisions as part of the Christian T-O tradition, but I would suggest that a more likely source would be the cross-in-circle Egyptian hieroglyph for 'town' and the quartering of the circular *templum* in Roman town-founding rites (described by Varro, *De lingua latina*, VII, 7): see Joseph Rykwert, *The Idea of a Town: The Anthropology of Urban Form in Rome, Italy, and the Ancient World* (London: Faber and Faber, 1976), pp. 46 and 192.

69  The four extant illustrated manuscripts of Adomnán's text and the five illustrated manuscripts of Bede's shorter version are listed in Wilkinson, *Jerusalem Pilgrims before the Crusades*, pp. 193–7. See also Adomnán, *Adamnan's De locis sanctis*, ed. Denis Meehan, (Dublin: Dublin Institute for Advanced Studies, 1958).

70  Vienna, Österreichische Nationalbibliothek, Vindobonensis MS 458, fol. 17$^v$.

71  Adomnán, *De locis sanctis*, 2.1, v 228, quoted by Wilkinson, *Jerusalem Pilgrims*, p. 96. The identity of Arculf, the French bishop who is supposed to have landed on the shores of the Scottish island of Iona on his way back to France from Palestine, remains unelucidated and some scholars see him as no more than 'a literary fiction', created, presumably, by Adomnán: see Thomas O'Loughlin, 'Palestine in the aftermath of the Arab conquest: The earliest Latin account', in Swanson (ed.), *Holy Land, Holy Lands*, pp. 78–89, esp. p. 87. See also Thomas O'Loughlin, 'Adomnán and Arculf: The case of an expert witness', *Journal of Medieval Latin*, 7 (1997), 127–46.

72  Abbot Daniel, *The Life and Journey of Daniel Abbot of the Russian Land*, trans. W. F. Ryan, in J. Wilkinson, with J. Hill and W. F. Ryan (eds), *Jerusalem Pilgrimage 1099–1185*, Hakluyt Society, 2nd series, 167 (London: Hakluyt Society, 1988), pp. 120–71, esp. p. 122.

73  Nasir-i-Khusrau, *Diary of a Journey through Syria and Palestine by Nâsir-i-Khusrau*, Palestine Pilgrims' Text Society, 4 (London: Palestine Pilgrims' Text Society, 1897), p. 27; Muhammad al Idrisi, 'Muhammad al Idrisi', in Wilkinson, Hill and Ryan (eds), *Jerusalem Pilgrimage 1099–1185*, pp. 223–7, esp. p. 124.

74  Johannes Poloner, *Description of the Holy Land: By John Poloner*, trans. Aubrey Stewart, Palestinian Pilgrims' Text Society, 6 (London: Palestine Pilgrims' Text Society, 1894), p. 26.

75  For reproductions, see Nebenzahl, *Maps of the Bible Lands*, plates 17 and 18.

76  Johannes Phocas, *The Pilgrimage of Johannes Phocas*, trans. Aubrey Stewart, Palestine Pilgrims' Text Society, 5 (London: Palestine Pilgrims' Text Society, 1897), p. 3. Wilkinson, however, gives a different reading ('we must attempt, as best we can, to paint a picture, using words on our canvas': Wilkinson, Hill and Ryan (eds), *Jerusalem Pilgrimage 1099–1185*, p. 315).

77 O'Loughlin, 'Palestine in the aftermath of the Arab conquest'.

78 On the place of maps in travel, see Catherine Delano-Smith, 'Milieus of mobility: Itineraries, routes and roads', in J. R. Akerman, *Maps on the Move: Cartography for Travel and Transportation*, Twelfth K. Nebenzahl Jr Lecture in the History of Cartography, 1996 (Chicago: University of Chicago Press for the Newberry Library, forthcoming).

79 François Micheau, 'Les itinéraires maritimes et continentaux des pèlerinages vers Jerusalem', *Occident et Orient au X<sup>e</sup> siècle: Actes du IX<sup>e</sup> congrès de la Societé des Historiens Médiévistes de l'Enseignement Supérieur Public, Dijon, 2–4 juin, 1978*, Publications de l'Univérsité de Dijon, 57 (Paris: Société des Belles Lettres, 1979), pp. 79–104.

80 Trans. from the Latin transcription in Miller, *Mappaemundi*, v, p. 8.

81 'Physician's handbook: Astrological and medical compendium, with pilgrim's guide from London to Jerusalem and itinerary of the Holy Land', Christie's Auction House, London, *Sales Catalogue*, 29 November 1999, p. 9. I am grateful to Tony Campbell for drawing this item to my attention and to Natalie Taylor for her help.

82 Charts were not used in north-western Europe until the sixteenth century. See Tony Campbell, 'Portolan charts from the late thirteenth century to 1500', in Harley and Woodward (eds), *History of Cartography*, i, pp. 371–463.

83 John Wilkinson gives this reading but notes that there is a variant ('by the narrow sea'): Wilkinson, Hill and Ryan (eds), *Jerusalem Pilgrimage 1099–1185*, p. 122 and n. 3. C. W. Wilson gives 'following the coast windings' in Abbot Daniel, *The Pilgrimage of the Russian Abbot Daniel*, ed. C. W. Wilson, Palestine Pilgrims' Text Society, 4 (London: Palestine Pilgrims' Text Society, 1897), p. 4.

84 Anna Comnena, *The Alexiad of Anna Comnena*, trans. from the Greek by E. R. A. Sewter (Harmondsworth: Penguin Books, 1969), pp. 414–15.

85 Fabri, *Wanderings*, i, p. 135.

# 7

## *Reviving the crusade: Sanudo's schemes and Vesconte's maps*

**(》**

Evelyn Edson

O N 28 May 1291, the Christian-held city of Acre on the Eastern Mediterranean coast fell to Mamluk troops under the leadership of the Sultan
of Egypt, al-Ashraf. On that day, the culmination of a seven-week siege, the
seaside tower of the Templars was successfully assaulted and those remaining inside were slaughtered. 'Everywhere there was fear, panic and groans
of death', wrote Marino Sanudo. All the elements fought against the city:
'the land was soaked with blood, the water was full of drowned people, fire
consumed the buildings, and the air was black with smoke . . . Thus all Syria
was lost'.[1] Those who managed to escape fled to Sidon or to Cyprus, and the
sultan ordered the city razed. In a few days what had been a bustling commercial city of 20,000 was reduced to a smouldering ruin.[2]

There had been plenty of warning of the disaster to come. In 1287 the
coastal city of Latakia had fallen, and in 1288 Tripoli followed. The citizens of
Acre, including William of Beaujeu, the master of the Temple, had begged
the West for reinforcements. Although distracted by a crusade in Sicily, the
Pope managed to raise funds to send a fleet of Venetian galleys, supported
by ships from Aragon, to the aid of the threatened city. Reaching Acre
in August 1290 and finding no immediate action at hand, some of the would-
be crusaders returned home. Others, eager to take up arms against the
infidel, started a riot in the market-place and killed a number of Muslim
merchants. This atrocity was the pretext for the Mamluk assault on the city
in April 1291.

After Acre's fall the other coastal cities followed in short order: Sidon,
Tyre, Haifa, Beirut, Tortosa. In August the Templars abandoned their great
fortress, the Chastel Pèlerin, on the coast south of Haifa. The nearest remaining toehold to the mainland was the island of Ruad near Tortosa, which the
Templars held for another twelve years. The fleeing Christians found refuge
on the island of Cyprus, still in Frankish hands under King Henry II. Others,

not so lucky, flooded the slave markets of Cairo and Damascus, where the price of a slave-girl dropped to a drachma.[3]

When the news reached Pope Nicholas IV in August 1291, he promptly issued an encyclical, *Dirum amaritudinis calicem* ('Fearful cup of bitterness'), to announce the disaster to the world and to call for immediate action to recover the lost Holy Land. Despite the fact that other Christian possessions in the Holy Land had been taken, it was the loss of Acre that captured Europe's attention, not only owing to its importance as chief port and capital of the Latin kingdom, but also because of its heroic defence. To modern historians the fall of Acre has served as a date for the 'end of the crusades', but to contemporaries this was not at all clear.[4] The crusading movement had always been episodic, with gains and losses and periods of inactivity. Over the next half-century there was considerable planning and preaching for another crusade, which seemed forever imminent. One of its leading proponents was the scion of a Venetian merchant family, Marino Sanudo, who composed a book-length proposal for action.

## MARINO SANUDO (C. 1270–1343) AND THE *LIBER SECRETORUM*

Marino, born about 1270 in Venice, was a member of the prominent Sanudo (or Sanuto) family, one branch of which, under the enterprising Marco, had established itself in the Aegean shortly after the Fourth Crusade. With their headquarters on the island of Naxos, the Sanudos styled themselves the Dukes of the Archipelago, and took advantage of their strategic position for shipping in the East. The resources of the Greek islands were fairly limited, but Naxos produced fruit, sweet wine and other agricultural products in quantity sufficient for export.

Marino Sanudo used the additional name 'Torsello', the name of an island in the Venetian lagoon, and is usually styled 'The Elder' today, to distinguish him from a later famous Marino Sanudo, the diarist who chronicled life in sixteenth-century Venice.[5] Our Marino's father was a member of the Venetian Senate, and the young Sanudo was attached to the entourage of the doge Giovanni Dandolo. He tells us that he travelled extensively in the East: in Palestine, Negroponte (Euboea), in Romania (Greece), Egypt, Cyprus, Armenia and Rhodes.[6] He had been in Acre as a teenager about 1285. In 1304 he was at the court of Palermo, and later in the same year went to Rome, where he was attached to the suite of Cardinal Ricardo Petroni of Siena. He was involved in business affairs, both of his immediate family and as an agent for the Sanudi of Naxos, but in Venice the distinction between business and politics was blurry, and more than one modern historian has suggested that he was employed abroad as an agent of the Venetian Republic.[7] He himself insisted that he was not controlled by any king, prince, or city, but acted of his own free will.[8]

Venetian interest in the Levantine trade and the whole crusading project was deep and intense. Venice had seized control of the Fourth Crusade in 1204 and directed it to suit its ends, but all along it was Venetian ships that often transported crusaders and pilgrims to the East. Here one could buy an entire pilgrim's 'outfit', complete with bed-roll and provisions, along with a boat ticket. In Acre Venetians controlled an extensive walled quarter of the city, where there were warehouses, palaces for wealthy families and their own church, consulate and bath-house. Since the early twelfth century the Venetians of Acre had enjoyed considerable privileges, including exemption from most taxes in the kingdom of Jerusalem. The government of the colony consisted of a governor and council sent from Venice, with the assistance of a local council. Acre was a centre not only of commerce, but of manufacturing, as local workmen were employed in the luxury industries of fine weaving and glassmaking.[9] A map of Acre, included in Marino's book, shows the city before its fall with its Genoese, Pisan, German and Venetian quarters and its many Christian churches and monasteries, as well as the headquarters of the great military Orders, such as the Templars, Teutonic Knights, and Hospitallers (Figure 7). The map also shows its formidable defences, which were to hold out against onslaught by land and sea for seven weeks in 1291. Surely Acre must have seemed indestructible, and we hear that the Venetian residents continued to acquire property in the city right up to the eve of its fall. David Jacoby has described the 'atmosphere de relative insouciance' among the Venetians of Acre as late as 1290, adding 'The Latins had hardly any sense of the greatness of the danger which menaced them'.[10]

We do not know when Sanudo conceived the idea of his campaign to restore western rule in the Holy Land. Was it when he heard the unbelievable news of the fall of Acre, where he had lived in the thriving Venetian colony only a few years before? Or did he become inspired by his patron Ricardo of Siena, a well-known proponent of the revival of the crusade?[11] In any case, by 1307 he had written a book, *Conditiones Terrae Sanctae*, which put forward his strategy for reconquest. The heart of his plan was an embargo against Egypt. Church funds were to finance a fleet of ten galleys (or maybe seven or five would do, if ten were too expensive) to patrol the Egyptian coast, barring all trade in or out. This was not a new idea, but in the past enforcement of a trade ban had depended on the penalty of excommunication. Christians could always buy their way out of this, while Muslims were not impressed. Sanudo's idea was to put real teeth into the policy by stationing an avenging fleet in the eastern Mediterranean Sea.

*Conditiones Terrae Sanctae* became the first part of an expanded work, *Liber secretorum fidelium crucis super Terrae Sanctae recuperatione et conservatione* ('Book of secrets for faithful crusaders on the recovery and retention of the Holy Land'). In 1321 we find Sanudo in Avignon, presenting his book to

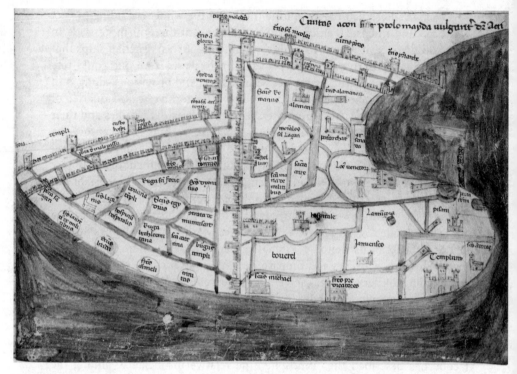

7 Acre. Here one sees Acre before its destruction in 1291. The city is ringed with walls and divided into various sectors, some of which were occupied by self-governing groups of Europeans. The tower of the Templars, the last stronghold to fall, is at the lower right. The Venetian sector (*locus venetorum*) is marked by a castle with a flag near the harbour.

Pope John XXII. The Pope, in recognisable bureaucratic style, rewarded Sanudo with some money and luxurious garments, and appointed a commission to look into it. The book ended up on the shelf, but at least one member of the commission took it to heart: Paolino Minorita, the Bishop of Pozzuoli, who freely adapted parts of its for his own history.[12]

Marino Sanudo's proposal was one of nearly thirty such documents circulating in Europe in the early fourteenth century.[13] Ramon Llull, the Master of the Hospital, the Master of the Templars, an Armenian prince, a French government official, a Dominican missionary and the Bishop of Leon were among those who obliged the Pope in his request for advice on the implementation of a successful recovery mission. In previous centuries there had been other requests and other responding documents, but one characteristic of the fourteenth-century ones was a great emphasis on strategy and practical means. Having lost its base on the mainland, any crusading mission must be super-organised if it was to achieve its goal. Of all this raft of proposals Sanudo's is one of the most detailed and practical. Like a good Venetian businessman he spells out expenses – provisions for each galley-load of soldiers per month and per year, for example[14] – and he consistently refers to his project as 'the business [negotium] of the Crusade'. Whereas some earlier pamphleteers had focused on such nebulous goals as general repenting of sins and restoring peace to squabbling European powers, Sanudo concentrated on the bottom line.

Thus it is not surprising that he began his project with economic warfare. He observed that much of Egypt's wealth derived from its position as middleman in the lucrative spice trade from Asia to Europe. These valuable cargoes were sent to Aden, and then to Chus on the western shore of the Red Sea. They were transported by camel caravan to the Nile just below the First Cataract, and then were sent by boat to Cairo and on to Alexandria, where western merchants bought them. The sultan took one-third of their value in taxes, in addition to the profits his merchants were reaping. Sanudo suggested that westerners deal instead with the Mongols of Persia, transporting the eastern cargoes through their territory. Though shipping charges would be higher, because they would be travelling by land, merchants would escape the exorbitant taxes of Egypt and thus deprive its government of a major source of its income.[15] Sanudo also detailed the disastrous consequences to Egypt if its sources of wood, iron and pitch were cut off, as these were essential to shipbuilding. Egyptians also relied on the West for gold and silver, which were needed to carry on the trade with the hard-currency markets of India.[16] He observed that the native Egyptians were poor soldiers, and that the military forces employed by the sultan, the very ones which had expelled the Christians from Palestine, were actually slaves purchased from both Christian and pagan countries and imported by sea.[17] All these important military resources could be denied the sultan by means of an effective blockade. In fact, Sanudo went still further and argued that there should be no trade at all with the infidel, either by land or by sea, in order to bring down the regime, because, he argued, disobedient Christians, pretending to deal in permitted goods, would treacherously bring in forbidden items. This may have been a lesson he learned from his sojourn in Acre, the center of illicit trade with Egypt.[18]

After two or three years of the naval blockade, Sanudo thought Egypt would be sufficiently weakened for the Christians to assault them with the second step of his plan, which was to launch a small professional force against the sultan. The huge unwieldy general crusades of the previous century had been ineffective. In Sanudo's opinion a 'passagium particolare' would be able to conquer where the 'passagium generale' had failed. This force of 15,000 foot and 300 horse would establish a beach-head on the island of Rosetta on the Egyptian coast. Sanudo thought it should be led by Venetians because of their seafaring experience, their many colonies in the East (particularly in the Aegean islands and Greece) and the similarity of the Egyptian coast to Venice, with its rivers, islands, lagoons and swamps. He admitted that other nations were also good sailors, especially those from the Baltic and North Sea ports,[19] but thought that a force of mixed nationality might have problems acting together. For one who had experienced the intense inter-communal hostility in Acre, this was an apt observation.[20]

And finally, after Egypt was secured, a more general crusade would be announced. This force would go on to reconquer the Holy Land, and maybe even the Byzantine Empire, back in the hands of the 'schismatic' Greeks since 1261. The funds for the last effort would be raised and its participants recruited by a major preaching campaign in Europe. Sanudo asked the Pope to preach the crusade 'in mundi climatibus universis cum solemnitate maxima' (in all the regions of the world with the greatest solemnity). He thought princes, barons and nobles should contribute money or forces, especially those who were enjoying the fruits of church property.[21] Money was needed to finance those who could not afford to pay their own way, and for the expenses of siege engines and other weapons. Once Egypt was laid low, the crusaders would move on to take the Holy Land.

Along with Sanudo's specific details, lists of equipment and supplies and expenses, he provided a set of maps to guide the would-be conquerors. The maps were part of his first edition presented to the Pope, either part of the book itself or as a separate atlas – Sanudo says he gave the Pope two books. The maps were the work of Pietro Vesconte, a Genoese mapmaker established in Venice since 1311, and were an innovative combination of the traditional maps of the world and the Holy Land with the charts of seafaring merchants.[22] As Sanudo made other copies of his book, which he sent to other European rulers, the maps included (like the text) underwent some variation.

There is some confusion as to exactly which maps appeared in the original version of the work. Sanudo says in his introductory letter that there are four: a map of the Mediterranean, one 'of sea and land', one of the Holy Land, and one of the land of Egypt.[23] However, the manuscript that is generally believed to be the one handed to Pope John, now Vatican City, Biblioteca Apostolica Vaticana, MS Vat. lat. 2972, contains six maps, showing the Black Sea, the southern half of the Balkan peninsula and the African coast, the Eastern Mediterranean and Arabia, Italy with part of the Dalmatian and French coasts and north Africa, western Europe including Denmark and the British Isles, and a world map. Only two of these correspond to Sanudo's rather vague description of his cartographic offering. Degenhart and Schmitt have suggested that the maps Sanudo describes are those found in the atlas made and signed by Pietro Vesconte in 1320. This manuscript is now also in the Vatican Library (Vatican City, Biblioteca Apostolica Vaticana, MS Pal. lat. 1362a).[24] Five of the maps make up a marine chart of the Mediterranean and Black seas and the British Isles ('map of the Mediterranean'), and the others are a world map ('map of sea and land'), a map of the Holy Land and a map of the Eastern Mediterranean which is part sea chart and part land map ('map of Egypt'). The city maps of Jerusalem and Acre were apparently not worth mentioning. If there was a second copy of Sanudo's book, it appears to have been lost.[25] Nearly identical maps appear in various combinations in the numerous manuscripts of Sanudo's work (see 'Note on the maps' below, pp. 151–2).

For a long time Sanudo was thought to have been the author of his own maps and thus a pioneer in the development of cartography.[26] Since the late nineteenth century the honour has been transferred to Pietro Vesconte, thanks to the work of Konrad Kretschmer, who revealed the identity between Vesconte's productions and the maps in Sanudo's books. Vesconte, who signed some of his works, tells us he is from Genoa, but by 1318 he was working in Venice. His 1311 chart is the oldest signed and dated marine chart that survives from the Middle Ages. Elsewhere, he even leaves us what appears to be a portrait of himself, laying out the structure of a marine chart on a piece of parchment spread out on his drawing table.[27] He appears to have been the inventor of the atlas, a group of maps designed to be seen together. The oldest of these dates from 1313, and by 1321, in his collection of maps for Sanudo, he has put all the maps in his atlas into the same scale. His works date from 1311 to 1325. Either he ceased to be active at this time, or perhaps he was the same man as Perrino Vesconte, who produced a similar atlas in 1327.

Most scholars now accept Vesconte as the maker of Sanudo's maps, but we cannot know the extent of the collaboration between Vesconte and Sanudo from any other source than their works. The close relationship between Sanudo's text and the maps and the careful design of the maps to suit his overall purpose, argue that he must have had significant input into the content, if not the design, of the maps. As for alternative views, Robert Almagià offered the opinion that the original conception of the world map at least was Paolino Minorita's.[28] The essence of his attribution turns on the date 1320 (MCCCXX), the date written in Roman numerals on Vesconte's source atlas (Vatican City, Biblioteca Apostolica Vaticana, MS Pal. lat. 1362a). Since the sheet is torn at this point, Almagià argues that there could have been additional digits on the date. He goes on to say that Paolino's *Satyrica historia* (Vatican City, Biblioteca Apostolica Vaticana, MS Vat. lat. 1960), though mostly dating to from post-1334 (Benedict XIII is included in the list of popes), incorporates a tract, 'De mapa mundi', and a sketch of the world map made before 1320. The text and map are nearly though not entirely congruent.

Paolino's map is a rough and inexpert drawing, which has led to the conclusion that it is a copy of Sanudo/Vesconte's original, but Almagià sees Paolino as the creator of the unusual and new world format, later refined by the professional mapmaker. It is difficult to resolve this question with finality, but the majority of scholars attribute the map to Vesconte. Its many interesting qualities lead one to wish to know more about its ultimate sources.

## THE MAPS IN SANUDO'S *LIBER SECRETORUM*

A world map (Figure 8) appears in the Vesconte atlas of 1320,[29] and in most Sanudo manuscripts. Oriented to the east with the three continents of the inhabited, known world surrounded by a narrow strip of Ocean, it looks at first glance like eleventh- and twelfth-century *mappaemundi*. But if we compare it with its famous predecessor, the Hereford *mappamundi* (c. 1300), some interesting developments are apparent. The Black and Mediterranean sea coasts reflect the geographical forms of the marine chart, rather than the more abstract style employed on the Hereford and other *mappaemundi*. In fact, Vesconte's world map is the first surviving example of the clear blending of the *mappamundi* and marine chart. The oldest surviving marine or portolan chart is the Pisa Chart of *c.* 1290, but it is now believed that such charts were in existence at least one hundred years before that.[30] In addition, Vesconte's world has an open Indian Ocean, which appears as an extension of the Red Sea/Persian Gulf. The south-east coast of Africa curves around to form its southern shore. In this area there are a number of islands, which have not been positively identified, but seem to represent the sources of the Indian spice trade. One island has a forest of pepper trees, another is inhabited by pirates, and a third ('island of Linga, dicitur Kamar') may refer to a river port and island in the Malacca Straits. The important Red Sea ports of Chus and Aden are also shown. On the African coast can be found ginger ('zinziber') and nutmeg ('noçe'). Other interesting features of the map are the Gulf of Guinea in west Africa, a landlocked Caspian Sea, and a peninsular Scandinavia. The Holy Land is not enlarged, unlike the treatment it receives on the Hereford *mappamundi*, but is represented by just a few place names (Syria, Jerusalem). Conventional features of the map include a reference to the stronghold of Gog and Magog in northern Asia and notes on the uninhabitability of the far north and south, but there is no Paradise, which was a staple in thirteenth-century world maps.[31] Vesconte's map appears to owe something to the Arabic tradition, particularly the world maps of the twelfth-century cartographer al-Idrisi, who showed a similar configuration of the Indian Ocean.[32] It seems likely that Sanudo, with his extensive travels in the East, might have seen a copy of al Idrisi's world map and brought it to show Vesconte.

The world map is surrounded by an anonymous descriptive geographical text organised in four parts – treating the three continents and the islands. The shape of the text (with Asia on top and twice the size of the other continents, Europe to the left, Africa to the right) mirrors the configuration of the map.[33] There is little correspondence between the geographical names on the map and those in the text, which is more traditional. For example, the text lists a number of 'tribes' in eastern Europe, long since moved on and converted into settled nations. The anonymous author of the text cites ancient authorities, Isidore (seventh century) and Honorius Augustodunensis (early twelfth century). In addition there are historical and literary references to the adventures of Jason in the Black Sea and to the conquests of Alexander the Great. In the section on islands, only islands in the Mediterranean and North Atlantic are named, not those of the Indian Ocean shown on the map. A few lines below the map, apparently by Sanudo, acknowledge its limitations: 'One must know that a mappa mundi of this type is not drawn so that it shows everything, since this would be impossible.'[34] In a written text such as his book, the author suggests, more detail can come to light.

The world map has little to do with the main mission of Sanudo's book and may be regarded as an ornamental addition which would be pleasing to the learned. Sanudo himself was anxious to be considered erudite and peppered his writings with classical and biblical references. His immediate audience, the papal court at Avignon and subsequently the other courts of Europe, would have appreciated this aspect of his work. The one possible function of the world map, however, was to illustrate the point Sanudo makes about the declining strength of Christianity in the world.[35] He begs his reader to consider what a small space of the earth is inhabited by Christians. In Asia there is only Armenia, and it is constantly under siege. Even in Europe Spain is partly under Saracen rule, while eastern Europe is dominated by schismatic Greeks. Looking at the world map one could see this sorry state of affairs more vividly.

The map of the Eastern Mediterranean (Figure 9), which shows the main theatre of operations for Sanudo's proposed campaign, is a combination of a marine chart and a map of the interior. In some manuscripts (though not in the one illustrated here) it is covered with rhumb lines radiating from compass roses, in the style of the marine chart. Lined up along the southern coast of Asia Minor, and the shores of Palestine and Egypt and the island of Cyprus, is a series of names of ports. On the coast of Palestine these are accompanied by indications of distances in miles. In the interior, much more vaguely indicated, are larger features such as the Tigris and Euphrates rivers and the countries of Mesopotamia, Persia and Chaldea. The Arabian Sea is shown with its two arms, the Red Sea and the Persian Gulf.

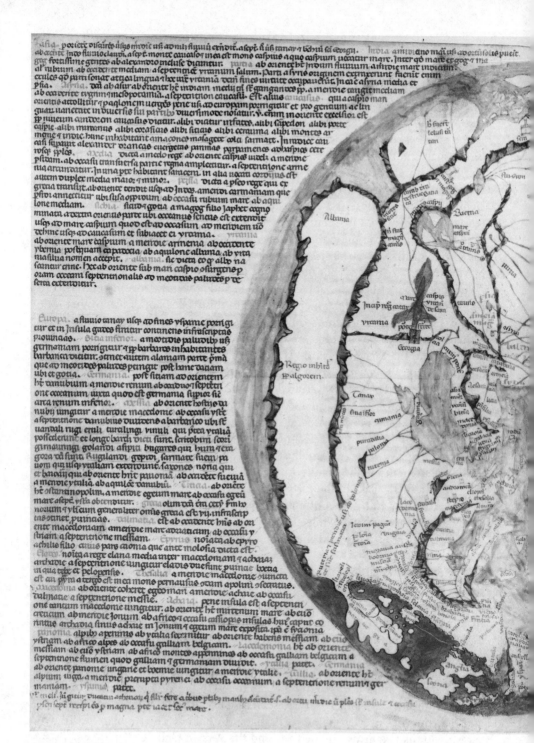

*this page and facing*]
8 World map. The map is orientated to the east with the Indian Ocean on the upper right. Africa is the

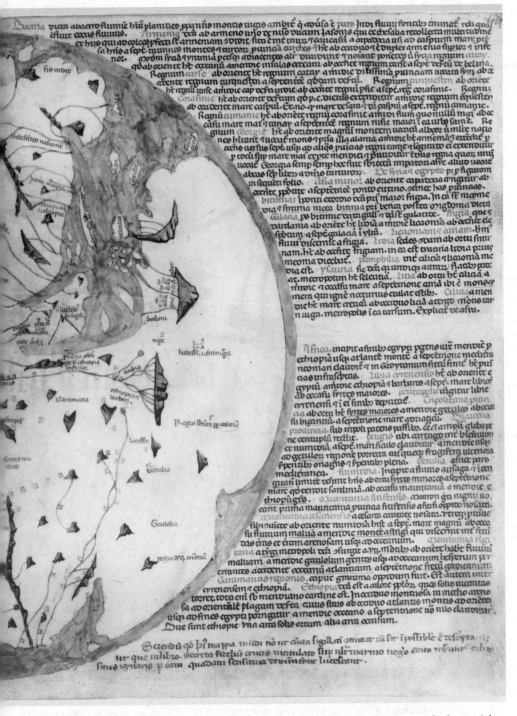

continent which occupies most of the right side of the map. Note the Gulf of Guinea at the lower right. This manuscript has a dedication to Robert VII, Count of Boulogne and Auvergne (r. 1313–24).

*this page and facing*]

9 Eastern Mediterranean. Orientated to the east, this map uses the style of the marine chart to depict the southern coast of Asia Minor, Cyprus, and the coasts of Syria and Egypt. On the Syrian coast the numbers represent distances in miles. At the upper right is the Red Sea and Persian Gulf leading from

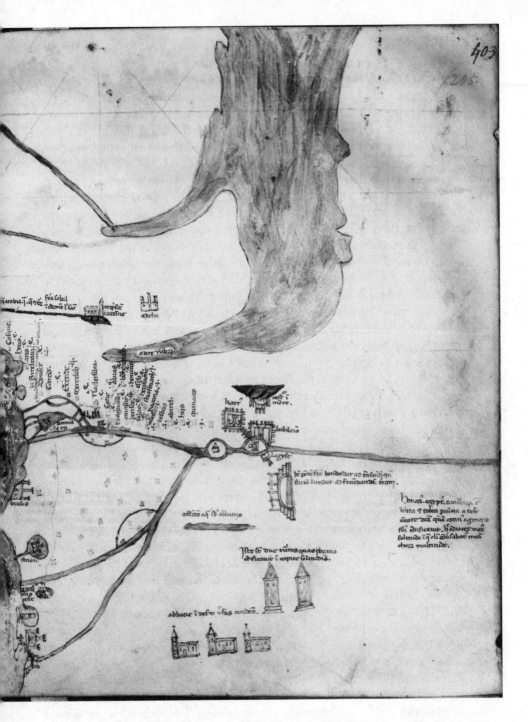

the Arabian Sea. Mecca and the monastery of St Catherine at Sinai may be seen on the Arabian peninsula. The upper half of the map is a vague delineation of the Tigris and Euphrates rivers. On the lower right one can see the configuration of the Nile. Above the river is an itinerary for a land journey from Gaza to Cairo.

The line-up of coastal towns, which is generally quite correct, can also be followed in book II part 4 of the *Liber secretorum*, where Sanudo repeats the same names and sailing distances, adding the specific navigational details which he surely took from a portolan or written set of sailing directions. We have examples of these documents dating back to classical times.[36] They typically include lists of ports, distances and wind directions (and, later, compass directions), as well as notes on sailing hazards, such as large rocks or sandbars. Sanudo's text is derived from a text circulating in Europe since the mid-thirteenth century.[37] He notes: 'Laoycia or Licia has a good harbour with a chain and an entrance on the northwest side, at the opening of which, on the northwest, there is a tower'. He also mentions features which can be seen from a ship, such as: 'From Tyre to the White Cape it is ten miles, sailing south by southwest. This cape is high and above it are very high mountains, which are called Bellinae by the local inhabitants.'[38] This section is devoted to sea travel, whereas in book III, where Sanudo he covers the same area, he describes travel by land. Book III also includes more details of the interior and gives biblical references, which are lacking in the itinerary section of book II. The map was a combination of the two approaches.

Going on to Egypt,[39] Sanudo gives information which would be useful for his invading force, that is, the depth of water in the various branches of the Nile, the extent to which each entrance is fortified and the availability of provisions, such as fruits, grain and fish. On some versions of the map, such as the one reproduced here, are shown not only the configuration of the Nile (up which Sanudo hoped the crusaders would eventually sail), but also a series of towns and villages along two alternative land routes between Gaza and the city of Cairo, with distances indicated. This feature of the map follows the text in book III, part 14, Chapter iii, where Sanudo gives the same information. On some other versions of this map, little boxes are shown in this area, but no names are given.[40]

The most notable features of the map of the Holy Land (Figure 10) are its detail and the rectangular grid which overlies it. The mapmaker has attempted to draw it to scale: he notes that each square of the grid represents one league (or two miles) on a side. There are many references in the text to distances and days' journeys, which are consistent with the distances represented by the squares on the map. The grid lines are also locational and are keyed to book III, part 14, Chapter iii, where Sanudo gives a detailed description of the sites of the Holy Land. 'In row one, square seventy-six' he tells us we will find Petra of the Wilderness or Monreal, and so we do. With the map before us we can (laboriously) follow his verbal description with its added information: in the sixth row, thirteenth square is Sueta 'from whence came Bildad the Shuhite', and in the twelfth row, sixty-seventh space is Massada (Masada) 'an impregnable fortress built by Herod'.[41] Despite its array of scientific certainty, there are many errors of location, some of which are detailed by Lieutenant-Colonel Conder of the Royal Engineers in his prefix to a translation of this part of *Liber secretorum*.[42] Conder notes that the country is too wide on the north in proportion to the south and that the area east of the Jordan is shifted too far to the north. While Pietro Vesconte is usually believed to have been the maker of Sanudo's maps, the Holy Land example makes clear that their collaboration was extremely close, with an almost perfect correspondence between map and text. Since the written description was added to Sanudo's book after its presentation to the Pope, Almagià believes that it was completely based on the map.[43]

Sanudo does not tell us which places he personally visited, and his written work owes much to previous travel writers of the Holy Land, such as Burchard of Mount Sion, whose description of the Holy Land dates from the 1280s.[44] Burchard had attempted a geometric outlay of space, which is often compared with Sanudo. In his work, however, Burchard uses the city of Acre as a starting point and describes a series of sectors radiating out from that city to the north, east and south, giving distances. No map matching Burchard's arrangement of spaces survives, except for a simple sketch in a late manuscript[45] – and following his description is difficult. An interesting precursor to the Sanudo map of Palestine, though it lacks the grid, is found in a late thirteenth-century copy in Florence's Archivio di Stato. It has a similar arrangement of places though not so many names.[46] A similar, even earlier copy of this map, is in the Biblioteca Laurenziana, also in Florence. Paul Harvey calls these maps 'Burchardus maps', because of the similarity of the place names and descriptive phrases used in his text,[47] but, with one exception, they are large, free-standing maps not associated with any text. Röhricht's palaeographical analysis puts one of them a century earlier than Burchard, which seems to imply that, if there is a 'Burchard map', his work was not entirely original.[48]

Another map of Palestine, which can bear comparison with Vesconte/Sanudo's, was made by Matthew Paris, the thirteenth-century chronicler of St Albans Abbey in England. Matthew uses units of a day's journey to establish some sort of scale along the coast and includes many modern names as well as biblical sites (Lot's wife, the ditch where Adam was made). These two early attempts at a spatially accurate geographical representation of the Holy Land suggest that Vesconte/Sanudo may have built on an established tradition.[49] Even though they may not have been entirely original, what is definitely revolutionary about Sanudo is that his maps were not made for Bible study, or even pious pilgrimage, but for practical, strategic uses.

In many manuscripts Sanudo includes a city map of Acre (see Figure 7) as it appeared before its fall. Here we see the elaborate rings of fortifications, including the large Templar tower on the coast, the last to fall, and the so-called Turris Maledicta, whose capture was thought to be the beginning of

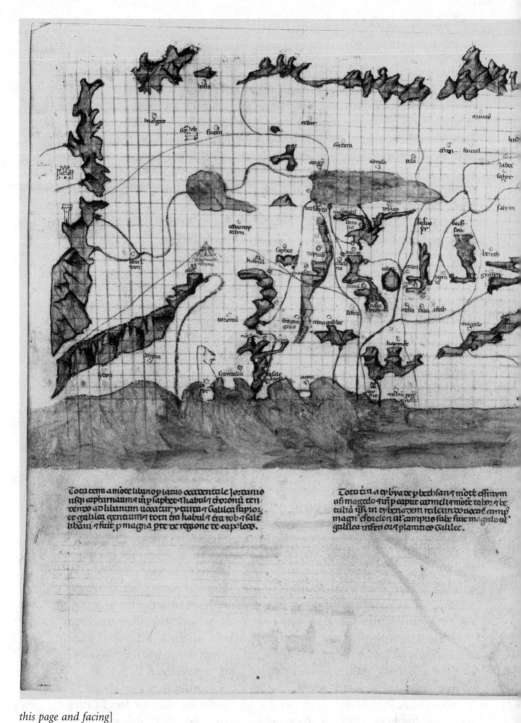

Tota terra a mōte libano plauis ocidentale Jordauis
usqꝫ capharnaum ꝗ in p saphet ꝗ habul ꝗ chorōnu ten
tendo ad libanum uocatur. y cuita ꝗ Galilea suplor
ce galilea gentaium totn tra habul ꝗ tra tob ꝗ sale
libani ꝗ fuit p magna pte de regione te capoloes.

Tota tīn a tybria de p bethsan ꝗ mōtē effraym
usꝗ magedo ꝗui p caput carmeli ꝗ mōte tabor ꝗ ter
culta isꝫ in tyberiadem reducunt ad nos de campl
magn eloreton ul campus sate sue magedo ul
galilea inferi ori ꝗ plammtes Galilee.

*this page and facing*]
**10** Holy Land. Orientated to the east, this map shows the Holy Land from Sidon in the north-west to

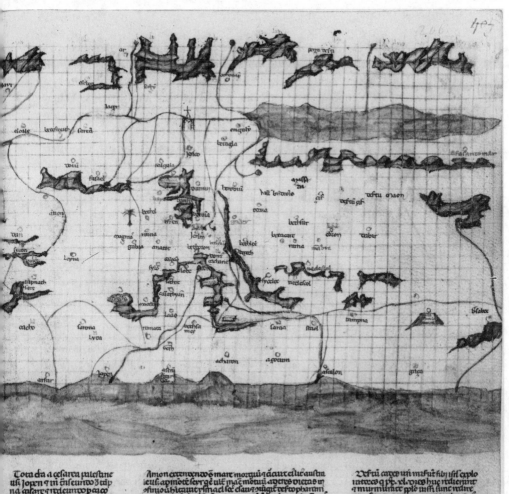

the end. The city is divided into walled sectors with the Venetians occupying the prime real estate near the outer harbour, extending to the small inner harbour, which could be defended with a chain. A war had broken out between the Venetians and the Genoans over this land in 1258. When the Venetians were triumphant, they vented their wrath by tearing down the Genoese tower. This tower, which appears on Matthew Paris's map of Acre, is not on Sanudo's map, as it had vanished by his time.[50] The map shows the churches, the monasteries, the military orders, the arsenal and the office of the patriarch or papal representative in Acre, as well as the sectors controlled by the different nationalities: Pisans, Genoese, Venetians, Germans. Of course Sanudo knew that this world had ceased to exist. Most touchingly, the Gothic doorway of the Church of Sant' Andreas, shown near the harbour, had been dismantled and moved to Cairo, where it served to ornament the tomb of al-Ashraf, the conqueror of Acre. Perhaps Sanudo imagined that after the recovery of the Holy Land, Acre could be restored to its former glory.

The map of Jerusalem is less modern than that of Acre, but still it is the first map to show Jerusalem, accurately reflecting its physical configuration, although it is not drawn to scale. The traditional medieval map of Jerusalem, the *Situs Hiersolymitae*, was circular (though the city itself was not), and highly pictorial (see Figure 5). The various versions sometimes show pilgrims arriving at the city or crusader knights on horseback outside.[51] On Vesconte's map the city is an irregular form. Pictures include a grove of trees for the Mount of Olives, more trees for the Garden of Gethsemane, and the fig tree cursed by Christ, all to the east of the city. Some churches and other buildings are represented pictorially, while the house of the Last Supper shows a long, rectangular table. Places on the map mostly reflect events in the life of Jesus, such as the road Christ rode into Jerusalem, the house of Pilate and the potter's field which was bought with Judas's betrayal money. An unusual feature is the emphasis on the water supply of the city. Eight different water sources are shown, from the torrent of Cedron to the springs of Siloam, Rogel and Gyon. A note at the bottom of the map describes how the water from the lower spring of Gyon was diverted into the city to form the Piscina Interior, where it served as a source of water in time of siege. This information is taken from Burchard's account, which is repeated in Sanudo's text.[52] Although the walls of the city are drawn in, there is no attempt to label the various fortifications and gates. Of course, Jerusalem was of little strategic importance and came rather late in Sanudo's scheme of conquest. In the text Sanudo makes some notes on modern conditions in the city, such as the tower near the Golden Gate 'which the Saracen priests are accustomed to ascend to proclaim the law of Mohammed'.[53] Nothing like this is indicated on the map.

## MARINE CHARTS

Only two of Sanudo's manuscripts include a set of marine charts. These cover the Black Sea, Mediterranean and North Atlantic/North Sea coasts, and are identical with those made on other occasions by Pietro Vesconte. One set appears in the Vatican manuscript (Vatican City, Biblioteca Apostolica Vaticana, MS Vat. lat. 2972), which is thought to have been Sanudo's presentation copy to Pope John XXII. The other is in the British Library manuscript (London, British Library, Additional MS 27376), which has the largest set of maps (nine) of any Sanudo manuscript. In other copies of his work he concentrated on the maps which were most strategically relevant to his project: the maps of the Eastern Mediterranean and the Holy Land and the city plans of Acre and Jerusalem. The world map appears in all but one manuscript, perhaps to set the scene.

Sanudo's maps are not mere flourishes to dress up his books, which are in any case lavishly illustrated and carefully produced, but are intended as tools for his crusaders. All his maps have a sense of *travelled* space, and in his text he frequently gives a sense of motion from place to place, giving direction, distance and, occasionally, features that can be seen. While he admits that a map can never be as detailed as a verbal description, it is clear that a map makes it easier to visualise a region. Employing one of the best-known marine cartographers of his day, he puts the tools of sailors and merchants into the hands of crusaders to enable them to carry out his scheme. His use of maps is the first surviving example of maps being designed for strategic purposes in western Europe since classical times. From a late Roman source, *Epitoma rei militaris* of Vegetius, Sanudo had a reference for the importance of written as well as graphic itineraries in war.[54] Writing about armies on the march, Vegetius said that the general:

> Should have itineraries of all regions in which war is being waged written out in the fullest detail, so that he may learn the distances between places by the number of miles and the quality of roads, and examine short-cuts, by-ways, mountains and rivers, accurately described. Indeed, the more conscientious generals reportedly had itineraries of the provinces in which the emergency occurred not just annotated but illustrated as well, so that they could choose their route when setting out by the visual aspect as well as by mental calculation.[55]

Sanudo used Vegetius as one of his principal sources for battle strategy, frequently quoting his maxims with approval and backing them up with classical and modern examples.

From 1321 until the end of his life in 1343 Sanudo continued to campaign tirelessly for his crusade. He made and sent copies of his proposal to all the leading powers of Europe: King Robert of Naples; the French ambassador Louis of Clermont; King Charles IV of France; King Philip VI of France;

Edward II of England; Bishop Durand of France; William, Count of Hainault; Robert, Count of Boulogne; and other cardinals, bishops, and French nobles.[56] He also carried on a voluminous correspondence, sending letters all over Europe and western Asia, frequently following up with a personal visit. Tyerman calls him a fourteenth-century lobbyist.[57] As circumstances changed, he altered his proposals to suit the times. For example, as the Turkish threat increased, he shifted his animosity from the Byzantine Empire to the Turks, and campaigned for the creation of the anti-Turkish league in the 1330s. He was now even willing to correspond with the Byzantine Emperor, Andronicus Palaeologus, in the face of their common threat. The death of Pope John XXII in 1334 and the outbreak of the Hundred Years' War between France and England brought an end to the flurry of crusading projects of the early fourteenth century, and Sanudo died without ever seeing his plan put fully into effect. Perhaps he died still believing that it could have succeeded, if only it had been tried. In his will he left his books and maps to the Dominican monastic library of St John and St Paul in Venice, with instructions that they should be sent to Rome by the first reliable agent.

If we read his words, it seems as though his motive was primarily religious. Again and again he refers to the fact that the Holy Land had received the 'precious drops of Christ's blood', and thus should be rescued from the clutches of the infidel. His animosity towards the Muslim faith was extreme. He accurately lists some of the chief practices of the faith (prayer five times a day, abstention from pork) and even quotes from the Qur'an, but he mistakenly asserts that Muhammad thought himself to be the Messiah. His main charge against Islam, similar to his hostility to the Greek Orthodox Church, was that Islam enticed people away from the 'true faith', that is, Roman Catholic Christianity.[58] Perhaps only such fanaticism could have kept him going all those years.

If Sanudo's scheme had succeeded, there is no question that Venice would have benefited economically, after the initial losses during the embargo. Sanudo may have had in mind the glory days after the Fourth Crusade, when the Sanudi, as well as other Italians, had ranged about the Eastern Mediterranean, annexing territory at will. But it is not clear that his proposals or all his politicking bore any official stamp from the Venetian Republic. This does not mean there was none, for the Venetian government was notoriously secretive, and Sanudo held a number of official posts in the city. Where his Venetian businessman's character most clearly emerges, however, is in the nature of his proposals with their practical details of finance, equipment and supply. No Venetian trading venture would ever put to sea, as some of the early crusaders had done, buoyed only by their hopes and faith. As for the success of the disorganised First Crusade, Marino put it down to miraculous divine aid.[59] For his crusade he bore in mind that the Lord helps those who help themselves.

The combined resources of the written portolan directions and the graphic geographical representation are his most original contribution to the project. He packs in as much information as he can find about locations and their characteristics, distances, sailing conditions, local resources. The departing expedition could plan their route with precision, reducing the inevitable vagaries of sea travel to a minimum. Sanudo was well aware of the importance of his maps. In his letters to his many powerful correspondents, he frequently mentioned the maps. In a 1332 letter to King Philip VI of France, he wrote:

> Whosoever exercises the leadership of the crusade must wholeheartedly follow the directions as proposed in the *Book of Secrets*. The crusade leader should study and pay close attention to the map of the world, and pay very careful attention to the maps showing Egypt, the Mediterranean and the Holy Land. If these precautions are followed, with the help of God, this venture will come to a victorious conclusion.[60]

### NOTE ON THE MAPS

There are nine surviving manuscripts of Marino Sanudo's *Liber secretorum* which contain maps, out of a total of nineteen. All were made during his lifetime. The maps were doubtless expensive to reproduce. In some of his letters Sanudo says he will send them if requested. It is also possible that the maps became separated from some of these manuscripts.[61]

The manuscripts with maps are the following:

*Brussels, Bibliothèque Royale, MS 9404–5*. Five maps: world, Eastern Mediterranean, Holy Land, Antioch, Jerusalem.

*Brussels, Bibliothèque Royale, MS 9347–8*. Same five maps.

*Florence, Biblioteca Laurenziana, Plut. XXI.23*. Four maps: World, Eastern Mediterranean, Jerusalem, Acre. Maps are unfinished.

*Florence, Biblioteca Riccardiana, MS 237*. Four maps: Eastern Mediterranean, Holy Land, Jerusalem, Acre.

*London, British Library, Additional MS 27376*. Nine maps: four marine charts (Mediterranean, Black Sea, northern Europe including the British Isles), world, Eastern Mediterranean, Holy Land, Jerusalem, Acre.

*Naples, Biblioteca Nazionale, MS V.F. 35*. One map: Eastern Mediterranean.

*Oxford, Bodleian Library, MS Tanner 190*. Five maps: world, Eastern Mediterranean, Holy Land, Jerusalem, Acre.

*Vatican City, Biblioteca Apostolica Vaticana, MS reg. 548*. Five maps: World, Eastern Mediterranean, Holy Land, Jerusalem, Acre.

*Vatican City, Biblioteca Apostolica Vaticana, MS Vat. lat. 2972.* Six maps: world, four marine charts, Eastern Mediterranean.

Some of the same maps appear in the following manuscripts:

*Paris, Bibliothèque Nationale, MS lat. 4939.* This is Paolino Minorita's *Chronologia magna.* Five maps: world, Eastern Mediterranean, Holy Land, Jerusalem, Acre.

*Vatican City, Biblioteca Apostolica Vaticana, MS. Vat. lat. 1960.* Paolino Minorita, *Satyrica historica.* Five Sanudo maps: world, Eastern Mediterranean, Holy Land, Jerusalem, Antioch. This manuscript also includes maps of Italy and Venice.

*Vatican City, Biblioteca Apostolica Vaticana, MS. Pal. lat. 1362a.* Ten maps: world, five marine charts, Holy Land, Jerusalem, Acre. This is Pietro Vesconte's atlas of 1320.

*Venice, Biblioteca Marciana, MS lat. Z. 399.* Paolino Minorita, *Chronologia magna.*

The maps are quite consistent from copy to copy, although a few improvements appear over time, for example, a refinement of the Scandinavian peninsula. All Sanudo's manuscripts date from his lifetime and were clearly presentation copies that he sent to the powerful and influential of Europe.

## NOTES

1 Marino Sanudo Torsello, *Marino Sanutus dictus Torsellus: Liber secretorum fidelium crucis,* in J. Bongars (ed.), *Gesta Dei per Francos,* 2 vols (Hanover: Typis Wechelianis apud heredes Johannis Aubrii, 1611); repr. with introduction by Joshua Prawer (Toronto: University of Toronto Press, 1972), III. 12. xxi and xxii, pp. 231–2. Prawer's edition comes with five of Sanudo's maps, reproduced in colour, but lacks the letters which appear in Bongars's edition. The page numbers are the same.
2 Hans E. Mayer, *The Crusades* (Oxford: Oxford University Press, 1972), p. 273.
3 Steven Runciman, *The Kingdom of Acre and the Later Crusades,* in *History of the Crusades,* 3 vols (Cambridge: Cambridge University Press, 1954), iii, p. 420.
4 Sylvia Schein, *Fideles crucis: The Papacy, the West and the recovery of the Holy Land, 1274–1314* (Oxford: Clarendon Press, 1991), pp. 1 and 73.
5 Available in 58 volumes: Marino Sanuto, *I diarii,* ed. Rinaldo Fulin *et al.,* 58 vols (Venice: F. Visentini, 1879–1903).
6 Sanudo, *Liber secretorum,* Introduction, p. 3.
7 A. Laiou, 'Marino Sanudo Torsello, Byzantium and the Turks: The background to the anti-Turkish league of 1332–34', *Speculum,* 45 (1970), 374.
8 Sanudo, *Liber secretorum,* introduction, p. 3.
9 Frederic C. Lane, *Venice: A Maritime Republic* (Baltimore: Johns Hopkins University Press, 1973), p. 72.
10 David Jacoby, 'L'expansion occidentale dans le Levant: Les Vénitiens à Acre dans le second moitié du treizième siècle', *Journal of Medieval History,* 3 (1977), 245.

11  Christopher J. Tyerman, 'Marino Sanudo Torsello and the last crusade: Lobbying in the fourteenth century', *Transactions of the Royal Historical Society*, 5th series, 32 (1982), 59.

12  The relationship between Paolino Minorita and Sanudo is discussed in Bernhard Degenhart and Annegrit Schmitt, 'Marino Sanudo und Paolino Veneto: Zwei Literaten des 14. Jahrhunderts in ihrer Wirkung auf Buchillustrierung und Kartographie in Venedig, Avignon und Neapel', *Römisches Jahrbuch für Kunstgeschichte*, 14 (1973), 1–137. See also Nathalie Bouloux, *Cultures et savoirs géographiques en Italie au XIVe siècle* (Turnhout: Brepols, 2002), esp. pp. 45–68. This appears to have been their first meeting, and they remained in communication for the rest of their lives. Paolino has been credited with the creation of some of the maps, notably by Roberto Almagià, *Monumenta cartographica Vaticana*, 4 vols, i: *Planisferi, carte nautiche e affini dal secoli XIV al XVII esistenti nella Biblioteca Apostolica Vaticana* (Vatican City: Biblioteca Apostolica Vaticana, 1944), p. 4. It seems most likely, however, that the maps were already in existence before he and Sanudo met.

13  Antony Leopold, *How to Recover the Holy Land: The Crusade Proposals of the Late Thirteenth and Early Fourteenth Centuries* (Aldershot: Ashgate, 2000).

14  Sanudo, *Liber secretorum*, I. 4. vii, pp. 30–1.

15  *Ibid.*, I. 1. iv and vi, pp. 24–5.

16  *Ibid.*, I. 4. i–ii, pp. 27–8.

17  *Ibid.*, I. 3. ii, p. 27.

18  *Ibid.*, I. 4. i–ii, pp. 27–8. Jacoby ('L'Expansion occidentale') calls Acre 'une place de choix' for illegal trade with Egypt.

19  Sanudo, *Liber secretorum*, II. 4. xviii, pp. 72–3.

20  *Ibid.*, II. 1. ii, pp. 35–6.

21  *Ibid.*, II. 4. xix, p. 74.

22  Vesconte's authorship was first established by Konrad Kretschmer, *Die italienischen Portolane des Mittelalters: Ein Beitrag zur Geschichte der Kartographie und Nautik* (Reinheim: Lokay, 1909; repr. Hildesheim: G. Olms, 1962), pp. 113–16.

23  Sanudo, *Liber secretorum*, ed. Prawer, p. 1.

24  Degenhart and Schmitt, 'Marino Sanudo and Paolino Veneto', 68–9.

25  Almagià (*Planisferi*, p. 22) thinks that Vatican City, Biblioteca Apostolica Vaticana, MS Vat. lat. 2971 was the second book. Its maps had been lost as early as the sixteenth century.

26  This view is repeated by A. S. Atiya, *The Crusade in the Later Middle Ages* (London: Butler & Tanner, 1938; repr. New York: Kraus, 1965), p. 123.

27  This little portrait appears in his atlas now in Venice, Museo Civico, Collezione Correr, Port. 28.

28  Almagià, *Planisferi*, pp. 4–7. David Woodward gives the maps to Vesconte ('Medieval mappaemundi', in J. B. Harley and David Woodward (eds), *Cartography in Prehistoric, Ancient, and Medieval Europe and the Mediterranean: The History of Cartography* (in progress), i (Chicago: University of Chicago Press, 1987), pp. 314–15, 333), as does Paul Harvey ('Local and regional cartography in medieval Europe', in Harley and Woodward (eds), *History of Cartography*, i, pp. 473, 475). Dilke believes (without giving his reasons) that Sanudo and not Vesconte developed the grid map (Oswald Dilke and Margaret Dilke, 'Mapping a crusade', *History Today*, 39 (1989), 31–5). Tony Campbell ('Portolan charts', p. 409) refers to Almagià's theory about Paolino. Marcel Destombes, *Mappemondes 1200–1500*, catalogue prepared by the Commission des Cartes Anciennes de L'Union Géographique Internationale (Amsterdam: N. Israel, 1964), also accepts Almagià's theory, but gives no new evidence to support it.

29 This is Vatican City, Biblioteca Apostolica Vaticana, MS Pal. lat. 1362a. Figure 8 shows the world map from Oxford, Bodleian Library, MS Tanner 190, fols 203ᵛ–204.

30 Patrick Gautier Dalché, *Carte marine et portulan au XIIe siècle: Le Liber de existencia riverarium et forma maris nostri Mediterranei (Pise, circa 1200)* (Rome: École Française de Rome, 1995), pp. ix–xi and *passim*.

31 Alessandro Scafi, 'Paradise: The essence of a mappamundi', in P. D. A. Harvey (ed.), *The Hereford World Map: Medieval World Maps and their Context* (London: The British Library, forthcoming).

32 Tadeusz Lewicki, 'Marino Sanudos Mappa Mundi (1321) und die runde Weltkarte von Idrisi (1154)', *Rocznik Orientalistyczny*, 38 (1976), 169–96.

33 Bouloux, *Culture et savoirs géographiques*, pp. 65–6. She thinks Vesconte may have been the author of this text, which appears in his atlas of 1320 (*ibid.*, p. 50).

34 This text appears on most manuscript versions of the world map and is reprinted in Sanudo, *Liber secretorum*, ed. Prawer, p. 285.

35 Sanudo, *Liber secretorum*, I. 5. i, pp. 31–2.

36 Lionel Casson (ed. and trans.), *Periplus maris Erythraei* (Princeton: Princeton University Press, 1989) is an edition of such a portolan. Found in a tenth-century manuscript, it is thought to date from the first century CE.

37 Almagià (*Planisferi*) says it is a fragment of a 1296 portolan, a copy of which is found in the Deutsche Staatsbibliothek, Berlin (MS Hamilton 396), which in turn is based on the 'Compasso da Navegare'). On the latter see Tony Campbell, 'Portolan charts', pp. 382–3.

38 Sanudo, *Liber secretorum*, II. 4. xxv, pp. 85–6.

39 *Ibid.*, p. 87.

40 For example, London, British Library, Additional MS 27376, and Vatican City, Biblioteca Apostolica Vaticana, MS Vat. lat. 2972. In Almagià's opinion, the labelled itinerary which appears on the Oxford map is the original edition ('Edition A'), and the names were omitted in subsequent versions (Almagià, *Planisferi*, p. 19).

41 Sanudo, *Liber secretorum*, III. 14. iii, pp. 275–6.

42 'Note on the maps', in Marino Sanudo, *Secrets for True Crusaders to Help them Recover the Holy Land*, trans. Aubrey Stewart, Palestine Pilgrims' Text Society, 12 (London: Palestine Pilgrims' Text Society, 1896; repr. New York: AMS Press, 1971), pp. ix–xii. Conder has also provided the footnotes on geographical issues which accompany this translation.

43 Almagià, *Planisferi*, p. 19.

44 Burchard of Mount Sion, *Burchard of Mount Sion: A Description of the Holy Land*, trans. Aubrey Stewart, annotated by C. R. Conder, Palestine Pilgrims' Text Society, 12 (London: Palestine Pilgrims' Text Society, 1896; repr. New York: AMS Press, 1971). For a fuller account of the experience of pilgrims to the Holy Land, see Catherine Delano-Smith in Chapter 6 above.

45 Hamburg, Staats- und Universitatsbibliothek, Cod. Geogr. 59, fol. 13 (sixteenth century). The map is a half-circle with Acre in the centre and wind lines radiating from it.

46 The map was discovered by Reinhold Röhricht and is reproduced in his 'Karten und Pläne zur Palästinakunde aus dem 7. bis 16. Jahrhundert', *Zeitschrift des Deutschen Palästina-Vereins*, 14 (1891), 8–11.

47 Paul D. A. Harvey, 'The biblical content of medieval maps of the Holy Land', in Dagmar Unverhau (ed.), *Geschichtsdeutung auf alten Karten: Archäologie und Geschichte*, Wolfenbütteler Forschungen, 101 (Wiesbaden: Harrassowicz, 2003), pp. 56–63.

48 The map bound with Burchard's text is Florence, Biblioteca Laurenziana, Plut. LXXVI, no. 56, fols 97ᵛ–98ʳ (fourteenth century).

49 This map can be found at Oxford, Corpus Christi College, MS 2*. It was originally bound in a Bible. On the map, see Evelyn Edson, 'Matthew Paris's "other" map of Palestine', *Map Collector*, 66:1 (1994), 18–22, and P. D. A. Harvey, 'Matthew Paris's maps of Palestine', in Michael Prestwich, Richard Britnell and Robin Frame (eds), *Thirteenth Century England*, 8 (Woodbridge: Boydell and Brewer, 2001), pp. 165–77.

50 Matthew Paris's map of Acre appears on his two maps of the Holy Land: London, British Library, Royal MS 14. C. VII, fols. 4ᵛ–5ʳ; and Cambridge, Corpus Christi College, MS 16, fols iiᵛ–iiiʳ and MS 26, fols iiiᵛ–ivʳ.

51 Illustrated in P. D. A. Harvey, *Medieval Maps* (London: The British Library, and Toronto: University of Toronto Press, 1991), p. 90.

52 Burchard, *A Description of the Holy Land*, pp. 67–71; Sanudo, *Liber secretorum*, III. 14. ix, pp. 255–6.

53 *Ibid.*, III. 14. lx, p. 256.

54 Sanudo, *Liber secretorum*, III. 15. v and vi, p. 265.

55 Vegetius, *Epitome of Military Science*, ed. and trans. N. P. Milner, Translated Texts for Historians, 16 (Liverpool: Liverpool University Press, 1993), iii. 6, p. 71.

56 Tyerman, 'The last crusade', 65.

57 As indicated by Tyerman's subtitle to 'Marino Sanudo Torsello and the last crusade': 'Lobbying in the fourteenth century'.

58 Sanudo, *Liber secretorum*, III. 3. iv–v, pp. 125–7.

59 *Ibid.*, II. 2. i, p. 37.

60 This letter is reprinted in F. Kunstmann, 'Studien über Marino Sanudo den Älteren mit einem Anhang seiner ungegedruckten Briefen', *Abhandlungen, Phil.-Historische Classe, Königliche Bayerische Akademie der Wissenschaften*, 7 (1853), p. 794. The translation is by Frank Frankfort, 'Marino Sanudo Torsello: A social biography', unpublished PhD dissertation, University of Cincinnati, 1974, p. 223.

61 The sources for information about the manuscripts are Kretschmer, *Die italienischen Portolane des Mittelalters* (pp. 112–16), Prawer in his introduction to Sanudo, *Liber secretorum* (pp. xv–xviii), Almagià, *Planisferi* (pp. 1–23) and Degenhart and Schmitt, 'Marino Sanudo and Paolino Veneto' (pp. 21–6).

# 8

## *The diversity of mankind in* The Book of John Mandeville

**◖◗**

### Suzanne Conklin Akbari

IN A VOLUME devoted to travel literature, *The Book of John Mandeville* occupies a peculiar place: it is, first of all, doubtful that the writer actually travelled into the eastern regions he so memorably describes; moreover, the identity of the author is in doubt, in spite of the fact that he identifies himself as 'I, Iohn Maundevylle, knight . . . born in Englond in the town of Seynt Albones'.[1] What justifies the inclusion of *The Book of John Mandeville* in the present volume is not the validity of the traveller's observations, but rather his readers' enthusiastic reception of this portrait of the world. The work first appeared in the mid-fourteenth century in an Old French version; almost immediately, however, translations into other European vernaculars and Latin began to appear, along with a variety of redactions and adaptations.[2] This extraordinary popularity, which persisted well into the seventeenth century, illustrates the power of the text to capture the imagination and to intersect with a range of cultural currents: exploration, nationalism and even affective piety.

In this chapter I will examine how the author of *The Book of John Mandeville* presents the people located at the fringes of the species of mankind, found particularly in Ethiopia and India – that is, the so-called 'monstrous races' – and the human populations living closest to them. While individual monstrous prodigies were thought to be unique departures from the norm, the monstrous races were seen as a naturally occurring extreme on the spectrum of human bodily diversity. The ideal body, engendered by a perfectly temperate climate, lay at one end of the spectrum, the monstrous races on the other. In between them lay the full span of human diversity, including the fair-skinned people formed by the extremely cold northern climates, and the dark-skinned people generated in the torrid south. The bodily diversity of mankind anatomised and celebrated in medieval texts is certainly different from modern theories of race, formulated in the wake of the Enlightenment; nonetheless, as I will show, medieval systems of categorisation laid the foundations for modern distinctions between those who are 'naturally' slaves and those who are 'naturally' their masters. There is, moreover, a crucial distinction between medieval and modern discourses of bodily diversity: that is, the language of wonder found in medieval texts. The wondrous quality of the human beings located at the margins of the known world served not only to stimulate curiosity but also to create the image of a unified and harmonious world, shaped by the wisdom of its maker. This view of the significance of the wonders of nature had been expressed by Augustine in the early Middle Ages; late medieval accounts, however, such as *The Book of John Mandeville*, highlight the desirability and fascination of these wonders, taking the reader along with the narrator on a kind of virtual journey, in which the wonders of the frontier serve to reflect (and magnify) both the traveller's homeland and the traveller himself.

## MEDIEVAL CATEGORIES AND THE DISCOURSE OF RACE

Well before the seventeenth century, when (according to Foucault) one might to expect to find the systems of categories that make up a discourse, we find in Mandeville's *Book* an elaborate system of classification, one which integrates religious, geographical, linguistic and bodily difference into a carefully balanced and unified 'order of things'. This fact begs two questions. First, can the system of classification found in Mandeville's work and in related texts (such as medieval maps and encyclopaedias) be considered elements of a discourse, in the Foucauldian sense? Second, can the categories of bodily difference (a source of fascination for medieval as for modern readers) be considered equivalent to early modern and Enlightenment definitions of racial difference? Recent attempts to interpret the depiction of bodily difference – of 'race' – in medieval texts have tended to oversimplify a complicated matter. Some readers do not distinguish between difference constituted in terms of religion and difference constituted in terms of race, in part because these categories so frequently overlap in the medieval texts themselves. This has led Andrew Fleck, for example, to suggest that Christian and Muslim difference in Mandeville's *Book* may be read in terms of Abdul JanMohamed's theory of the 'Manichean allegory' of racial difference. (The same strategy is used by Lynn Ramey in her study of Muslims in medieval French literature.)[3] Other readers homogenise the 'Saracen' body found in medieval texts, characterising it exclusively in terms of monstrosity and excess in spite of the fact that a countermodel of the desirable Saracen – the admirable pagan knight and his beautiful sister – is presented as an equally fascinating alternative.[4] The category of bodily difference in medieval texts can be understood only in tandem with other categories of difference, for the construction of these categories is dialectical: one cannot emerge without the presence of the other. Religion, nation and race are intricately intertwined yet distinct modes of categorising the differences between self and other.

As John Block Friedman and David Williams have shown, medieval texts explain the existence of the monstrous races in two different ways: monstrosity is either the consequence of the damnation of outcasts such as Cain or Canaan, or a manifestation of the diversity of nature.[5] The former line of explanation draws upon biblical and theological sources; the latter upon Pliny's *Natural History*, known in a variety of adaptations throughout the Middle Ages. The former depicts racial difference as inborn, the product of genealogical descent; the latter depicts racial difference as the product of environment. *The Book of John Mandeville* features both of these very different explanations of how bodily difference is occasioned, drawing upon a wide range of sources, including the encyclopaedia of Bartholomaeus Anglicus. It is not this combination, however, that sets the *Book* apart from other medieval treatments of the monstrous races. Instead, *The Book of John Mandeville* stands out by virtue of the system of the world which governs the text, so that the monstrous races are incorporated into a finely balanced – although by no means homogeneous – world. Paradoxically, unity appears only within diversity. In order to provide a context for my reading of Mandeville, I will provide a brief account of how bodily diversity – what might be called race – was understood by thirteenth- and fourteenth-century writers.[6]

With the reintroduction of the Aristotelian corpus during the thirteenth century, accompanied by the rich commentaries of Muslim philosophers such as Avicenna and Averroës, the view of natural diversity inherited from Pliny (by way of Solinus and Isidore) was substantially altered. It was no longer sufficient to describe and label the heterogeneous range of monstrous races and fabulous animals; instead, it became necessary to categorise them, to account for how their unusual features had come to be, and to explain how bodily differences such as skin colour shaded off into monstrosity. The importance of climate in determining the natural diversity of mankind is emphasised in both the astronomical and the medical tradition. In the *De sphaera*, a popular treatise based on Ptolemy's cosmology, the astronomer Sacrobosco explains that Ethiopia must be located at the equator, that is, in the torrid zone, 'for [the inhabitants] would not be so black if they were born in the temperate habitable zone' (see Figure 11).[7] His commentators, influenced by Aristotelian explanations of causation and change, elaborated on this passage with enthusiasm. One early thirteenth-century commentator launches into a digression on the physiology of the people of Ethiopia: 'An example of the blackening of Ethiopians is the cooking of golden honey. First it is golden, then reddish, and finally by long cooking it becomes black and bitter, and that which was at first sweet is now salty. And it is just this way all

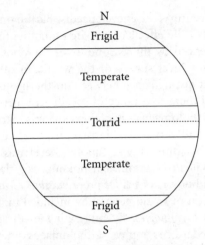

11 Climatic zones (after Macrobius)

over Ethiopia.' Their blood is drawn to the surface of the skin by the great heat, where it becomes 'black and bitter, and in this way it can be clearly seen why the Ethiopian is black'. Several other commentators and glossators include comparable elaborations on this same passage in the *De sphaera*.[8]

Turning from the astronomical tradition to the medical, we find that writers such as Avicenna and Haly Abbas (known in the west through the *Pantegni*, a translation by Constantinus Africanus) similarly explain the blackness of the inhabitants of the southern regions in terms of natural process. In a passage frequently paraphrased by other writers, Constantinus explains that the northern regions near the pole are cold and dry, and therefore the water and air are especially clear, and the bodies of the inhabitants are healthy and of a pleasing colour, the women's bodies soft and the men's strong. The northern climate also has negative consequences, however: the women conceive only rarely (because they are 'frigid') and give birth with difficulty, because of the dryness of the climate, which is reflected in their bodily complexion. The northerners vomit easily, and have a good appetite. The southern regions are precisely the opposite: being hot and humid, the bodies of the inhabitants are black in colour and tend to be phlegmatic. This humour impairs their digestion, and because their natural bodily heat is dissipated through their pores, they are soft-bodied, become drunk easily, and are prone to dysentery and diarrhoea. Southern women conceive more easily, but also miscarry frequently.[9] In the *Pantegni*, as throughout the medical tradition, the ideal body is the temperate body, in which the qualities of heat and cold, moisture and dryness, are in perfect balance.

In the thirteenth century, the encyclopaedist Bartholomaeus Anglicus took up the explanations of the effects of climate on bodies found in the medical tradition and, influenced by the astronomy of Sacrobosco, integrated these views into his geographical survey of the world; in other words, he took medical theories that distinguished between northern and southern bodies in general, and applied them to a range of specific countries. Like *The Book of John Mandeville*, Bartholomaeus's encyclopaedia was extremely popular both in its Latin original and vernacular translations; the late fourteenth-century English translation by John Trevisa (quoted here) was among the earliest titles printed by William Caxton. Bartholomaeus's description of world geography, found in book 15 of his *De proprietatibus rerum*, follows in rough outline the description of world geography included by Isidore of Seville in his seventh-century *Etymologies*. By integrating medical and astronomical theories with the standard geography, Bartholomaeus differs significantly from his contemporary encyclopaedist Vincent of Beauvais, who follows Isidore quite slavishly. Though Vincent is clearly familiar with the theories of Avicenna and Constantinus Africanus, and even quotes the pertinent passages else-where in his vast encyclopaedia,[10] he does not draw out their implications for the geographical sections. In each section of *his* geography, however, Bartholomaeus takes pains to note the correspondence of climate to the bodily nature of the inhabitants of a given land. Those of the northern countries, such as Albania and Almania ('Germany'), for example, are large-bodied and fair-skinned, with blond, straight hair, while those of the southern countries, such as Ethiopia and Libya, have smaller bodies, with dark skin and 'crisp' hair.[11] Monstrosities – that is, bodies 'wondirful and horribilche yshape [formed]'[12] – are found here, in the torrid regions, where excess of heat affects conception and gestation.

Yet Bartholomaeus goes still further, for in his geography he repeatedly emphasises not just the diversity of mankind, but its balance: each climatic extreme, each geographical location, has its opposite, or (one might say) its complement. Thus he writes of Gallia that 'by the dyuersite of heuene, face and colour of men and hertes and witte and quantite of bodyes ben dyuers (different). Therefor Rome gendreth heuy men, Grece light men, Affrica gyleful men, and Fraunce kyndeliche (naturally) fers men and sharpe of witte'.[13] In his entry on Europe, we see the binary opposition that underlies this exuberant diversity:

Yif this partie of the worlde be lesse than Asia, yitte is it pere therto [equal to it] in nombre and noblete of men, for as Plius seithe, he [i.e. the sun] fedeth men that ben more huge in bodie, more stronge in myghte and vertue, more bolde of herte, more faire and semeliche of shappe, thanne men of the cuntres and londes of Asia other of Affrica. For the sonne abideth longe ouer the Affers, men of Affrica, and brennen and wasten humours and maken ham [them] short of body, blacke of face, with crispe here. And for spirites passe outte atte pores that ben open, so they be more cowardes of herte.

An the cuntrarye is of men of the northe londe: for coldenes that is withoute stoppeth the pores and breedeth humours of the bodye maketh men more ful and huge; and coolde that is modir [mother] of whitnesse maketh hem the more white in face and in skynne, and vapoures and spirites ben ysmyten [driven] inwarde and maken hatter withinne and so the more bolde and hardy.[14]

This binary opposition of northern and southern bodies is not particularly innovative: it appears in the *Pantegni*, as well as in the writings of Avicenna and Albertus Magnus. What is unusual, however, is Bartholomaeus's praise of the 'semeliche' bodies of the 'bolde and hardy' northern men, and denigration of the southern men who are 'cowardes of herte'. Here, not the temperate mean but the northern extreme is presented as the beautiful and desirable ideal.

The balanced diversity, based on a series of binary oppositions, found in the encyclopaedia of Bartholomaeus Anglicus is echoed in the heterogeneous world of Mandeville.[15] This world is balanced in every way: astronomically, climatically, in the marvellous symmetry of its wonders and in the variable physiology of its inhabitants. Mandeville remarks that the North Star, which sailors use to navigate, has its corresponding pole star in the southern hemisphere: their star, he says, 'appereth not to us. And this sterre that is toward the north (that we clepen [term] the lodesterre) ne appereth not to hem'.[16] The climatic extremes, too, are balanced, as the author shows in considering those lands that lie at the periphery of the seven climates: that is, India, located in the far south-east, and England, located in the extreme north-west (see Figure 12). He explains that 'The superficialtee of the erthe is departed [divided] in vii parties [sections] for the vii. planetes, and tho parties ben clept clymates. And oure parties be not of the vii. clymates, for thei ben descendynge toward the west betwene high toward the roundness of the world. And there ben the yles of Ynde, and thei ben ayenst [opposite to] vs that ben in the lowe contree, and the vii. clymates strecchen hem environynge the world.'[17] The wonders of the world are balanced as well: Mandeville describes an amazing fruit, found in farthest India. It looks like a melon, but when ripe, it opens to reveal a little lamb inside, so that people eat 'bothe the frut and the best'. But this marvel, far from being an anomaly uniquely found in the exotic Orient, is simply an example of the balanced diversity of nature: Mandeville tells his eastern guides about the barnacle geese, animals that grow on trees in the British Isles. They respond with amazement: 'hereof had thei also gret meruayle [amazement], that summe of hem trowed it were an inpossible thing to be' (Chapter 29).[18] Wonders are found at each end of the climatic extremes, balanced in accord and harmony.

This overarching structure of the world is common to both Bartholomaeus Anglicus's encyclopaedia and Mandeville's *Book*, and is most comprehensively

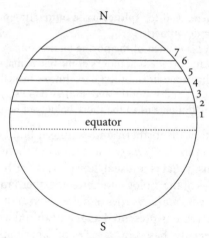

12 The seven climates of the northern
temperate zone (after Ptolemy)

expressed with regard to the populations of the earth. An overall north–
south dichotomy governs the human geography of the world both in
Bartholomaeus's text and in Mandeville's. We have already seen this binary
opposition in Bartholomaeus's encyclopaedia, in his comparison of the robust,
fair men of the north with the weak, dark men of the south. A similar
dichotomy governs Mandeville's *Book*. The first half of the text recounts the
pilgrimage to Jerusalem; beginning with Chapter 16, however, the author
promises to lead his reader in a wide-ranging tour of the lands lying to the
east of Jerusalem, declaring, 'Now is tyme yif it lyke you for to telle you of
the marches and iles and dyuerse bestes and of dyuerse folk beyond theise
marches'.[19] This chapter and the following one use the north–south binary,
familiar from Bartholomaeus, to give an overall shape to the world: in Chapter
16, Mandeville contrasts the land of Albania, where 'the folk ben whitere . . .
than in other marches', with Libya, where there is 'gret hete of the sonne'. In
the following chapter, Mandeville juxtaposes Amazonia, in the far north,
with Ethiopia, where the people are 'blake' of skin, become 'lyghtly dronken
and han [have] but litille appetyt to mete. And thei han comounly the flux of
the wombe [intestines]' (Chapters 16, 17).[20] Mandeville's description of the
inhabitants of Libya and Ethiopia corresponds to medical accounts of typical
southern physiology (as described in the works of Constantinus Africanus,
Avicenna and Albertus Magnus), but is applied to specific countries, following
the precedent set by Bartholomaeus Anglicus.

Climate governs not only the form and physiology of the body, but the
behavioural predispositions of the nation. Mandeville makes this clear using

another binary opposition, this time contrasting the men of India, located in the first climate of the far south-east, with those of England, in the seventh climate of the far north-west:

> Men of Ynde han this condicoun of kynde, that thei neuere gon [go] out of here owne contree, and therfore is ther gret multitude of peple. But thei ben not sterynge ne mevable [lit. movable] because that thei ben in the first clymat, that is of Saturne; and Saturne is slough and litille mevynge . . . And for because that Saturne is of so late sterynge [stirring], therfore the folk of that contree that ben vnder his clymat han of kynde no wille for to meve ne stere to seche straunge places.
>
> And in oure contrey is alle the contrarie, for wee ben in the seventhe clymat that is of the mone, and the mone is of lyghtly mevynge [very readily mobile] . . . And for that skylle it yeueth [gives] vs wille of kynde [by nature] for to meve lyghtly and for to go dyuerse weyes and to sechen [seek] strange thinges and other dyuersitees of the world, for the mone envyrouneth the erthe more hastyly [circles . . . more rapidly] than ony other planete (Chapter 18).[21]

Ordinarily, both extremes of behaviour – one sluggish, one errant – would be undesirable. This can be seen in Henry Daniel's presentation of the same climatic categories, where those in the climate governed by Saturn are 'dry and malicious and unwys', while those in the climate governed by the 'unstedfast' moon 'nevermare wyll be rewled'.[22] In Mandeville's text, however, the desire 'to go dyuerse weyes' is a virtue, at least in the eyes of the narrator, who leads his readers on a vicarious tour of the world, urging them to seek out and discover for themselves 'many mo dyuersitees of many wondirfulle thinges thanne I make mencoun of' (Chapter 34).[23]

The binary oppositions that make up the marvellous diversity of the world are, paradoxically, evidence of its fundamental harmony, as illustrated by Bartholomaeus's description of unity in diversity as a kind of natural music:

> The world is made of many thingis compowned and contrariouse, and yit in itsilf it is one. The worlde is one in noumbre and tale and nought many worldes . . . The worlde of the whiche we speketh at this tyme is not diuers in itsilf nothir departid in substaunce, though contrariousnesse be founde in parties therof, touchinge contrariousnesse of the qualitees. For the worlde hath most nedeful acord ['harmonia'] al itsilf, and as it were acorde of musik . . . Herof it folewith that the world is wondirful bicause of chaunginge therof . . . Nothing in the schappe of the worlde is so vile nothir so lowe nothir partykel, in the whiche schinyth noght praysinge of God in mater and in vertu and in schap. For in the mater and schappe of the worlde is some difference, but that is with acorde and most pees.[24]

Mandeville echoes this sentiment, applying it particularly to the diversity of mankind: describing how the inhabitants of the torrid climates in India find relief from the 'gret hete' by walking about stark naked, he remarks that this apparently 'foul' sight is actually beautiful, for 'nothing is foul that is of kyndely nature' (Chapter 20).[25] It is important, however, to stress that while this view of the harmonious diversity of mankind may seem ideal and even utopian, it contains within it the elements of an intellectual system, based on the relationship of climate to physiology, that could be used to justify the subjugation of peoples and would be used, eventually, as part of the justification for the institution of slavery. As early as the sixteenth century, the philosopher Jean Bodin suggested that the principles of political admini-stration should be tailored to match the predisposition of different national groups. That is, forms of government must vary depending upon the tractability of each national group, whose behavioural characteristics were in turn determined by their climate; here, Bodin uses Aristotelian notions concerning the role of climate in human development and applies them pragmatically to the question of how to govern most effectively.[26] By the late sixteenth and early seventeenth centuries, as Joyce Chaplin has shown, Aristotelian climatic theories were applied to the native populations of North America. These so-called 'Indians' were, supposedly, identical to the Indians in India: they tended by virtue of their climate to be prone to disease, easily drunk (like the Ethiopians) and generally debauched. Their extermination in the wake of European settlement was thus rationalised as biological destiny.[27] Finally, climatic theory was used to explain the suitability of Africans for slavery, until climate-based explanations of their 'natural' inferiority were supplanted, during the eighteenth century, by theories based primarily on the role of heredity.[28]

In *The Book of John Mandeville*, bodily diversity is accounted for in terms of both heredity and climatic influence; the latter cause, however, is pre-dominant. The rise of the 'monstrous races' is, on the one hand, explained as the consequence of the curse placed by Noah on the descendants of Ham following the Great Deluge; their monstrous features, on the other hand, are *also* explained as the natural consequence of the climatic extremes found in Ethiopia and India. In each land described, climate is adduced as the cause of the physiology of the inhabitants. This is especially well illustrated in Mandeville's account of the land of the Pygmies, where the people are all only a few spans in height; this is appropriate to their climate. Curiously, however, when men of normal stature come to live there, their offspring are also of diminutive stature, like the Pygmies. The reason for this, says Mandeville, is that 'the nature of the lond is such' (Chapter 22).[29] Here, climate governs the physiology not only of the native inhabitants, but of those who merely pass through. This would suggest that the effects of climate are mutable: in other words, that the bodily diversity of mankind is not essential, but rather subject to variation.

In this, Mandeville resembles Albertus Magnus, who in his *De natura loci* suggests that if Ethiopians were removed from the first climate to the fourth or fifth climate (that is, to more temperate climates: see Figure 12), within a few generations they would be altered: their offspring would have white skin and all the other attributes of the northern climates.[30] Yet Albertus is unusual in his strict application of Aristotelian theory to the description of human physiology; more common is a composite of climatic theory and genealogical descent. This can be seen, for example, in Bartholomaeus Anglicus, who generally adheres to a climate-based theory of human diversity; in his entry on 'Pictavia', however, he inserts heredity into his analysis of the inhabitants. Their qualities are a peculiar combination of what might be found in more northern and more southern climates; Bartholomaeus explains, however, that this is 'no wondir', for the men of Pictavia are of mixed descent, a combination of 'Pictes' and 'Frenshe men'. They have the qualities of each nation, qualities which were first formed by 'kynde of clymes' and subsequently combined through heredity.[31] Here, two seemingly mutual exclusive theories of human diversity – environment and heredity – are yoked together.

The same is true of Mandeville's *Book*, where the diversity of mankind is accounted for not only through the natural operation of the climates, but also through genealogical descent. In keeping with a long tradition, Mandeville attributes the rise of the monstrous races to the descent from Ham, the accursed son of Noah:

> The fendes of Helle camen many tymes and leyen with the wommen of his [that is, Ham's] generacoun and engendred on hem dyuerse folk, as monstres and folk disfigured, summe withouten hedes, summe with grete eres [ears], summe with on [one] eye, summe geauntes, sum with hors feet, and many other of dyuerse schapp ayenst kynde. And of that generacoun of Cham ben comen the paynemes and dyuerse folk that ben in yles of the see be all Ynde (Chapter 24).[32]

In this text, environment and heredity are yoked uneasily together to explain the genesis of the monstrous races, the 'dyuerse folk' located at the margins of the world. They are deformed and darkened owing to their descent from Ham; but they are also deformed and darkened owing to their genesis in the torrid climates. This inconsistent rationalisation is similar to the incompletely theorised notion of race characteristic in pre-eighteenth-century accounts of racial difference.

It is now possible to return to the two questions with which we began. First, can the account of the bodily diversity of mankind found in texts such as Mandeville's *Book* and the encyclopaedia of Bartholomaeus Anglicus be considered constitutive elements in a pre-modern discourse of race? If by a discourse we mean a system of naming and categorisation, which specifies what is normal and beautiful in contradistinction to what is pathological and ugly, then we certainly have a discourse manifest in these medieval texts.[33] For Bartholomaeus, the harmonious diversity of nature includes both the strong and 'semeliche' bodies of northerners and the weak bodies, prone to illness, of southerners. For Mandeville, the wanderlust of the English, born in the climate of the moon, is clearly superior to the inertia of the Indians, born in the climate of Saturn. But what about the second question? Can medieval categories of bodily difference be considered equivalent to early modern and Enlightenment definitions of race? The answer, again, is yes; for before the eighteenth century, when theories of race based on the role of heredity came to predominate, writers produced climate-based explanations of the causes of bodily diversity that bear a close resemblance to those found in thirteenth- and fourteenth-century texts.[34] From the thirteenth century to the late seventeenth century, we find heredity and environment variously and inconsistently identified as the causes of bodily diversity; by the eighteenth century, however, we find a conception of bodily diversity that sees physical and behavioural differences as essential, fixed and immutable – rooted in the very existence of the individual. Historians such as William Evans have therefore been wrong to claim that the integration of climate models with Noachid genealogy as the justification for enslaving black Africans emerges only in the fifteenth century, adapted by the Portuguese from Muslim attitudes toward non-Muslim African nations, the so-called 'Banu Ham' or 'sons of Ham'.[35] On the contrary, well before the period of the European slave trade in Africa, a system of knowledge had been developed which would facilitate and ra-tionalise the process to come. In this case at least, the discourse of race came to exist before the exercise of power in the colonial setting.

### WONDERS OF NATURE AND THE WONDERFUL SELF

Until this point, we have been concerned with the similarities between modern and medieval discourses of race; it is now time to focus on a profound difference between the two, that is, the language of wonder central to medieval presentations of bodily diversity. As Lorraine Daston and Katherine Park have shown, the experience of wonder can be subdivided into several aspects, including not only the sense of amazement caused by an apparent violation of the laws of nature, but also the disturbing sense of stubborn frustration that accompanies the failure to resolve a conundrum. In general, wonder appears at the moment when the attempt to rationalise, to participate in and thus help to generate a unifying discourse fails: as Daston and Park put it, 'To register wonder was to register a breached boundary, a classification subverted'.[36] In *The Book of John Mandeville*, this experience takes place above all in India, where the marvellous diversity encountered there is progressively assimilated into an overarching system, only to overflow finlly the boundaries of the discourse that seeks to contain it. The regenerative multiplicity of India produces, as its mirror image, the notion of an English homeland that is at once unified and, like the traveller himself, dominant over the world extended before it.

There are, moreover, other distinctions to be made in the medieval experience of wonder. As Daston and Park point out, individual monstrous births (or 'prodigies') were clearly distinguished from the monstrous races: the former were a unique and destabilising violation of the laws of nature, while the latter were manifestations of the magnificent diversity of the created world.[37] This distinction can be compared to that made by the medieval encyclopaedist Gossouin, who distinguishes between eclipses of the sun which 'comen by nature' and those caused directly by God, who 'may all thinge chaunge and deffete at is playsir'.[38] Like the supernatural eclipse at the moment of the Crucifixion, the monstrous prodigy was a sign of divine intervention in the natural order. The medieval understanding of monstrosity is further illuminated by the distinction between 'mirabilia', things which cause wonder simply because they are not understood, and 'miracula', things which are actually contrary to or beyond nature. As Caroline Bynum points out, that which initially seems to be a 'miraculum' may, on closer inspection, prove to be rationally explicable, rather than a violation of the laws of nature.[39] Finally, a distinction must be drawn between what might be termed the 'naive' and the 'knowing' sense of wonder: that is, between the sense of amazement experienced upon encountering a phenomenon that, on first inspection, seems to defy the dictates of nature, and the subsequent amazement experienced when that phenomenon is revealed to be simply a manifestation of the orderly processes of nature, comprehended on a larger scale. This last distinction is crucial to *The Book of John Mandeville*, where the presence of a variety of monstrous races and marvellous phenomena generates in the narrator (and in the reader) a naive sense of wonder. That sense of naive wonder is widened by the discovery that a rule which should normally hold true appears to be violated in nature. Such discoveries extend beyond the experience of observing the monstrous races; they occur, for example, when the animal or plant life of a given location does not correspond to what that territory ought to produce, according to the predictions of the natural philosophers. Finally, an additional level of wonder – what might be termed 'knowing' wonder – is experienced when the naive sense of wonder is replaced as a result of the discovery that the apparent violation of nature's laws is, in fact, part of the orderly workings of nature. This experience is akin to the wonder engendered by 'mirabilia' as described by Bynum, with the difference that the experience is not a humbling one, as the traveller witnesses the power of God, but an exalting one, as the traveller inhabits an almost divine perspective, surveying the world spread out before him.

These different senses of wonder can be illustrated in Mandeville's *Book*. To begin with, the wonder generated by the 'mirabilia', which testifies to the power of God, is encountered early in the narrative, when the narrator relates how, during his peregrinations in Egypt, he heard tell of a great marvel. A hermit encountered a 'monstre' having the body of a man above the navel, and the body of a goat below. The translator of the Middle English version found in the Cotton manuscript glosses the passage as follows: 'that is to seyne [say], a monstre is a thing disformed ayen kynde [contrary to the nature] bothe of man or of best or of ony thing elles and that is cleped a monstre'. Because it is 'ayen kynde', that is, unnatural, a monster offers a glimpse into the enigmatic workings of nature; it is, as it were, a tear in the fabric of creation. This definition of monstrosity is fundamentally Augustinian, as can be seen in the subsequent fate of the monster: as the redactor of the Cotton manuscript goes on to relate, 'the monster . . . besoughte [begged] the heremyte that he wolde preye God for him, the whiche that [he who] cam from Heuene for to sauen [save] alle mankynde, and was born of a mayden, and suffred passioun and deth, as wee wel knowen, be [by] whom wee lyuen and ben [exist]. And yit [still] is the hede with the ii. hornes of that monstre at Alisandre [Alexandria] for a merueyle' (Chapter 7).[40] The body of the beast becomes a devotional object, its deformity a testament to the omnipotence of the divine maker, who can violate the laws of nature at will.

The monstrous races described in the later parts of Mandeville's *Book*, remarkable for the sheer number of their kinds as well as in strangeness of their features, similarly testify to the omnipotence of the God who made them; they differ, however, from the goat-man encountered by the hermit in Egypt in that they are not singular departures from normal human development. On the contrary, their monstrosity is the natural consequence of their location, for their bodies (like those of the white-skinned inhabitants of northern Europe, and the dark-skinned bodies of the Ethiopians) are shaped by their environment, where the overabundance of heat causes predictable defects in conception and gestation. Climate produces bodily diversity, ranging from the monstrous races at the fringes of the known world to those races found at the extreme ranges of the habitable zone, whose bodies are less dramatically altered by the effects of heat and cold. As Bartholomaeus Anglicus puts it, in keeping with medieval medical theory, 'in the north lond ben men hiye of stature and faire of shappe; by coldenesse of the owtwarde ayer the pores ben stopped and the kynde hete is holde [retained] withynne, and by vertue thereof the stature is hoge [huge] and the shappe of body faire and semely. And . . . men of the south lond ben contrarie to men of the north londe in stature and in shappe'.[41] Not just men, but animals of the north are naturally large in size and white in colour: in northern countries like Albania and Almania, therefore, the land is populated with 'huge' dogs and 'huge' fair-skinned men,[42] while southern countries like Ethiopia and Libya have dark inhabitants, small in stature, with both men and beasts 'wondirful and horribleche yshape [formed]'.[43]

India, however, is even more wonderful than these torrid regions of Libya and Ethiopia, for it contains not only those monstrous races whose bodies are 'wonderliche yshape', along with 'beestes wondirliche yshape', but also another kind of wonderful sight: it contains men of 'grete stature', men whose appearance would be perfectly normal in the colder climes of the north, but which is dramatically out of place in the deep south. 'Huge beestes' and 'grete houndes' are found not in the far north, as climatic theory would dictate, but 'in longe space toward Ethiopia'.[44] It is natural to find 'gret houndes' in chilly Albania;[45] the 'grete houndes' found in steamy India, however, are dramatically out of place. In *The Book of John Mandeville*, this marvellous phenomenon is amplified still more, for the author describes India as a land that contains men and beasts extraordinary owing not only to their unnatural stature, but to their white colour: in spite of the extreme heat, the narrator finds in India 'huge' snails, 'gret white wormes', and 'lyouns alle white and als grete as oxen' (Chapter 21).[46] In Bartholomaeus's account of India and, still more, in Mandeville's account, the experience of wonder is occasioned precisely by the fact that the climatic model is violated; this is quite different from the experience of wonder occasioned by the sight of the monstrous races, for there the initial sense of wonder (generated by the apparent violation of natural order) is replaced by an intellectual understanding of how climatic extremes naturally give rise to monstrosity. The wonder occasioned by the normal-seeming inhabitants of the extreme climate of India is, conversely, not followed by rational resolution; it is an open-ended response to a marvel which remains inexplicable.

Mandeville's depiction of the fair-skinned inhabitants of India has yet another purpose: that is, to characterise India as at once an extreme aspect of the world and a microcosm of it. This can be seen in his lengthy description of the inhabitants of India, who are 'alle pale. And the men han thynne berdes and fewe heres, but thei ben longe'. The straight hair of the inhabitants, like their fair skin, violates the climatic norm according to which those dwelling under the greatest heat of the sun have dark skin and 'crisp' hair. Mandeville goes on, following the account in the *Relatio* by the Franciscan friar Odoric of Pordenone, completed in 1330, to write that 'In that lond ben many fairere wommen than in ony other contree beyonde the see'; he departs from Odoric to add, 'therfore men clepen that lond Albanye because that the folk ben white' (Chapter 22).[47] This is extraordinary: Mandeville has taken the convention, found in the encyclopaedic tradition, of naming northern lands 'Albania' owing to 'the [white] coloure of men',[48] and applied it to its direct opposite, the torrid south-eastern region.[49] In so doing, he constructs an image of India which is not only diverse and multiple, but also self-sufficient, a little world unto itself.

By creating an image of India as microcosm, Mandeville also creates a counter-image of England, a land which he depicts as the reciprocal or 'contrarie' of India in several different places in his *Book*. We have earlier noted the opposition of India, where the inert inhabitants of the first climate stay put (in imitation of Saturn), to its 'contrarie', England, where the lively inhabitants of the seventh climate love to wander and explore (in imitation of the moon). Mandeville reinforces this opposition in his discussion of the geographical position of England relative to Prester John's Land, the most plenteous and lush location in all of India. Following a common tradition found in the encyclopaedias and on many *mappaemundi*, Mandeville states that Jerusalem is the centre of the world, while England and Prester John's Land are equidistant from it: 'For our londe is in the lowe partie of the erthe toward the west, and the lond of Prestre Iohn is the lowe partie of the erthe toward the est and han [have] there the day whan wee haue the nyght, and also high to the contrarie thei han the nyght whan wee han the day' (Chapter 20).[50] Like two weights placed on either side of a fulcrum, the 'contraries' of England and Prester John's Land balance one another, and contribute to the perfect symmetry of nature. This is the final sense of wonder experienced in the *Book*, a 'knowing' wonder which exalts the traveller who can see the whole world at once, and whose place in the world is correspondingly magnified.

By characterising India as a microcosm of the whole world, Mandeville is necessarily making a statement about the nature of England: it too is a 'little world', sufficient unto itself. As the 'contrarie' of India, however, it is not a territory to be explored and claimed by others, but a seed-bed for generations of explorers who will set out to wander the world, to explore and exercise dominion. This view of the special role of England, while developed to a new level by Mandeville, is not without precedent in the writings of the encyclopaedists and astronomers. Bartholomaeus Anglicus, for example, uses his entry on 'Anglia' as an opportunity to propagandise on behalf of his homeland. England's name is 'ab angulo dictam', that is, 'a londe sette in the eende or a cornere ['angulo'] of the worlde'; but then Bartholomaeus goes on to praise England as the most fertile and fruitful corner of the world ('angulus orbis').[51] In one of his rare interventions while translating Bartholomaeus, John of Trevisa expands upon his original by explaining that, if England is a corner, it is 'the plenteuouseste corner of the world, ful ryche a londe that unnethe it nedeth helpe of any londe, and everyche lond nedeth helpe of Inglonde'.[52] A similarly gratuitous encomium of England appears in Robertus Anglicus's thirteenth-century commentary on the *De sphaera* of Sacrobosco: after noting Sacrobosco's observation that England lies at the margin of the seventh climate, Robertus writes a lengthy and poetic passage asserting that England is a land of 'unfailing fertility . . . fecund in every kind of metal', where 'varied crops spring in their season from the rich glebe'. There, 'grass grows for the animals and flowers of varied colours distribute honey to the roving bees' ('indeficienti fertilitate ... omni enim genere metalli fecunda'; 'animalium pascibus gramina conveniunt et advolantibus apibus flores diversorum colorum mella distribuunt').[53] *The Book of John Mandeville* is thus one in a sequence of writings which claim to offer a scientific, empirical view of the natural world, but which include at the heart of this supposedly objective picture a loving portrait of the writer's own nation.

These texts participate in a dramatic paradigm shift which took place during the later Middle Ages. In the categorising of peoples, monstrosity and normality had long been defined as opposite terms on a continuous spectrum: monstrous races were at one end, 'normal' people at the other end, with the weak, darkened southerners and the savage, pale northerners located along the continuum. Here, the region of normality, as it were, was located in the central temperate climates. By the thirteenth century, however, when Bartholomaeus Anglicus wrote his encyclopaedia, a new value was assigned to the northerly climates, especially to that north-west 'corner' ['angulo'] inhabited by the English. During the fourteenth century, this paradigm shift was completed, as a series of texts, including *The Book of John Mandeville*, redefined the region of normality, moving it from the temperate fourth climate to the north-western extreme of the seventh climate. Instead of a binary opposition of north and south, a new opposition of north–west and south–east was created, with this new 'Orient' conveying many of the properties formerly associated with the south (dry, hot terrain, with cowardly and morally lax inhabitants). Thus in Gower's *Confessio amantis*, for example, we find a description of how desert lands are located 'in occident as for the chele [cold], / in orient as for the hete'.[54] This new paradigm is Anglo-centric: though it appears in texts not written in English (Anglo-Norman French in the case of Mandeville, Latin in the case of Bartholomaeus Anglicus and Robertus Anglicus), all of these include explicit accounts of the 'natural' superiority of the territory of England and the people who inhabit it.[55]

Finally, the balanced cosmography essential to *The Book of John Mandeville* places the narrator himself at a peculiar vantage point: when he describes the overall shape of the world, in which 'alle the parties of see and of lond han here appositees habitables or trepassables [traversable] and yles of this half and beyond half' (Chapter 20),[56] he inhabits a position outside the world itself, seeing (as it were) from a God's-eye view. At other moments in *The Book*, however, he is clearly immersed in the world he experiences, side-by-side those he meets and with whom he converses. This traveller is at once intimately involved in the foreign lands he passes through and starkly outside them, at a vantage point far away. His claim to tell the truth is based both on objective, intellectual authority and personal, eyewitness experience. *The Book of John Mandeville* thus illustrates the double perspective of the traveller, who is both just beside the people, places and things he encounters, and also far away from them, surveying the world at arm's length.

## NOTES

An earlier version of the first part of this chapter was presented at the International Congress for Medieval Studies, Kalamazoo, MI, 2–5 May 2002. Thanks are due to the session organiser, Maura Nolan, and the audience members there, as well as to E. Ruth Harvey and Richard Raiswell, who read and commented on the complete essay.

1 John Mandeville [Jean de Mandeville], *Le livre des merveilles du monde*, ed. Christiane Deluz, Sources d'histoire médiévale, 31 (Paris: CNRS, 2000), p. 92 (prologue); *idem*, *Mandeville's Travels*, ed. Michael C. Seymour (Oxford: Clarendon Press, 1967), p. 3 (edited from London, British Library, MS Cotton Titus C. xvi). In the interest of concision, quotations in this chapter are from the Middle English text. For the reader's convenience, however, references to text quoted in the chapter are supplied both from Deluz's edition of the Anglo-Norman text (*Livre des merveilles*), and from Seymour's edition of the Middle English text: the page number in Deluz's edition is cited first, followed by the page number in Seymour's edition. For a useful assessment of the ongoing debate regarding the identity of the author and the extent of his travels, see Deluz's introduction to *Livre des merveilles*, pp. 7–14.

2 For a survey of the versions, see Deluz's introduction to *Livre des merveilles*, pp. 28–36; Iain Macleod Higgins, *Writing East: The 'Travels' of Sir John Mandeville* (Philadelphia: University of Pennsylvania Press, 1997), pp. 20–5; Michael C. Seymour, *Sir John Mandeville*, Authors of the Middle Ages, 1 (Aldershot: Variorum, 1993), pp. 37–49.

3 Andrew Fleck, 'Here, there, and in between: Representing difference in the *Travels* of Sir John Mandeville', *Studies in Philology*, 97 (2000), 390, 398; Lynn Tarte Ramey, *Christian, Saracen, and Genre in Medieval French Literature* (London: Routledge, 2001), pp. 11–12.

4 Jeffrey Jerome Cohen, 'On Saracen enjoyment: Some fantasies of race in late medieval France and England', *Journal of Medieval and Early Modern Studies*, 31 (2001), 119–21.

5 John Block Friedman, *The Monstrous Races in Medieval Art and Thought* (Cambridge, MA: Harvard University Press, 1981); David Williams, *Deformed Discourse: The Function of the Monster in Mediaeval Thought and Literature* (Montreal and Kingston: McGill-Queen's University Press, 1996).

6 On the merits of understanding the presentation of bodily diversity in medieval texts in terms of 'race', see Thomas Hahn's introductory essay 'The difference the Middle Ages makes: Color and race before the modern world' in the special issue of the *Journal of Medieval and Early Modern Studies*, 31 (2001), ed. Thomas Hahn, 1–37.

7 Lynn Thorndike, *The Sphere of Sacrobosco and its Commentators* (Chicago: University of Chicago Press, 1949), pp. 107, 137. For a survey of classical and medieval schemas dividing the earth into climates, see Ernst Honigmann, *Die sieben Klimata und die Poleis episemoi: Eine Untersuchung zur Geschichte der Geographie und Astrologie im Altertum und Mittelalter* (Heidelberg: Carl Winter, 1929).

8 The commentary quoted is possibly by Michael Scot; see Thorndyke, *The Sphere of Sacrobosco*, p. 334 (Latin text; trans. mine). Commentaries with comparable elaborations on the Ethiopians include the thirteenth-century anonymous commentary in Cambridge, Gonville and Caius MS 137, fol. 46b (Thorndyke, *The Sphere of Sacrobosco*,

p. 461); another anonymous commentary preserved in two thirteenth-century manuscripts, Oxford, Bodleian Library, Canon Misc. MS 161 and Princeton University Library, Garrett MS 99 (Thorndyke, *The* Sphere *of Sacrobosco*, p. 439); and the fifteenth-century commentary by John de Fundis (Thorndyke, *The* Sphere *of Sacrobosco*, p. 50).

9  Constantinus Africanus, *Pantegni*, lib. 5, cap. 9 ('De mutatione aeris propter regiones'); in *Omnia opera Ysaac* (Lyons: s.n., 1515), fols 19ᵛ–20ʳ (second foliation). It should be noted that medical tradition varies with regard to whether the northern climate is essentially dry (as in the *Pantegni*) or moist (as in Avicenna's *Liber canonis*).

10  Vincent of Beauvais, *Speculum naturale*, 4. 110, quoting Constantinus Africanus; *Speculum naturale*, 6. 18, quoting Avicenna, *Liber canonis*, lib. 1, doct. 2, summa 1, cap. 11; published edn (Venice: per Paganum de Paganis, 1507; repr. Luca: Antonio Guinta, 1562, fol. 32ʳ). The *Speculum naturale* appears in Vincent of Beauvais, *Speculum quadruplex sive Speculum maius* (Duaci: Baltazaris Belleri, 1624; repr. Graz: Akademische Druck- und Verlagsanstalt, 1964); see cols 303, 380–1.

11  See the Latin text in Bartholomaeus Anglicus, *De proprietatibus rerum* (Frankfurt: apud Wolfgangum Richterum, 1601; repr. Frankfurt: Minerva, 1964), Chap. 15. 7, p. 627; Chap. 15. 15, p. 630; Chap. 15. 52, p. 649; Chap. 15. 91, p. 671; also the late fourteenth-century Middle English of John Trevisa, in *On the Properties of Things: John Trevisa's Translation of 'Bartholomaeus Anglicus*, De proprietatibus rerum', ed. Michael C. Seymour *et al.*, 3 vols (Oxford: Clarendon Press, 1975–78), ii, pp. 728, 732, 754, 779. In the interest of concision, only the Middle English text is quoted in this chapter. For the reader's convenience, however, references in the notes are to the chapter and page numbers in the Latin text (Frankfurt, 1601), and to the page numbers in Seymour's edition of the Middle English text.

12  Bartholomaeus Anglicus, *De proprietatibus rerum*, Chap. 15. 52, p. 649; *On the Properties*, p. 754.

13  Bartholomaeus Anglicus, *De proprietatibus rerum*, Chap. 15. 66, p. 657; *On the Properties*, p. 763. This is an elaboration of Isidore, *Etymologies*, 9. 2. 105: 'Inde Romanos graves, Graecos leves, Afros versipelles, Gallos natura feroces atque acriores ingenio pervidemus, quod natura climatum facit': in *Etymologiarum sive Originum libri XX*, ed. W. M. Lindsay (Oxford: Clarendon Press, 1911). The passage appears not in Isidore's geography, but in his book on languages and cities.

14  Bartholomaeus Anglicus, *De proprietatibus rerum*, Chap. 15. 50, p. 648; *On the Properties*, pp. 752–3. The balanced contraries of mankind are central to Bartholomaeus's overall presentation of the natural world: see, for example, the balanced 'oppositions of beast against beast' noted by D. C. Greetham, 'The concept of nature in Bartholomaeus Anglicus', *Journal of the History of Ideas*, 41 (1980), 663–77, at 670. My thanks to Richard Raiswell for this reference.

15  On the use of Bartholomaeus's encyclopaedia in *The Book of John Mandeville*, see D. C. Greetham, 'The fabulous geography of John Trevisa's translation of Bartholomaeus Anglicus' *De proprietatibus rerum*', unpublished PhD dissertation, City University of New York, 1974, pp. 190, 316, 325 n. 46.

16  *Livre des merveilles*, p. 333; *Mandeville's Travels*, p. 132.

17  *Livre des merveilles*, pp. 340–1; *Mandeville's Travels*, p. 137.

18  *Livre des merveilles*, pp. 427–8; *Mandeville's Travels*, p. 191.

19  *Livre des merveilles*, p. 286; *Mandeville's Travels*, p. 101.

20  *Livre des merveilles*, pp. 287–8, 304; *Mandeville's Travels*, pp. 106, 114–15. Other encyclopaedic works are sometimes adduced as sources for these passages, including Pliny, Honorius of Autun, Gossouin and Brunetto Latini; the account of southern physiology found in Mandeville, however, appears in none of them.

21 *Livre des merveilles*, pp. 312–13; *Mandeville's Travels*, pp. 119–20. Cf. the commentary on Sacrobosco written (in 1271) by Robertus Anglicus: in his thirteenth lecture Robertus explains that, just as part of India is outside the range of the seven climates, so too part of England lies outside the range; he does not, however, discuss the influence of Saturn and the moon on the climates, as does Mandeville. See Thorndike, *The Sphere of Sacrobosco*, pp. 187, 191 (Latin text); pp. 236, 240 (trans.). A closer parallel to Mandeville's formulation can be found in the *Summa judicialis de accidentibus mundi*, written in 1347–48 by John of Ashenden: Johannes Eschuid, *Summa astrologiae judicialis* (Venice: Franciscus Bolanus, J. Sanctiter, 1489), fol. 42$^r$ (tr. 1, dist. 8, cap. 1). On the influence and wide dissemination of John's work, see Lynn Thorndike, *A History of Magic and Experimental Science*, 4 vols (New York: Columbia University Press, 1923–34), iii, pp. 325–46.

22 Henry Daniel, *Liber uricrisiarum*, London, Wellcome Library, Sloane MS 1101, fol. 60$^v$; this passage corresponds closely to the schema used by John of Ashenden, cited in n. 21 above. I am very grateful to E. Ruth Harvey for showing me this passage in her transcription of Daniel's treatise.

23 *Livre des merveilles*, p. 478; *Mandeville's Travels*, p. 228.

24 Bartholomaeus Anglicus, *De proprietatibus rerum*, Chap. 8. 1, pp. 369–70; *On the Properties*, pp. 443–4.

25 *Livre des merveilles*, p. 331; *Mandeville's Travels*, p. 131.

26 Marian J. Tooley, 'Bodin and the medieval theory of climate', *Speculum*, 28 (1953), 64–83, at 80–1.

27 Joyce E. Chaplin, 'Natural philosophy and an early racial idiom in North America: Comparing English and Indian bodies', *William and Mary Quarterly*, 54 (1997), 229–52, at 236–8.

28 Kenan Malik, *The Meaning of Race: Race, History, and Culture in Western Society* (Houndmills and London: Macmillan, 1996), pp. 79–84.

29 *Livre des merveilles*, p. 365; *Mandeville's Travels*, p. 152. The source for the passage is Odoric of Pordenone, but the explanation of the cause (that is, the 'nature of the lond') is original to Mandeville. Cf. Odoric, 'Relatio', 24. 2, in *Sinica Franciscana*, 6 vols, i: Anastasius van den Wyngaert (ed.), *Itinera et relationes fratrum minorum saeculi XIII et XIV* (Florence: Quaracchi, 1929), pp. 468–9.

30 'Licet autem huiusmodi nigri aliquando nascantur etiam in aliis climatibus, sicut in quarto vel in quinto, tamen nigredinem accipiunt a primis generantibus, quae complexionata sunt in climatibus primo et secundo, et paulatim alterantur ad albedinem, quando ad alia climata transferuntur': Albertus Magnus, *De natura loci*, 2. 3; in *Opera omnia*, 37 vols, v, part 2, ed. Paul Hossfeld (Monasterii Westfalorum: Aschendorff, 1980), p. 27.

31 Bartholomaeus Anglicus, *De proprietatibus rerum*, Chap. 15. 122, p. 689; *On the Properties*, p. 768.

32 *Livre des merveilles*, p. 379; *Mandeville's Travels*, pp. 160–1. Cf. Isidore, *Etymologiae*, 9. 2. 127: 'Aethiopes dicti a filio Cham, qui vocatus est Chus, ex quo originum trahunt. Chus enim Hebraica lingua Aethiops interpretatur'. On the association of Ham with the southern climates, see Suzanne Conklin Akbari, 'From due east to true north: Orientalism and orientation', in Jeffrey Jerome Cohen (ed.), *The Postcolonial Middle Ages* (New York: St Martin's Press, 2000), pp. 19–34, at pp. 22–3.

33 On whether the term 'discourse' (in the Foucauldian sense) can be used to describe medieval culture, see Suzanne Conklin Akbari, 'Orientation and nation in the *Canterbury Tales*', in Kathryn L. Lynch (ed.), *Chaucer's Cultural Geography* (London: Routledge, 2002), pp. 102–34, at pp. 102–3, 112, 124. As Malik points out, there is no

'simple "definition" of "race". The concept of race is too complex and multi-faceted to be reduced to single, straightforward definitions. Different social groups and different historical periods have understood race in radically different ways . . . [Race] is not an expression of a single phenomenon or relationship. Rather it is a medium through which the changing relationship between humanity, society, and nature has been understood' (*The Meaning of Race*, p. 71).

34  See the survey of pre-modern theories of race in part one of Ivan Hannaford, *Race: The History of an Idea in the West* (Washington, DC: Woodrow Wilson Center, 1996).

35  William McKee Evans, 'From the land of Canaan to the land of Guinea: The strange odyssey of the "Sons of Ham"', *American Historical Review*, 85 (1980), 15–43, at 39. Part of Evans's argument that medieval Muslim societies 'lived in a racially stratified society' in spite of their 'seeming lack of color prejudice' is built on the shaky ground of an anachronistic analogy with nineteenth-century Latin American culture (*ibid.*, p. 31 and n. 51). See also David Brion Davis, who argues that 'the "Hamitic myth" played a relatively minor role in justifying black slavery until the late eighteenth and the nineteenth centuries' (*Slavery and Human Progress* (Oxford: Oxford University Press, 1984), p. 337 n. 144), and the rejoinder to Davis in Robin Blackburn, 'The Old World background to European colonial slavery', *William and Mary Quarterly*, 54 (1997), 65–102, at 94–5.

36  Lorraine Daston and Katherine Park, *Wonders and the Order of Nature, 1150–1750* (New York: Zone, 1998), pp. 109–33, at p. 14.

37  Daston and Park, *Wonders*, pp. 48–57.

38  Quoted in the Middle English translation of Caxton; see *Caxton's Mirrour of the World*, 3. 7; ed. Oliver H. Prior, Early English Text Society, e.s., 110 (Oxford: Oxford University Press, 1913), pp. 141–3.

39  Caroline Walker Bynum, 'Miracles and marvels: The limits of alterity', in Franz J. Felten and Nikolas Jaspert (eds), *Vita religiosa im Mittelalter: Festschrift für Kaspar Elm zum 70. Geburtstag* (Berlin: Duncker and Humblot, 1999), pp. 801–17, at pp. 803–7.

40  *Livre des merveilles*, p. 150; *Mandeville's Travels*, pp. 33–4. On the significance of monstrosity according to Augustine, see Daston and Park, *Wonders*, pp. 39–41; Jean Céard, *La nature et les prodiges: L'insolite au XVIe siècle* (Geneva: Droz, 1977), pp. 21–9.

41  Bartholomaeus Anglicus, *De proprietatibus rerum*, Chap. 14. 1, p. 593; *On the Properties*, p. 694.

42  Bartholomaeus Anglicus, *De proprietatibus rerum*, Chap. 15. 7, 15, pp. 627, 630; *On the Properties*, pp. 728, 732.

43  Bartholomaeus Anglicus, *De proprietatibus rerum*, Chap. 15. 52, p. 649; *On the Properties*, p. 754; cf. 'wondirliche yshape', *De proprietatibus rerum*, Chap. 15. 91, p. 671; *On the Properties*, p. 779.

44  Bartholomaeus Anglicus, *De proprietatibus rerum*, Chap. 15. 73, pp. 661–2; *On the Properties*, pp. 770–1.

45  Bartholomaeus Anglicus, *De proprietatibus rerum*, Chap. 15. 7, p. 627; *On the Properties*, p. 728.

46  *Livre des merveilles*, pp. 349, 353; *Mandeville's Travels*, pp. 142, 145.

47  *Livre des merveilles*, pp. 359–60; *Mandeville's Travels*, p. 149. Cf. Odoric of Pordenone, *Relatio*, 19. 2, p. 458.

48  Bartholomaeus Anglicus, *De proprietatibus rerum*, Chap. 15. 7, p. 626; *On the Properties*, p. 728.

49  Cf. Isidore, *Etymologies*, 14. 3. 34.

50  *Livre des merveilles*, p. 336; *Mandeville's Travels*, p. 134.

51 Bartholomaeus Anglicus, *De proprietatibus rerum*, Chap. 15. 14, pp. 631–2; *On the Properties*, p. 734.

52 On the fidelity of Trevisa's translation, see Traugott Lawler, 'On the properties of John Trevisa's major translations', *Viator*, 14 (1983), 267–88.

53 Robertus Anglicus, thirteenth lecture, in Thorndyke, *The Sphere of Sacrobosco*, p. 187 (Latin text), p. 236 (trans.).

54 John Gower, *Confessio amantis*, book 7, lines 582–3, in *The Complete Works of John Gower*, ed. G. C. Macaulay, 4 vols (Oxford: Clarendon Press, 1901), ii. On the development of the East–West binary during the late fourteenth century, see Akbari, 'From due east', pp. 28–31.

55 This point renders the question of the nationality of the author of *The Book of John Mandeville* all the more perplexing: see Deluz's intelligent survey of the debate in *Livre des merveilles*, pp. 7–16.

56 *Ibid.*, p. 336; *Mandeville's Travels*, p. 134.

# 9

## Travels with Margery: pilgrimage in context

❰❱

### Rosalynn Voaden

... & euer it cam a-geyn so fast þat sche myth not rest ne qwiet han in hir mende but euyr was labowred & comawnded to gon ouyr þe see.[1]
(... and it always came again so quickly that she could not rest, or have quiet in her mind, but was always laboured and commanded to go over the sea).

From a single point at Lynn, one can still observe key reference points of Margery's life: the Guildhall, the church of St Margaret, and the lane leading down to a river which suggests – through the peculiar bowing of its horizon – the allure of the beyond.[2]

MARGERY Kempe was a laywoman and visionary, born at the close of the fourteenth century, who lived in Lynn, on the east coast of England. Though married and the mother of fourteen children, pilgrimage was a continuous and vital part of her religious praxis. Her restless nature resisted both spiritual and geographical boundaries, and she was prepared to face risk and hardship to respond to 'the allure of the beyond' in both senses. This chapter will argue that pilgrimage and travel undertaken for spiritual ends were predominant forces in shaping Margery's spiritual expression, and that ultimately they provided the lens through which she understood and articulated the story of herself and her divinely ordained purpose. I will first offer some background on Margery Kempe and her *Book*, describing both her spiritual and secular life, and arguing for Lynn, one of the principal ports on the east coast of England, as a major influence in her life. I will then consider pilgrimage in late medieval England, both how it was organised practically and how it functioned as a spiritual exercise. Against this backdrop I will discuss the nature of Margery's two major pilgrimages – both eastward bound, though the first was metaphorically east to the more traditional destinations of Rome and the Holy Land, while the second was geographically due east to holy sites in northern Europe. Finally, I will explore how both of these spiritual journeys acted as a formative influence on Margery's understanding of herself as a visionary and on the expression of her spirituality in her *Book*.

## MARGERY KEMPE: HER *BOOK* AND HER LIFE

Margery Kempe was the daughter of one well-to-do and influential merchant and the wife of another (rather less influential and well-to-do) who lived during the closing years of the fourteenth century and the first four decades of the fifteenth in Lynn, in Norfolk. Her *Book*, the first autobiography in English,[3] details her life and spiritual aspirations in an apparently indiscriminate mixture, including her 'madness' following the birth of her first child, her conversations with Christ and the Virgin Mary, the response of her neighbours to the would-be holy woman in their midst and the protracted negotiations with her husband to have a chaste marriage (protracted enough to allow for the production of fourteen children).[4] It also offers frequent and lengthy descriptions of pilgrimage. Margery was a restless soul – in all meanings of that phrase – and much of her time seems to have been consumed visiting shrines, holy sites and devout persons throughout England and Europe. These pilgrimages both formed and expressed her devotional praxis; travel was the means whereby she discovered different forms of piety, it offered an opportunity to develop and test her presentation as visionary and holy woman, and it was a venue for spiritual performance.

In spite of all her striving, Margery had a mixed reception in her lifetime, as a neighbour, as a fellow traveller and as a visionary. Her fellow citizens of Lynn criticised her for hypocrisy and gossiped about her marriage and treatment of her husband. Her companions on pilgrimage humiliated her and deserted her en route. Her incessant 'crying and roaring' whenever she thought of Christ's Passion elicited hostile responses from lay and clergy alike. She was several times accused of heresy and of being a Lollard, no light thing at a time when England felt under threat from heretical movements, and parliament had in 1401 passed the statute *De haeretico comburendo*, providing for the burning of convicted heretics.[5] However, when St Margaret's Church was on fire, it was on Margery that the citizenry called to save it. When a young mother went mad after the birth of her child, it was to Margery that the distraught husband came for help. Her fellow pilgrims sought Margery's prayers during storms at sea. And Margery cites numerous highly placed clerics who praise her piety and support even some of her unconventional desires and practices, such as wearing white clothes, traditionally the garb of virgins or pious widows. Although it must be remembered that this is a tale told by Margery, she does not, as might be expected, and, indeed, as was usual in the writings of medieval women visionaries, offer a burnished version of a pious performance.[6] We get, instead, a warts-and-all representation, a representation which permits insight into her self-fashioning. Her negative reception by her contemporaries is generally constructed as her opportunity for *imitatio Christi*, the imitation of the suffering and humiliation undergone by Christ during his Passion which was a dominant aspect of late medieval popular devotion. Her positive experiences are construed as approbation of her chosen way of life. There can be little doubt that Margery was not an easy person to be with – she is irritating and self-righteous and always has the last word (at least, in her *Book*). However, we can see in her rendition of her life the forces at play in fourteenth-century religion, and the way in which the piety of this particular woman was formed.

Margery's spirituality was predominantly formed by affective piety, a form of devotion originated largely by the Franciscans, which encouraged an imaginative and empathetic response to the events of Scripture, particularly to Christ's Nativity and Passion. The faithful were enjoined to envision these events in great detail and living colour, even to insert themselves in the scriptural drama as bit-player or onlooker. So Margery imagines the Virgin Mary showing her how she swaddles her son, and describes herself making a pot of soup to comfort the Virgin after the Crucifixion.[7]

Since the discovery of Margery's autobiography in 1934 scholars have argued consistently that her spirituality is far more reminiscent of continental visionaries and holy women, particularly those of Germany and the Low Countries, than it is of English devotion.[8] The *Book* refers to Margery's having had read to her 'Seynt Brydys [Birgitta's] boke' (*The Liber Celestis of St Bridget of Sweden*), and the scribe refers to Marie d'Oignies when he is trying to make sense of Margery's chronic weeping.[9] Margery herself manifests a desire to emulate Birgitta in piety.[10] There are two additional holy women whose influence on Margery can arguably be detected in the text, although she mentions neither by name. She could well have encountered accounts of these women while on pilgrimage: Angela of Foligno during her first pilgrimage to Jerusalem and Rome, and Dorothea of Montau while she was in Prussia on her second pilgrimage. Both are discussed below. Certainly, there is no doubt that pilgrimage and life in Lynn exposed Margery to forms of spiritual life and devotional praxis which resonated with her, and which she adopted and adapted to reflect her own spirituality.

### LATE MEDIEVAL LYNN: GATEWAY TO 'THE BEYOND'

Diagonally opposite St Margaret's Church in present-day King's Lynn, in the courtyard of Thoresby College, is a slate marker indicating the location of the medieval quay.[11] St Margaret's Church, Margery Kempe's parish church, where she worshipped, experienced revelations and engaged in intimate conversations with Christ, was thus mere metres away from the hustle and bustle of a major international port, where merchants and traders, pilgrims and travellers from all over England and all over Europe met and mingled, bringing with them not only material goods for import and export but also tales of distant lands, of different lives and spiritual attitudes. Margery Kempe's daily life and devotional praxis were profoundly influenced by this cosmopolitan atmosphere.[12]

Lynn was one of the foremost ports of England during the thirteenth century, close after Boston, which was second only to London.[13] Although its importance declined somewhat in the fourteenth century, it was still an important port for both trade and travel. In the late fourteenth century Lynn was a prosperous and bustling city of about five thousand, boasting two large markets.[14] With the rise of the Hanseatic league in the late fourteenth century, German merchants came to dominate the trade routes and became a visible presence in Lynn. Although there was no Hanse *Kontor* (headquarters) in Lynn at this time, Hanse merchants had been granted liberties in Lynn from 1271, and it is clear that the Germanic influence was pervasive in the town.[15] The extent of this influence is evident in the Germanic style of the memorial brasses in St Margaret's commemorating two mayors from the late fourteenth century.[16] Trade was not just one-way, either; Lynn merchants established a headquarters in Danzig for trade in Prussia and the Baltic. There was an English church in Danzig, and there is evidence of both German and English traders marrying local women.[17]

It was not only material goods that passed through Lynn – travellers and pilgrims also embarked from its quays. In 1405, Philippa, daughter of Henry IV, sailed from Lynn to marry Eric, King of Norway and Denmark. And it was at Lynn that the first Birgittine nuns landed, en route from the mother house in Vadstena, Sweden, to the monastery at Syon, newly established in 1415 by Henry V.[18] This event must have had great significance for Margery, given her identification with Birgitta of Sweden. Lynn was thus a conduit for new ideas, beliefs and practices, particularly those originating in northern Europe.[19] Among these imports were religious texts, inspirational tracts and accounts of the lives and visions of holy people. Margery Kempe's unconventional, un-English piety was undoubtedly shaped by her exposure to these influences.

## PILGRIMAGE IN LATE MEDIEVAL ENGLAND

Pilgrimage, both to holy sites and to the shrines of saints, has always been a part of Christian devotion; it has also always been viewed by the Church with some ambivalence. Although the impulses to visit the location of scriptural events, or to pray – or give thanks – for a miracle at a shrine were perceived as laudable, the subversive potential of the dislocation involved was also understood. As Victor and Edith Turner have famously observed, pilgrimage is a liminal period, when the participants are removed from their accustomed physical and social states and where a new kind of *communitas*, a 'social antistructure', can develop.[20] The Church's control over this particular act of devotion was restricted; being away from home, pilgrims had unaccustomed latitude in their choice of confessors and performance of spiritual exercises. Many clerics condemned pilgrimage, arguing that would-be pilgrims would be better off following a pilgrimage of the mind and spirit throughout their lives, and giving to the poor the considerable money which would have been expended.[21] However, the Church also encouraged pilgrimage; it offered both a spiritual outlet and a major economic resource. Pilgrimage sites were sources of enormous revenue for the Church as well as for local merchants, innkeepers and vendors of transportation. Pilgrimage was given a major boost in 1095, when Urban II introduced the practice of indulgence. Affective piety, with its focus on the humanity of Christ, fostered the desire to see the places associated with his life; and by the fourteenth century, pilgrimage to the three major sites of Christendom – Jerusalem, Rome and Santiago de Compostela – had become a virtual package tour industry. Tours were well established, organised and profitable, with standard itineraries and guaranteed turn-around time for the ships.[22] Although many pilgrims were sincere and devout, many more were seduced by a desire to see the world, and pilgrimage became increasingly secularised.[23] One has only to consider the dubious piety of most of Chaucer's Canterbury pilgrims.

Secular governments as well as the Church had reservations about the numbers of pilgrims roaming around Europe. English wars with France and Spain, with the resultant fear of spies and desire to limit the export of bullion, led secular authorities to require licences for all travellers apart from authorised merchants.[24] Gradually, ship owners started to acquire group licences for transporting groups of pilgrims, particularly those travelling to Compostela, a journey which could be accomplished almost entirely by sea.[25]

Popular as it was, pilgrimage was still arduous and dangerous. Sea voyages involved overcrowding, seasickness, bad food and the threat of shipwreck and pirates. Travellers on overland routes faced sporadic or continuing wars, bandits, verminous inns and villainous innkeepers, theft, difficult terrain, inclement weather and unreliable guides.[26] Land journeys were slow and lengthy. One historian has estimated that a medieval rider on the road from Calais to Rome could cover thirty miles a day.[27] Another suggests that a mixed group of pedestrians and riders could cover about twenty miles a day. In the late thirteenth century, it was reckoned that the overland trip to either Rome or Compostela took sixteen weeks – a long time away from the comforts of home.[28] For obvious reasons, the journey part of pilgrimage was frequently constructed as an *imitatio Christi*, offering the pilgrim a chance to suffer as Christ had done.

Pilgrimage was also expensive, and could easily consume a year's income for a member of the merchant class. The return journey from Venice to Jaffa alone cost around fifteen pounds; a carpenter's wages at that time in England were about twelve pounds a year.[29] Pilgrims either would have to carry large sums of money, and face the risk of theft and the difficulties of changing currency en route, with the attendant possibility of being cheated, or could arrange for bills of exchange.[30] In either case they could well run out of money and find themselves reduced to begging and staying in pilgrim hostels.[31]

Despite its mixed reputation and the dangers and discomforts it presented, pilgrimage could still be a profoundly significant spiritual exercise. For the truly devout, the opportunity to walk where Christ had walked and to see relics of his life overshadowed all other considerations. For Margery, and countless others, pilgrimage was an inextricable part of their devotion.

### MARGERY KEMPE: PILGRIMAGE TO THE HOLY LAND AND ROME

Margery always attributes her impulse to go on pilgrimage to divine inspiration; pilgrimage forms part of the spiritual path which Christ lays out for her early in her life as a visionary: 'As sche was in þes desyres, owyr Lord bad hir in hir mend ii ȝer er þan sche went þat sche schuld gon to Rome, to Iherusalem, & to Seynt Iamys'[32] ('While she had these desires, our Lord bade her in her mind that she should go to Rome, to Jerusalem and to St James'). The prospect of this fervently desired pilgrimage impels her to put her spiritual life in order by negotiating an agreement with her husband to live chastely:

> 'Grawntyth me þat ȝe schal not komyn in my bed, & I grawnt ȝow to qwyte yowr dettys er I go to Ierusalem. & makyth my body fre to God so þat ȝe neuyr make no chalengyng in me to askyn no dett of marimony aftyr þis day whyl ȝe leuyn, & I schal etyn and drynkyn on þe Fryday at ȝowr byddyng'. Than seyd hir husbond a-ȝen to [hir], 'As fre mot ȝowr body ben to God as it hath ben to me.'[33]
> ('Agree not to come into my bed and I agree to quit your debts before I go to Jerusalem. And make my body free to God so that you never challenge me nor ask for the matrimonial debt after this day, as long as you live, and I will eat and drink on Friday as you ask.' Then her husband said again to her, 'May your body be as free to God as it has been to me.')

Although the urging of Margery's divine travel agent was doubtless compelling, Margery's readiness to embark on such a momentous journey can be attributed to two additional factors: her familiarity with travel, and the affective nature of her piety.

The thought of a forty-year-old woman setting off in 1413 on an arduous journey of a thousand miles through a war-torn Europe, over the Alps and across the Mediterranean to the Holy Land, a journey that would take months and largely be undertaken on foot or by wagon, compels our amazement. It was also unusual for a woman, especially a laywoman travelling without her husband, to undertake the pilgrimage to Jerusalem – women tended to restrict themselves to domestic pilgrimage.[34] The journey to Jerusalem was generally acknowledged to be the most dangerous that could be undertaken.[35] However, travellers' tales must have prepared Margery for the ordeal. She would have spoken with merchants and travellers, with pilgrims both setting out and returning, and would have been aware of the trials that awaited her.[36] She would also have been prepared, to a certain extent at least, to deal with them. By the time Margery embarked on her first overseas pilgrimage the popularity of pilgrimage had given rise to a large number of guidebooks, some of which focused on the practicalities of the journey – where to sleep, how to change money, where bandits might lurk – while others described the sights, sacred and otherwise, to be seen. Still other guidebooks combined both. Donald Howard informs us that there are 526 extant accounts of pilgrimage to Jerusalem written between 1100 and 1500.[37] He suggests that many of these would have circulated locally; it is highly likely, therefore, that Margery, living in a port town, would have heard some of these accounts. A fifteenth-century poem attesting in boisterous rhyme to the unpleasantness of sea travel ('Cooke make redy anoon our mete / Our pylgryms haue no lust to ete') also suggests that pilgrimage literature was widespread and readily available.[38]

One of the most important practical preparations for pilgrimage concerned, not surprisingly, money. In addition to meeting the cost of the pilgrimage itself, pilgrims were enjoined to pay all their debts and make their wills before embarking. 'He that be a pilgrim oweth first to pay his debts, afterwards to set his house in governance, and afterwards to array himself and take leave of his neighbours and go forth', stated the London preacher Richard Alkerton, writing just before Margery embarked.[39] That Margery followed this advice is evident in her *Book*:

Whan tyme cam þat þis creatur xuld vysiten þo holy placys wher owyr Lord was whyk & ded . . . sche preyd þe parysch preste of þe town þer sche was dwellyng to sey for hir in þe pulpyt þat, yf any man er woman þat clemyd any dette of hir husbond or of hir þei xuld come & speke wyth hir er sche went, & sche, wyth þe help of God, xulde makyn a-seth to ech of hem þat þei schuldyn heldyn hem content.[40]

(When the time came for this creature to visit the holy places where our Lord was quick and dead . . . she asked the parish priest of the town where she was dwelling to say for her in the pulpit that, if any man or woman claimed any debt of her husband or herself, they should come and speak with her before she went, and she, with the help of God, would make satisfaction with each of them, so that they should be content.)

The second way in which Margery would have been prepared for her pilgrimage is through her devotional praxis. The affective piety that stimulated her meditations focused specifically and in great detail on the events of Christ's life. This detailed anticipation is of paramount importance when considering the nature of her experience in the Holy Land, especially in comparison with her later journey to northern Europe. She, like other devotees of this form of spiritual exercise, had already visited in her imagination the sites associated with Christ's life; the actual visit just confirmed her expectations.

Margery's expectations were also shaped by her devotional reading; she was particularly influenced by the revelations of Birgitta of Sweden (c. 1303–73), and modelled herself on Birgitta to a great extent. Her admiration for Birgitta is demonstrated by the fact that she tried to visit her house while she was in Rome, and claims to have spoken to her maid.[41] Birgitta made a pilgrimage to Jerusalem in 1372 in her late sixties, when she visited the major sites and received a vision of the painless manner in which the Virgin Mary gave birth to the Christ Child.[42] Margery's Jerusalem visit parallels that of Birgitta. To some extent this would have been inevitable, given the guided tours which the Franciscans conducted for pilgrims. However, Margery's account of her visit echoes Birgitta's in the same way that much of her spiritual life and many of her visions echo Birgitta's, suggesting strongly that when Margery visited Jerusalem she saw what Birgitta had prepared her to see.

It is therefore evident that, when Margery at the age of forty set out on her pilgrimage to the Holy Land and to Rome, she was prepared in both spiritual and practical ways. She had paid her own and her husband's debts, taken proper leave of her household and her confessor and knew what to anticipate. She took with her a maid, and a considerable sum of money – Sanford Meech, one of the original modern editors of *The Book*, estimates that she had at least thirty-six pounds in cash, which should have allowed her to travel in comfort.[43] Since she refers twice to 'hir gold' being held by a fellow pilgrim, it seems that she had not arranged for a letter of credit or bill of exchange.[44] She knew her ultimate destination, and the sites she expected to see. It is not known how she made contact with a ship, and whether she set out with a group of pilgrims or just met up with them at the port or on board. It is evident, however, from the subsequent account, that she did travel with a group which stayed the same all the way to Venice, at least. There is little information available about the process whereby pilgrims knew when and from where ships were sailing, although word of mouth seems to have been the most likely means.[45]

She embarked from Yarmouth, probably in the autumn of 1413, and landed in Zierikzee, in Zealand, in the Netherlands, a standard starting point for the overland journey to Venice, where special galleys took pilgrims on to Jaffa.

They obviously crossed the Alps during the winter months, and in Venice waited thirteen weeks for the ship to the Holy Land; these ships usually sailed in late spring or early summer.[46] The only stops on the route that Margery names are Constance and Bologna; however, from Zierikzee she may well have travelled through the diocese of Liège, home to Marie d'Oignies and a remarkable community of Beguine holy women in the thirteenth century.[47] These women dedicated their lives to Christ, were self-supporting, and lived together in informal communities. Their spirituality was affective, focused on the humanity of Christ. In both their way of life and their piety, Beguines were akin to what Margery aspired to.[48] It is certainly possible that on her passage through Liège Margery heard stories of these holy women and appropriated elements of their spirituality to her own piety.

Margery tells almost nothing of her journey to Venice, which is surprising to the modern reader in view of both the novelty of the experience and the rigours of the road. If a winter crossing of the Alps did not excite comment, surely nothing physical would. This pattern continues throughout all her pilgrimages, and has caused some critics to wonder if she even went to these places, so marked is her lack of interest in her physical whereabouts. Donald Howard remarks, 'There is not in her book a scintilla of traveller's curiosity, so we get no bananas, giraffes or elephants from Margery'.[49] This is hardly fair to Margery, though. There are two reasons for the blinkers she dons while travelling. The first is the medieval attitude toward *curiositas* (curiosity): clearly distinguished from *sapientia* (wisdom) and *scientia* (knowledge), it was categorised as a vice. Indulgence in *curiositas*, it was believed, was morally dangerous, excited the senses and signified an unstable attitude of mind.[50] The devout pilgrim should resist *curiositas* as a tool of the devil and focus on the destination alone, as Santo Brasca, an Italian pilgrim to Jerusalem, wrote in 1481, 'A man should undertake this voyage solely with the intention of visiting, contemplating and adoring the most Holy Mysteries . . . and not with the intention of seeing the world, or from ambition, or to be able to say "I have been there" or "I have seen that" in order to be exalted by his fellow men.'[51] That this was Margery's attitude is clear from the paucity of descriptions; what she records is her response to the sights, not the sights themselves.

The second reason for the blinkers is that Margery constructs her pilgrimage in *imitatio Christi*, as she does so much of her life, and for her this was achieved through humiliation. She mapped the humiliation she felt onto Christ's Passion, and consequently what she recalls of the journey is less scenery than suffering. The source of her humiliation was her fellow pilgrims, and it is their ill-treatment of her which animates and directs her account. They scorned her, ignored her, stole her money, and refused to sit at table with her, and some of them abandoned her. Her maid deserted her, and other pilgrims cut her gown off at the knees and forced her to wear a white canvas smock, like a fool.[52] Her narrative of the journey vacillates between tales of wrongs done to her and accounts of the approbation she received for her piety and her suffering from various churchmen and devout persons along the way. It was always the non-English people she encountered, for example the innkeeper at their hostel, who recognised and validated her spirituality and devotional praxis; this is a recurrent theme throughout both pilgrimages.[53] Terence Bowers argues convincingly that in the particular enactment of *imitatio Christi* on her pilgrimage to Rome, in their mocking and abuse of Margery, it is her fellow English pilgrims who adopt the roles of Christ's persecutors.[54]

Margery's humiliation and rejection was vastly increased when she began to be overcome by irresistible crying and roaring, often accompanied by writhing and thrashing on the ground. This first occurred during her tour of the Holy Land. At Calvary, the site of the Crucifixion, she had a vision of the crucified Christ which precipitated the first of these uncontrollable episodes.[55] They continued for about ten years and were the cause of much hostility levelled against her. Her entire tour of the Holy Land is viewed through the lens of her dramatic responses to the sites and events of Christ's life. She fell down and sobbed in the Holy Sepulchre, she climbed Mount Quarantine, where Christ fasted for forty days, and experienced empathetic thirst, and she visited the burial place of the Virgin Mary, where she had a vision in which Christ and his mother praised her weeping and writhing.[56]

As suggested earlier, apart from her emotional responses, Margery's tour was quite conventional and in all likelihood modelled on that of Birgitta of Sweden. The Franciscans, who dominated the pilgrim trade in the Holy Land, led pilgrims on guided tours of the principal sites: Calvary, the Church of the Nativity, the river Jordan, Mount Quarantine. This being so, there was little scope for individualised experience. In many ways the Franciscans both generated the pilgrims' initial expectations, through the influence they had on affective piety, and then confirmed those expectations through the inevitably selective nature of their tour.

Margery travelled in the Holy Land for three weeks before returning to Venice with her group.[57] At this point they refused to travel with her any further, and thus began the desperate search for travelling companions which characterises not only the remainder of this pilgrimage but also her travels in northern Europe. Travelling alone, dependent on others for guidance, transportation and, often, money, heightened Margery's insecurity and mental suffering, and her greater vulnerability increased her fear for her physical safety.

On her way home, Margery visited Assisi and Rome. While in Assisi, she may well have heard from the Franciscans of Angela of Foligno (c. 1248–

1309), a visionary whose life and devotional praxis bear some startling resemblances to Margery's. Foligno, Angela's home town, is only a few miles from Assisi. Hope Emily Allen speculates that Margery may have been told of Angela by the Franciscans in the Holy Land, their accounts an attempt to explain her weeping and writhing.[58] Another possible pathway of influence is suggested by Paul Lachance, editor of Angela's works, who suggests that in the late medieval period these were well received among the Beguines of the Low Countries, where, as noted earlier, Margery travelled.[59] Whatever the source, although Margery never mentions Angela by name, a strong case can be made that during her pilgrimages she learned of this visionary and that her evolution as a holy woman may have been profoundly influenced by Angela of Foligno.

Margery was in Rome from the early autumn of 1414 until some time after Easter of the following year, long enough to become embedded in the life of expatriate pilgrims and clerics in that city and to generate among this community the heady mixture of hostility and praise which nourished her conflicted desire for abjection and for approbation. The most significant event for her during this time was undoubtedly her mystical marriage to the Godhead, which occurred on 9 November 1414 in the Apostles' Church in Rome.[60] Although it is not evident how her being in Rome precipitated this event, it may well be that Margery's liminal status as a pilgrim and her separation from home – and, not incidentally, her earthly husband – created the necessary psychic space for divine union to occur. It may be, also, that she was influenced by stories heard on her travels of other holy women, such as Angela of Foligno, Catherine of Siena and many of the Beguines of the Low Countries who had mystical marriages. Beyond these possible direct influences, though, it seems that the humiliation and danger Margery had encountered on pilgrimage, coupled with her exposure to the sites of Christ's life and Passion, moved her, in her own mind, to a closer attachment, even perhaps a greater sense of entitlement, to Christ. Her mystical marriage is a symbolic representation of her own sense of spritual growth.

Margery's trip home is only briefly recounted, with none of the anguished *imitatio Christi* which accompanied her outward trip. Her return, however, is anticlimactic, lacking any sense of accomplishment, especially when compared with the good form in which she set out. The unfocused and peremptory ending to the tale of Margery's pilgrimage to the Holy Land and Rome lends further support to the argument that Margery modelled her pilgrimage on the accounts of Birgitta and others, and that these models abandoned her on the way home. It was the preparation, the outward journey and the destination which featured in nearly all pilgrimage accounts. Consequently, for the tale of her return journey, Margery was left to her own devices and experiences, unmediated by the perceptions of others. Neither Margery's skills as a raconteur nor those of her scribe were sufficient to shape an appropriate ending for her journey. The effect on her *Book* of the lack of a narrative model can also be perceived in the account of her pilgrimage to northern Europe, discussed below.

## MARGERY KEMPE: PILGRIMAGE TO NORTHERN EUROPE

In her travels in northern Europe, Margery was very much the accidental tourist. Margery's second lengthy pilgrimage overseas, in 1433, recounted in *Liber II* of her *Book*, was very different from her first. This time, there was no prior divine warning that she was to go on pilgrimage, no eager anticipation, no preparations made, no debts paid, no prayers offered or leave given by her confessor. It was a spur-of-the-moment endeavour where Margery had no idea of where she was going, or why, other than that suddenly she 'was comawndyd in hir hert for to gon ouyr þe se'.[61] Margery's circumstances at this time go some way towards explaining this impetuosity. Her husband and son had recently died, and her German daughter-in-law had decided to return to her home town of Danzig (Gdansk). Perhaps travel offered Margery some prospect of relief or distraction, or a renewed sense of purpose. Whatever the reason, she impulsively decided to accompany her daughter-in-law – who was clearly less than happy with the idea – to Danzig.[62] It is possible that Margery felt an affinity for Prussia and Germany, as a result of the presence of Hanseatic merchants in Lynn, and the fact that her son had lived there for some time.[63] Be that as it may, one result of the unplanned nature of this pilgrimage to northern Europe is that it has a veracity, a ring of authenticity, which is arguably missing from the account of the pilgrimage to the Holy Land. In this account we do learn something of conditions on the road, of storms and war, of lousy travelling companions and sleeping in barns. And our compassion is stirred for this sixty-year-old woman with an injured foot, struggling to keep up with her guide, terrified of being abandoned in an unknown country at war with her own.

With such a hasty departure, Margery evidently left without much money or a licence to travel. She must first have been largely dependent on her daughter-in-law, then, after leaving Danzig, on strangers, begging for rides and sleeping at times by the road. Her journey was apparently aimless. Margery seems to have left without a clear purpose or destination for this journey, and it is here that the most significant difference from her pilgrimage to the Holy Land is evident. Although she did visit the shrines of Wilsnak and Aachen, she seems to have learned of their existence en route – these were not popular pilgrimage destinations for the English, and she probably had no model or prior knowledge to shape her expectations.[64] Another important factor is that, in contrast with her pilgrimages to the Holy Land and to Compostela, on this journey she travelled only sporadically with pilgrims. There is certainly no sense of her being part of a group of pilgrims with the same destination, sharing and reinforcing each other's expectations. She records no pious or emotional response to the relics, merely stating baldly, in both cases, that she was there.

The focus of this pilgrimage is therefore not on the shrines or holy places. Whereas in her account of the Holy Land she does describe the places she visited, especially in terms of their scriptural significance, and does record – often in lengthy detail – her own responses to the sites, this time, in northern Europe, the focus is almost completely on Margery's trials.[65] Her real relationship to the journey was to her own humiliation and hardship, or, less often, to the approbation she received. The physical fearfulness evident in her earlier pilgrimage is intensified here – not surprisingly, given her increased age, infirmity and consequent vulnerability. The theme of danger is established early in the account, when she describes the terrible tempests that blew the ship off course, forcing it onto the Norwegian coast. Shipwreck was something of a convention in pilgrimage miracle stories, but Margery's fear is palpable; this was one occasion when she did not emulate Birgitta, who was shipwrecked and continued her journey as if nothing untoward had happened.[66]

The ultimate destination of the ship was Danzig, a Hanse town on the Baltic with strong links with Lynn. They landed there after Easter in 1433. Margery stayed there five or six weeks, still evidently a thorn in her daughter-in-law's side.[67] Danzig was a centre of veneration for Birgitta of Sweden,[68] and it is likely that Margery spent some of her time there visiting sites connected with the saint. In Danzig she almost certainly would have heard of Dorothea of Montau (1347–94), a local visionary whose life and spirituality are remarkably similar to Margery's, and who died only a few decades before Margery's sojourn there.[69] Dorothea spent the last year of her life as an anchorite at the cathedral at Marienwerder, near Danzig. Her piety was legendary in Prussia, and there was a flourishing local cult centred on her anchorite's cell.

Margery left Danzig rather abruptly, impelled by God's command and by the suggestion of 'a man' that she should accompany him on pilgrimage to Wilsnak, in Prussia.[70] The first part of the journey, from Danzig to Stralsund, was to be by boat, to avoid Pomerelia, Pomerania and Neumark, territories ruled by the Teutonic Knights and currently under attack by Poland. However, Margery encountered an obstacle leaving Danzig because she lacked the necessary permission to travel. Eventually, a Lynn merchant came to her aid and obtained leave for her to travel, whereupon Margery and her escort sailed for Stralsund, with Margery in constant terror of shipwreck and storms.[71]

They landed and set out overland to Wilsnak, a distance of 110 miles, and the chronicle of persecution and humiliation began. Her escort tried to abandon her, she felt surrounded by enemies, and her injured foot made walking difficult. They were evidently travelling alone and on foot, sleeping by the side of the road or on straw in barns. Eventually, after leaving Wilsnak, Margery's guide succeeded in deserting her, and she fell in with various groups of companions on her way to Aachen, a journey which probably took three to four weeks.[72] Her travelling companions, like her destinations, seem to have been largely random. At one point she was reduced to travelling with a group of poor people who periodically stripped naked to search themselves for nits – which they generously shared with her. Humiliated though she was, she was too afraid of travelling alone to abandon them until they reached Aachen. On this northern European journey, Margery's fears were almost obsessively focused on sexual assault; she was afraid to sleep alone, and sought out women or monks as travelling companions wherever possible.[73] Her panic when even these threatened to leave her is eloquent testimony to the perils of pilgrimage for an elderly woman, travelling alone. Shorn of the formal structure of her Jerusalem pilgrimage, her northern European pilgrimage heightened her identification with the sufferings of Christ in a way less influenced by Franciscan devotional praxis than by her own sense of vulnerability in a hostile environment, subject to the kindness and curses of strangers.

Margery's northern European pilgrimage ended at Calais, after a journey of about two months. In all she had been away from early April until probably mid-August 1433. Her voyage from Calais to Dover was another tempest-tossed ordeal which seems to mark the end of her travel 'ouyr þe see'. While the period after she returned home to Lynn was not exactly a time of 'emotion recollected in tranquillity' – tranquillity being foreign to Margery's nature – it certainly was a time of recollection, as she and her scribe worked together on the composition of her *Book*.

### THE CONSEQUENCES OF PILGRIMAGE

Margery's second scribe commenced extensive revisions of *Liber I* in 1436, and began the writing of *Liber II* in 1438.[74] Since her northern European pilgrimage preceded the final revision and writing of her *Book* by only a short period of time, it is highly likely that the religious ideas and spiritual attitudes which Margery encountered during this journey would have been uppermost in her mind as she recounted her life story for the benefit of her scribe. This last pilgrimage, then, was arguably of great significance in determining her self-presentation and influencing the focus of the entire book. It could be that its spontaneous generation, the lack of preparation and the random itinerary reflect a stage in Margery's development when she had moved beyond the structures and dictates of affective piety, and was impelled to follow her own spiritual compass. And then, by launching herself into the unknown, she travelled still further towards the complete identification with Christ for which she so ardently yearned. She discovered meaning in the apparently random persecution, humiliation and suffering which she had undergone on her travels by mapping them onto Christ's Passion and constructing her own life in *imitatio Christi*.

Another factor of significance in the timing of the writing of the book is that Margery had recently encountered – perhaps for the second time – the spirituality of the holy women and Beguines of Germany, Prussia and the Low Countries, with their Christocentric affective piety and bodily devotion. This was a spirituality which resonated with her own predilections, so radically different from the more muted piety of England, and which gave definition and approbation to her own devotional praxis as she reflected on her life and then gave voice to it in her *Book*.

Living in Lynn, a busy port on the eastern edge of England, Margery was aware of both the practical requirements and the spiritual promise inherent in journeying further east – to Jerusalem and then, towards the end of her life, to northern Europe. Just as a telescope brings distant objects into focus so that they become part of the immediate environment and enrich one's perception of the world, so, for Margery Kempe, pilgrimage and travel for spiritual ends brought into her world distant lives and different devotional practices, diverse forms of spirituality and new ways to suffer for Christ. Travel therefore provided the lens through which she came to understand herself and her life, and consequently was of paramount importance in shaping her presentation of herself in her text as visionary and holy woman.

### NOTES

I would like to thank Jocelyn Lear for her invaluable assistance with research for this essay.

1 Margery Kempe, *The Book of Margery Kempe*, ed. S. B. Meech and H. E. Allen (Oxford: Oxford University Press, 1940), p. 226. All quotations are from this edition; all translations are my own. For a full translation of the text, see *The Book of Margery Kempe*, ed. and trans. L. Staley (New York: Norton, 2001).

2 D. Wallace, *Chaucerian Polity: Absolutist Lineages and Associational Forms in England and Italy* (Stanford: Stanford University Press, 1997), p. 392 n. 3.

3 Margery was illiterate, and dictated her *Book* to two different scribes; see Margery Kempe, *Book*, pp. 1–6 for the second scribe's *proem*. For the role of the scribes, see R. Ellis, 'Margery Kempe's scribe and the miraculous books', in H. Phillips (ed.), *Langland, the Mystics and the Medieval English Religious Tradition* (Cambridge: D. S. Brewer, 1990), pp. 161–75.

4 There is a thriving industry in Margery Kempe criticism, which includes several useful general studies of the text. See C. W. Atkinson, *Mystic and Pilgrim: The Book and the*

*World of Margery Kempe* (Ithaca: Cornell University Press, 1983); K. Lochrie, *Margery Kempe and Translations of the Flesh* (Philadelphia: University of Pennsylvania Press, 1991); S. J. McEntire (ed.), *Margery Kempe: A Book of Essays* (New York: Garland Publishing, 1992), S. Beckwith, *Christ's Body: Identity, Culture and Society in Late Medieval Writings* (London: Routledge, 1993). For works dealing specifically with Margery and pilgrimage see Atkinson, *Mystic and Pilgrim*; D. Dyas, *Pilgrimage in Medieval English Literature, 700–1500* (Cambridge: D. S. Brewer, 2001); J. Helfers, 'The mystic as pilgrim: Margery Kempe and the tradition of nonfictional travel narrative', *Journal of the Rocky Mountain Medieval and Renaissance Association*, 13 (1992), 25–45; T. Bowers, 'Margery Kempe as traveler', *Studies in Philology*, 1:47 (2000), 1–28. For a discussion of the rationale behind Margery's apparently indiscriminate revelations of details of her life, see R. Voaden, *God's Words, Women's Voices: The Discernment of Spirits in the Writing of Late-Medieval Woman Visionaries* (York: York Medieval Press, 1999), pp. 109–57.

5  Margery's one-time parish priest, William Sawtre, was the first person to be executed under this statute (Atkinson, *Mystic and Pilgrim*, pp. 103–4). It is unlikely that Margery was tainted by association; although it is possible that conversations with Sawtre early in her spiritual career could have contributed to the unconventional aspects of Margery's piety, she does not manifest any affiliation with Lollard practices or beliefs. An excellent study of Margery Kempe in the context of early fourteenth century English heresy-hunting is Beckwith, *Christ's Body*.

6  Margery's scribe undoubtedly played a role in formulating the *Book*, though the amount of editorial control he exercised is debatable, and certainly the finished product bears little resemblance to the lives of Margery's models, such as Birgitta of Sweden and Marie d'Oignies. See Voaden, *God's Words*, pp. 109–54 for a discussion of the forces at work in the construction of Margery Kempe.

7  Margery Kempe, *Book*, pp. 209 and 195.

8  *Ibid.*, pp. liii–lxi; J. Dillon, 'Holy women and their confessors or confessors and their holy women? Margery Kempe and continental tradition', in R. Voaden (ed.), *Prophets Abroad: The Reception of Continental Holy Women in Late-Medieval England* (Cambridge: D. S. Brewer, 1996), pp. 115–40; U. Stargardt, 'The Beguines of Belgium, the Dominican nuns of Germany, and Margery Kempe', in T. J. Heffernan (ed.), *The Popular Literature of Medieval England* (Knoxville: University of Tennessee Press, 1985), pp. 275–313.

9  Margery Kempe, *Book*, pp. 143 and 153.

10  *Ibid.*, p. 47.

11  This marks the location of the quay in the thirteenth century. During subsequent centuries, the build-up of silt and rubbish led the east bank of the river Ouse to shift, so that the current river bank is about sixty metres west of the medieval quay (*King's Lynn: The First Thousand Years*, King's Lynn Blue Badge Guides (King's Lynn: King's Lynn Town Guides, 1997), p. 13). However, there can be no doubt that at the end of the fourteenth century St Margaret's would still have been in the centre of quayside activity.

12  Margery probably grew up in a house on Bridgegate (now High Street) which parallels the quays on the river Ouse and runs between the two principal market places (C. Scott Stokes, 'Margery Kempe: Her life and the early history of her Book', *Mystics Quarterly*, 25:1–2 (1999), 9–68, at 19; see also D. H. Owen (ed.), *The Making of King's Lynn: A Documentary Survey* (London: Oxford University Press, 1984), pp. 185–7).

13  E. Carus-Wilson, 'The medieval trade of the ports of the Wash', *Medieval Archaeology*, 6–7 (1962–3), 182–201, at 182.

14 D. S. Ellis, 'Margery Kempe and King's Lynn', in McEntire (ed.), *Margery Kempe: A Book of Essays*, pp. 139–63, at p. 143. This essay offers a detailed description of Lynn during Margery's lifetime, including information about her extended family and their role in the town.

15 T. H. Lloyd, *England and the German Hanse, 1157–1611: A Study of their Trade and Commercial Diplomacy* (Cambridge: Cambridge University Press, 1991), p. 91; *King's Lynn: The First Thousand Years*, p. 13. The latter dates the building of the Hanseatic *Kontor* to 1475. A *Kontor* was almost a self-contained community, with wharves, warehouses, halls, residences and taverns. The Hanseatic warehouse in Lynn can still be seen – it is just behind St Margaret's Church.

16 Carus-Wilson, 'Ports of the Wash', 196.

17 Scott Stokes, 'Margery', 14–15.

18 *Ibid.*, p. 13.

19 It is no surprise that south-east England, to which Lynn formed the gateway, was the source of much religious turmoil and secular unrest in the fourteenth century. Quite apart from William Sawtre, there was considerable Lollard activity in this area; Norwich had special pits for the burning of heretics. Additionally, Essex and Cambridge were the hotbeds of the Peasants' Uprising in 1381.

20 V. Turner and E. Turner, *Image and Pilgrimage in Christian Culture: Anthropological Perspectives* (New York: Columbia University Press, 1978), pp. 1–39 and 250.

21 See Dyas, *Pilgrimage*, pp. 141–4 and 236–42 for ecclesiastical opposition to geographic pilgrimage. See also S. Schein, 'Bridget of Sweden, Margery Kempe and women's Jerusalem pilgrimages in the Middle Ages', *Mediterranean Historical Review*, 14:1 (1999), 44–58, at 46–9.

22 W. R. Childs, 'The perils, or otherwise, of maritime pilgrimage to Santiago de Compostela in the fifteenth century', in J. Stopford (ed.), *Pilgrimage Explored* (York: York Medieval Press, 1999), pp. 123–43, at p. 133.

23 Helfers, 'Mystic', 42.

24 On letters patent for English pilgrims see Bowers, 'Margery', 5.

25 Childs, 'Perils', pp. 130–2.

26 Technically, pilgrims were under the protection of both Church and lay authorities; what practical security this offered is open to doubt (Childs, 'Perils', pp. 125–6).

27 F. M. Stenton, 'The road system of medieval England', *The Economic History Review*, 7:1 (1936), 1–21, at 16.

28 Childs, 'Perils', p. 128.

29 Margery Kempe, *Book*, pp. 286–7 n. 64/13–16. For more details on the cost of pilgrimage, see J. Sumption, *Pilgrimage: An Image of Medieval Religion* (Totowa, NJ: Rowman and Littlefield, 1975), pp. 203–10. For the cost of land travel, see also Childs, 'Perils', p. 129.

30 Margery Kempe, *Book*, pp. 286–7 n. 64/13–16.

31 Sumption, *Pilgrimage*, pp. 203–9.

32 Margery Kempe, *Book*, p. 32. Margery goes on pilgrimage to Compostela in the summer of 1417, probably on a 'package tour' (*ibid.*, pp. 105–10).

33 *Ibid.*, p. 25. This episode occurred in 1413, at which time John and Margery had been married for about twenty years and had produced fourteen children.

34 Scott Stokes, 'Margery', 30–1; J. Brefeld, *A Guidebook for the Jerusalem Pilgrimage in the Late Middle Ages: A Case for Computer-Aided Textual Criticism* (Hilversum: Verloren, 1994), p. 15.

35 Sumption, *Pilgrimage*, p. 182. See pp. 175–84 for horror stories of attacks on pilgrims throughout the Middle Ages.

36 Margery was also privy to more specialised knowledge of what she would have to deal with. Her confessor prophesied how she would suffer, be deserted by her fellow pilgrims and be brought to safety by a hunchbacked man, all of which came to pass (Margery Kempe, *Book*, p. 60).

37 *Writers and Pilgrims: Medieval Pilgrimage Narratives and their Posterity* (Berkeley: University of California Press, 1980), p. 17.

38 'The pilgrims [*sic*] sea-voyage', in F. J. Furnivall (ed.), *The Stacions of Rome* (New York: Greenwood Press, 1969; originally pub. London: Early English Text Society, 1876), pp. 38–40.

39 Quoted in Sumption, *Pilgrimage*, p. 168.

40 Margery Kempe, *Book*, p. 60.

41 *Ibid.*, p. 95.

42 M. Tjader Harris (ed.), *Birgitta of Sweden: Life and Selected Revelations* (New York: Paulist Press, 1990), pp. 202–6. This was a highly influential vision, affecting subsequent iconographic representations of the Nativity. Before Birgitta's vision, in artistic representations Mary is depicted lying down with the Christ Child either on her breast or in the manger beside her – as a normal mother might appear after birth. Birgitta's vision led to the depiction of Mary kneeling before the child.

43 Margery Kempe, *Book*, p. 286 n. 64/13–16.

44 *Ibid.*, pp. 62 and 64.

45 Childs, 'Perils', p. 132.

46 Margery Kempe, *Book*, p. 284 n. 60/18–19.

47 Scott Stokes, 'Margery', 32.

48 For the Beguines of Liège, see Juliette Dor, Lesley Johnson and Jocelyn Wogan-Browne (eds), *New Trends in Feminine Spirituality: The Holy Women of Liège and their Impact* (Turnhout: Brepols, 1999). For connections between Margery and Beguine spirituality, see Stargardt, 'Beguines'.

49 Howard, *Writers*, p. 35.

50 Christian K. Zacher, *Curiosity and Pilgrimage: The Literature of Discovery in Fourteenth-Century England* (Baltimore: Johns Hopkins University Press, 1976), p. 20.

51 Quoted in Zacher, *Curiosity*, p. 42.

52 Margery Kempe, *Book*, pp. 61–4.

53 *Ibid.*, p. 62.

54 Bowers, 'Margery', 18–20.

55 Margery Kempe, *Book*, p. 70.

56 *Ibid.*, pp. 71–4.

57 *Ibid.*, p. 75.

58 *Ibid.*, p. 73 n. 73/28.

59 Angela of Foligno, *Angela of Foligno: Complete Works*, trans. P. Lachance (New York: Paulist Press, 1993), pp. 112–13.

60 Margery Kempe, *Book*, pp. 86–9.

61 *Ibid.*, p. 226.

62 Margery frequently complains of her daughter-in-law's hostility (*ibid.*, pp. 228 and 231).

63 Ute Stargardt details Margery's demonstrated affinity for Germans, and explores the possibility that she may have spoken some German ('Beguines', p. 305).

64 The shrine at Wilsnak housed three consecrated hosts sprinkled with blood which were purported to have survived the fire which destroyed the church in 1383 (Margery Kempe, *Book*, p. 344 n. 232/10–11). The shrine at Aachen was the repository of the smock worn by the Virgin Mary when she gave birth, Christ's swaddling clothes, the

cloth which held the head of John the Baptist and the loincloth Christ wore on the cross. Every seven years these were exhibited for a two-week period surrounding St Margaret's Day; Margery's visit coincided with such an exhibition (*ibid.*, p. 346 n. 237/31).

65 The same apparent lack of interest in the destination of pilgrimage is also evident in her account of her journey to Compostela; her experience at the shrine merits barely four lines of text, the bulk of the account being a chronicle of her problems and the hostility she encounters.

66 *Ibid.*, p. 344 n. 233.

67 *Ibid.*, p. 231.

68 Birgitta is still venerated in Gdansk. In the 1970s and 1980s St Birgitta's Church was the spiritual centre of the Solidarity movement (U. Stargardt (trans.), *The Life of Dorothea von Montau, a Fourteenth Century Recluse* (Lewiston: Edwin Mellen Press, 1997), p. 9 n. 12). The celebrations in Rome in 1991 commemorating the 600th anniversary of Birgitta's canonisation included a contingent from the Gdansk shipyards, complete with brass band.

69 Stargardt, 'Beguines', p. 307. For a detailed analysis of the similarities between the two texts see *idem*, 'The influence of Dorothea von Montau on the mysticism of Margery Kempe', PhD dissertation, University of Tennessee, 1981.

70 Margery Kempe, *Book*, p. 232.

71 *Ibid.*, p. 232.

72 *Ibid.*, pp. 346–8 n. 237/34–7.

73 For a discussion of Margery's sexual fears and attitudes, see R. Voaden, 'Beholding men's members: The sexualizing of transgression in *The Book of Margery Kempe*', in P. Biller and A. J. Minnis (eds), *Medieval Theology and the Natural Body* (York: York Medieval Press, 1997), pp. 175–90.

74 Her first scribe is described as an Englishman by birth who had married a German and lived in Germany before returning to England with his wife and child, when he lived with Margery and wrote the first part of her revelations. He then died (Margery Kempe, *Book*, p. 4). It is certainly possible that this first scribe was Margery's son, although he is not identified as such.

# 10

## *Of smelly seas and ashen apples:*
## *two German pilgrims' view of the East*

**()**

Anne Simon

### INTRODUCTION

Yet all the country round about is full of trees and great fruits, exceeding fair to
see; but when these fruits are plucked and broken open, they are full of dust
and ashes within, and for three days the hands of him who plucked them
cannot be rid of a vile stench; for even all the country round about it is full of
God's curse.[1]

THIS DESCRIPTION of the Dead Sea, taken from the pilgrimage report by
Ludolf von Sudheim (1350), is echoed one hundred and thirty years later
by another German pilgrim to the Holy Land, Hans Tucher, who wrote: 'The
stench by the Dead Sea is vile, yet many pretty trees are to be found there
which bear fruit that is large, attractive and appealing, just like nice apples.
However, when you pick them, on the inside these fruit are full of dust
and emit an evil smell.'[2] By the Dead Sea stood the five cities of Sodom
and Gomorrah, synonymous with sexual perversion (Genesis 19:1–11) and
destroyed by fire and brimstone (Genesis 19:24–5). Both authors explicitly
connect the overwhelming stench of the Dead Sea and its inability to support
life to the evil practised in these cities, evil which was, even in the late fifteenth
century, strong enough to contaminate the surrounding land and vegeta-
tion.[3] Apples recall Original Sin and the Fall of Man, of which the vice
that led ultimately to the destruction of Sodom and Gomorrah was but one
manifestation. Given their deceptive appeal, they may also symbolise the
vanity of all earthly appearances, especially in comparison with the eternal
truths to which pilgrimage bears witness.

Whilst the Dead Sea really does smell atrocious, the overlaying of the biblical
past on to the travellers' present and the viewing of landscape through the
filter of the Bible constitute features common to medieval pilgrimage reports.
A further feature is the similarity and interdependence of many accounts,

characteristics that affect their status as authentic documents of lived experience.[4] Hence this examination of the pilgrimage reports by Ludolf von Sudheim and Hans Tucher will focus on the following issues: the practicalities of travel, the authors' response to the experience of travel; the veracity of lived experience versus the veracity of the literary text; the shaping of the journey and of the perception of the outside world by preconceptions derived from the Bible; and the at times uneasy jostling of immersion into the sacred past of the shrines against the sharp reality of discomfort on the journey, imprisonment, assaults by hostile Saracens, financial extortion, heat and the impact on the senses of the Orient. Finally, both men are sharp observers of the world around them and describe in considerable detail not just the shrines but the societies encountered, trade and the political realities that governed travel in the fourteenth and fifteenth centuries, such as the loss of the Holy Land by western Christendom and the domination of the Mediterranean by the Turks. Moreover, Tucher occasionally notes his own personal responses, so his pilgrimage report is an interesting record both of Muslim society in the Holy Land and Egypt and of an individual's response to a different culture. I shall also refer to the account by the Dominican friar Felix Fabri from Ulm, who undertook two pilgrimages (1480 and 1483) and who drew on Tucher's account in compiling his own, the *Eigentlich Beschreibung*.

### LUDOLF VON SUDHEIM

Ludolf von Sudheim is believed to have been *Rector* in Sudheim, a small place near Lichtenau in the diocese of Paderborn, Westphalia. His work, the Latin version of which was the first pilgrimage report to be printed in Germany, is dedicated to the Bishop of Paderborn, Baldwin of Steinfurt. At the time of his journey Ludolf may have been chaplain to a German knight in the service of the King of Armenia. He travelled through the Holy Land, Egypt and Syria between 1336 and 1341. His account was written in Latin (the oldest known manuscript dates from *c.* 1380), and circulated widely in manuscript (forty-four manuscripts are extant). It was translated into Low and High German (eight manuscripts and seven manuscripts respectively) and eventually published, probably in Augsburg, some time around 1468.[5] The first German edition appeared in 1473 in Ulm; it was followed by a second in Augsburg around 1476. Further editions followed; the text was also reprinted in all four editions of *Das Reyßbuch deß Heyligen Lands* (1584, 1609, 1629 and 1659), initially published by Sigmund Feyerabend. Manuscript and printing history thus suggest that Ludolf's work was one of the most popular early German pilgrimage reports.

Closer consideration of the text itself reveals a broad underlying principle to its structure, though details remain open to debate.[6] Ludolf starts with a preface which sets out his reasons for writing, tackling head-on the thorny question of veracity and first-hand experience:

> Howbeit, let no one suppose that I beheld with my eyes each several one of the things which I intend to put into this book, but that I have happily extracted some of them from ancient books of history, and that some things I have heard from the lips of truthful men, all of which in whatsoever places they are written or found, I have decided to trust to the judgement of the discreet reader . . . and at this present day I could put in yet more, which I pass over because of ignorant cavillers and scoffers, lest I should tell anything which they could not believe, and for which I would be held by them for a liar; for to ignorant cavillers and scoffers, who are not worthy to know anything at all, everything seems incredible and passing belief. (p. 2)

First-hand experience is not construed as essential to the veracity of the text, though reliable sources are. By trusting the reader Ludolf is giving the former a stake in defending the text as true and creating an ally against the 'cavillers and scoffers', themselves dismissed as unworthy of the text and by implication of the truths to which it bears witness. Ludolf then gives a glowingly emotive description of the Holy Land's importance in biblical history and hence in mankind's salvation, culminating in the veiled suggestion that it should be reclaimed from the Saracens through a crusade.

Ludolf starts the account proper with the necessity of obtaining papal permission for the journey, in other words, with practical preparations.[7] He lists a number of possible land routes before concentrating on the sea route across the Mediterranean. The section called 'The Mediterranean Sea' ushers in a series on subjects such as 'The Peril called "Gulph"',[8] 'The Peril of shoals' and 'Perils by Fish'. Thus the actual narration of the sea route is preceded by a list of risks encountered on it, a strategy which may derive from a desire for comprehensiveness or from the traveller's desire to show off by enumerating dangers braved and conquered. It derives further purpose from the *imitatio Christi*: the trials and tribulations suffered by pilgrims en route to the Holy Land allowed them to relive Christ's suffering.[9] Ludolf seems to envisage Genoa as the port of departure, for he describes Corsica, Sardinia and Sicily, which do not lie on the route from Venice. Several sections may be devoted to one topic, as when Ludolf describes Sicilian towns and volcanoes separately from the island as a whole. Greece and Cyprus form the subsequent focus of the narrative, with paragraphs devoted to various islands, towns and places of interest. After arrival in Alexandria the narrative takes a tremendous leap to Tripoli, then works back down the Palestinian and Egyptian coasts to Alexandria and Cairo (see Figures 1 and 2).

Then begins the journey through the Sinai desert via St Catherine's monastery to Bethlehem and Jerusalem. This route is not common in pilgrimage reports, especially later ones; usually pilgrims landed in Jaffa and rode straight to Jerusalem from there. Ludolf himself draws attention to the change in route and attributes it to the recent destruction of Jaffa by the sultan (p. 49). Common or not, there can be no doubt that a contemporary reader would have recognised in the route described the history of salvation as presented in the Old and New Testaments, starting with the Exodus and proceeding to the Birth and Crucifixion of Christ. Indeed, the function of the text as an aid to meditation may have dictated this ordering of the material, rather than the actual sequence of Ludolf's journey. Further support is lent to this thesis by the sequence of shrines within the holy city itself. This starts with the Temple of the Rock, the place of Abraham's sacrifice of Isaac, prefiguring the Crucifixion. It proceeds to the Castle of David, seen as the ancestor of Christ; the Church of the Holy Sepulchre on Calvary' the place of the Crucifixion' the Tomb of Christ and the tombs of the first kings of Jerusalem, Godfrey of Bouillon and his brother Baldwin, showing that the Christian crusading past that determines Ludolf's narrative is a consequence of Christ's death, and linking the biblical past with the present of both traveller and reader. The sequence concludes with Sion, the place of the Last Supper, of Christ's apparition to his disciples after the Resurrection and of the descent of the Holy Spirit. In other words, these events link the pre-Crucifixion past to the post-Crucifixion future, Christian mission and Christian salvation, and in so doing further reinforce the justification for a crusade. After devoting more space to shrines round Jerusalem, including the valley of Josaphat where Judgement Day will occur, and the Mount of Olives, scene of the Ascension, Ludolf describes first the Jordan, site of Christ's baptism and the initiation into the Christian Church through the cleansing of sins, and then places in the north of the country. He finishes with Damascus and records, in the mountains of Lebanon, 'a vast multitude of Christians conforming to the Latin rite and the Church of Rome, many of whose bishops I have seen consecrated by Latin archbishops, and who ever long with singular eagerness for the coming of Crusaders and the recovery of the Holy Land' (p. 135). Thus the work both starts and finishes on the idea of a crusade: the incentive and the hope for one since Christians in the Holy Land are both a cause to be embraced and potential allies in the enterprise.

This analysis shows that the way underlies the narrative structure, even if not so plainly as in works from the fifteenth and sixteenth centuries. In Ludolf's case it leads up to a climax in Jerusalem: Crucifixion, Resurrection, Ascension and Judgement Day, the end of history as man knows it and start of eternity. The passages on the Lebanon return the narrative to its starting point by resuming and reinforcing the theme of a crusade (implicit in the lament over Acre (pp. 50–61)) to rescue the land of Christian salvation from the hands of the infidel.[10] Furthermore, the structure supports Ludolf's avowed aim in writing his account. As well as honouring Bishop Baldwin of Paderborn, Ludolf intends to give a more detailed, accurate and well-founded picture of the Holy Land than many others lacking his experience of the country. Thus his chosen route enables him to include the maximum amount of information in a reasonably logical sequence, while the division into short sections facilitates rapid and focused reference. It also enables the reader to follow the journey as it unfolds. Nowhere, however, does Ludolf claim to be writing in order to help or encourage others to undertake a pilgrimage, a claim found, for example, in Tucher.

Ludolf's ordering of his material in sections and under headings is a narrative principle which does not immediately reflect the straightforwardly linear progression of the journey found in late medieval accounts. This organisation of the text may be interpreted in various ways.[11] First, one may assume that a strict division of the material served to master the richness, diversity and possible threat posed by experiences in an East that was ruled by enemies of the Christian faith. In other words, the literary form indirectly expresses the feeling of being overwhelmed by the Other and an attempt to reassert control by dividing the material and the experience itself into manageable sections. However, from Ludolf's prologue it becomes clear that his work was written some years after his journey, so at a time when first impressions had been digested and may even have faded. Moreover, the ordering of the material is reminiscent of that in medieval encyclopaedias, which have as their basic structural principle the six days of the Creation.[12] Thus, second, it may well be that in using this established structure Ludolf wanted to borrow established authority for his work and hence reinforce its credibility and authority in turn. Finally, the structure may, in accordance with the aim of an encyclopaedia, have been intended to facilitate access by the reader to all information on a subject included in this particular text.[13]

Credibility and authority also derive from personal experience, in which Ludolf's narrative is rooted from the start and which is his justification for writing. Thus he begins his work with the remark: 'Now, I have dwelt in those parts for an unbroken space of five years, being both by day and by night in the company of kings and princes, chiefs, nobles and lords' (p. 1). He locates the narrative firmly in his own personal past to guarantee its validity: 'I have caught quails . . . on board ship, but they straightaway died. Yet in all the parts in which I have been beyond the seas, I have never seen a stork; but once in a monastery of Minorites I saw a stork which was held to be a wonder for size' (p. 19).

Moreover, Ludolf refers repeatedly to people he has known. Thus his status as eyewitness to their actions becomes a source of authority for his written account. About the wealth of the local aristocracy on Cyprus, for example, he writes: 'The princes, nobles, barons, knights, and citizens of Cyprus are the richest in the world ... But they spend it all in hunting. I knew a count of Jaffa who kept more than five hundred hounds, every pair of which dogs, according to the custom of those parts, had a servant of their own, to keep them clean, bathe them, and anoint them, which must needs be done to hunting dogs in those parts' (p. 43).

Ludolf's observing eye also registers mercantile activity and is first attracted by the wealth of the citizens of Famagusta: 'In a warehouse in this city there is more aloeswood than five carts can carry; I say nothing about spices, for they are as common there as bread is here, and are just as commonly mixed and sold' (pp. 42–3). He continues: 'There are also in Cyprus exceeding rich citizens and merchants, and no wonder, seeing that Cyprus is the furthest (east) of all Christian lands, wherefore all ships both great and small, and all merchandise of whatsoever kind and from whatsoever country, must needs come first of all to Cyprus, and can in no wise pass by it' (pp. 43–4). Cyprus, then, is located not just in terms of Christian geography but also in terms of its position on the trade map of the East.[14] Trade also links the present of Ludolf's journey to the past of Christian crusader dominance in the Holy Land, for, in his description of Acre, the last crusader stronghold to fall to the Saracens (1291), Ludolf highlights its pre-eminence as a centre of trade and the wealth of its merchants:

> There also dwelt in Acre the richest merchants under heaven, who were gathered together therein out of all nations; there were Pisans, Genoese, and Lombards, by whose accursed quarrels the city was lost, for they also bore themselves like nobles. There dwelt therein also exceeding rich merchants of other nations, for from sunrise to sunset all parts of the world brought merchandise thither, and everything that can be found in the world that is wondrous or strange used to be brought thither because of the nobles and princes who dwelt there. (p. 53)

Damascus, however, surpasses all other cities; here more than anywhere else the reader has a sense of the far-flung trade routes that covered and drew together Occident and Orient:

> It stands on the place where Cain killed his brother Abel, and is an exceeding noble, glorious, and beauteous city, rich in all manner of merchandise, and everywhere delightful, but more by artificial than by natural loveliness, abounding in foods, spices, precious stones, silk, pearls, cloth-of-gold, perfumes from India, Tartary, Egypt, Syria, and places on our side of the Mediterranean, and in all precious things that the heart of man can conceive. (p. 129)[15]

Whilst the description of trade in Acre is obviously part of a strategy of lament and memory intended to stir the feelings of Christians in the West, cumulatively the various descriptions of merchant activity impart to the reader a map of the Mediterranean and the Orient different from that inscribed with the history of salvation and the crusades. The underlying map is one of a web of trade routes spreading from India to the Mediterranean, of the creation by trade of communities which cut across national and religious boundaries, of long-term knowledge and cultural interaction on a level quite distinct from the hostility of recent crusading history.[16]

As established earlier, though, Ludolf's pilgrimage report is based not just on personal experience and observation. His inclusion of material from classical authors and of stories from more or less reliable eyewitnesses is a practice common to pilgrimage reports and an inherent part of the literary structure of the pilgrimage experience.[17] Indeed, in the case of oral sources, such as sailors, Ludolf himself has to vouch for their credibility.[18] In other words, he uses the authority he has himself established as author to lend authority to other sources, and the strategy he chooses, though itself a topos, is intended to shut down disbelief. Ludolf's text does not, therefore, transmit an immediate impression of either the experience of travel or the process of observing and reacting to foreign cultures but rather one that has been selected and compiled from various sources and omits as much as it includes. Furthermore, whilst Ludolf includes his experiences, he refrains from recording his feelings and reactions; thus no conclusions as to his state of mind during the voyage may be drawn.

Yet it is in this very absence that the key to understanding Ludolf's experience of pilgrimage and encounter with the Other lies: the author steps back behind his text because his emotions are unimportant in comparison with the shrines and the testimony they bear to Christ's life and ministry.[19] That is above all the case in the description of the Holy Land, where the landscape is a physical map of the biblical past and man's need for tangible proof of it: 'Also near Bethlehem there is a great cave in the rock, into which a great number of bodies of the Innocents were cast, and this rock has been almost entirely carried away by pilgrims' (p. 96).[20] Ludolf's text is a record of the physical changes wrought on the Holy Land by Christian devotion and indicates how the present of the pilgrims could impact on the past of their faith. The shift in temporal levels (between present and past) is accompanied by one in emphasis: it is not just the validity of the literary record of lived experience that is important but also the pilgrims' need for evidence of the validity of the biblical past.[21]

Nevertheless, missing from this and indeed many other pilgrimage reports is any explicit expression of personal piety or jubilation on finally seeing the places of Christ's ministry so familiar from the Bible. In Jerusalem, for example, Ludolf describes the Church of the Holy Sepulchre, which he likens to the cathedral of Munster in Westphalia, with detailed matter-of-factness:

> The inside of this church is very much like the cathedral of Munster in Westphalia, especially in the choir . . . In front of the choir, on the west side, stands a small double chapel which has as it were three doors, and wherein three altars seem to have stood. From this chapel one goes into another chapel, wherein is Christ's sepulchre, through a low and small doorway, arched semicircularly, and made so that one must enter it with a bent back. This chapel is semicircularly vaulted; it has no window, and in it is Christ's sepulchre. The length of this chapel and sepulchre is about nine palms, the width of the chapel about seven palms, and the height of the chapel is about twelve palms. Christ's sepulchre is cut out of the solid rock, but lest it should be defiled or carried away by pilgrims, it is covered with other stones of white marble. (pp. 103–5)

The unadorned style means that the reader is responding more directly to the relics and shrines themselves rather than the author's response to them. As pilgrimage reports were intended, amongst other things, to enable people at home to recreate a pilgrimage spiritually and emotionally or, indeed, to re-enact one physically, with buildings in the home town being designated the Church of the Holy Sepulchre, Mary's birthplace, and so on, the precise, detailed descriptions of the holy sites perform an essential function.[22] The comparison to home, something found in most reports, also has the function of linking sacred past and secular present and of bringing the sacred into the reader's everyday life. It does so by making the physical reality of the Holy Land or Egypt more tangible, presenting it in terms of the reader's own visual and spatial experience and giving him access to the sacred, or even just the foreign, through his own home world. Michael Baxandall stresses the active nature of the interior visualisation of holy stories by the pious 'practised in spiritual exercises that demanded a high level of visualisation of, at least, the central episodes of the lives of Christ and Mary'.[23] Images of such stories constituted the basis of what Baxendall terms 'a visualizing meditation'.[24] Indeed, quoting from the *Zardino de oration* (1454) Baxandall makes clear how superimposing the holy onto the familiar aided devotion:

> The better to impress the story of the Passion on your mind, and to memorise each action of it more easily, it is helpful and necessary to fix the places and people in your mind: a city, for example, which will be the city of Jerusalem – taking for this purpose a city that is well known to you. In this city find the principal places in which all the episodes of the Passion would have taken place – for instance, a palace with the supper-room where Christ had the Last Supper with the Disciples . . . When you have done all this, putting all your imagination into it, then go into your chamber. Alone and solitary, excluding every external thought from your mind, start thinking of the beginning of the Passion, starting with how Jesus entered Jerusalem on the ass.[25]

By facilitating the visualisation of the physical and spiritual geography of the Holy Land and Egypt, Ludolf is aiding his readers' active meditation and prayer.

On the other hand, whilst contemporary landscape and architecture are read as documents of the distant biblical past, they may also be read as documents of the more recent crusading past. In addition to his lengthy description of the glories of Acre and the heart-rending account of its fall (pp. 54–61), attributed in part to quarrels amongst its Christian citizens,[26] Ludolf frequently mentions the ruined remains of crusader settlements, members of the military orders and other individual Christians left over, as it were, in the Holy Land:

> This same city [Caesarea], on recovery of the Holy Land, came into the possession of a certain knight of these parts, named De Horne, whose son-in-law's widow was living even in my own time, for I have often seen her and talked upon this subject with her. Going on from Caesarea, one comes to what once was a fair city, but now is deserted, called Pilgrims' Castle, which of old was called Assur. This city was given to the Templars by Godfrey de Bouillon, the first Christian king of Jerusalem, for a memorial of himself. (pp. 64–5)

In this way Ludolf's pilgrimage report becomes not just a confirmation of the biblical past but a chronicle of recent Christian engagement with the Holy Land, the result of beliefs generated by events recorded in the Bible. It documents architectural and human traces on the landscape which serve, amongst other things, as both memorial to and reinforcement of the Christian claim to it. Thus Ludolf's journey becomes the movement through physical geography and temporal geology on at least three, possibly four layers: the era of the Bible; that of the crusades; that of Ludolf's present; and that of the reader's present with the biblical and historical knowledge he or she brings to bear on the text. Ludolf's work is therefore a type of literary excavation. As Mary Campbell puts it: 'Like an archaeologist, the Christian pilgrim is looking for the past, but it is a past made up of singular events and personalities, individual epiphanies, incarnations, and martyrdoms. Places are referred to as "witnesses" of those events and people, and pilgrims in turn are witnesses of those places seen *as* events.'[27] Awareness of the crusades – as both acquisition and loss – runs like a unifying thread through the narrative, reinforcing the implicit appeal for a renewed campaign to win back the Holy Land for Christendom, rebuild the ruins and thereby restore the glorious past.

If pilgrims, then, read the Holy Land through the filter of their faith, Ludolf might be expected to observe members of other faiths through the filter of the Catholic Church. However, Ludolf displays tolerance towards other religions. The Mamluk rulers of Egypt controlled the Holy Land, and one might be forgiven for expecting a more pronounced hatred of Islam, such as is found, for example, in the pilgrimage report of the Dean of Mainz Cathedral, Bernhard von Breidenbach.[28] However, Ludolf seems to acknowledge Muslim piety:

The Saracens pay the greatest reverence to the Lord's Temple, keeping it exceed-ingly clean both within and without, and all alike entering it unshod. They call it 'the holy Rock', not 'the Temple,' and therefore they say to one another, 'Let us go to the holy Rock.' . . . I have heard it said of a truth by Saracen renegades that no Saracen presumes to touch that rock, and that Saracens journey from distant lands to devoutly visit it. (p. 98)

His tolerance may stem from the fact that some external forms of Muslim veneration for their holy places are recognisable and acceptable to a Latin Christian. Where the divergence in culture is too great, alienation is dis-cernible. It is provoked, for example, by the Bedouins encountered in the desert en route from Sinai to Hebron. The description of their 'diabolical' appearance may reflect the fear, loneliness and vulnerability experienced by pilgrims in what must have been a completely new and alien landscape:

In this wilderness there is exceeding great scarcity of water, and countless people dwell therein like wild beasts . . . They never eat bread, unless some pilgrims chance to give them some, or unless it be brought to them more than twelve days' jour-ney; for they neither sow nor reap, but live like wild beasts, and their faces are very dreadful to look upon, black and bearded; they are very fierce and swift, and on the backs of their dromedaries they can go as far as they please in one day, seeking for the places where water may be found. (p. 90)

Even if the characteristics singled out for description reflect the facts, swarthiness and ugliness are signs of the diabolic with which the genuinely strange and threatening are associated. Bedouins live outside regulated urban communities, dress differently, and enjoy a way of life that must have been completely incomprehensible to pilgrims.

As Jeffrey Richards points out, the Devil, sexual deviation, heresy and disease were very closely connected in medieval thought, and outsiders – groups excluded from and by the Church and society – were in their turn identified by and labelled with these characteristics.[29] In the pilgrimage accounts traces of this attitude can be found: what is strange, non-Christian and hence potentially threatening is connected not just to the Devil but, for example, to nudity and lasciviousness:

Near Paphos once stood Venus's Castle, where they used to worship the idol Venus, and travel from distant lands to visit her gates, and thither all noble lords and ladies and young damsels gathered together in that castle. It was in this temple that the first step was taken towards the ruin of Troy; for Helen was taken when on her way to this temple. Moreover, all damsels and girls used to make vows in this temple for marriage and husbands, wherefore in Cyprus men are more lustful by nature beyond those of all other lands, for if earth from Cyprus, and more especially from the place where Venus's Castle used to stand, be placed beneath a man's head as he sleeps, it will throughout the whole night dispose him to lust. (p. 39)

Of course, this borders on the fantastic. It cannot be denied that a certain element of the fabulous and mythological is present in Ludolf's report. In fact, there is a stock of legends drawn on by many authors. Helen of Troy, for example, is frequently mentioned, as are dragons and unicorns.[30] In addition Ludolf includes flying fish which hatch out of apples in England and Ireland (p. 18), and the inhabitants of Corsica who cure themselves of snake bites with their own spittle and pass this gift on to others.[31] The fantastic shades into religious superstition, such as the belief in the power to aid nursing mothers with Mary's milk (scraped off a rock in the cave in Bethlehem where she and the infant Christ hid from Herod) or the power to cure fever with twigs from bushes like the burning bush in which God appeared to Moses. The for-us-unlikely is not questioned, possibly because in God's Creation everything is possible. The Bible itself bears witness to the existence of giants (Genesis 6:4); fantastic creatures were documented in classical and oriental travel literature and depicted on the margins of medieval *mappaemundi*.[32] Besides this, the exotic was essential to the poetics of the Other, especially of the Orient, as Wolfram von Eschenbach's *Parzival*, *Herzog Ernst* and the Alexander story show. In his description of the fabulous Ludolf is fulfilling his readers' expectations, which in part determine his literary portrayal of travel. The conventions of the genre demand that the protagonist encounter the strange and wonderful, the survival of which enhances his prestige as well as providing excitement and entertainment for his reader. Furthermore, there is often a core of truth: flying fish do exist, even if they do not hatch out of apples. The attempt to describe an experience outside the writer's and reader's normal mental and linguistic world can make something seem fabulous which is not really so, as illustrated by Ludolf's description of whales in the Mediterranean:[33]

> [T]he same sailor told me not to wonder, because there was in the sea a fish a mile long, which was four thousand six hundred miles [*sic*] wide in the narrowest part ... I have seen three such fishes off Sardinia. They puffed out water with their breath into the air in vast quantity, further than a crossbow could shoot, and made a noise like thunder. Moreover, in my time near the isle of Tortosa, such a fish while chasing other little fishes cast himself up on the dry land, driving a great wave of water before him, and when the water ran back into the sea the fish remained on dry land, and fed all the dwellers in those parts with his flesh and fat. (p. 17)

In fact, Ludolf's account is a perfectly accurate description of whale behaviour.

If Ludolf has a chiffre for the Otherness of the foreign and the fear it inspires, this symbol is the recurrent motif of poison. While poisonous animals doubtless existed, poison is above all an attribute of the snake:

In this country the serpent called *tyrus* is found and taken, whence what is called tyriac (treacle) gets its name, for it is chiefly made thereof.[34] This is a serpent not half an ell long, as thick as a man's finger, of a yellow colour mixed with red, and it is blind. No cure for its poison is known except cutting off the bitten limb. When it is angry it puts out its tongue like a flame of fire, and one would think that it was fire indeed, save that it does not burn the creature; it sets up the hair on its face like an angry boar, and its head at such times grows bigger. Were it not blind I believe that no man could escape from it, for I have heard from those whose trade it is to catch these serpents that if they bit a man's horse, they would kill the rider. (p. 117)

The snake is the symbol *par excellence* of Satan, and this species, the thyriac, a sort of viper, is caught near Sodom and Gomorrah. In other words, the medieval cleric Ludolf senses his vulnerability as a traveller in a foreign country and the threat posed by its Otherness most keenly in the place which in the Bible is defined by vice and destroyed by God for its wickedness. The snake, made more threatening by its colour symbolism (red, the Devil's colour) and fire (shades of Hell), is related to the ashen apples as a symbol of mankind's Fall, from which the pilgrimage forms part of the long journey of redemption.

### HANS TUCHER

Let us turn next to Hans Tucher. Tucher was a member of a Nuremberg patrician family. In 1476 he became a member of the town council in place of his elder brother Endres, who entered a Carthusian monastery. Hans Tucher was made *Bürgermeister* in 1480. In May 1479 he embarked on a pilgrimage to the Holy Land in the company of another Nuremberg patrician, Sebald Rieter. After almost a year's absence (until March 1480), on their return each of them wrote an account of his journey. In doing so Rieter was following a family tradition most recently upheld by his father, Sebald senior, whose visits to Rome in 1450, Santiago in 1462 and the Holy Land in 1464 are recorded in the family chronicle; the latter provided material for his son's and Tucher's accounts.[35]

In undertaking the journey to the Holy Land the two men were following not only a strong local tradition – in the Middle Ages more pilgrims went from Nuremberg and Lübeck to the Holy Land than from any other German city – but in Rieter's case a strong family one.[36] While Rieter's report was, like those of his predecessors, probably meant for the edification of family and friends rather than a wider public, Tucher's appeared in print in Augsburg in 1482. By 1486 it had seen six more editions.[37] Other pilgrims such as Felix Fabri and the Dean of Mainz Cathedral, Bernhard von Breidenbach, drew on it in compiling their reports. In fact, it was amongst the most widely read pilgrimage accounts of the Middle Ages[38] and was, like Ludolf's, reprinted in *Das Reyßbuch deß heyligen Lands.*

Tucher's report reveals, first, a strong will to organise the narrative clearly and logically; second, skill in integrating material from various sources. Structurally, his work falls into two distinct parts. The first encompasses the journey to and through the Holy Land; a history of the kings of Jerusalem which he tells us is copied from chronicles in the monastery library on Sion;[39] practical advice for the journey; and an itinerary from Nuremberg to Jerusalem.[40] In the second part we find the crossing of the desert to St Catherine's monastery and places linked to Moses and the Exodus; tours of Cairo and Alexandria; a list of two empires and twenty kingdoms in Christendom taken from Rieter senior (and copied in the popular prose novel *Fortunatus*, printed by Johann Otmar in Augsburg in 1509); and more useful travel tips. Thus the structure is balanced: two descriptions of journeys and the destinations once reached, complemented by 'historical' and practical background information and linked by advice on food and equipment for Sinai. Throughout the description of the voyage to the Holy Land the reader is prepared step by step for the climax, Jerusalem. Each visit to the shrines in Venice and the Mediterranean foreshadows the tour of the Holy City. The culmination is reached in the procession round the Church of the Holy Sepulchre and the chance to see places at the heart of the Christian faith. Jerusalem is balanced by St Catherine's monastery on Sinai, and Venice (trading port and point of departure for the exotic unknown) by Cairo and above all Alexandria (trading port and point of departure for the familiar and mundane). A gradual secularisation of subject matter is evident – perhaps a reflection of the farewell to the Holy Land and pilgrim's identity and return to everyday life at home. Moreover, Egypt was less weighted with events connected to the life of Christ, so pilgrims may have felt more open to 'worldly' topics and freer to record them.

Although not all pilgrims went to Sinai, similar elements, arising from the structure of the journey itself, are present in many late medieval and early modern pilgrimage reports. In Tucher's work dates such as 'On the second day of the month of July, the day of Our Lady' (fol. 351$^r$) introduce new sections of the narrative and constitute its ordering framework, which thus comes to be dominated by the passage of (contemporary rather than historical) time. In other contemporary or later accounts this is more pronounced, so that parts of the narrative consist purely of a date in the margin and a brief entry such as '15th. September. Taken ill'.[41] The use of dates as an ordering principle may reflect the pilgrims' taking with them of writing materials to make diary-like notes which then form the basis of the finished work;[42] it also enables the reader to participate mentally and emotionally in the gradual build-up to Jerusalem and re-create for himself the whole unfolding of the pilgrimage.

Now we turn to Tucher's skill in integrating into the narrative material from other sources, including legendaries, chronicles, mythology, other pilgrimage reports, oral traditions and information passed on by monks, guides and local inhabitants. As noted in the discussion of Ludolf, this is standard practice in pilgrimage reports, and sources, apart from oral ones and the chronicles in the library on Sion, are not acknowledged. Such additional information is doubtless intended to give the reader as rounded a picture of pilgrimage to the Holy Land as possible; it also serves to enliven the work. Tucher achieves cohesion by telling the reader all about each place as he comes to it in the course of the journey. When the pilgrims visit Bethlehem, for example, the sites where Christ was born or Jerome translated the Bible are noted straight away (fol. 357$^v$). Similarly, Tucher's description of Rhodes immediately calls for the relevant, if garbled, classical mythology: that the island acted as a launching pad for the destruction of Troy, caused by the presence there of a ram with a golden fleece (fol. 351$^v$). Tucher may have copied this from Ludolf, who gives a similarly worded and similarly confused version.[43] Such an integrating approach may in part be prompted by the need to present useful facts in a form easily followed by a readership without a family tradition of pilgrimage or a family guide to consult as well as by the intention to publish. The results are two-fold: details of the voyage, relics and incidents en route are readily memorable for being immediately connected to a place or story; and a clear and therefore informative picture of pilgrimage emerges. This in turn facilitates mental reconstruction of the pilgrimage for the reader at home and its use as a starting point for private meditation in a way similar to that already observed in Ludolf's narrative.

Tucher is concise, thorough and methodical, taking care to clarify to the reader concepts which may be unfamiliar to him. The same assiduousness is demonstrated in Tucher's awareness of his surroundings: he explains the Mamluk system of government in Cairo in some detail, and the history of the Hospitallers on Rhodes, their role in combatting the Turkish menace and their aid to Christians escaping from slavery or imprisonment in Turkey (fols 351$^v$–352$^r$). In this he draws on Ludolf for some of his information, though the crusading past is not superimposed on to the present of the narrative to the same extent as in the former. Tucher allows more insight into the actual course of the pilgrimage and the formalities it entails than Ludolf, one being the visit to the Grand Calin ('Groß Calin') to draw up the contract for the journey to Sinai (fols 362$^v$–363$^r$). The reader also gains some insight into the hardships of the journey, as when Tucher portrays the pilgrims' exhaustion on having to walk into Rama carrying their gear. He writes: 'And when we had arrived within a distance of about two fields from Rama we had to dismount from our donkeys and enter the town on foot and each one of us had to carry his bags or gear. And the weather was really hot and we became very tired walking into the city in all the dust in this way, for the heathens allow no Christian to ride in' (fol. 352ᵛ). These hardships may explain his fondness for his creature comforts. The following quotation is taken from his list of provisions for Sinai: 'There were nine of us who drank wine and we had six barrels with us, each of which held one and a half quarts, and in Gazera [Gaza] we bought wine made of currants while we were there. However, even then we had barely enough to cover our needs until we got to Cairo, as wine saves a man's life on a journey' (fol. 362ᵛ). Tucher stresses the need to ensure an ample supply of wine and recommends, in as much loving detail as he devotes to the shrines, the best means of transporting it, though this may reflect his experience as a merchant.

However, wine forms the staple ingredient in many of his remedies for the ills of shipboard life themselves part of the lengthy lists of equipment and provisions for the journey. Such tips cover everything from currency to diet to clothing to medication. Thus Tucher includes prescriptions for remedies against sea-sickness and constipation; recommends ordering a garment like those worn by Muslim merchants so as to be less conspicuous; and advocates wooden stirrups as iron ones tend to be stolen; a straw mattress and feather quilt; a chamber pot (also useful when being sick on board ship); green ginger, coriander and aniseed for the digestion; cooking equipment; butter (fifteen to twenty pounds per person); candles; twice-baked bread; hens; dried fish; vinegar; plenty of fresh water; and so on (fols 361ᵛ–362ʳ). He suggests taking a wooden chest to store one's belongings but also to sleep on at night as the floor is covered in fleas. As currency Tucher recommends 'Ducaten de Zeckea', remarking that used coins are not viewed favourably in the Muslim world; also four or five ducats' worth of new Venetian shillings as they are useful for tipping in the Holy Land.[44] As well as providing advice on supplies, Tucher lists the price of passage (different according to type of ship) and the duties and taxes pilgrims have to pay. He warns that ships' captains tend to stint on food and that pilgrims should take plenty of their own provisions; also that they secretly load merchandise with which to trade, even though they are not supposed to. Tucher's concern with comfort on the voyage leads him to recommend the best place on the galley for those who suffer from sea-sickness, namely behind the mast in the middle of the deck (fols 373ᵛ–374ʳ). All this information may, of course, stem from the merchant's experience of long-distance travel.

The travellers' few creature comforts may have cushioned the physical and emotional hardship of being away from home, since one thing to emerge from Tucher's report is his sense of vulnerability, caused by his removal from his secure home environment and intensified by his being at the mercy of guides whose language he could not speak and who were probably set on exploiting him and his fellow travellers. Nowhere is it more acute than in the crossing of the Sinai desert, which Tucher describes at considerable length. Here the rather restricted style, the repeated use of a small number of adjectives and nouns – 'wild', 'sandy', 'harsh', 'wide', 'sandhills', 'sandwaves', 'sandheaps' – tellingly if unintentionally convey the sheer plodding monotony of the pilgrims' progress, something which in itself becomes a metaphor for man's struggle through this life to hoped-for salvation.[45] Most severe is the sense of isolation felt by men from one of Europe's largest and busiest cities:

> On 29 September, a Wednesday, on the Eve of St Michael's Day, four hours before dawn, we continued our journey from there, travelling through a rough stony type of landscape and especially through a long deep ravine in a chalk-white rocky mountain landscape, wild and unusual . . . And in seven days we did not see a single stranger and we saw very few animals or birds. During the day we saw in the hills many tumbledown stone houses which had once been inhabited by hermits in the desert. (fols 364$^{r-v}$)

As for Ludolf, the past of earlier Christian settlement of the Holy Land breaks the surface of the narrative, and the Bedouins embody all that is threatening because so alien. They lurk on the edges of his description of the desert, always ready to attack European travellers: 'We had to keep very still there without fire or smoke and several of us had to keep watch at night because of the Arabs who lie in wait there all the time and rob passing caravans' (fol. 364$^r$). Indeed, fear of the Arabs was not limited to Christians: on the first day of their journey across the desert Tucher's party are joined by a Turkish merchant and his companions, who have waited several days for them in Gaza so as to cross the desert in greater safety (fol. 363$^v$). However, Tucher is also capable of a more differentiated view of the Bedouins, one that demonstrates some engagement with them on a human level: 'We carried with us a large number of biscuits or twice-baked bread to give to the Arabs. They are a poor miserable people who suffer greatly from hunger and thirst' (fol. 364$^r$).

As well as compassion for others, Tucher reveals something of himself to the reader, relating several incidents in which he plays a central role and is proud of it, such as his mounting of a sundial on to the Franciscan monastery church on Sion, a visible and lasting reminder of his presence in Jerusalem:

> For the monks on Sion I erected a sundial on their church so that they might always be able to tell what time of day it was when the sun shone. They were really pleased and delighted with the sundial. It hardly ever rains during the year, only in November and December. I put the dial up for them on the south side of the church at such a height that it can show all twelve hours and be seen from many parts of the monastery. (fol. 359$^r$)

Thus Tucher inscribes his presence on the Holy City in the same way the hermits did on the desert or, indeed, the crusaders with their fortifications did on the Holy Land.[46] Matters more personal still are mentioned, for example, his tiredness and need to rest during the ascent of Sinai or, an aspect of pilgrimage rarely touched on in the accounts, his need for privacy: 'Item: in Venice buy six ells of coarse black linen cloth as well. It is good for use as a curtain. When you lie on your chest you can hang that in front of you so that no one can watch everything you do, for example, when you get up or go to bed or get dressed or undressed' (fol. 374ʳ). In this remark above all a more clearly developed notion of the self as an individual distinct from other people may be seen.[47] This self-awareness and integration of self into the narrative constitute the main difference between Tucher's account and that by Ludolf. Ludolf may refer to himself as an observer, but never as an agent actively responding to and leaving his mark on the landscapes and people he encounters.

Whilst Tucher does mention trade, he does not allow it as much space in his narrative as one might expect. Discussion of it is largely confined to the section on Alexandria, where Tucher and his party stay in the *fondaco* belonging to the Venetian merchants. One of the most important merchant cities in the Middle Ages, Nuremberg had trading connections stretching from the Baltic to Cracow and Lemberg in Poland to Flanders to Hungary. Venice was Nuremberg's leading trading partner; Nuremberg merchants had their own chamber in the Fondaco dei Tedeschi in Venice.[48] The close relations between the two cities are mirrored in the text: many of the Venetian merchants are known to Tucher personally; he and his party are well treated; and the Venetians instantly intervene when Tucher and his companion Otto Spiegel are incarcerated (fol. 369ᵛ). Little information emerges from Tucher's account about the type of wares passing through Alexandria; more space is devoted to what appears to be the annual custom of imprisoning foreign merchants and forcing them to buy pepper at vastly inflated prices in return for their release.[49] Felix Fabri is more informative than Tucher about both local and long-distance trade. For example, he describes traders in the Church of the Holy Sepulchre doing good business with the pilgrims locked in for the night by selling them precious stones, paternosters, rings, crucifixes and so on (fol. 88ᵛ). In Alexandria, as part of a lengthy description of trade in that city, Fabri notes the import of over 10,000 ducats' worth of hazelnuts from Christendom (fol. 187ᵛ). On the return journey to Venice the pilgrims are given salted fish that has been caught in the Danube and bought in Alexandria, imported there by Turkish merchants. Fabri remarks: 'But what can possibly escape merchants that their hands do not distribute throughout the world. The Danube that flows past Ulm also flows through Turkey. There the Turks catch huge quantities of fish, salt them and transport them over the sea and to Venice' (fol. 197ᵛ).[50] As noted in the discussion on Ludolf's work, trade cuts through boundaries of race and religion. Indeed, pilgrimage itself was a kind of business, the pilgrims 'buying' a religious experience and spending enough money to affect local economies along pilgrimage routes.[51]

Finally, Tucher's work is enriched by his evident interest in architecture, stemming doubtless from his personal background: his brother Endres had been a master builder before entering the Carthusian monastery, and Hans himself sat on the commission for the building of the towers of St Sebaldus in Nuremberg. He always demonstrates a keen eye for detail, whether it be the layout of Cairo and its sultan's palace (fols 368ᵛ–369ʳ), the disintegrating splendour of Alexandria (fols 369ᵛ–370ʳ) or the intricately embroidered tapestries donated by Philip of Burgundy to the Franciscan monastery on Sion (fol. 353ᵛ). Most unusual of all, he undertakes to describe the Church of the Holy Sepulchre not merely through a brief reference to a known building but through a step-by-step comparison with St Sebaldus in Nuremberg:

> Item: after that the procession continued further round the Temple as if in St Sebaldus's you went up in front of St Kunigunde's altar and in front of the wedding door as far as the sacristy. There stands a chapel in the rock. Inside it stands an altar. That is the spot where the Almighty God was kept prisoner while His Holy Cross was made ready for Him. At that place are indulgences worth seven years and seven quarantines [sets of forty days]. (fol. 354ʳ)[52]

Tucher thereby presents the heart of the Christian faith to his reader in an immediately tangible way, aiding the latter's imaginative recreation of the procession round the shrines and bringing the religious experience of pilgrimage more forcefully into his everyday life. This presentation of the sacred in concrete form has a further effect: through the close identification of St Sebaldus's with the holiest place in Christendom, some of the latter's sanctity is transferred to the Nuremberg church, so that it becomes 'holier' and capable of inspiring more intense personal devotion.[53]

### CONCLUSION

What conclusions may be drawn from this analysis? How authentic a record of the lived experience of travel can texts like Ludolf's and Tucher's be, predetermined as they are by the mental and spiritual map of their authors and selectively cobbled together out of various sources? Their nature as literary documents does not make the narrator's personal experience of the journey or his record of it any less authentic. The purpose of pilgrimage literature was certainly different from that of the modern travel guide. Indeed, the copying from various sources, including other pilgrimage reports, means that each work is complete in itself and thus offers the most authentic, authoritative picture of the journey and its destination possible. Taken on its own, as a text performing a particular function, each work has an inherent veracity and validity, attempting to point to an eternal truth of greater value than mere personal experience in a deceptive and transient world. Strictly speaking, especially in earlier texts, it does not matter whether authors have been to a particular site or not: its truth is not dependent on *their* having seen it *personally*. Theological necessity dictates its presence, and for it to have been recorded by someone is sufficient.

Fabulous elements – or, indeed, Ludolf's deadly viper – may simply be a chiffre for the Otherness and potential threat of an unknown world when language fails, a code familiar to and thus readily understood by those at home. Pilgrims were removed from their usual frame of reference, vulnerable and struggling to come to grips with a reality outside their experience. In a land where the ultimate miracle, God's Incarnation and Resurrection, had taken place anything was possible, even unicorns or giants buried in the desert – Tucher visits the giant's grave (fol. 364$^r$). Eternal biblical truths, or even the apocryphal legends derived from them, were certainties to cling to, not to question, a means of organising confusing information according to a secure model. This chapter has argued that pilgrims move on various time levels: their own, that of the Bible, that of the crusades and possibly that of their own family history, its transmitted knowledge in turn predetermining their impressions and literary record of the Holy Land. The pilgrims' time level is filled with the nausea, stench and cramped conditions of the sea voyage, irritation at bad food, uncomfortable lodgings, illness, exhaustion, dishonest guides and Muslim hostility; that of the Bible by sacred truths which promise release from temporal suffering; that of the crusades by buildings, tombs, ruins and memories which link the two. Movement, in the form of tours of the shrines or excursions to Bethlehem or the Jordan, takes pilgrims back into the hallowed past, which is superimposed on their present, as is evident in the initial description of the Dead Sea.

This preoccupation with the past may explain the patchiness of profound engagement with and exploration of foreign cultures encountered on the voyage. The culture in which pilgrims like Ludolf are interested is primarily their own, namely Christian and biblical. Of course interaction must have taken place, but it lies tantalisingly beneath the surface of their texts, since ethnography was the purpose of neither the journey nor its written record. One finds at best traces: for example the Templars in the mountains of Israel who were taken captive at the fall of Acre and have been sawing wood for the sultan for so long they do not know their Order has been suppressed (*Description*, pp. 117–18); or the noblewoman Margaret of Sicily, sister of a canon of the Church of the Holy Sepulchre, who helps in the pilgrim hospital run by the Hospitallers and is viewed favourably by the sultan because of her usefulness (*Description*, pp. 106–7). In Ludolf one finds an odd example not so much of cultural exchange as of cultural appropriation:

Out of this Church of St Mary the Saracens have now made a church of their own. Yet all the story of Anna and Joachim and the Blessed Mary's birth remains to this day right nobly painted on the front of the church. This painting in my time used to be all devoutly and religiously explained to Christians by an old Saracen woman named Baguta. She used to dwell over against the church, and declared that the picture of Joachim stood for Mahomet, and the painting of the trees for paradise, wherein Mahomet kissed girls, and she referred the whole of the painting to Mohammed, and set it forth with fervour, and would tell many more and more wondrous stories about Mahomet with tears in her eyes. (pp. 100–1)

Tucher includes more observation of non-Christian culture in his work, though at times he foregrounds cultural conflict rather than exchange, such as attacks on Christians within the city of Jerusalem itself or on the road from Jaffa to Rama, where pilgrims are stoned to death by Arabs in the villages. Tucher himself is knifed in the neck in Alexandria and then thrown into gaol, an incident reported with remarkable matter-of-factness (fol. 369ᵛ). By contrast, it is a point of pride with Tucher that once most of his travelling companions have left Jerusalem to return home, he and the others left behind are allowed to wander round the city unmolested and given access to shrines not normally open to Christians.

Trade must have enabled not just the exchange of merchandise but also the encounter of cultures. Galleys and caravans criss-cross the texts and the pilgrims' experience of the Orient, overlapping and merging before moving beyond the margins of the pilgrims' spiritual and mental maps to the vague geography of India and countries further east. However, one of the most striking exchanges to be found in either text brings the reader down to a startlingly mundane level of domestic detail, far removed from spiritual or mercantile quest of any sort: 'It should be noted that between Morocco and Spain the Mediterranean Sea flows out to the ocean through an arm scarce a quarter of a mile in breadth; wherefore upon one bank there stands a Christian woman and on the other bank a heathen woman washing their clothes, and wrangling and quarrelling with one another' (Ludolf, *Description*, p. 9).

## NOTES

My thanks to the Arts Faculty Research Fund, University of Bristol, for a grant which enabled me to carry out research for this chapter at the Herzog August Bibliothek, Wolfenbüttel. I thank Nigel Harris of the Department of German, University of Birmingham, for inviting me to give the paper to the Medieval Society at Birmingham on which this chapter is based.

1 Ludolf von Sudheim [Ludolph von Suchem], *Ludolph von Suchem's Description of the Holy Land and of the Way Thither: Written in the Year 1350*, trans. Aubrey Stewart, Palestine Pilgrims' Text Society, 27 (London: Palestine Pilgrims' Text Society, 1895),

pp. 116–17. All quotations will be taken from this translation, and page numbers given in the text.

2 Hans Tucher, *Verzeichnuß der Reyß zum Heyligen Land*, in *Das Reyßbuch deß Heyligen Lands* (Frankfurt am Main: Johann Feyerabend for Sigmund Feyerabend, 1584), fols 349ᵛ–374ᵛ, at fol. 359ᵛ. All quotations will be taken from this version of the text; the translations are my own.

3 The past evil of Sodom and Gomorrah as well as its present consequences are recorded by other pilgrims such as Felix Fabri, who sees in the Dead Sea open and visible signs of God's wrath, though they do not prevent him and his companions from wading out into it (Felix Fabri, *Eigentlich Beschreibung der hin vnnd wider farth zu dem Heyligen Landt* ([s.l., s.n.], 1557), fol. 103ᵛ). E. D. Hunt points out that the third-century presbyter and martyr Pionius already read the landscape of Judaea as a testament to God's anger: 'For Pionius the biblical fate of Sodom and Gomorrah was revealed as present reality in the landscape of contemporary Palestine, and with it a foretaste of the biblical wrath of God still to come' ('Were there Christian pilgrims before Constantine?', in J. Stopford (ed.), *Pilgrimage Explored* (York: York Medieval Press, 1999), pp. 25–56, at p. 25).

4 Scholarship has made much of the stylistic similarity of pilgrimage reports and their interdependence. See Martin Sommerfeld's classic study of pilgrimage literature, 'Die Reisebeschreibungen der deutschen Jerusalempilger im ausgehenden Mittelalter', *Deutsche Vierteljahrsschrift*, 2 (1924), 816–51; Dietrich Huschenbett, 'Die Literatur der deutschen Pilgerreisen nach Jerusalem im späten Mittelalter', *Deutsche Vierteljahrsschrift*, 59 (1985), 29–46; and Christiane Hippler, *Die Reise nach Jerusalem: Untersuchungen zu den Quellen, zum Inhalt und zur literarischen Struktur der Pilgerberichte des Spätmittelalters*, Europäische Hochschulschriften, series 1, 968 (Frankfurt am Main, Bern and New York: Lang, 1987); see also Mary Campbell, ' "The object of one's gaze": Landscape, writing and early medieval pilgrimage', in Scott D. Westrem (ed.), *Discovering New Worlds: Essays on Medieval Exploration and Imagination* (New York and London: Garland Publishing, 1991), pp. 3–15.

5 The Latin version was printed in Augsburg in 1468, probably by Heinrich Eggesteyn. A second Latin edition by the same publisher dates from the same period (Strasburg: [Heinr. Eggesteyn, *c.* 1475–80] ); then in 1483 Ludolf's account was published in Gouda by Gheraert Leeu (before 11 June 1484) as the third item in a compendium comprising Marco Polo, Ludolf and *Mandeville's Travels*. The German translation (*Das bůch von dem weg*) was published by Johannes Zainer in 1473. See Thomas Freller, 'Ein Osnabrücker Kleriker auf Malta: Ludolphs von Suchen Itinerar und der heilige Paulus: Neue Aspekte spätmittelalterlicher Fremdwahrnehmung', *Jahrbuch der Gesellschaft für Niedersächsische Kirchengeschichte*, 94 (1996), 139–51; Kurt Ruh (ed.), *Die deutsche Literatur des Mittelalters: Verfasserlexikon* (Berlin and New York: Walter de Gruyter, 1977–), v, cols 984–6; Ludolf von Sudheim, *Ludolfs von Sudheim Reise ins Heilige Land*, ed. Ivar von Stapelmohr, Lunder Germanische Forschungen, 6 (Kopenhagen: C. W. K. Gleerup, 1913; repr. Lund: Ohlsson, 1937); idem, *Ludolphi, rectoris ecclesiae parochalis in Suchem, de itinere Terrae Sanctae liber*, ed. Ferdinand Deycks, Bibliothek des Litterarischen Vereins in Stuttgart, 25 (Stuttgart: Litterarischer Verein, 1851).

6 See Dietrich Huschenbett, '*Von landen und ynseln*: Literarische und geistliche Meerfahrten nach Palästina im späten Mittelalter', in Norbert Richard Wolf (ed.), *Wissensorganisierende und wissensvermittelnde Literatur im Mittelalter: Perspektiven ihrer Erforschung: Kolloquium 5.–7. Dezember 1985* (Wiesbaden: Reichert, 1987), pp. 189–207; and Gerhard Wolf, 'Die deutschsprachigen Reiseberichte des Spätmittelalters', in Peter J. Brenner (ed.), *Der Reisebericht* (Frankfurt am Main: suhrkamp, 1989), pp. 81–116.

7 He does not, however, offer the very practical advice on provisions, clothes, etc. found in Tucher, Sebald Rieter junior, Felix Fabri (*Eigentlich Beschreibung*, fol. 13ᵛ) or Conrad Grünemberg (see Reinhold Röhricht and Heinrich Meisner (eds), *Deutsche Pilgerreisen nach dem Heiligen Lande* (Berlin: Weidmannsche Buchhandlung, 1880), pp. 146–61).

8 This is from the Italian *colpo di vento* and seems to mean a gust of wind.

9 Debra J. Birch points out that Jacques de Vitry, for example, returns repeatedly to the 'penitential nature of the pilgrim's journey'. See Debra J. Birch, 'Jacques de Vitry and the ideology of pilgrimage', in J. Stopford (ed.), *Pilgrimage Explored*, pp. 79–93, at p. 84.

10 Jacob von Bern, travelling in 1346–47, lists and laments all the cities lost by the crusaders on account of their sinfulness (Röhricht and Meisner (eds), *Deutsche Pilgerreisen*, p. 58).

11 Ludolf von Sudheim followed Wilhelm von Boldensele in the organisation of his material (Ruh (ed.), *Verfasserlexikon*, v, col. 985). However, this does not invalidate my observations, as Ludolf made a conscious decision to adopt this structure.

12 Christl Meier, 'Grundzüge der mittelalterlichen Enzyklopädik', in Ludger Grenzmann and Karl Stackmann (eds), *Literatur und Laienbildung im Spätmittelalter und der Reformationszeit* (Stuttgart: Metzler, 1984), pp. 467–500.

13 This is not the same as saying that Ludolf intended his coverage to be comprehensive. We have seen that at the start of his work (p. 2) he identifies selectivity and credibility as guiding principles of his narrative.

14 For an account of the interdependence of pilgrimage and trade see Marie-Luise Favreau-Lilie, 'Die Bedeutung von Wallfahrten, Kreuzzügen und anderen Wanderungsbewegungen (z.B. Gesellenwanderungen) für die Kommunikation in Mittelalter und früher Neuzeit', in Hans Pohl (ed.), *Die Bedeutung der Kommunikation für Wirtschaft und Gesellschaft: Referate der 12. Arbeitstagung der Gesellschaft für Sozial- und Wirtschaftsgeschichte vom 22.–25.4.1987 in Siegen, Vierteljahrschrift für Sozial- und Wirtschaftsgeschichte*, Beiheft 87 (Wiesbaden and Stuttgart: Steiner, 1989), pp. 64–89.

15 Ulrich Leman from St Gallen is also impressed by the wealth of Damascus and its citizens, mentioning a recently deceased merchant whose wealth was assessed at 300,000 ducats and who was far from being the richest. Leman is particularly impressed by the spices and precious stones imported from India and by the international character of the city, where merchants from all Christian nations, India, Egypt, Turkey and Syria can be found. He says he that whilst in Syria he saw setting out on one day fifteen thousand camels laden with merchandise for India. This gives an impression of the extent of international trade in the late fifteenth century. See the extract from Ulrich Leman's account in Röhricht and Meisner (eds), *Deutsche Pilgerreisen*, pp. 102–10, at pp. 107–8.

16 'The Mediterranean world functioned in some respects as a single economy . . . East and west were not simply hostile worlds whose contact was sharply constrained by religious differences and military confrontation' (David Abulafia, 'The impact of the Orient', in Dionisius A. Agius and Ian Richard Netton (eds), *Across the Mediterranean Frontiers: Selected Proceedings of the International Medieval Congress, University of Leeds, 10–13 July 1995, 8–11 July 1996* (Turnhout: Brepols, 1997), pp. 1–40, at p. 39.

17 Martin Sommerfeld first draws attention to this practice in 'Die Reisebeschreibungen'.

18 For example, he describes one sailor (who tells a particularly tall story about a young man's being bitten in half by a large fish he was trying to stare down) as 'exceedingly notable' (p. 15).

19 Mary B. Campbell, *The Witness and the Other World: Exotic European Travel Writing 400–1600* (Ithaca, NY, and London: Cornell University Press, 1988).

20 Felix Fabri also notes that he took home with him stones and pieces of all the shrines, claiming not to have damaged any of them (fol. 89ᵛ).

21 'Biblical locations function as "witnesses", they are "shown", produced in evidence, as confirmation of the sacred history represented in them' (Hunt, 'Christian pilgrims', p. 35).

22 See G. Liebe, 'Die Wallfahrten des Mittelalters und ihr Einfluß auf die Kultur', *Neue Jahrbücher für das Klassiche Altertum, Geschichte und Deutsche Literatur*, 1 (1898), 149–60. Old Testament descriptions of the Ark of the Covenant or Temple of Solomon may provide the model for them.

23 Michael Baxandall, *Painting and Experience in Fifteenth-Century Italy* (Oxford: Oxford University Press, 1972; paperback 1974), p. 45.

24 *Ibid.*, p. 46.

25 *Ibid.*

26 This topos enjoyed considerable longevity, as in his prologue to the *Reyßbuch deß heyligen Lands* Sigmund Feyerabend cites unity amongst Christian princes as the main prerequisite for the recapture by Christendom of the Holy Land from the Turks (fol. vʳ).

27 Campbell, *The Witness and the Other World*, p. 19.

28 Bernhard von Breidenbach, *Peregrinatio in Terram Sanctam* (Mainz: Erhard Reuwich, 11 February 1486).

29 Jeffrey Richards, *Sex, Dissidence and Damnation: Minority Groups in the Middle Ages* (London and New York: Routledge, 1991).

30 In the desert en route to Sinai, Felix Fabri sights what he and other pilgrims think is a camel; however, they are assured by their Arab guides that it is a unicorn, and Fabri apparently accepts this, as he makes no further comment (fol. 133ʳ). Almost one hundred years later the Augsburg physician and botanist Leonhard Rauwolf also sees a unicorn in the desert.

31 Ludolf writes: 'These same give to men the power of curing with their spittle any who may have been bitten by serpents or asps. When they confer this power upon any man they take a glass full of wine, and drink thereof first, and then put therein a good deal of their spittle, and if he who is offered to drink thereof is seized with loathing, they thereupon mix earth with the wine, and give it to him who would receive this power or grace' (p. 21). Freller claims that, owing to the confused state of cartography at this period, Ludolf has mixed up Corsica and Malta, for the abilities described are normally linked to the legends associated with St Paul's shipwreck on Malta (Freller, 'Ein Osnabrücker Kleriker', 146–50).

32 See Rudolf Wittkower, 'Marco Polo and the pictorial tradition of the Marvels of the East', in Rudolf Wittkower (ed.), *Allegory and the Migration of Symbols* (London: Thames & Hudson, 1977), pp. 75–92; and *idem*, 'Marvels of the East: A study in the history of monsters', *Journal of the Warburg and Courtauld Institutes*, 5 (1942), 159–197; also in Wittkower (ed.), *Allegory and the Migration of Symbols*, pp. 45–74.

33 This passage follows on a description by Ludolf's sailor source of a fish so big it had tried to swallow a boat and had left stuck in the hold a tooth 'as thick as a beam, and three cubits long' (p. 17).

34 The word 'treacle' is derived from Greek 'the-riake' (from 'the-rion') and means a medicinal salve originally used as an antidote to poison and venomous bites. 'Theriac' is an antidote to poison, especially the bite from a poisonous snake. Konrad von Megenburg in *Das Buch der Natur* maintains that before Christ's birth no cure existed for the bite of the snake, so venomous was it. However, a particularly nasty specimen was hung on the Cross next to Christ, from which day onwards this species has, through the Blood of Christ, the ability to act as an antidote against all types of poison

except a bite from another snake of the same species. My thanks to Dr Nigel Harris, Department of German, University of Birmingham, for drawing my attention to this. It is interesting that Hans Tucher recommends spreading theriac on the teeth, tongue and lips as a remedy for the pestilential air at sea (*Verzeichnuß*, fol. 361$^v$).

35 See Reinhold Röhricht and Heinrich Meisner (eds), *Das Reisebuch der Familie Rieter* (Tübingen: Litterarischer Verein Stuttgart, 1884).

36 Favreau-Lilie discusses Lübeck's strong involvement in the Third Crusade as well ('Die Bedeutung', p. 66).

37 According to Ruh (ed.), *Verfasserlexikon*, ix, cols 1127–32, nine editions of Tucher's work were published between 1482 and 1488.

38 Röhricht and Meisner (eds), *Reisebuch*, p. 3.

39 The account of the crusades and kings of Jerusalem is lengthy and detailed and provides, so to speak, the first part of the story that Ludolf concludes with his account of the fall of Acre. Read together, the two texts provide a reasonably complete account of crusading history and its main players.

40 For more on this itinerary see Randall Herz, 'Zwei Druckfassungen eines Itinerars und ihre Abhängigkeiten', *Gutenberg-Jahrbuch*, 78 (1998), 101–4.

41 Albrecht von Löwenstein, *Pilgerfahrt gen Jerusalem*, in *Das Reyßbuch deß heyligen Lands*, fols 188$^v$–212$^v$, at fol. 196$^r$. For Klaus Niehr the growing tendency to date experience precisely as a means of attesting to its authenticity results from an inflation in the claims personally to have seen something. See Klaus Niehr, ' "als ich das selber erkundet vnd gesehen hab" ': Wahrnehmung und Darstellung des Fremden in Bernhard von Breydenbachs *Peregrinationes in Terram Sanctam* und anderen Pilgerberichten des ausgehenden Mittelalters', *Gutenberg-Jahrbuch*, 76 (2001), 269–300, at 282.

42 Thus Tucher writes, 'After that buy writing material, paper and ink so that when you are underway you can write as a distraction from boredom and describe what you see on the journey' (*Verzeichnuß*, fol. 374$^r$). Felix Fabri notes at one point that he has forgotten the words of a prayer that the King of Hungary's chaplain composed for a plaque to hang on the wall in the Roman Catholic church on Sinai because he did not note them down in his little book (fol. 149$^v$). This signals a literarisation of the journey. In other words, the intention to record the journey and to create a monument to the Holy Land in the traveller's memory and in literary form is present from the start; and possibly the act of writing shapes the way in which the traveller perceives and experiences the landscape and cultures through which he is travelling.

43 Ludolf writes: 'It was from this isle that first came the destruction of the noble city of Troy, for they say that there lived the ram with the golden fleece, of whom one reads at greater length in the histories of Troy' (p. 34). Tucher's version may, in turn, have been copied by Felix Fabri, who refers to a 'geldenen schepper' on account of which Troy was destroyed (fol. 23$^v$), only to break off hastily with the remark that he does not wish to write about such 'heathen poetic things'.

44 See also Andrew Jotischky on suitable currency for travel in the Holy Land in Chapter 5 above, pp. 91, 103n.20.

45 In a letter to his brother Endres written in Jerusalem on 6 August 1479 Tucher, having described the pilgrims' preparations, expresses his lack of enthusiasm for the trip to Sinai: 'Und mir ist das hercz gering dorzu' ('And my heart really is not in it'). See Randall Eugene Herz, 'Briefe Hans Tuchers d. Ä. aus dem Heiligen Land und andere Aufzeichnungen', *Mitteilungen des Vereins für Geschichte der Stadt Nürnberg*, 84 (1997), 61–92, at 71.

46 Pilgrims inscribed their presence quite literally: Fabri's list of ten articles on how a pilgrim should behave in the Holy Land includes the stipulation that members of the

nobility ('die edlen') should not scratch or paint with charcoal their coats-of-arms or rhymes on the walls (fol. 33$^v$).

47 This awareness of the self and, more strikingly, of the contribution of travel to self-knowledge, is found in Felix Fabri. When describing the characteristics of the Order of the Holy Sepulchre which put it above other Orders of knighthood, Fabri says the following: 'But the most useful thing is that one learns that whilst on a pilgrimage a man gets to know himself better in thirty weeks than in thirty years in other circumstances. In all my days I have never been able to see myself more clearly than on the journey and especially on board ship. On board everything inside a man is stirred, virtue and wonder' (fol. 72$^v$). (The German has 'wunder', which could also mean 'curiosity'.)

48 See Gerhard Hirschmann, 'Das Nürnberger Patriziat', *Aus sieben Jahrhunderten Nürnberger Stadtgeschichte: Ausgewählte Aufsätze von Gerhard Hirschmann: Festgabe zu seinem 70. Geburtstag*, ed. Kuno Ulshöfer, Nürnberger Forschungen, 25 (Nürnberg: Selbstverlag des Vereins für Geschichte der Stadt Nürnberg, 1988), pp. 123–42, at pp. 127–8.

49 The sum given is 110 ducats instead of 50, or 70 ducats a 'Sport', though I have been unable to ascertain exactly what quantity this is. Tucher also describes in some detail the amount the Venetians pay the sultan alone in taxes and duties (2,000 ducats the previous year) and how they recoup the extra costs by adding them to the price of goods they sell on (fol. 371$^r$).

50 Felix Fabri is also discussed by Elka Weber in Chapter 2 and Catherine Delano-Smith in Chapter 6 above, pp. 40, 47, 107, 123n.3 and 126n.32.

51 See E. S. Hunt and J. M. A. Murray, *History of Business in Medieval Europe, 1200–1550* (Cambridge: Cambridge University Press, 1999), pp. 67–8.

52 Was this inspired by the similar technique in Ludolf's account? In his letter to Endres of 6 August Hans Tucher includes a version of this description which, as Herz points out, forms the basis for the printed version. See Herz, 'Briefe Hans Tuchers d. Ä.', 66–70. This letter has been preserved for us in Endres's own hand-written copy, which he kept with his copy of Hans's printed account (*ibid.*, p. 63). At the end of the letter, Endres Tucher comments: 'When the letter copied here arrived everyone wanted to hear it, both lay and clergy, so that it became quite torn and damaged, with the result that I copied it and included it here as a memorial' (*ibid.*, p. 72). This gives some idea of the status of a pilgrim, even in a merchant city like Nuremberg, the wealth of which was based on long-distance trade. It also demonstrates the piety – and possibly curiosity about foreign countries – characteristic of late medieval Germany.

53 For more on this see Joel Raba, 'Das Weltbild der mittelalterlichen und frühneuzeitlichen russischen Reisenden', *Forschungen zur osteuropäischen Geschichte: Konferenz zur Geschichte des Moskauer Reiches*, Osteuropa-Institut an der Freien Universität Berlin, Historische Veröffentlichungen, 38 (Wiesbaden: Harrassowitz, 1986), pp. 20–41.

# 11

## Late medieval Spanish travellers in the East: Clavijo, Tafur, Encina and Tarifa

( )

### Barry Taylor

ALTHOUGH SPAIN can lay claim (not undisputed) to the earliest medieval travel narrative, the *Itinerarium Egeriae* of the fourth to sixth centuries, and although the Spaniard Benjamin of Tudela (*fl.* 1161) left a famous account of his travels in the East, the focus of this chapter will be journeys by Spanish travellers, two to the Holy Land and two beyond, taken between the beginning of the fifteenth century and the beginning of the sixteenth.[1] I shall begin with a brief account of these four travellers and their travels, and go on to examine a number of topics present in each text in order to bring out some of the distinctive qualities of each. Two of these authors, Clavijo and Tafur, are well known outside Hispanism thanks to some excellent English translations, while Encina and Tarifa are much less familiar.

The *Embajada a Tamorlán* is the record of an embassy sent by Henry III of Castile to Tamerlane.[2] The ambassadors left Puerto de Santa María (near Cadiz) on 21 May 1403, sailing via Cadiz, Tangiers, Malaga, Cartagena, Ibiza, the Straits of Bonifazio (between Corsica and Sardinia), Gaeta and Messina, reaching Greece at Calamo, then via Rhodes, Chios, Mitylene, Troy, the Dardanelles, Gallipoli and the Sea of Marmora, landing at Constantinople, where they stayed for some time. They departed for Trebizond, but were forced by storms at sea to spend the winter at Pera, from where they set out in March 1404. Their route took them next to Trebizond, Arzinjan, Mount Ararat, Khoy, Tabriz, Zanjan, Sultaniyah, Tehran, Ray, Firuzkuh, Damghan, Bustam, Jajarm, Isfarayin, Nishnapur, Meshed, the Merv oasis, Balkh, the Oxus, Tirmiz and Tamerlane's capital Samarkand, where they arrived on 31 August 1404, staying until 21 November. On their return journey the ambassadors followed a slightly different route, reaching the Spanish court at Alcalá de Henares on 24 March 1406.

The ambassadors were Ruy González de Clavijo, Fray Alfonso Páez de Santa María and Gómez de Salazar, with an entourage of eleven. Opinion varies as to the authorship of the *Embajada*. The text refers variously to 'the ambassadors' in the third person, to 'we' and on occasions 'I'. Gómez de Salazar, the king's 'guard', died en route at Nishapur on 26 July 1404 and so cannot have contributed to the whole work. The Dominican Fray Alfonso was 'master in theology', and Clavijo too had clerkly abilities: when his wife, Mayor Arias, wrote a poem lamenting their separation, he wrote a poem in reply.[3] It is not possible to adjudicate between single and collaborative authorship, and I shall refer to the author of the *Embajada* as Clavijo. Of the travellers studied here, Clavijo is probably best regarded as a historical source by modern scholars.[4] He also enjoyed the greatest medieval reception.[5]

Taking advantage of the truce between John II of Castile and the Moors of Granada, Pero Tafur left Sanlúcar de Barrameda in late 1435, following the Spanish coast to Gibraltar, Cadiz, the Barbary Coast, Ceuta, Malaga, Cartagena, the Balearics, Genoa, San Lorenzo, Sestri Levante, Pisa, Florence, Venice, Rome (described at length), Viterbo, Perugia, Assisi, Gubbio, Rimini, Ravenna and Venice. From here he sailed in a pilgrim ship for Parenzo, Zara, Ragusa, Corfu, the Gulf of Patras, the Isthmus of Corinth, Cythera, Crete, Rhodes, Jaffa and Jerusalem. After the Holy Land he went on to Cyprus, up the Nile to Cairo, Mount Sinai and the Red Sea, and returned to Cairo. He next went via Alexandria and Cyprus to Rhodes (where he was almost drowned), Troy, the Dardanelles and Pera to Constantinople (described at length). Next he went to Adrianople, Trebizond, Kaffa and Tartary, then back to Constantinople, Mytilene, Salonica, Ragusa, Ancona, Spalato, Parenzo and Venice (the subject of a long account). Tafur's route home took him via north Italy, Germany, the Low Countries, Germany, Poland, Vienna, Buda, north and south Italy (he was in Ferrara on 16 January 1439) and Sardinia. At this point the manuscript ends.[6]

Don Fadrique Enríquez de Ribera, Marqués de Tarifa (1476–1539), set out for Jerusalem on 24 November 1518, accompanied by his major-domo Don Alonso de Villafranca, a chaplain and eight servants. He left Bornos (near Seville) for Valencia, Montserrat, Montpellier, Marseilles, St-Maximin, Briançon, Turin, Milan, Ferrara and Padua, arriving in Venice on 12 May 1519. Thence he went to Zakynthos, Kythira, Rhodes, Cyprus, Jaffa and Jerusalem. He left Jerusalem on 20 August 1519, the return journey taking in Rome and Avignon and describing an arc through north and west Spain to arrive in Seville on 30 October 1520.[7]

Juan del Encina, choirmaster of Salamanca, court dramatist and poet and a figure of the transition between the Middle Ages and the Renaissance in Spain, became an associate of Tarifa on his pilgrimage.[8] Encina set out independently of Tarifa from Rome, 'one third of the way through' 1519 ('Terciado ya el año de los diez y nueve, / después de los mil y quinientos encima': lines 369–70, my translation), visiting Loreto, Ancona and Venice (described with wonder), where he met Tarifa. Encina's account, the *Tribagia* alias *Viaje de Jerusalem*, takes the form of 1,704 lines of *arte mayor*, a stately metre associated with exalted narrative or moral themes; it is one of the first Spanish travel accounts to use verse. Preserved with the *Tribagia* are six shorter poems on his pilgrimage.

### THE PURPOSE OF MAKING AND RECORDING THE JOURNEY

Clavijo's journey is explicitly a diplomatic mission, and this purpose may explain the bureaucratic and non-judgemental style of his report. Tarifa and Encina identify themselves as pilgrims. As Chaucer's pilgrims witness, pilgrimage need not have been undertaken in a purely religious spirit, but we may note that Encina is most insistent on his personal need to do penance, dedicating some 250 lines (lines 105–360) to the state of his soul, and there seems to be no reason to doubt his motivation. Tafur is the most unconventional of the four travellers: neither pilgrim nor diplomat, he declared that he intended in travelling to acquire knightly prowess by being proved by hardship and to learn statecraft by comparing the governments of various states.

The *Embajada* survives in four manuscripts (a respectable number for an Old Spanish text), none of them de luxe, and an edition of 1582. Tafur's text appears to have had little circulation in its own time, leaving only one, post-medieval, manuscript, and this is incomplete at the end. It was first printed in 1874. The pilgrimage accounts of Tarifa and Encina circulated together. Biblioteca Nacional, Madrid, 17,510 is a workaday copy: because of its scruffy appearance it has been thought to be the original journal of the expedition.[9] In contrast, Biblioteca Nacional, Madrid, 9355 is a de luxe manuscript.[10] Tarifa had his work printed in 1521 (with Encina's), and there were further editions in 1580, 1606 and 1608.

Each of our travellers felt the need to write down his travels. The purpose of our travel texts is somewhat harder to determine, and not only because only one of them, Tafur's, has a prologue. It is generally accepted that, for instance, Columbus's purpose in describing his voyages was to sell the idea of an empire in the Indies to Ferdinand and Isabella, so he stressed that the natives were suitable for evangelisation and the land was rich in natural resources. Clavijo's account, we may presume, started life as a report for his master Henry of Castile. However, it also enjoyed circulation outside the confines of royal archives: of the manuscript witnesses, all are codices rather than state papers, and appear therefore to have been published.

Tafur chose to address his prologue to Don Fernando de Guzmán, 'comendador mayor de la Orden de Calatrava'.[11] Although Tafur does not indulge in blatant self-glorification, it is possible that his purpose was to describe his experiences as a self-portrait of interest in itself.

Tarifa's book conforms to the model of pilgrim narratives, in which the pilgrim bears witness to the monuments of Christianity so that his readers can experience them vicariously. Encina too imbues his book with elements from the tradition of the *meditationes vitae Christi*,[12] for the benefit of the devout reader at home. Although there is no documentary proof, it seems to me likely that Encina enjoyed the patronage of Tarifa (witness his praise of the marquis, lines 449–56), and this would seem to be sufficient motivation for writing.

## THE ROLE OF THE AUTHOR AND HIS TREATMENT OF THE HISTORICAL BACKGROUND

In general and to varying degrees, the role of the traveller is to observe, to react and to suffer. Clavijo concentrates on the first; his reactions are limited to pronouncing certain sights a 'marvel'; and his references to the difficulties of travel are stoically taciturn. These features may be attributable to Clavijo's role as a diplomat or to the multiple authorship of the *Embajada*. Tafur is more prominent in his narrative, including anecdotes and expressing his interest in women, presumably because his relatively unstructured travels allowed more room for exploring byways both literal and literary. Tarifa, in accordance with the pilgrim tradition, is self-effacing. Encina is the most given to lamentation over great matters (that Jerusalem is in the hands of Muslims) and small (at being overcharged); two eight-line stanzas are given over to a series of anaphoras on 'peligro', the dangers suffered by the pilgrim (lines 1537–52).

Geography as a focus of history is essential to the pilgrimage, and all our travellers are informed by this connection. Even the secular travellers are interested in Christian relics (e.g. those of Pera and Constantinople described at length by Clavijo, pp. 61–93, 129–37) and biblical sites (Tafur, p. 78). Such monuments are commonly termed 'mysterios' (e.g. Tarifa, fol. 75ᵛ; Encina, line 950). Outside religious sites, a visit to Troy leads Clavijo to expatiate on the Trojan War (pp. 54, 294).

Tarifa is the most interested in gathering documents: he quotes (fol. 37ʳ), apparently verbatim, the contract between the pilgrims and their carrier (in order to enumerate the carrier's several breaches of contract), the epitaphs (in translation) of Godfrey of Bouillon and Baldwin at Jerusalem (fol. 60ᵛ; also given by Encina in Latin between lines 1024 and 1025), and the rule of the Knights of St John at Rhodes (fols 109ᵛ–152ʳ).

In order better to brief his royal master, Clavijo includes full accounts of the political history of the Mongol Empire, not necessarily linked to place (pp. 50–3, 85–7). His historical passages may well reflect what the ambassadors were told at each point: 'The people here told us that . . .' (p. 141). By such phrases I understand Clavijo to be identifying his sources rather than dissociating himself from them. Comparative politics are a stated theme of Tafur's book, and the government of Venice merits praise from him (pp. 165–6) and from Tarifa (fol. 31ᵛ).

## WONDERS, SCEPTICISM AND EYEWITNESS ACCOUNTS

Although the Plinian tradition of monstrous races and fabulous beasts was alive is the literary culture of late medieval Spain – in fact, fabulous travellers' tales far outnumber truthful ones in manuscripts and printed editions – its role in these travellers' accounts is much reduced.[13]

One element from fantastic literature which Clavijo cannot have seen for himself is the Amazons, which he nevertheless describes in his usual documentary style:

> Some fifteen days' march from Samarqand, and in the direction of China, lies a country that is inhabited by Amazons, and these women hold the custom of admitting no men to live with them. At a certain season of the year however with the consent of their elders, the younger mothers take their daughters and proceed with them to the countries thereto lying adjacent. Here the men on their coming invite all to stay in their houses and the maidens go to those men they prefer, eating and drinking as of their household, and now living with them. (pp. 293–4)

'Maravilla' is a staple of Clavijo's vocabulary, used to refer to gardens, extremes of heat and cold, storms and architecture (including the tents of Samarkand). He typically comments of the mosaics of the cloister of Santa Maria of Peribletos: 'Among the rest was to be seen here the Jesse Tree showing the descent of the Blessed Virgin Mary, and this so wonderfully displayed and richly wrought that he who sees it never can have seen the like elsewhere' (p. 67).[14]

Clavijo does describe inanimate natural curiosities, such as a natural stone picture at Constantinople:

> On this slab there appears, formed naturally and not wrought by human art either of sculpture or of painting, the perfect figure of the most Blessed Virgin Mary, who holds our Lord Jesus Christ in her arms . . . These figures . . . are not drawn or painted with any pigment, nor graven in the stone artificially, but are entirely natural and of its substance; for the stone evidently was formed thus by nature with this veining and marking in it which so clearly depict those Persons whose figures now appear upon its surface. (p. 75)

This trusting attitude contrasts with that of Tarifa's regarding a comparable picture at Bethlehem: 'on an inner wall, growing right out of the marble, is figured in red a man's head with a long beard and monkish cowl which they say is the head of St Jerome; but it is merely a natural feature of the marble' ('y no es sino cosa natural del marmol', fols 75$^v$–76$^r$, my translation). For Clavijo the picture is marvellous because there has been no human intervention; for Tarifa it is to be dismissed because its resemblance to a portrait is merely coincidental.

Tafur himself makes no claim to have seen any monsters. However, they do play a role in his book, albeit a confined one. At Mount Sinai he meets the famous Italian traveller Niccolo de Conti, who regales him with a long passage of traveller's tales (pp. 87–95). Tafur enquires if he has ever seen the Plinian monsters, but Conti can only claim to have seen a white elephant, a giant multi-coloured ass and a unicorn (p. 92).

Our travellers commonly use phrases such as 'dizen que' ('they say that'). For García Martín, Tarifa's usage when referring to relics is an indication of his scepticism,[15] but it is more likely an indication of the source of his information. Tarifa is capable of a degree of scepticism, but this is generally made abundantly clear. In Sinai, the pilgrims are shown the body of St Catherine, 'but I was told by the majordomo of that house ... that the truth was that the body of St Catherine was not there ...' (fol. 56$^r$). On the same subject, Tafur's comments are enigmatic, amounting to a raised eyebrow: 'I did not see the body [of St Catherine], because they are not accustomed to show it, and, indeed, the place is not convenient for seeing it, but it appeared to me, from its size, that the body must be greater by a span than the tallest women who could be found in the world today' (p. 83). In the Mediterranean section of his journey, Clavijo describes the fortifications of various ports at which he did not land. He is thus punctilious in recording only what he could see from a vantage point out at sea.

### THE OTHER

For Nilda Guglielmi, the traveller is always marginalised.[16] Encina's anxiety at the decay of the biblical sites can make him appear like a disgruntled modern tourist whose experience does not live up to his guidebook. However, such distress pays tribute to his powers of observation, which mark him out from earlier pilgrims such as Egeria, who filters out the contemporary Palestine and focuses only on biblical history. The following exemplifies the absence of the Other in Egeria:

> And so when we had left the bush [from which God spoke to Moses] they began always to show us the other sites. They showed us the place where the children of Israel camped for the days when Moses went to the mountain. They also showed us the place where the [golden] calf was constructed, because a large stone is now set there. And as we went, we saw ahead of us the mountain peak which cast a shadow over the whole of the valley, from which holy Moses saw the children of Israel dance when they had made the calf.[17]

We may compare with this Encina's address to the Patriarch of Jerusalem:

> As an eyewitness / who has been in Jerusalem, / I give you your Patriarchate's complaint, / as a memoir and list, / against Mahomet, who oppresses it / without there being anyone to resist him.
>
> The inn where I stayed / while in Jerusalem, / as many know well, / was the Patriarchate . . . The patriarchal house / Mahomet has in his charge, / and this has enabled him / to turn it into a dungheap, / nay, he / treats it as a brothel / and administers it badly. It is in Jerusalem, / next to the Holy Sepulchre, / full of thistles and lamentation; / it is clothed / in dishonour and contempt, / desolate, alone and sad, / devoid of all good. Full of cobwebs, / windows and doors broken, / the walls almost open / displaying its insides; / it calls on God / and on you, Sir, / in its strange anxieties. (poem LX, lines 9–42)

However, neither Clavijo nor Tafur – perhaps more sophisticated – expresses any sense of alienation from his strange surroundings.[18] Indeed, Tafur consistently presents himself as an insider – 'I there presented myself to the Marquis, lord of the city [Ferrara], and remained three days' (p. 32) – stressing the network of contacts that has enabled him to move from one centre of power to another. (This aspect of his text as a curriculum vitae suggests that Tafur may be attempting to sell himself to his dedicatee Don Fernando de Guzmán, whom he conceived as a potential patron.) Clavijo's relaxed attitude to the Other may be derive from the fact that, despite the difficulties of his journey, he enjoys the privileges of diplomatic status.

## RELIGION

Describing the Greeks of Trebizond, Clavijo notes that they 'are devout people, but in matters of faith they hold to many errors' (p. 113). In general, however, Clavijo is at pains to be objective in his handling of religion. Encina is much more judgemental: he expresses discomfort at the sight of non-European Christians. The houses of Annas and Caiaphas 'are now churches and in the power of the Moors; / they are maintained by Christians not white but dark, / their habits and faces between white and black. / Let us leave aside their beliefs, whether sound or unsound, / it suffices that they have the names of Christians' (lines 713–18). In the Holy Sepulchre 'there are many nations of Christians . . . Most of them seem to be Indians, / their habits and faces more ugly than beautiful; / but as regards enjoying the Holy Sepulchre / they are all neighbours and brothers in Christ' (lines 857–64). At Bethlehem, 'the high altar of this monastery, / although it is the Latins', is held by the Greeks, / where they say their services, and come and go there, / even though our people think it an insult' (lines 1409–12). More blatantly, Tarifa distinguishes the practices of the various Christian groups present at Jerusalem, and does not hesitate to pronounce them heretics (fols 97ᵛ, 99ʳ–). Whatever their opinions, our travellers do not merely denigrate the beliefs of others without attempting to show some knowledge of them. Encina is the traveller with the strongest crusading instincts. In a shorter poem ('¡Jerusalem, Jerusalem, / descanso y fin de nuestro bien!', poem LVIII) he prays God to inspire Pope Leo X to regain the Holy Land. Clavijo and Tafur show no interest in non-Christian religions.

Like all writers, our travellers make use of comparisons when describing the unfamiliar. According to Tafur, the Granaries of Joseph 'must be much higher than the Great Tower at Seville' (p. 78); the city of Kaffa is 'as large as Seville, or larger' (p. 132); the ears of the elephant 'resemble a shield, and the head is like one of those great jars which hold six arrobas' (p. 78); the giraffe 'in general appearance . . . is like a stag' (p. 79); the columns in St Mark's Square 'are as high as towers' (p. 122); some of the men of the court of the Grand Turk wear 'hats made like those worn at rustic merry-makings in Burgos' (p. 127).

In Clavijo's account, wine bottles are wrapped in cloths 'as white as winding-sheets'; a knight's plume is 'like a peacock's tail'; Constantinople is of similar size to Seville, and Pera to Triana, a district of Seville; Samarkand is 'slightly larger than Seville'. His measurements are also sometimes comparative: 'as long as a mass lasts', 'two crossbow shots in distance', 'twice as high as a man could throw a stone'.

The purpose of Clavijo's first two comparisons quoted is to stress or praise the qualities indicated; the rest, and all of Tafur's, are honest attempts to explain the Other.[19]

## TRADE AND MONEY

Clavijo describes currency and taxes. He notes the stocks in the streets of Constantinople which are used to punish traders who give short measure (p. 88). Tafur is a nobleman, but his interest in trade was such as to mislead the historian Henri Pirenne to call him a merchant;[20] he admires the speed with which the Venetians deal with bills of exchange (p. 32) and is a frequenter of markets (pp. 100–1). Encina is the most money-conscious of our travellers, complaining in a short poem in lingua franca of the extortions of the *mucaros*, traders who supplied pilgrims with goods.[21] He also contends that the Venetian economy is being harmed by Portuguese trade with the Spice Islands (lines 401–4).

## STRUCTURE AND STYLE

In both structure and style these books are unelaborated. The diary structure – with historical digressions – is essential to the travel genre. Clavijo and

Tarifa carefully record dates and distances, while Tafur and Encina are less punctilious: Tafur, alone among our travellers, gives no dates.[22] The concern with noting long distances (in leagues) is essential to primitive works of geography such as the fourth-century Peutinger Table.[23] The interest in counting the number of steps between monuments or the number of stairs climbed (e.g. Tarifa, fol. 72$^r$, Encina, line 1290) may be intended to aid the reader to visualise the scene and link his prayers or meditations to the number of paces taken in his imagination.

In style, Clavijo's fondness for cliché has been seen as symptomatic of officialese, but overuse of words and phrases such as 'dicho' ('aforesaid'), 'muy bien fecho' ('very well made'), 'del mundo' ('[most] in the world'), 'cosa maravillosa de ver' ('a marvellous thing to see') and 'muy', 'mucho' ('very', 'much') is equally a feature of early prose in general.

Tafur seems to be more stylistically sensitive. He omits details of a caravan of camels 'as I do not wish to appear to speak extravagantly' ('demasiado', p. 90, i.e. 'too much'). He also gives his work a prologue, showing literary pretensions. Encina invests his verse with a prosaic quality.

It has been pointed out that the accounts of cities given by our travellers – describing the antiquity and founders of the city, its situation and fortifications, the fertility of its land and waters, the customs of its inhabitants, its buildings and monuments, its famous men, with the use of comparisons throughout – conform to the model of the *laus urbis* prescribed in medieval Latin rhetoric.[24] This is not impossible, as there is no reason to doubt that our authors had a Latin education, but I feel the elements of such descriptions are well-nigh universal.

The travel book was not an imitable category in medieval rhetoric, and in general the similarities between travel texts must be attributable to independent solutions to similar problems. Nor do our travellers cite classical authorities. However, there is some evidence that some of our authors were aware of their predecessors. Tafur met Niccolo de' Conti (pp. 84–6) and mentions when, by the Don, his route coincides with that of 'the ambassadors of King Enrique . . . when they went to the court of Timur-Beg' (p. 135). (Jiménez de la Espada claims that Tafur married a daughter of Clavijo.)[25]

Tarifa formed a library of travel books (Marco Polo), guides to Rome (*Mirabilia Romae* and others), geographical works (Ptolemy), maps and historical works concerning the areas which he visited (Josephus, Fontano's *Destruction of Rhodes*) which may have suggested models.[26]

### WOMEN AND CLOTHES

All our authors are aware of women and avoid both the medieval stereotypes of the good and the evil female and the modern cliché of the oriental houri. In fact, most comments of a sexual nature refer to European women. Landing at Rovino, Encina reports the strange phenomenon that 'most of the women are all lame' (the contradiction is his: 'do son las mugeres, las mas, coxas todas', line 497). Tarifa remarks on the veiled women of Venice (fol. 27ᵛ), and reports Venetian pre-nuptial customs: 'When a man marries, they first send a female relative of his to see his intended naked, to see if she has any secret defect. Afterwards they record her height, figure ["gordura"] and facial features, all in writing. And when they are going to marry, they measure and look her over again, and if they do not find her as is in the document, they are consternated ["desconciertanse"]' (fol. 31ᵛ).

Tafur has some caddish elements: offered a rank crocodile skin as a souvenir by the governor of Damietta, he remarks, 'I would rather have carried away the governor's pretty daughter' (p. 103); he comments on the barbers of Cairo 'who serve the women in that which they are wont to cleanse secretly at the baths' (p. 100). At the baths in Basle, 'they think nothing of men and women bathing together quite naked . . . I frequently threw silver coins into the bath, and [a lady's] maids dived for them. One can well imagine what it was they held in the air when they put down their heads' (p. 185). But he makes a point of showing that he is a gentleman: at Sluys he is approached at mass by a lady who takes him to her house and offers him her daughters, saying that she had eaten nothing for many days 'except a few small fish'. Having extracted a promise that they will never make such an offer again, Tafur gives them six Venetian ducats and leaves (pp. 200–1). In the East, Clavijo is unaroused by Tamerlane's polygamy; as Lawrance remarks:

> In his description of the Khanum's stately entrance at the great feast to honour the ambassadors in Timur's own pavilion, he makes no comment on the presence of the Khan's seven other wives, but is struck by the women's unveiled and blanched faces, dyed hair, magnificent feathered coiffure, and jewel-encrusted dresses. Even when the Khanum shows him her sleeping quarters he takes more interest in her jewelry than in the great silk divan bed.[27]

In this respect our travellers share the broader medieval aesthetic which was more interested in fabrics and jewels, which could express status, than in the body which they adorned, as witness Clavijo's portrait of the governor of Arzinjan:

> The Governor was dressed in a robe of blue Zaytuni stuff, embroidered in gold thread, and on his head he wore a very high hat, adorned with jewels and other ornament. On the crown of his hat was a golden crest set in a fold, and from this crest depended two tresses of crimson horse-hair each in three plats, and these came down below the neck resting on either side upon the shoulders. This style of head-dress with the horse-hair tresses is the fashion now established by Timur

[i.e. Tamerlane]. The Governor was a man of fine presence and may have been about forty years of age with a brownish-yellow complexion, and he had a black beard. (p. 123)[28]

### ANIMALS

Clavijo and Tafur write vivid descriptions of exotic animals – the elephant, the giraffe and the crocodile – which have become anthology pieces. Although rare in medieval Spain, these animals were not unknown there. In 1260 King 'Alvandexaver' of Egypt sent Alfonso X of Castile an elephant and a giraffe ('azorafa'); and crocodile skins were part of the medieval pharmacopoeia.[29] However, the sight of these creatures alive was a novelty. Clavijo writes:

> These elephants were very black and their skins had no hair except indeed at the tail which is hairy as is that of the horse, where the hairs are of silky texture . . . Their bodies are clumsily built; they have no grace of form, and it is as though each were a great sack that had been stuffed out full. At the ankle-joint the leg comes down quite straight, as is the case with the buffalo, but with the elephant the legs, both the pair before and the pair behind, are equally huge of size. The foot is round and plump, with the five toes, each with its black nail not unlike a human toe nail . . . The ears are very large, round in shape and the rim is as it were notched . . . He must fetch up the food to his mouth with his trunk when he would eat, and with it he will catch hold of the grass and pluck it off, cutting it short as with a knife, [and] carrying it to his mouth . . . So we see it is with his trunk the elephant purveys all his needs; and hence his trunk is never still but ever kept in motion, coiling and uncoiling like a snake. (pp. 262–6)[30]

This is clearly an eyewitness account, accurate enough in its detail to identify the elephant as Indian. Only in one respect does Clavijo appear to be influenced by tradition: his comparison of the elephant's tail to a horse's recalls the line drawings in the fifteenth-century manuscript of *Calila e Digna* (the fables of Bidpay translated from the Arabic), in which elephants sport genuine pony tails.[31] Tafur too describes the elephant (p. 79), but succumbs to old wives' tales when he claims, 'They have a very hard skin, and if they are wounded they put them where the moon shines on them, and the next day they are healed'.

Tafur's portrait of a giraffe likewise has the tang of authenticity, except when he reports 'they say that these creatures live to a great age, and that this one has been there more than 200 years' (p. 79).[32]

### CONCLUSION

Are our travellers tourists? The term of course is pejorative and anachronistic, perhaps corresponding in medieval terms to curiosity.[33] Tafur has been called a tourist,[34] and we might even accuse him of sex tourism in the baths of Basle. Encina's complaints about accommodation conditions suggest a bourgeois expectation that travel will be comfortable and good value for money. However, our travellers' serious attitude to travel and their desire to learn about the places they visit acquit them of charges of tourism.

What did these travellers get out of their travels? Were they transformed? Tafur's prologue claims that experience effects changes in the traveller: 'From the practice of travelling into foreign lands a man may reasonably hope to attain proficiency in that which prowess demands. Thus hidalgos may grow stout-hearted where, being unknown, they are beset by hardship and peril, striving to show themselves worthy of their ancestors, and by their own deeds to make their virtue known to strangers' (p. 19).

Tafur took home some slaves which he bought in Kaffa (p. 133), Clavijo and his colleagues had the satisfaction of a mission accomplished, and Tarifa and Encina had reduced their time in purgatory. None of them, unsurprisingly, shows any signs of broadened horizons or even less of going native. They bear out Seneca's disenchanted maxim: 'Magis quis veneris quam quo interest'.[35]

## NOTES

1 For a survey and bibliography, see Barry Taylor, 'Los libros de viajes de la Edad Media hispánica: Bibliografía y recepción', in *Actas do IV Congresso da Associação Hispânica de Literatura Medieval* (Lisboa: Cosmos, 1991–3), i, pp. 57–70. Benjamin of Tudela is discussed by Elka Weber in Chapter 2, above.

2 References will be to the excellent annotated translation by Guy Le Strange, Ruy González de Clavijo, *Embassy to Tamerlane 1403–1406*, The Broadway Travellers (London: Routledge, 1928), as it is the most manageable edition. *Embajada a Tamorlán*, ed. Francisco López Estrada, Nueva colección de libros raros o curiosos, 1 (Madrid: Consejo Superior de Investigaciones Científicas, 1943) is a model of editing but is not as reader-friendly. This edition is updated in the series Clásicos Castalia, 242 (Madrid: Castalia, 1999). All these editions have maps of the itinerary: López Estrada's 1943 edition following p. cxiv, his 1999 edition facing p. 81, and Le Strange's edition facing pp. 43, 111 and 165.

3 On the ambassadors, see Clavijo, *Embajada*, ed. López Estrada (1999), pp. 30–2. Clavijo's poem is in *Cancionero de Juan Alfonso de Baena*, ed. Brian Dutton and Joaquín González Cuenca, Biblioteca filológica hispana, 13 (Madrid: Visor, 1993), pp. 798–802.

4 See Margaret Wade Labarge, *Medieval Travellers: The Rich and Restless* (London: Hamish Hamilton, 1982), pp. 127–31, who in addition comments: 'it was a most extraordinary trip for any medieval man and far beyond the usual pattern of diplomatic travel' (*ibid.*, p. 131).

5 See Clavijo, *Embajada*, ed. López Estrada (1943), pp. ix–xxxiii; Taylor, 'Los libros de viajes', pp. 65–6.

6 Edition used: Pero Tafur, *Travels and Adventures 1435–1439*, ed. and translated with an introduction by Malcolm Letts, The Broadway Travellers (London: Routledge, 1926). There are editions of the Spanish original, *Andanças e viajes de Pero Tafur*, ed. Marcos Jiménez de la Espada, Colección de libros españoles raros o curiosos, 8 (Madrid:

Miguel Ginesta, 1874), and ed. José María Ramos, Biblioteca clásica, 265 (Madrid: Hernando, 1934).

7 Edition used: Fadrique Enríquez de Ribera, Marqués de Tarifa, *Este libro es de el viaje q[ue] hize a Jerusalem* (Lisbon: Antonio Alvarez, 1608). This is studied by Pedro García Martín, *La cruzada pacífica: La peregrinación a Jerusalén de don Fadrique Enríquez de Ribera*, Libros del buen andar, 44 (Barcelona: Serbal, 1997).

8 Edition of the *Tribagia* used: Juan del Encina, *Obras completas*, ed. Ana M. Rambaldo, Clásicos castellanos, 218–20, 227, 4 vols (Madrid: Espasa-Calpe, 1978–83), ii, pp. 187–243. See the studies by M. Isabel Hernández González, 'El viaje y el descubrimiento: Hacia una lectura devocional de la *Tribagia* de Juan del Encina', in Javier Guijarro Ceballos (ed.), *Humanismo y literatura en tiempos de Juan del Encina*, Acta salmanticensia: Estudios filológicos, 271 (Salamanca: Ediciones Universidad de Salamanca, 1999), pp. 367–78, and César Domínguez, *Juan del Encina, el peregrino: Temas y técnicas de la 'Tribagia'*, Papers of the Medieval Hispanic Research Seminar, 31 (London: Department of Hispanic Studies, Queen Mary and Westfield College, 2000).

9 It is described by Josefina Mateu Ibars, 'Peritaje paleográfico del ms. 17510 de la Biblioteca Nacional de Madrid', *Revista de Literatura Medieval*, 7 (1995), 72–92.

10 See the description by Vicenç Beltran, 'El *Viaje a Jerusalén* del Marqués de Tarifa: Un nuevo manuscrito y los problemas de composición', in Rafael Beltrán (ed.), *Maravillas, peregrinaciones y utopías: Literatura de viajes en el mundo románico* (Valencia: Publicacions de la Universitat de València, Departament de Filologia Espanyola, 2002), pp. 171–85, and the illustrations in García Martín, *La cruzada pacífica*.

11 On Guzmán, see Tafur, *Andanças e viajes*, ed. Jiménez de la Espada, pp. 455–7.

12 Hernández, 'El viaje y el descubrimiento', pp. 370–6.

13 On fabulous tales, see Taylor, 'Los libros de viajes'.

14 Quoted by López Estrada, in Clavijo, *Embajada*, ed. López Estrada (1999), p. 47.

15 García Martín, *La cruzada pacífica*, pp. 63, 85, 140.

16 Nilda Guglielmi, *Guía para viajeros: Oriente, siglos XIII–XV* (Buenos Aires: Programa de Investigaciones Medievales, Consejo Nacional de Investigaciones Científicas y Técnicas, 1994), p. 11.

17 Egeria, *Journal de voyage*, ed. and French trans. by Hélène Pétré, Sources chrétiennes, 21 (Paris: Editions du Cerf, 1948), pp. 112–14 (my trans.); Mary B. Campbell, *The Witness and the Other World: Exotic European Travel Writing, 400–1600* (Ithaca, NY, and London: Cornell University Press, 1988), pp. 20–33.

18 Jeremy Lawrance contrasts the open-mindedness of Clavijo with the anti-Turkish literature ('Europe and the Turks in Spanish literature of the Renaissance and early modern period', in Nigel Griffin *et al.* (eds), *Culture and Society in Habsburg Spain: Studies Presented to R. W. Truman by his Pupils and Colleagues on the Occasion of his Retirement* (London: Tamesis, 2001), pp. 17–33).

19 On comparisons in Clavijo, see Clavijo, *Embajada*, ed. López Estrada (1943), pp. ccxx–ccxxi; on measures, *ibid.*, pp. ccxxxii–ccxxxiii.

20 Quoted by Letts in Tafur, *Travels and Adventures*, p. 16.

21 Text in Encina, *Obras completas*, poem LXII, pp. 268–70; see the study by R. O. Jones, L. P. Harvey and Keith Whinnom, 'Lingua franca in a *villancico* by Encina', *Revue de Littérature Comparée*, 41 (1967) 572–9. Tarifa also refers to them (pp. 82–3), and Encina in the *Tribagia*, lines 593–6.

22 Letts, in Tafur, *Travels and Adventures*, p. v.

23 P. D. A. Harvey, *Medieval Maps* (London: The British Library; and Toronto: University of Toronto Press, 1991), pp. 6–7.

24 Miguel Angel Pérez Priego, 'Estudio literario de los libros de viajes medievales', *Epos*, 1 (1984), 217–38, at p. 227.
25 In his edition of Tafur, *Andanças e viajes*, p. xix n. 6.
26 M. Carmen Alvarez Márquez, 'La biblioteca de don Fadrique Enríquez de Ribera, I Marqués de Tarifa (1532)', *Historia, Instituciones, Documentos*, 13 (1986), 1–39.
27 Lawrance, 'Europe and the Turks', p. 17, quoting pp. 258–60, 268–71.
28 As E. Jane Burns observes, '[T]he courtly body can be understood . . . as a set of clothes that make, mark, delimit, and define the body presumed to lie beneath . . . there is no body in any foundational sense prior to the garments placed upon it' (*Courtly Love Undressed: Reading through Clothes in Medieval French Culture* (Philadelphia: University of Pennsylvania Press, 2002), p. 12); Susan Crane comments, 'The body is costumed, and clothing, not skin, is the frontier of the self' (*The Performance of Self: Ritual, Clothing and Identity during the Hundred Years War* (Philadelphia: University of Pennsylvania Press, 2002), p. 6) (I thank Rosamund Allen and Rosalind Field for help in locating these references). See also Rosemary Morris, *The Character of King Arthur in Medieval Literature*, Arthurian Studies, 4 (Cambridge: D. S. Brewer, 1982), Chap. 7: 'Personal attributes' (pp. 119–29).
29 For Alfonso, see Cayetano Rosell (ed.), *Crónica de los reyes de Castilla*, Biblioteca de autores españoles, 66 (Madrid: Rivadeneyra, 1875), Chap. 9, p. 8. The crocodile skin became an attribute of the apothecary, as witness *Romeo and Juliet*, V. i. 37, 42–4: 'I do remember an apothecary . . . and in his needy shop a tortoise hung, / an alligator stuff'd, and other skins / of ill-shap'd fishes'.
30 In the first line quoted here Le Strange has 'camel' (reflecting a Spanish reading 'camello') for 'horse' ('cauallo'). López Estrada in both Clavijo, *Embajada* (1943), p. 189 and Clavijo, *Embajada* (1999), p. 293 has 'cauallo'.
31 John E. Keller and Robert W. Linker, *Iconography in Medieval Spanish Literature* (Lexington: University Press of Kentucky, 1984), p. 49.
32 See also his account of the crocodile, pp. 69–70.
33 On this theme, see Christian K. Zacher, *Curiosity and Pilgrimage: The Literature of Discovery in Fourteenth-Century England* (Baltimore: Johns Hopkins University Press, 1976).
34 César Domínguez, 'El relato de viajes como intertexto: El caso particular de las crónicas de cruzada', in Rafael Beltrán (ed.), *Maravillas, peregrinaciones y utopías*, pp. 187–210, at p. 195.
35 Seneca, *Epistulae*, 38. The meaning, but not the form, is rendered in Robin Campbell's edition of Seneca, *Letters from a Stoic*, Penguin Classics (Harmondsworth: Penguin, 1969), p. 76: 'Where you arrive does not matter so much as what sort of person you are when you arrive there'.

# Bibliography

**( )**

## PRIMARY SOURCES

'Abd al-Latif al-Baghdadi, *Fi 'ilm ma ba'd al-tabi'a. Maqalat al-Lam: 'Abd al-Latif al-Bagdadis Bearbeitung von Buch Lamda der aristotelischen Metaphysik*, ed. and with commentary by A. Neuwirth (Wiesbaden: Steiner, 1976).

——, *Relation de l'Egypte par Abd Allatif, médecin arabe de Bagdad*, trans. M. Silvestre de Sacy (Paris: Imprimerie impériale, chez Treuttel et Würtz, 1810).

——, *The Eastern Key: Kitab al-Ifadah wa'l-I'tibar of 'Abd al-Latif al-Baghdadi*, trans. K. F. Zand, J. A. Videan and I. E. Videan (London: George Allen and Unwin, 1964).

Abbot Daniel, *The Life and Journey of Daniel Abbot of the Russian Land*, trans. W. F. Ryan, in Wilkinson, Hill and Ryan (eds), *Jerusalem Pilgrimage 1099–1185*, pp. 120–71.

——, *The Pilgrimage of the Russian Abbot Daniel*, ed. C. W. Wilson, Palestine Pilgrims' Text Society, 4 (London: Palestine Pilgrims' Text Society, 1897).

Abu 'Umar al-Kindi, *The Governors and Judges of Egypt*, trans. Rhuvon Guest (Leiden: Brill, 1912).

Abu al-Fida', *Annales A. H. 536*, ed. M. Reinaud, Recueil des Historiens des Croisades, Historiens Orientaux I (Paris: Académie des Inscriptions et Belles Lettres, 1872).

*Acta Honorii III et Gregorii IX (1216–41)*, ed. A. L. Tautu CICO, 3 (Vatican: Typis Polyglottis Vaticanis, 1950).

*Acta Innocentii Papae IV (1243–54)*, ed. T. Haluscynskyj and M. Wojnar CICO, 4 (1 and 2) (Rome: Pontificia Commissio ad Redigendum Codicem Iuris Canonici Orientalis, 1966).

*Actus beati Francisci et sociorum eius*, ed. P. Sabatier (Paris: Fischbacher, 1902).

Adam of Bremen, *Gesta Hammaburgensis ecclesiae pontificum*, ed. B. Schmeidler, MGHSS, rerum Germanicarum in usum scholarum, 2 vols (Hanover: [s.n.], 1917).

Adomnán [Adamnan], *Adamnan's De locis sanctis*, ed. Denis Meehan (Dublin: Dublin Institute for Advanced Studies, 1958).

——, *De locis sanctis*, ed. L. Bieler, Corpus Christianorum series latina, 175 (Turnhout: Brepols, 1965), pp. 175–234.

Alberic of Trois Fontaines, *Chronica*, ed. F. Schaffer-Boichorst, MGHSS, 35 (Munich, 1874).

Albertus Magnus, *De natura loci*, in *Opera omnia*, 37 vols, v, part 2, ed. Paul Hossfeld (Monasterii Westfalorum: Aschendorff, 1980).

Albrecht von Löwenstein, *Pilgerfahrt gen Jerusalem*, in *Das Reyßbuch deß Heyligen Lands* (Frankfurt am Main: Sigmund Feyerabend, 1584), fols 188ᵛ–212ᵛ.

Angela of Foligno, *Angela of Foligno: Complete Works*, trans. P. Lachance (New York: Paulist Press, 1993).

Angelo da Spoleto, *De fratribus minoribus visitantibus captivos in Babilonia*, in Golubovich (ed.), *Biblioteca*, iii, pp. 68–72.

Anna Comnena, *The Alexiad of Anna Comnena*, trans. from the Greek by E. R. A. Sewter (Harmondsworth: Penguin Books, 1969).

Anthony de Reboldis, *Itinerarium*, in Golubovich (ed.), *Biblioteca*, iii, p. 337.

Avicenna, *Liber canonis*, ed. Andrea Bellunello (Venice: per Paganum de Paganis, 1507; repr. Luca: Antonio Guinta, 1562).

Babylonian Talmud, ed. I. Epstein, trans. Maurice Simon, 35 vols, Tractate *Moed Qatan*, Tractate *Berakhot* (London: Soncino Press, 1952, 1960).

Baha' al-din Ibn Shaddad, *The Rare and Excellent History of Saladin or al-Nawadir al-Sultaniyya wa'l-Mahasin al-Yusufiyya*, trans. D. S. Richards (Aldershot: Ashgate, 2001).

Barron, W. R. J. and Glyn S. Burgess (gen. eds), *The Voyage of Saint Brendan: Representative Versions of the Legend in English Translation* (Exeter: University of Exeter Press, 2002).

Bartholomaeus Anglicus, *De proprietatibus rerum* (Frankfurt: apud Wolfgangum Richterum, 1601; repr. Frankfurt: Minerva, 1964).

——, *On the Properties of Things: John Trevisa's Translation of 'Bartholomaeus Anglicus, De proprietatibus rerum'*, gen. ed. Michael C. Seymour, 3 vols (Oxford: Clarendon Press, 1975–78).

Bede, *Bede: On the Tabernacle*, ed. and trans. Arthur G. Holder, Translated Texts for Historians, 18 (Liverpool: Liverpool University Press, 1994).

——, *Bede: On the Temple*, ed. and trans. with notes by Seán Connolly, introduction by Jennifer O'Reilly, Translated Texts for Historians, 21 (Liverpool: Liverpool University Press, 1995).

Benjamin of Tudela, *The Itinerary of Benjamin of Tudela*, ed. and trans. Marcus Nathan Adler (London: Henry Frowde, 1907; repr. as *The Itinerary of Benjamin of Tudela: Travels in the Middle Ages*, with introductions by Michael A. Signer, 1983, and A. Asher, 1840 (New York: Joseph Simon, 1983).

Bernhard von Breidenbach, *Peregrinatio in Terram Sanctam* (Mainz: Erhard Reuwich, 11 February 1486).

Boehmer, H. (ed.), *Analekten zur Geschichte des Franciskus von Assisi*, 6 vols, i: *Regula non bullata* (Tübingen and Leipzig: J. C. B. Mohr, 1904).

Bordeaux Pilgrim, *Itinerary from Bordeaux to Jerusalem*, trans. Aubrey Stewart, Palestine Pilgrims' Text Society, 1 (London: Palestine Pilgrims' Text Society, 1887; repr. New York: AMS Press, 1971).

Brocardus, pseudo-, *Directorium ad passagium faciendum*, ed. C. Kohler, RHC Docs Arms, 2 (Paris: Académie des Inscriptions et Belles Lettres, 1967).

*Bullarium Franciscanum*, ed. J. H. Sbaralea, 5 vols (Rome: Typis Sacrae Congregationis de Propaganda Fide, 1898).

Burchard of Mount Sion, *Burchard of Mount Sion: A Description of the Holy Land*, trans. Aubrey Stewart, annotated by C. R. Conder, Palestine Pilgrims' Text Society, 12 (London: Palestine Pilgrims' Text Society, 1896; repr. New York: AMS Press, 1971).

——, *Descriptio Terrae Sanctae*, in J. C. M. Laurent (ed.), *Peregrinatores medii aevi quatuor*.

Burchardus Argentoratensis, *De statu Egypti vel Babylonie*, in S. de Sandoli, *Itinera Hierosolymitana Crucesignatorum (saec. xii–xiii)*, 4 vols, Pubblicazioni dello Studium Biblicum Franciscanum, 24 (Jerusalem: Studium Biblicum Franciscanum, 1978–84), ii, pp. 392–414.

Buzurg ibn Shahriyar, *'Aja'ib al-Hind*, ed. Yusuf al-Sharuni (London: Riad El-Rayyes Books, 1990).

——, *Captain Buzurg ibn Shahriyar of Ram Hormuz: The Book of The Wonders of India, Mainland, Sea and Islands*, ed. and trans. G. S. P. Freeman-Grenville (London and The Hague: East-West Publications, 1981).

*Cancionero de Juan Alfonso de Baena*, ed. Brian Dutton and Joaquín González Cuenca, Biblioteca filológica hispana, 13 (Madrid: Visor, 1993).

Casson, Lionel (ed. and trans.), *Periplus maris Erythraei* (Princeton: Princeton University Press, 1989).

Caxton, William, *Caxton's Mirrour of the World*, ed. Oliver H. Prior, Early English Text Society, e.s., 110 (Oxford: Oxford University Press, 1913).

*Chronicon de Lanercost*, ed. J. Stevenson (Edinburgh: Maitland Club, 1839).

Clavijo: see González de Clavijo.

Constantinus Africanus, *Pantegni*, in *Omnia opera Ysaac* (Lyons: s.n., 1515), fols $1^r$–$144^r$.

*Crónica de los reyes de Castilla*, ed. Cayetano Rosell, Biblioteca de autores españoles, 66 (Madrid: Rivadeneyra, 1875).

Daniel the Abbot: see Abbot Daniel.

Dawson, C. H. (ed.), *The Mongol Mission: Narratives and Letters of the Franciscan Missionaries in Mongolia and China in the Thirteenth and Fourteenth Centuries* (London: Sheed and Ward, 1955).

*De adventu patriarchae Indorum ad urbem sub Calisto papa IIo*, ed. in F. Zarncke, 'Der Patriarch Johannes von Indien und der Priester Johannes', *Abhandlungen der Philologisch-Historischen Classe der Königlich Sächsischen Gesellschaft des Wissenschaften*, 7 (Leipzig: bei S. Hirzel, 1879), 837–46; repr. in Beckingham and Hamilton (eds), *Prester John*, pp. 29–38.

Dicuil, *Liber de mensura orbis terrae* ed. J. J. Tierney and L. Bieler (Dublin: Dublin Institute for Advanced Studies, 1967).

Egeria, *Journal de voyage*, ed. and French trans. Hélène Pétré, Sources chrétiennes, 21 (Paris: Editions du Cerf, 1948).

Encina, Juan del, *Obras completas*, ed. Ana M. Rambaldo, Clásicos castellanos, 218–20, 227, 4 vols (Madrid: Espasa-Calpe, 1978–83).

Enríquez de Ribera, Fadrique, Marqués de Tarifa, *Este libro es de el viaje q[ue] hize a Jerusalem* (Lisbon: Antonio Alvarez, 1608).

Ernoul, *La chronique d'Ernoul*, ed. L. de Mas Latrie (Paris: Societé de l'Histoire de France, 1871).

Fabri, Felix, *Eigentlich Beschreibung der hin vnnd wider Farth zu dem Heyligen Landt* ([s.l., s.n.], 1557).

——, *The Book of the Wanderings of Brother Felix Fabri*, trans. Aubrey Stewart, Palestine Pilgrims' Text Society, 2 vols (London: Palestine Pilgrims' Text Society, 1887–97; repr. New York: AMS Press, 1971).

——, *Fabri evagatorium in Terra Sanctae, Arabiae et Egypti peregrinationem*, ed. Conrad Dieter Hassler, 3 vols (Stuttgart: Societas Literaria Stuttgardiensis, 1843–49).

Fidenzo of Padua, *Liber recuperationis Terrae Sanctae*, in Golubovich (ed.), *Bibliotheca*, i, pp. 1–60.

Flint, V., 'Honorius Augustodunensis, *Imago mundi*', *Archives d'Histoire Doctrinale et Littéraire du Moyen Age*, 49 (1982), 1–151.

Friedberg, E. (ed.), *Corpus iuris canonici*, 2 vols (Leipzig, 1879–81; repr. Union, NJ: Lawbook Exchange, 2000).

Furnivall, F. J. (ed.), *The Stacions of Rome* (New York: Greenwood Press, 1969; originally pub. London: Early English Text Society, 1876).

Gerard de Frachet, *Vitae fratrum ordinis Praedicatorum*, IV, 1; ed. B. Reichert, *MOPH*, 1 (Rome: Institutum Historicum Fratrum Praedicatorum Romae, 1897).

Gibb, H. A. R. (ed.), *The Life of Saladin, from the Works of 'Imad ad-Din and Baha' ad-Din* (Oxford: Clarendon Press, 1973).

Golubovich, G. (ed.), *Biblioteca bio-bibliografica della Terra Santa e dell' Oriente francescano*, 5 vols (Florence: Quaracchi, 1906–27).

González de Clavijo, Ruy, *Embajada a Tamorlán*, ed. Francisco Lopez Estrada, Nueva colección de libros raros o curiosos, 1 (Madrid: Consejo Superior de Investigaciones Ciéntificas, 1943).

——, *Embajada a Tamorlán*, ed. Francisco Lopez Estrada, Clásicos Castalia, 242 (Madrid: Castalia, 1999).

——, *Embassy to Tamerlane 1403–1406*, trans. Guy Le Strange, The Broadway Travellers (London: Routledge, 1928).

Harris, M. Tjader (ed.), *Birgitta of Sweden: Life and Selected Revelations* (New York: Paulist Press, 1990).

Henry Daniel, *Liber uricrisiarum*, London, Wellcome Library, Sloane MS 1101.

Honorius Augustodunensis, *De imagine mundi libri tres*, book I, cc. viii–xxi, xxxii–xxxiii, in J.-P. Migne (ed.), *PL*, 172 (Paris: apud Garnieri Fratres, 1895).

Hugeburc, *The Life of St. Willibald*, trans. J. Wilkinson, in Wilkinson, *Jerusalem Pilgrims before the Crusades*, pp. 124–38.

Ibn Abi Usaybi'ah, *'Uyun al-anba' fi tabaqat al-atibba'*, ed. Nizar Rida (Beirut: Maktabat al-Hayat, 1965); ed. Basil 'Uyun al-Sud (Beirut: Dar al-Kutub al-'Ilmiyyah, 1998).

Ibn al-'Arabi, *Le dévoilement des effets du voyage = Kitab al-isfar 'an nata'ij al-asfar*, ed. and trans. Denis Gril (Paris: Editions de l'Éclat, 1994).

Ibn Battuta, *The Travels of Ibn Battuta, AD 1325–1354*, trans. H. A. R. Gibb and C. F. Beckingham, 5 vols (index vol. ed. A. D. H. Bivar), The Hakluyt Society, series 2, vols 110, 117, 141, 178 and 190 (London: Hakluyt Society, 1958–2000).

Ibn Fadlan, *Voyage chez les Bulgares de la Volga*, trans. Marius Canard (Paris: Sindbad, 1988).

al-Idrisi, *Géographie d'Edrisi traduit de l'arabe en français*, ed. P. A. Jaubert, 2 vols (Paris: Imprimerie Royale, 1836–40).

al Idrisi, Muhammad, 'Muhammad al Idrisi', in Wilkinson, Hill and Ryan (eds), *Jerusalem Pilgrimage 1099–1185*, pp. 223–7.

Innocent III, *Regesta Innocentii III*, in J. P. Migne (ed.), *PL*, 216 (Paris: apud Garnieri Fratres, 1855).

Isidore of Seville, *Etymologies (Etymologiae)*, in *Etymologiarum sive Originum libri XX*, ed. W. M. Lindsay, 2 vols (Oxford: Clarendon Press, 1911).

*Itinerarium cuiusdam Anglici*, in Golubovich (ed.), *Biblioteca*, iv.

Jacques de Vitry, *Historia Orientalis*; ed. F. Moschus as *Jacobi de Vitriaco libri duo quorum prior Orientalis, sive Hierosolymitanae, alter, Occidentalis historiae* (Douai: Balthazar Bellerus, 1597; repr. Farnborough: Gregg International Publishers, 1971).

Jacques de Vitry, *Lettres de Jacques de Vitry*, ed. R. B. C. Huygens (Leiden: Brill, 1960); new edn, *Lettres de Jacques de Vitry, 1160/70–1240, Évêque de S. Jean d'Acre*, ed. R. B. C. Huygens, Corpus Christianorum Continuatio Medievalis, 171 (Turnhout: Brepols, 2000).

James of Verona, *Liber peregrinationis Fratris Jacobi da Verona*, ed. R. Röhricht in *Revue de l'Orient Latin*, 3 (1895), 155–303.

Joannes Eschuid [John of Ashenden], *Summa astrologiae judicialis* (Venice: Franciscus Bolanus, J. Sanctiter, 1489).

John Gower, *Confessio amantis*, in *The Complete Works of John Gower*, ed. G. C. Macaulay, 4 vols, (Oxford: Clarendon Press, 1901), i–ii.

John Mandeville [Jean de Mandeville], *Le livre des merveilles du monde*, ed. Christiane Deluz, Sources d'histoire médiévale, 31 (Paris: CNRS, 2000).

——, *Mandeville's Travels*, ed. Michael C. Seymour (Oxford: Clarendon Press, 1967).

John of Joinville, *The Life of St Louis*, trans. R. Hague (London: Sheed and Ward, 1955).

John Trevisa, *On the Properties of Things: John Trevisa's Translation of 'Bartholomaeus Anglicus, De proprietatibus rerum'*, ed. Michael C. Seymour *et al.*, 3 vols. (Oxford: Clarendon Press, 1975–78).

Joinville: see John of Joinville.

Jordan Catalani, *Mirabilia descripta: The Wonders of the East*, trans. H. Yule, The Hakluyt Society, lst series, 31 (London: Hakluyt Society, 1863).

Kaeppeli, T. and P. Benoit, 'Un pèlerinage dominicain inédit du XIVe siècle: Le *Liber de locis et conditionibus Terrae Sanctae et sepulcro* d'Humbert de Dijon OP (1332)', *Revue Biblique*, 62 (1955), 513–40.

Kohler, C. (ed.), RHC Docs Arms, 5 vols (Paris: Imprimerie Nationale, and Farn-borough: Gregg Press, 1869–1906).

Langland, William, *Will's Visions of Piers Plowman, Do-Well, Do-Better and Do-Best*, ed. George Kane and E. Talbot Donaldson (London: Athlone Press, 1975).

Laurent, J. C. M. (ed.), *Peregrinatores medii aevi quatuor* (Leipzig: J. C. Hinrichs, 1864, 2nd edn 1873).

Lemmens, L. *Die Franziskaner im Heiligen Lande* (Münster: [s.n.], 1919).

Leo Marsicanus, *Chronicon monasterii Cassinensis*, ed. W. Wattenbach, MGHSS, 7 (Hanover: [s.n.], 1846).

*Les pelerinaiges por aler en Iherusalem*, in Michelant and Raynaud (eds), *Itinéraires à Jérusalem*, pp. 89–103.

*L'estoire d'Eracles empereur et la conqueste de la terre d'Outremer* in *Guillaume de Tyr et ses continuateurs*, 2 vols, ed. P. Paris (Paris: Librairie de Firmin-Didot et Cie, 1879–80).

*Liber canonis*, lib. 1, doct. 2, summa 1, cap. 11 (Venice, 1507, fol. 32$^r$).

*Litterae encyclicae magistrum generalium ordinis Praedicatorum 1233–1376*, ed. B. M. Reichert, MOPH, 5 (Rome: Institutum Historicum Fratrum Praedicatorum Romae, 1900).

Lopez, Robert S. and Irving W. Raymond, *Medieval Trade in the Mediterranean World: Illustrative Documents Translated with Introductions and Notes* (London: Oxford University Press, 1955).

Ludolf von Sudheim [Ludolph von Suchem], *Ludolph von Suchem's Description of the Holy Land and of the Way Thither: Written in the Year 1350*, trans. Aubrey Stewart, Palestine Pilgrims' Text Society, 27 (London: Palestine Pilgrims' Text Society, 1895).

——, *Ludolphi, rectoris ecclesiae parochialis in Suchem, de itinere Terrae Sanctae liber*, ed. Ferdinand Deycks, Bibliothek des Litterarischen Vereins in Stuttgart, 25 (Stuttgart: Litterarischer Verein, 1851).

——, *Ludolfs von Sudheim Reise ins Heilige Land*, ed. Ivar von Stapelmohr, Lunder Germanische Forschungen, 6 (Kopenhagen: C. W. K. Gleerup, 1913; repr. Lund: Ohlsson, 1937).

Macrobius, *Commentary on the Dream of Scipio*, trans. W. H. Stahl (New York and London: Columbia University Press, 1952).

Margery Kempe, *The Book of Margery Kempe*, ed. S. B. Meech and H. E. Allen (Oxford: Oxford University Press, 1940).

——, *The Book of Margery Kempe*, ed. and trans. L. Staley (New York: Norton, 2001).

Marino Sanudo Torsello, *Marino Sanutus dictus Torsellus: Liber secretorum fidelium crucis*, in J. Bongars (ed.), *Gesta Dei per Francos*, 2 vols (Hanover: Typis Wechelianis apud heredes Johannis Aubrii, 1611); repr. with introduction by Joshua Prawer (Toronto: University of Toronto Press, 1972).

Marino Sanuto, *Secrets for True Crusaders to Help them Recover the Holy Land*, trans. Aubrey Stewart, with 'Note on the maps' by C. R. Conder, Palestine Pilgrims' Text Society, 12 (London: Palestine Pilgrims' Text Society, 1896; repr. New York: AMS Press, 1971).

Marino Sanuto (the Diarist), *I diarii*, ed. Rinaldo Fulin *et al.*, 58 vols (Venice: F. Visentini, 1879–1903).

Martiniano Roncaglia, *Storia della provincia di Terra Santa*, i: *I Francescani in Oriente durante le crociate (sec. XIII)* (Cairo: Centro di Studi Orientali, 1954).

Michelant, H. and G. Raynaud (eds), *Itinéraires á Jérusalem*, 2 vols, Société de l'Orient Latin, 20 (Paris: Société de l'Orient Latin, 1882).

Muhammad al Idrisi: see al Idrisi.

Nasir-i-Khusrau, *Diary of a Journey through Syria and Palestine by Nâsir-i-Khusrau*, Palestine Pilgrims' Text Society, 4 (London: Palestine Pilgrims' Text Society, 1897).

Niccolo da Poggibonsi, *Libro d'Oltramare*, ed. B. Bagatti (Jerusalem: Tipografia dei Francescani, 1945).

Nicholas of Lyra, *Postillae super Bibliam* [illustrated] (Nuremberg: Anton Koberger, 1481).

——, *Postilla super totam Bibliam* (Rome: Conradus Sweynheim and Arnoldus Pannartz, 1471–72).

Odoric of Pordenone, 'Relatio', in *Sinica Franciscana*, 6 vols, i: Anastasius van den Wyngaert (ed.), *Itinera et relationes fratrum minorum saeculi XIII et XIV* (Florence: Quaracchi, 1929).

Oliver of Paderborn, *Historia Damiatana*, in *Die Schriften des Kölner Domscholmasters, späteren Bischofs von Paderborn und Kardinal-Bischofs von S. Sabina Oliverus*, ed. H. Hoogeweg, Bibliothek des Litterarischen Vereins in Stuttgart, 202 (Tübingen: Litterarischer Verein Stuttgart, 1894).

Otto of Freising, *Chronica sive Historia de duabus civitatibus*, ed. A. Hofmeister, MGHSS, rerum Germanicarum in usum scholarum (Hanover and Leipzig: Hahn, 1912).

Paris, Matthew, *Chronica majora*, ed. H. R. Luard, Rolls Series, 7 vols (London: Longman & Co., 1872–83).

Paulus Orosius, *The Seven Books of History against the Pagans*, trans. R. J. Deferrari (Washington, DC: Catholic University of America Press, 1964).

Pegolotti, *La pratica della mercatura*, in Robert S. Lopez and Irving W. Raymond (eds and trans.), *Medieval Trade in the Mediterranean World: Illustrative Documents Translated with Introductions and Notes* (London: Oxford University Press, 1955).

*Pelrinages et pardouns de Acre*, in Michelant and Raynaud (eds), *Itinéraires à Jerusalem*, pp. 229–30.

Pfister, F., *Der Alexanderroman des Archipresbyters Leo* (Heidelberg: Carl Winter, 1913).

Phocas, Johannes, *The Pilgrimage of Johannes Phocas*, trans. Aubrey Stewart, Palestine Pilgrims' Text Society, 5 (London: Palestine Pilgrims' Text Society, 1897).

'Physician's handbook: Astrological and medical compendium, with pilgrim's guide from London to Jerusalem and itinerary of the Holy Land', Christie's Auction House, London, *Sales Catalogue*, 29 November 1999, p. 9.

Pliny, *The Natural History*, ed. and trans. W. H. Rackham *et al.*, 10 vols (London: Loeb Classical Librar, 1938–62).

Polo, Marco, *The Travels of Marco Polo*, trans. Ronald Latham (Harmondsworth: Penguin Books, 1958).

Poloner, Johannes, *Description of the Holy Land: By John Poloner*, trans. Aubrey Stewart, Palestine Pilgrims' Text Society, 6 (London: Palestine Pilgrims' Text Society, 1894).

Pseudo-Brocardus: see Brocardus.

——, *Ptolemy's Geography: An Annotated Translation of the Theoretical Chapters*, ed. and trans. J. Lennart Berggren and Alexander Jones (Princeton and Oxford: Princeton University Press, 2000).

*Qualiter*, in Wilkinson, Hill and Ryan (eds), *Jerusalem Pilgrimage 1099–1185*, pp. 90–1.

Qur'an: *The Holy Qur'an*, trans. and ed. A. Yusuf Ali, 2nd edn (USA: American Trust Publications, 1977).

Raynaud, Gaston (ed.), *Les Gestes des Chiprois*, RHC Docs Arms, 2 vols (Paris: Société de l'Orient Latin, 1869–1906); repr. as *Les Gestes des Chiprois*, Recueil de chroniques français aux XIII et XIV siècles (Osnabruck: Otto Zeller, 1968).

*Registres de Grégoire IX*, ed. L. Auvray, BEFAR, series 2:9, 4 vols (Paris: E. de Bocard, vice Fontemoing, 1896–1955).

*Registres d'Innocent IV*, ed. E. Berger, BEFAR, series 2:1, 4 vols (Paris: Thorin, 1884–1921).

Richard of Poitou, *Chronica*, ed. G. Waitz, MGHSS, 26 (Hanover, 1882).

Ricoldo of Monte Crucis, 'Epistolae V commentatoriae de perditione Acconis 1291', ed. R. Röhricht, *Archives d'Orient Latin*, 2 (1884), 264–96.

——, *Liber peregrinacionis*, in Laurent (ed.), *Peregrinatores medii aevi quatuor*, pp. 124–31.

Robertus Anglicus, Commentary on Sacrobosc in Thorndike, *The* Sphere *of Sacrobosco*, pp. 187–91 (Latin text), 236–40 (trans.).

Roger Bacon, *Opus maius*, ed. J. Bridges, 3 vols (Oxford: Clarendon Press, 1897–1900).

Röhricht, Reinhold and Heinrich Meisner (eds), *Das Reisebuch der Familie Rieter* (Tübingen: Litterarischer Verein Stuttgart, 1884).

——, *Deutsche Pilgerreisen nach dem Heiligen Lande* (Berlin: Weidmannsche Buchhandlung, 1880).

Saewulf, 'A reliable account of the situation of Jerusalem', ed. and trans. in Wilkinson, Hill and Ryan (eds), *Jerusalem Pilgrimage 1099–1185*, pp. 94–116.

Sandoli, S. de, *Itineraria Hierosolymitana crucesignatorum (saec. xii–xiii)*, 4 vols (Jerusalem: Pubblicazioni dello Studium Biblicum Franciscanum, 1978–84).

Sanudo: see Marino Sanudo.

Seneca, *Letters from a Stoic*, trans Robin Campbell, Penguin Classics (Harmondsworth: Penguin, 1969).

Simon of St Quentin, *Histoire des Tartares*, ed. J. Richard (Paris: Librairie Orientaliste Paul Geuthner, 1965).

Solinus, C. Julius, *Collectanea rerum memorabilium*, ed. T. Mommsen (2nd edn Berlin: Weidmann, 1895).

Stargardt, U. (trans.), *The Life of Dorothea von Montau, a Fourteenth Century Recluse* (Lewiston: Edwin Mellen Press, 1997).

Symon Semeonis, *Itinerarium Symonis Semeonis ab Hybernia ad Terram Sanctam*, ed. M. Esposito, Scriptores Latini Hiberniae, 4 (Dublin: Dublin Institute for Advanced Studies, 1960).

Tafur, Pero, *Andanças e viajes de Pero Tafur*, ed. Marcos Jiménez de la Espada, Colección de libros españoles raros o curiosos, 8 (Madrid: Miguel Ginesta, 1874); ed. José María Ramos, Biblioteca clásica, 265 (Madrid: Hernando, 1934).

——, *Travels and Adventures 1435–1439*, ed. and trans. with an introduction by Malcolm Letts, The Broadway Travellers (London: Routledge, 1926).

Tarifa: see Enríquez de Ribera.

Thomas of Celano, *Vita prima*, in E. Alençon (ed.), *S. Francisci vita et miracula* (Rome: Deschée, Lefebvre, 1906).

Tucher, Hans, *Verzeichnuß der Reyß zum Heyligen Land*, in *Das Reyßbuch deß Heyligen Lands* (Frankfurt am Main: Johann Feyerabend for Sigmund Feyerabend, 1584), fols 349$^v$–374$^v$.

Tudela: see Benjamin of Tudela.

Usamah Ibn Munqidh, *Kitab al-I'tibar*, trans. P. K. Hitti as *An Arab-Syrian Gentleman & Warrior in the Period of the Crusades* (New York: Columbia University Press, 2000).

——, *Usamah's Memoirs Entitled Kitab al-I'tibar*, ed. P. K. Hitti (Princeton: Princeton University Press, 1930; repr. Beirut: United Publishers, 1981).

Vegetius, *Epitome of Military Science*, ed. and trans. N. P. Milner, Translated Texts for Historians, 16 (Liverpool: Liverpool University Press, 1993).

Vincent of Beauvais, *Speculum naturale*, in *Speculum quadruplex sive Speculum maius* (Duaci: Baltazaris Belleri, 1624; repr. Graz: Akademische Druck- und Verlagsanstalt, 1964).

Walter the Chancellor, *The Antiochene Wars: A Translation and Commentary*, ed. and trans. T. S. Asbridge and S. B. Edgington (Aldershot: Ashgate, 1999).

Westrem, Scott D. (ed.), *Broader Horizons: A Study of Johannes de Witte de Hese's Itiner-arius and Medieval Travel Narratives* (Cambridge, MA: Medieval Academy of America, 2001).

Wilkinson, John, *Jerusalem Pilgrims before the Crusades* (Warminster: Aris and Phillips, 1977).

Wilkinson, J., with J. Hill and W. F. Ryan (eds), *Jerusalem Pilgrimage 1099–1185*, The Hakluyt Society, 2nd series, 167 (London: Hakluyt Society, 1988).

William Adam, *De modo Sarracenos extirpandi*, ed. C. Kohler, RHC Docs Arms, 2 (Paris: Imprimerie Nationale, 1906).

William of Rubruck, *The Mission of Friar William of Rubruck*, ed. P. Jackson with D. Morgan, The Hakluyt Society, 2nd series, 173 (London: Hakluyt Society, 1990).

William of Tyre, *Chronicon*, ed. R. B. C. Huygens, Identification des dates par H. E. Mayer et G. Rosch, Corpus Christianorum Continuatio Medievalis, 63, 63A (Turnhout: Brepols, 1986).

Wolfe, Michael (ed.), *One Thousand Roads to Mecca: Ten centuries of Travellers Writing about the Muslim Pilgrimage* (New York: Grove Press, 1997).

Zarncke, F., 'Der Briefe des Priesters Johannes an der byzantinischen Kaiser Emanuel', *Abhandlungen der Philologisch-Historischen Classe der Königlich Sächsischen Gesellschaft des Wissenschaften*, 7 (Leipzig: bei S. Hirzel, 1879), 873–934; repr. in Beckingham and Hamilton (eds), *Prester John*, pp. 40–102.

## SECONDARY SOURCES

Abulafia, David, 'The impact of the Orient', in Dionisius A. Agius and Ian Richard Netton (eds), *Across the Mediterranean Frontiers: Selected Proceedings of the International Medieval Congress, University of Leeds, 10–13 July 1995, 8–11 July 1996* (Turnhout: Brepols, 1997), pp. 1–40.

Adams, W. Y., *Nubia: Corridor to Africa* (London: Allen Lane, 1977).

Adler, Elkan Natan (ed.), *Jewish Travellers* (New York: Harmon Press, 2nd edn, 1966).

Akbari, Suzanne Conklin, 'From due east to true north: Orientalism and orientation', in Jeffrey Jerome Cohen (ed.), *The Postcolonial Middle Ages* (New York: St Martin's Press, 2000), pp. 19–34.

——, 'Orientation and nation in the *Canterbury Tales*', in Lynch (ed.), *Chaucer's Cultural Geography*, pp. 102–34.

——, 'Placing the Jews in Late Medieval English Literature', in Ivan Davidson Kalmar and Derek J. Penslar (eds), *Orientalism and the Jews* (Hanover, NH: University Press of New England, 2004).

Alexander, J. J. G., *A Survey of Manuscripts Illustrated in the British Isles*, i, *Insular Manu-scripts 6th to 9th Century* (London: Harvey Miller, 1978).

Allen, Roger, *The Arabic Literary Heritage* (Cambridge: Cambridge University Press, 1998).

Almagià, Roberto, *Monumenta cartographica Vaticana*, 4 vols: i, *Planisferi, carte nautiche e affini dal secoli XIV al XVII esistenti nella Biblioteca Apostolica Vaticana* (Vatican: Biblioteca Apostolica Vaticana, 1944).

Altaner, B., *Die Dominikanermissionen des 13 Jahrhunderts* (Habelschwerdt: Frankesbuch-handlung, 1924).

Alvarez Márquez, M. Carmen, 'La biblioteca de don Fadrique Enríquez de Ribera, I Marqués de Tarifa (1532)', *Historia, Instituciones, Documentos*, 13 (1986), 1–39.

Atiya, A. S., *Egypt and Aragon: Embassies and Diplomatic Correspondence between 1300 and 1330 AD* (Leipzig: F. A. Brockhaus, 1938); repr. in *Abhandlungen für die Kunde des Morgenlands*, 23 (Kraus reprint, 1966).

——, *The Crusade in the Later Middle Ages* (London: Butler & Tanner, 1938; repr. New York: Kraus, 1965).

Atkinson, C. W., *Mystic and Pilgrim: The Book and the World of Margery Kempe* (Ithaca: Cornell University Press, 1983).

Baldwin, M. W., 'Missions to the East in the thirteenth and fourteenth centuries', in Zacour and Hazard (eds), *The Impact of the Crusades on the Near East*, pp. 452–518.

Barber, M., *The New Knighthood: A History of the Order of the Temple* (Cambridge: Cambridge University Press, 1994).

—— (ed.), *The Military Orders: Fighting for the Faith and Caring for the Sick* (Aldershot: Ashgate, 1994).

Barber, Peter, 'The Evesham world map: A late medieval English view of God and the world', *Imago Mundi*, 47 (1995), 13–33, esp. 13–17.

Baxandall, Michael, *Painting and Experience in Fifteenth-Century Italy* (Oxford: Oxford University Press, 1972; paperback 1974).

Beckingham, C. F., *The Achievements of Prester John: An Inaugural Lecture at the School of Oriental and African Studies, London, 1966* (London: School of Oriental and African Studies, University of London, 1966); repr. in Beckingham and Hamilton (eds), *Prester John*, pp. 1–22.

——, 'An Ethiopian embassy to Europe, c. 1310', *Journal of Semitic Studies*, 14 (1989), 337–46; repr. in Beckingham and Hamilton (eds), *Prester John*, pp. 197–206.

—— and B. Hamilton (eds), *Prester John, the Mongols and the Ten Lost Tribes* (Aldershot: Ashgate Publishing Ltd, 1996).

Beckwith, S., *Christ's Body: Identity, Culture and Society in Late Medieval Writings* (London: Routledge, 1993).

Beltran, Vicenç, 'El *Viaje a Jerusalén* del Marqués de Tarifa: Un nuevo manuscrito y los problemas de composición', in Rafael Beltrán (ed.), *Maravillas, peregrinaciones y utopías: Literatura de viajes en el mundo románico* (Valencia: Publicacions de la Universitat de València, Departament de Filologia Espanyola, 2002), pp. 171–85.

Bencheikh, J. E., 'Le cénacle poétique du calife al-Mutawakkil (m. 247): Contribution à l'analyse des instances de légitimation socio-littéraires', *Bulletin d'Etudes Orientales*, 29 (1977), 33–52.

——, 'Les secrétaires poètes et animateurs de cénacles aux IIe et IIIe siècles de l'Hégire: Contribution à l'analyse d'une production poétique', *Journal Asiatique*, 263 (1975), 265–315.

Biller, P. and A. J. Minnis (eds), *Medieval Theology and the Natural Body* (York: York Medieval Press, 1997).

Birch, Debra J., 'Jacques de Vitry and the ideology of pilgrimage', in Stopford (ed.), *Pilgrimage Explored*, pp. 79–93.

Blackburn, Robin, 'The Old World background to European colonial slavery', *William and Mary Quarterly*, 54 (1997), 65–102.

Bosworth, C. E., 'Travel literature', in Meisami and Starkey (eds), *Encyclopedia of Arabic Literature*, ii, pp. 778–80.

Bouloux, Nathalie, *Culture et savoirs géographiques en Italie au XIVe siècle* (Turnhout: Brepols, 2002).

Bowers, T., 'Margery Kempe as traveler', *Studies in Philology*, 1:47 (2000), 1–28.

Boyle, J. A., 'The Il-Khans of Persia and the Christian West', *History Today*, 23:8 (1973), 554–63.

Bredero, Adriaan H., 'Jérusalem dans l'occident médiéval', in Gallois and Riou (eds), *Mélanges offerts à René Crozet*, pp. 259–71.

Brefeld, J., *A Guidebook for the Jerusalem Pilgrimage in the Late Middle Ages: A Case for Computer-Aided Textual Criticism* (Hilversum: Verloren, 1994).

Brenner, Peter J. (ed.), *Der Reisebericht* (Frankfurt am Main: suhrkamp, 1989).

Brincken, A.-D. von den, *Die 'Nationes Christianorum Orientalium' im Verständnis der lateinischen Historiographie*, Kölner Historische Abhandlungen, 22 (Cologne: Böhlau, 1973).

Brodersen, Kai, *Terra cognita: Studien zür römischen Raumerfassung* (Hildesheim: Olms, 1995).

——, 'The presentation of geographical knowledge for travel and transport in the Roman world', in Colin Adams and Ray Laurence (eds), *Travel and Geography in the Roman Empire* (London: Routledge, 2001), pp. 7–21.

Bruce Mitford, R. L. S., 'The art of the Codex Amiatinus', Jarrow Lecture, 1967, repr. in *Journal of the British Archaeological Association*, 3rd series, 32 (1969), 1–25.

Bull, Marcus, 'Origins', Chap. 2 of Riley-Smith (ed.), *The Oxford Illustrated History of the Crusades*, pp. 13–33.

Burnett, Charles, *The Introduction of Arabic Learning into England*, Panizzi Lectures 1996 (London: The British Library, 1997).

Burns, E. Jane, *Courtly Love Undressed: Reading through Clothes in Medieval French Culture* (Philadelphia: University of Pennsylvania Press, 2002).

Bynum, Caroline Walker, 'Miracles and marvels: The limits of alterity', in Felten and Jaspert (eds), *Vita religiosa im Mittelalter*, pp. 801–17.

Cahen, Claude, *The Formation of Turkey: The Seljukid Sultanate of Rum: Eleventh to Fourteenth Century*, ed. and trans. P. M. Holt (Harlow, Essex: Pearson, 2001).

Campbell, Mary B., *The Witness and the Other World: Exotic European Travel Writing, 400–1600* (Ithaca, NY, and London: Cornell University Press, 1988).

——, '"The object of one's gaze": Landscape, writing and early medieval pilgrimage', in Westrem (ed.), *Discovering New Worlds*, pp. 3–15.

Campbell, Tony, *The Earliest Printed Maps 1472–1500* (London: The British Library, 1987).

——, 'Portolan charts from the late thirteenth century to 1500', in Harley and Woodward (eds), *History of Cartography*, i, pp. 371–463.

Carus-Wilson, E., 'The medieval trade of the ports of the Wash', *Medieval Archaeology*, 6–7 (1962–3), 182–201.

Cary, G., *The Medieval Alexander* (Cambridge: Cambridge University Press, 1956).

Céard, Jean, *La nature et les prodiges: L'insolite au XVIe siècle* (Geneva: Droz, 1977).

Chaplin, Joyce E., 'Natural philosophy and an early racial idiom in North America: Comparing English and Indian bodies', *William and Mary Quarterly*, 54 (1997), 229–52.

Childs, W. R., 'The perils, or otherwise, of maritime pilgrimage to Santiago de Compostela in the fifteenth century', in Stopford (ed.), *Pilgrimage Explored*, pp. 123–43.

Christie, Niall, 'Crusade literature', in Suad Joseph *et al.* (eds), *The Encyclopedia of Women and Islamic Cultures* (Leiden: E. J. Brill, forthcoming).

Clanchy, Michael, 'Images of ladies with prayer books: What do they signify?', in Swanson, *The Church and the Book*.

Cohen, Jeffrey Jerome, 'On Saracen enjoyment: Some fantasies of race in late medieval France and England', *Journal of Medieval and Early Modern Studies*, 31 (2001), 113–46.

Cohn, Norman, *The Pursuit of the Millennium: Revolutionary Millenarism and Mystical Anarchists of the Middle Ages* (London: Paladin, 1970).

Connolly, Daniel, 'Imagined pilgrimage in the itinerary maps of Matthew Paris', *Art Bulletin*, 81 (1999), 598–622.

Crane, Susan, *The Performance of Self: Ritual, Clothing and Identity during the Hundred Years War* (Philadelphia: University of Pennsylvania Press, 2002).

Crichton, Michael, *Eaters of the Dead: The Manuscript of Ibn Fadlan Relating his Experiences with the Northmen in A.D. 922* (New York: Alfred A Knopf, 1976).

Cunliffe, Barry, *The Extraordinary Voyage of Pytheas the Greek: The Man who Discovered Britain* (London: Allen Lane, 2001).

Dajani-Shakeel, Hadiah, 'Some aspects of Muslim–Frankish Christian relations in the Sham region in the twelfth century', in Yvonne Yazbeck Haddad and Wadi Z. Haddad (eds), *Christian–Muslim Encounters* (Gainesville, FL: University Press of Florida, 1995), pp. 193–209.

Daniel, E. R., *The Franciscan Concept of Mission in the High Middle Ages* (Lexington: University Press of Kentucky, 1975).

Daston, Lorraine and Katherine Park, *Wonders and the Order of Nature, 1150–1750* (New York: Zone, 1998).

Davis, David Brion, *Slavery and Human Progress* (Oxford: Oxford University Press, 1984).

Degenhart, Bernhard and Annegrit Schmitt, 'Marino Sanudo und Paolino Veneto: Zwei Literaten des 14. Jahrhunderts in ihrer Wirkung auf Buchillustrierung und Kartographie in Venedig, Avignon, und Neapel', *Römisches Jahrbuch für Kunstgeschichte*, 14 (1973), 1–137.

Delacroix-Besnier, C., *Les Dominicains et la chrétienté grecque aux XIVe et XVe siècles*, Collection de l'École Française de Rome, 237 (Rome: École Française de Rome, 1997).

Delano-Smith, Catherine, 'Maps as science *and* art: Maps in sixteenth-century Bibles', *Imago Mundi*, 42 (1990), 65–83.

——, 'Milieus of mobility: Itineraries, routes and roads', in J. R. Akerman, *Maps on the Move: Cartography for Travel and Transportation*, Twelfth K. Nebenzahl Jr Lecture in the History of Cartography, 1996 (Chicago: University of Chicago Press for the Newberry Library, forthcoming).

—— and Roger J. P. Kain, *English Maps: A History* (London: The British Library, 1999).

Destombes, Marcel, *Mappemondes 1200–1500*, catalogue prepared by the Commission des Cartes Anciennes de l'Union Géographique Internationale (Amsterdam: N. Israel, 1964).

Dichter, B., *The Maps of Acre: An Historical Cartography* (Acre: Municipality of Acre, 1973).

Dilke, O. A. W., *Greek and Roman Maps* (London: Thames and Hudson, 1985).

——, 'Cartography in the Byzantine Empire', in Harley and Woodward (eds), *History of Cartography*, i, pp. 258–75.

——, 'Maps in the service of the state: Roman cartography to the end of the Augustan era', in Harley and Woodward (eds), *History of Cartography*, i, pp. 201–11.

Dilke, Oswald and Margaret Dilke, 'Mapping a crusade', *History Today*, 39 (1989), 31–5.

Dillon, J., 'Holy women and their confessors or confessors and their holy women? Margery Kempe and continental tradition', in R. Voaden (ed.), *Prophets Abroad: The Reception of Continental Holy Women in Late-Medieval England* (Cambridge: D. S. Brewer, 1996), pp. 115–40.

Domínguez, César, *Juan del Encina, el peregrino: Temas y técnicas de la 'Tribagia'*, Papers of the Medieval Hispanic Research Seminar, 31 (London: Department of Hispanic Studies, Queen Mary and Westfield College, 2000).

——, 'El relato de viajes como intertexto: El caso particular de las crónicas de cruzada', in Rafael Beltran (ed.), *Maravillas, peregrinaciones y utopías: literatura de viajes en el mundo románico* (Valencia: Publicacions de la Universitat de València, Departament de Filologia Espanyola, 2002), pp. 187–210.

Donkin, R. A., *Beyond Price: Pearls and Pearl-Fishing: Origins to the Age of Discovery*, (Philadelphia: American Philosophical Society, 1998).

Dor, Juliette, Lesley Johnson and Jocelyn Wogan-Browne (eds), *New Trends in Feminine Spirituality: The Holy Women of Liège and their Impact* (Turnhout: Brepols, 1999).

Dyas, D., *Pilgrimage in Medieval English Literature, 700–1500* (Cambridge: D. S. Brewer, 2001).

Edbury, P. W. and J. G. Rowe, *William of Tyre: Historian of the Latin East* (Cambridge: Cambridge University Press, 1988).

Edson, E., *Mapping Time and Space: How Medieval Mapmakers Viewed their World* (London: The British Library, 1997).

Edson, Evelyn, 'Matthew Paris's "other" map of Palestine', *Map Collector*, 66:1 (1994), 18–22.

Eickelman, Dale and James Piscatori (eds), *Muslim Travelers: Pilgrimage, Migration and the Religious Imagination* (Berkeley: University of California Press, 1990).

Eisenstein, J. D. (ed.), *Ozar Massaoth: A Collection of Itineraries by Jewish Travellers to Palestine, Syria, Egypt and Other Countries* (New York: J. D. Eisenstein, 1926, repr. Tel Aviv: J. D. Eisenstein, 1969); excerpts trans. in Adler (ed.), *Jewish Travellers*.

Elad, Amikam, *Medieval Jerusalem and Islamic Worship: Holy Places, Ceremonies, Pilgrimage* (Leiden: Brill, 1995).

Ellis, D. S., 'Margery Kempe and King's Lynn', in McEntire (ed.), *Margery Kempe: A Book of Essays*, pp. 139–63.

Ellis, R., 'Margery Kempe's scribe and the miraculous books', in H. Phillips (ed.), *Langland, the Mystics and the Medieval English Religious Tradition* (Cambridge: D. S. Brewer, 1990), pp. 161–75.

*Espansione del Francescanesimo tra Occidente e Oriente nel secolo XIII: Atti del VI Convegno Internazionale* (Assisi: Società Internazionale di Studi Francescani, 1979).

Evans, William McKee, 'From the land of Canaan to the land of Guinea: The strange odyssey of the "Sons of Ham"', *American Historical Review*, 85 (1980), 15–43.

Fahd, T., 'Sihr', in Gibb *et al.* (eds), *The Encyclopaedia of Islam*, ix, pp. 567–71.

Favreau-Lilie, Marie-Luise, 'Die Bedeutung von Wallfahrten, Kreuzzügen und anderen Wanderungsbewegungen (z.B. Gesellenwanderungen) für die Kommunikation in Mittelalter und früher Neuzeit', in Pohl (ed.), *Die Bedeutung der Kommunikation*, pp. 64–89.

Felten, Franz J. and Nikolas Jaspert (eds), *Vita religiosa im Mittelalter: Festschrift für Kaspar Elm zum 70. Geburtstag* (Berlin: Duncker and Humblot, 1999).

Fleck, Andrew, 'Here, there, and in between: Representing difference in the *Travels* of Sir John Mandeville', *Studies in Philology*, 97 (2000), 379–401.

Folda, J., 'Manuscripts of the *History of Outremer* by William of Tyre: A handlist', *Scriptorium*, 27 (1973), 90–5.

Frankfort, Frank, 'Marino Sanudo Torsello: A social biography', unpublished PhD dissertation, University of Cincinnati, 1974.

Freller, Thomas, 'Ein Osnabrücker Kleriker auf Malta: Ludolphs von Suchen Itinerar und der heilige Paulus: Neue Aspekte spätmittelalterlicher Fremdwahrnehmung', *Jahrbuch der Gesellschaft für Niedersächsische Kirchengeschichte*, 94 (1996), 139–51.

Friedman, John Block, *The Monstrous Races in Medieval Art and Thought* (Cambridge, MA: Harvard University Press, 1981).

—— and Kristen M. Figg, *Trade, Travel, and Exploration in the Middle Ages: An Encyclopedia* (New York: Garland Publishing Co., 2000).

Friedman, Mark, 'Jewish pilgrimage after the destruction of the Second Temple', in Rosovsky (ed.), *City of the Great King*, pp. 140–57.

Friedman, Yvonne, 'Women in captivity and their ransom during the crusader period', in Michael Goodich, Sophia Menache and Sylvia Schein (eds), *Cross-Cultural Convergences in the Crusader Period: Essays Presented to Aryeh Grabois on his Sixty-Fifth Birthday* (New York: Peter Lang, 1995), pp. 75–87.

Fürst, H., *Die Custodie des Heiligen Landes: Die Mission der Franziskaner im Heiligen Land und im Vorderen Orient* (Munich: Kommisariat für das Heilige Land, 1981).

Gallois, Pierre and Yves-Jean Riou (eds), *Mélanges offerts à René Crozet*, Cahiers de civilisation médiévale, supplement (Poitiers: Université de Poitiers, Centre d'études Supérieures de Civilisation Médiéval, 1996).

García Martín, Pedro, *La cruzada pacífica: La peregrinación a Jerusalén de don Fadrique Enríquez de Ribera*, Libros del buen andar, 44 (Barcelona: Serbal, 1997).

Gautier Dalché, Patrick, *Carte marine et portulan au XIIe siècle: Le Liber de existencia riverarium et forma maris nostri Mediterranei (Pise, circa 1200)* (Rome: École Française de Rome, 1995).

——, 'Connaissance et usages géographiques des coordonnées dans le Moyen Âge latin (du Vénérable Bède à Roger Bacon)', in Louis Callebat and Olivier Desbordes (eds), *Science antique, science médiévale (autour d'Avranches 235): Actes du colloque internationale (Mont-Saint-Michel, 4–7 septembre 1998)* (Hildesheim, Zürich and New York: Olms-Weidmann, 2000), pp. 401–36.

——, 'Décrire le monde et situer les lieux au XIIe siècle: L'expositio mappe mundi et la généalogie de la mappemonde de Hereford', *Mélanges de l'École Française Antiquité–Moyen Âge* (2001), 112–21.

Gibb, H. A. R. *et al.* (eds), *The Encyclopaedia of Islam*, 2nd edn, 11 vols and supplements (Leiden: E. J. Brill, 1954–2003).

Gil, Moshe, 'Aliya and pilgrimage in the early Arab period (634–1009)', *The Jerusalem Cathedra*, 3 (1983), 162–91.

Goitein, S. D., *A Mediterranean Society: The Jewish Communities of the Arab World as Portrayed in the Documents of the Cairo Geniza*, 5 vols (Berkeley: University of California University Press, 1969–88).

Golubovich, G., 'Disputatio Latinorum et Graecorum seu relatio Apocrisariorum Gregorii IX de gestis Nicaea in Bithynia et Nymphaeae in Lydia', *Archivum Franciscanum Historicum*, 12 (1919), 418–70.

Goodman, Jennifer R., *Chivalry and Exploration, 1298–1630* (Woodbridge: Boydell Press, 1998).

Graf, A., *Miti, leggende e superstizioni del medio evo*, 2 vols (Turin: E. Loescher, 1892–93).

Greetham, D. C., 'The concept of nature in Bartholomaeus Anglicus', *Journal of the History of Ideas*, 41 (1980), 663–77.

——, 'The fabulous geography of John Trevisa's translation of Bartholomaeus Anglicus' *De proprietatibus rerum*', unpublished PhD dissertation, City University of New York, 1974.

Grenzmann, Ludger and Karl Stackmann (eds), *Literatur und Laienbildung im Spätmittelalter und der Reformationszeit* (Stuttgart: Metzler, 1984).

Guglielmi, Nilda, *Guía para viajeros: Oriente, siglos XIII–XV* (Buenos Aires: Programa de Investigaciones Medievales, Consejo Nacional de Investigaciones Científicas y Técnicas, 1994).

Hackett, Jeremiah (ed.), *Roger Bacon and the Sciences: Commemorative Essays* (Leiden, New York and Cologne: Brill, 1997).

Haddad, Wadi' Z., 'The crusaders through Muslim eyes', *The Muslim World*, 73 (1983), 234–52.

Hahn, Thomas, 'The difference the Middle Ages makes: Color and race before the modern world', introduction to *Journal of Medieval and Early Modern Studies*, 31 (2001), ed. Thomas Hahn, 1–37.

Hambly, Gavin R. G. (ed.), *Women in the Medieval Islamic World: Power, Patronage and Piety* (New York: St Martin's Press, 1998).

Hamilton, Bernard, *The Latin Church in the Crusader States: The Secular Church* (London: Variorum, 1980).

Hamilton, B., 'A note on the manuscripts of the Latin text of the Prester John letter', in Beckingham and Hamilton (eds), *Prester John*, p. 39.

——, 'Continental drift: Prester John's progress through the Indies', in Beckingham and Hamilton (eds), *Prester John*, pp. 237–69.

——, 'Our Lady of Saidnaya: An Orthodox shine revered by Muslims and Knights Templar at the time of the crusades', in Swanson (ed.), *Holy Land, Holy Lands*, pp. 207–15.

——, 'The Armenian Church and the papacy at the time of the crusades', *Eastern Churches Review*, 10 (1978), 61–87.

Hannaford, Ivan, *Race: The History of an Idea in the West* (Washington, DC: Woodrow Wilson Center, 1996).

Harley, J. B. and David Woodward (eds), *Cartography in Prehistoric, Ancient, and Medieval Europe and the Mediterranean: The History of Cartography* (in progress), i (Chicago: Chicago University Press, 1987).

Hartog, François, *The Mirror of Herodotus: The Representation of the Other in the Writing of History* (Berkeley: University of California Press, 1988).

Harvey, P. D. A., *Mappa Mundi: The Hereford World Map* (London: Hereford Cathedral and The British Library, 1996).

——, *Medieval Maps* (London: The British Library; and Toronto: University of Toronto Press, 1991).

—— (ed.), *The Hereford World Map: Medieval World Maps and their Context* (London: The British Library, forthcoming).

——, 'Local and regional cartography in medieval Europe', in Harley and Woodward (eds), *History of Cartography*, i, pp. 464–501.

——, 'Matthew Paris's maps of Palestine', in Michael Prestwich, Richard Britnell and Robin Frame (eds), *Thirteenth Century England*, 8 (Woodbridge: Boydell and Brewer, 2001), pp. 165–77.

——, 'The biblical content of medieval maps of the Holy Land', in Dagmar Unverhau (ed.), *Geschichtsdeutung auf alten Karten: Archäologie und Geschichte*, Wolfenbütteler Forschungen, 101 (Wiesbaden: Harrassowicz, 2003), pp. 55–63.

——, 'The medieval grid maps of Palestine', unpublished paper read at the Nineteenth International Conference on the History of Cartography, Madrid, 1–6 July 2001.

——, 'The twelfth-century Jerome maps of Asia and Palestine', paper presented to the Seventeenth International Conference on the History of Cartography, Lisbon, 6–10 July 1997.

Hazard, H. W. (ed.), *The Fourteenth and Fifteenth Centuries*: K. M. Setton (gen. ed.), *A History of the Crusades*, iii (Madison, WI: University of Wisconsin Press, 1975).

Heffernan, T. J. (ed.), *The Popular Literature of Medieval England* (Knoxville: University of Tennessee Press, 1985).

Heinrichs, Wolfhart P., 'Abd al-Qahir al-Jurjani', in Meisami and Starkey (eds), *Encyclopedia of Arabic Literature*, i, p. 16.

Helfers, J., 'The mystic as pilgrim: Margery Kempe and the tradition of nonfictional travel narrative', *Journal of the Rocky Mountain Medieval and Renaissance Association*, 13 (1992), 25–45.

Hernández González, M. Isabel, 'El viaje y el descubrimiento: Hacia una lectura devocional de la *Tribagia* de Juan del Encina', in Javier Guijarro Ceballos (ed.), *Humanismo y literatura en tiempos de Juan del Encina*, Acta salmanticensia: Estudios filológicos, 271 (Salamanca: Ediciones Universidad de Salamanca, 1999), pp. 367–78.

Herz, Randall Eugene, 'Briefe Hans Tuchers d. Ä. aus dem Heiligen Land und andere Aufzeichnungen', *Mitteilungen des Vereins für Geschichte der Stadt Nürnberg*, 84 (1997), 61–92.

Herz, Randall, 'Zwei Druckfassungen eines Itinerars und ihre Abhängigkeiten', *Gutenberg-Jahrbuch*, 78 (1998), 101–4.

Higgins, Iain Macleod, *Writing East: The 'Travels' of Sir John Mandeville* (Philadelphia: University of Pennsylvania Press, 1997).

——, 'Defining the earth's center in a medieval "multi-text": Jerusalem in *The Book of John Mandeville*', in Sylvia Tomasch and Sealy Giles (eds), *Text and Territory: Geographical Imagination in the European Middle Ages* (Pennsylvania: University of Philadelphia Press, 1998), pp. 29–53.

——, 'Imagining Christendom from Jerusalem to Paradise: Asia in *Mandeville's Travels*', in Westrem (ed.), *Discovering New Worlds*, pp. 91–114.

Hillenbrand, Carole, *The Crusades: Islamic Perspectives* (Edinburgh: Edinburgh University Press, 1999).

Hippler, Christiane, *Die Reise nach Jerusalem: Untersuchungen zu den Quellen, zum Inhalt und zur literarischen Struktur der Pilgerberichte des Spätmittelalters*, Europäische Hochschulschriften, series 1, 968 (Frankfurt am Main, Bern and New York: Lang, 1987).

Hirschmann, Gerhard, 'Das Nürnberger Patriziat', *Aus sieben Jahrhunderten Nürnberger Stadtgeschichte: Ausgewählte Aufsätze von Gerhard Hirschmann: Festgabe zu seinem 70. Geburtstag*, ed. Kuno Ulshöfer, Nürnberger Forschungen, 25 (Nürnberg: Selbstverlag des Vereins für Geschichte der Stadt Nürnberg, 1988), pp. 123–42.

Honigmann, Ernst, *Die sieben Klimata und die Poleis episemoi: Eine Untersuchung zur Geschichte der Geographie und Astrologie im Altertum und Mittelalter* (Heidelberg: Carl Winter, 1929).

Hopkins, J. F. P., 'Geographical and navigational literature', in Young *et al.* (eds), *Religion, Learning and Science in the 'Abbasid Period*, pp. 301–27, bibliography on pp. 538–9.

Housley, N., *The Avignon Papacy and the Crusades* (Oxford: Clarendon Press, 1986).

——, *The Later Crusades, 1274–1580: From Lyons to Alcazar* (Oxford: Oxford University Press, 1992).

Howard, D., *Writers and Pilgrims: Medieval Pilgrimage Narratives and their Posterity* (Berkeley: University of California Press, 1980).

Huizinga, Johan, *The Autumn of the Middle Ages*, trans. Rodney J. Payton and Ulrich Mammitzsch (Chicago: University of Chicago Press, 1966; first published in Dutch in 1921).

Hulme, Peter and Tim Youngs (eds), *The Cambridge Companion to Travel Writing* (Cambridge: Cambridge University Press, 2002).

Humphreys, R. Stephen, *From Saladin to the Mongols* (Albany: State University of New York Press, 1977).

——, 'Munkidh', in Gibb *et al.* (eds), *The Encyclopaedia of Islam*, vii, pp. 557–80.

Hunt, E. D., 'Were there Christian pilgrims before Constantine?', in Stopford (ed.), *Pilgrimage Explored*, pp. 25–56.

Hunt, E. S. and J. M. A. Murray, *History of Business in Medieval Europe, 1200–1550* (Cambridge: Cambridge University Press, 1999).

Huschenbett, Dietrich, 'Die Literatur der deutschen Pilgerreisen nach Jerusalem im späten Mittelalter', *Deutsche Vierteljahrsschrift*, 59 (1985), 29–46.

——, '*Von landen und ynseln*: Literarische und geistliche Meerfahrten nach Palästina im späten Mittelalter', in Wolf (ed.), *Wissensorganisierende und wissensvermittelnde Literatur im Mittelalter*, pp. 189–207.

Ingram, Elizabeth M., 'Maps as readers' aids: Maps and plans in Geneva Bibles', *Imago Mundi*, 45 (1993), 29–44.

Irwin, R., 'How many miles to Babylon? The *Devise des chemins de Babiloine* redated', in Barber (ed.), *The Military Orders*, pp. 57–63.

Irwin, Robert, 'Usamah ibn Munqidh: An Arab-Syrian gentleman at the time of the crusades reconsidered', in J. France and W. G. Zajac (eds), *The Crusades and their Sources: Essays Presented to Bernard Hamilton* (Aldershot: Ashgate, 1998), pp. 71–87.

Jacoby, David, 'L'expansion occidentale dans le Levant: Les Vénitiens à Acre dans la seconde moitié du 13ème siècle', *Journal of Medieval History*, 3 (1977), 225–65.

Jones, R. O., L. P. Harvey and Keith Whinnom, 'Lingua franca in a *villancico* by Encina', *Revue de Littérature Comparée*, 41 (1967), 572–9.

Jotischky, Andrew, *The Carmelites and Antiquity: Mendicants and their Pasts in the Middle Ages* (Oxford: Oxford University Press, 2002).

——, *The Perfection of Solitude: Hermits and Monks in the Crusader States* (University Park, PA: Pennsylvania State Press, 1995).

Kedar, Benjamin Z., *Crusade and Mission: European Approaches toward the Muslims* (Princeton: Princeton University Press, 1984).

Kedar, B. Z., 'The *Tractatus de locis et statu sancte terre Ierosolimitane*', in J. France and W. G. Zajac (eds), *The Crusades and their Sources: Essays Presented to Bernard Hamilton* (Aldershot: Ashgate, 1998), pp. 111–33.

Keller, John E. and Robert W. Linker, *Iconography in Medieval Spanish Literature* (Lexington: University Press of Kentucky, 1984).

*King's Lynn: The First Thousand Years*, King's Lynn Blue Badge Guides (King's Lynn: King's Lynn Town Guides, 1997).

Kline, N. R., *Maps of Medieval Thought: The Hereford Paradigm* (Woodbridge: Boydell Press, 2001).

Kramer, Barbel, 'The earliest known map of Spain (?) and the Geography of Artemidorus of Ephesus on papyrus', *Imago Mundi*, 53 (2001), 115–20.

Kretschmer, Konrad, *Die italienischen Portlane des Mittelalters: Ein Beitrag zur Geschichte der Kartographie und Nautik* (Reinheim: Lokay, 1909; repr. Hildesheim: G. Olms, 1962).

Kunstmann, F., 'Studien über Marino Sanudo den Älteren mit einem Anhang seiner ungegedruckten Briefen', *Abhandlungen, Phil.-Historische Classe, Königliche Bayerische Akademie der Wissenschaften*, 7 (1853).

Kupfer, Marcia, 'The lost *mappamundi* at Chalivoy-Milon', *Speculum*, 66 (1991), 540–71.

——, 'The lost wheel map of Ambrogio Lorenzetti', *Art Bulletin*, 78:2 (1996), 286–310.

Labarge, Margaret Wade, *Medieval Travellers: The Rich and Restless* (London: Hamish Hamilton, 1982).

Laiou, A., 'Marino Sanudo Torsello, Byzantium and the Turks: The background to the anti-Turkish league of 1332–34', *Speculum*, 45 (1970), 374–93.

Lane, Frederic C., *Venice: A Maritime Republic* (Baltimore: Johns Hopkins University Press, 1973).

Lawler, Traugott, 'On the properties of John Trevisa's major translations', *Viator*, 14 (1983), 267–88.

Lawrance, Jeremy, 'Europe and the Turks in Spanish literature of the Renaissance and early modern period', in Nigel Griffin *et al.* (eds), *Culture and Society in Habsburg Spain: Studies Presented to R. W. Truman by his Pupils and Colleagues on the Occasion of his Retirement* (London: Tamesis, 2001), pp. 17–33.

Leaske, Nigel, *Curiosity and the Aesthetics of Travel Writing, 1770–1840* (Oxford: Oxford University Press, 2001).

Lemmens, L., *Geschichte der Franziskanermissconen* (Münster: Aschendorff, 1929).

Leopold, Antony, *How to Recover the Holy Land: The Crusade Proposals of the Late 13th and Early 14th Centuries* (Aldershot: Ashgate, 2000).

Lewicki, Tadeusz, 'Marino Sanudos Mappa Mundi (1321) und die runde Weltkarte von Idrisi (1154)', *Rocznik Orientalistyczny*, 37 (1976), 169–96.

Lewis, Suzanne, *The Art of Matthew Paris in the Chronica Majora* (Aldershot: Scolar Press with Corpus Christi College, Cambridge, 1987).

Liebe, G., 'Die Wallfahrten des Mittelalters und ihr Einfluß auf die Kultur', *Neue Jahrbücher für das Klassische Altertum, Geschichte und Deutsche Literatur*, 1 (1898), 149–60.

Lloyd, T. H., *England and the German Hanse, 1157–1611: A Study of their Trade and Commercial Diplomacy* (Cambridge: Cambridge University Press, 1991).

Lochrie, K., *Margery Kempe and Translations of the Flesh* (Philadelphia: University of Pennsylvania Press, 1991).

Loenertz, R.-J., 'Frère Jacques de Milan, missionaire en Orient au XIIIe siècle', *AFP*, 8 (1938), 274–84.

——, 'La societé des Frères Pérégrinants: Étude sur l'Orient dominicain', *AFP*, 45 (1975), 107–45.

——, 'Les missions dominicains en Orient au XIVe siècle', *AFP*, 2 (1932), 1–83.

Lozovsky, Natalia, *The Earth is our Book: Geographical Knowledge in the Latin West ca. 400–1000* (Ann Arbor: Michigan University Press, 2000).

Lynch, Kathryn L. (ed.), *Chaucer's Cultural Geography* (London: Routledge, 2002).

Makdisi, George, *The Rise of Colleges: Institutions of Learning in Islam and the West* (Edinburgh: Edinburgh University Press, 1981).

——, *The Rise of Humanism in Classical Islam and the Christian West, with Special Reference to Scholasticism* (Edinburgh: Edinburgh University Press, 1990).

Malik, Kenan, *The Meaning of Race: Race, History, and Culture in Western Society* (Houndmills and London: Macmillan, 1996).

Mann, J., *Texts and Studies in Jewish History Literature*, 2 vols (Cincinnati: Hebrew Union College Press, 1931).

Margolioth, M., *Halakhoth on the Land of Israel from the Genizah* (Jerusalem, 1974).

Mateu Ibars, Josefina, 'Peritaje paleográfico del ms. 17510 de la Biblioteca Nacional de Madrid', *Revista de Literatura Medieval*, 7 (1995), 72–92.

Mauriès, Patrick, *Cabinets of Curiosities* (London: Thames and Hudson, 2002).

Mayer, Hans E., *The Crusades*, trans. John Gillingham (Oxford: Oxford University Press, 1972).

McEntire, S. J. (ed.), *Margery Kempe: A Book of Essays* (New York: Garland Publishing, 1992).

McTiernan, John (director), *The 13th Warrior*, based on Michael Crichton, *Eaters of the Dead* (1976).

Meier, Christl, 'Grundzüge der mittelalterlichen Enzyklopädik', in Grenzmann and Stackmann (eds), *Literatur und Laienbildung*, pp. 467–500.

Meisami, Julie Scott, *Medieval Persian Court Poetry* (Princeton: Princeton University Press, 1990).

Meisami, Julie Scott and Paul Starkey (eds), *Encyclopedia of Arabic Literature*, 2 vols (London and New York: Routledge, 1998).

Micheau, François, 'Les itinéraires maritimes et continentaux des pèlerinages vers Jerusalem', *Occident et Orient au X^e siècle: Actes du IX^e congrès de la Société des Historiens Médiévistes de l'Enseignement Supérieur Public, Dijon, 2–4 juin, 1978*, Publications de l'Université de Dijon, 57 (Paris: Société des Belles Lettres, 1979), pp. 79–104.

Miller, Konrad, *Mappaemundi: Die ältesten Weltkarten*, 6 vols (Stuttgart: J. Roth, 1895–98).

Mollat du Jourdin, Michel, and Monique de la Roncière, *Sea Charts of the Early Explorers*, trans. L. leR. Dothan (London: Thames and Hudson, 1984).

Moorehead, A., *The Blue Nile* (London: New English Library, 1972).

Morgan, D. O., *The Mongols* (Oxford: Basil Blackwell, 1986).

Morray, David W., *The Genius of Usamah ibn Munqidh: Aspects of* Kitab al-I'tibar *by Usamah ibn Munqidh* (Durham: Centre for Middle Eastern and Islamic Studies, University of Durham, 1987).

Morris, Colin, 'Memorials of the holy places and blessings from the East: Devotion to Jerusalem before the crusades', in R. N. Swanson (ed.), *The Holy Land, Holy Lands, and Christian History*, 'Introduction' and pp. 90–109.

Morris, Rosemary, *The Character of King Arthur in Medieval Literature*, Arthurian Studies, 4 (Cambridge: D. S. Brewer, 1982).

Muldoon, J., *Popes, Lawyers and Infidels: The Church and the Non-Christian World 1250–1550* (Liverpool: Liverpool University Press, 1979).

Nebenzahl, Kenneth, *Maps of the Bible Lands: Images of Terra Sancta through Two Millennia* (London: Times Books, 1986); also published as *Maps of the Holy Land: Images of Terra Sancta through Two Millennia* (New York: Abbeville, 1986).

Netton, Ian R., *Golden Roads: Migration, Pilgrimage, and Travel in Mediaeval and Modern Islam* (Richmond, Surrey: Curzon Press, 1993).

——, *Seek Knowledge: Thought and Travel in the House of Islam* (Richmond, Surrey: Curzon Press, 1996).

—— 'Rihla', in Gibb *et al.* (eds), *The Encyclopaedia of Islam*, viii, p. 528.

Nicholson, Helen, 'Women on the Third Crusade', *Journal of Medieval History*, 23 (1997), 335–49.

Niehr, Klaus, '"als ich das selber erkundet vnd gesehen hab": Wahrnehmung und Darstellung des Fremden in Bernhard von Breydenbachs *Peregrinationes in Terram Sanctam* und anderen Pilgerberichten des ausgehenden Mittelalters', *Gutenberg-Jahrbuch*, 76 (2001), 269–300.

O'Loughlin, Thomas, 'Adomnán and Arculf: The case of an expert witness', *Journal of Medieval Latin*, 7 (1997), 127–46.

——, 'Living in the ocean', in Cormac Bourke (ed.), *Studies in the Cult of Saint Columba* (Dublin: Four Courts Press, 1997), pp. 11–23.

——, 'Palestine in the aftermath of the Arab conquest: The earliest Latin account', in Swanson (ed.), *Holy Land, Holy Lands*, pp. 18–89.

——, 'The plan of the New Jerusalem in the Book of Armagh', *Cambrian Medieval Celtic Studies*, 39 (2000), 23–38.

——, 'The view from Iona: Adomnàn's mental maps', *Peritia: The Journal of the Medieval Academy of Ireland*, 10 (1996), 98–122.

Oppenheimer, A'hron, 'Terumot and Ma'aserot', in Cecil Roth (editor-in-chief), *Encyclopedia Judaica*, 16 vols (New York: Macmillan, 1972–82).

Owen, D. H. (ed.), *The Making of King's Lynn: A Documentary Survey* (London: Oxford University Press, 1984).

Paviot, Jacques, 'La mappemonde attribuée à Jan van Eyck par Fàcio: Une pièce à retirer du catalogue de son oeuvre', *Revue des Archéologues et Historiens d'Art de Louvain*, 24 (1991), 57–62.

Pérez Priego, Miguel Angel, 'Estudio literario de los libros de viajes medievales', *Epos*, 1 (1984), 217–38.

Perruchon, J., 'Notes sur l'histoire d'Ethiopie: Extrait de la vie d'Abba Jean, 74e patriarche d'Alexandrie, relatif à l'Abyssinie (texte arabe et introduction)', *Revue Sémitique*, 7 (1899), 81–2.

Peters, R., 'Safar', in Gibb *et al.* (eds), *Encyclopaedia of Islam*, viii, p. 764.

Pflederer, Richard, 'Portolan charts: Vital tool in the age of discovery', *History Today*, 52:5 (May 2002), 20–7.

Phillips, H. (ed.), *Langland, the Mystics and the Medieval English Religious Tradition* (Cambridge: D. S. Brewer, 1990).

Piccirillo, M., *La custodia di Terra Santa e l'Europa: I rapporti politici e l'attivita culturale dei Francescani in Medio Oriente* (Rome: Il Veltro Editrice, 1983), pp. 95–116.

Pohl, Hans (ed.), *Die Bedeutung der Kommunikation für Wirtschaft und Gesellschaft: Referate der 12. Arbeitstagung der Gesellschaft für Sozial- und Wirtschaftsgeschichte vom 22.–25.4.1987 in Siegen, Vierteljahrschrift für Sozial- und Wirtschaftsgeschichte*, Beiheft 87 (Wiesbaden and Stuttgart: Steiner, 1989).

Prawer, Joshua, *The History of the Jews in the Latin Kingdom of Jerusalem* (Oxford: Clarendon Press, 1988).

Prestcott, F. M., *Jerusalem Journey: Pilgrimage to the Holy Land in the Fifteenth Century* (London, Eyre and Spottiswoode, 1954).

Pryor, J. H., 'The *Eracles* and William of Tyre: An interim report', in B. Z. Kedar (ed.), *The Horns of Hattin* (Jerusalem: Yad Izhak Ben-Zvi and London: Ashgate, 1992).

Raba, Joel, 'Das Weltbild der mittelalterlichen und frühneuzeitlichen russischen Reisenden', *Forschungen zur osteuropäischen Geschichte: Konferenz zur Geschichte des Moskauer Reiches*, Osteuropa-Institut an der Freien Universität Berlin, Historische Veröffentlichungen, 38 (Wiesbaden: Harrassowitz, 1986), pp. 20–41.

Ramey, Lynn Tarte, *Christian, Saracen, and Genre in Medieval French Literature* (London: Routledge, 2001).

Reid, Piers Paul, *The Templars* (New York: St Martin's Press, 2000).

Richard, J., *La papauté et les missions d'Orient au Moyen Age (XIIIᵉ–XVᵉ siècles)*, Collection de l'École Française de Rome, 33 (Rome: École Française de Rome, 1977).

——, 'Les missions chez les Mongoles aux XIIIe et XIVe siècles', in Simon Delacroix (gen. ed.), *Histoire universelle des missions catholiques*, 4 vols (1956–59), i: *Les missions des origines au XVIe siècle* (Paris: Grund, 1956), pp. 173–95.

——, 'The *Relatio de Davide* as a source for Mongol history and the legend of Prester John', in Hamilton and Beckingham (eds), *Prester John*, pp. 139–58.

Richards, D. S., 'al-Kindi, Abu 'Umar', in Meisami and Starkey (eds), *Encyclopedia of Arabic Literature*, ii, p. 451.

Richards, Jeffrey, *Sex, Dissidence and Damnation: Minority Groups in the Middle Ages* (London and New York: Routledge, 1991).

Riley-Smith, Jonathan, *The Atlas of the Crusades* (New York: Facts on File, 1991).

—— (ed.), *The Oxford Illustrated History of the Crusades* (Oxford: Oxford University Press, 1995).

Röhricht, Reinhold, 'Karten und Pläne zur Palästinakunde aus dem 7. bis 16. Jahrhundert', *Zeitschrift des Deutschen Palästina-Vereins*, 14 (1891), 8–11, 87–92, 137–41; 15 (1892), 34–9; 18 (1895), 173–82.

——, 'Marino Sanudo sen als Kartograph Palästinas', *Zeitschrift des Deutschen Palästina-Vereins*, 21 (1898), 84–128.

Roncaglia, Martiniano, *I Francescani in Oriente durante le crociate (sec XIII): Storia della provincia di Terra Santa* (Cairo: Centro di Studi Orientali, 1954).

Rosovsky, Nitza (ed.), *City of the Great King: Jerusalem from David to the Present*, (Cambridge, MA, and London: Harvard University Press, 1996).

Rubin, Rehav, *Image and Reality: Jerusalem in Maps and Views* (Jerusalem: The Hebrew University Magnes Press, 1999).

Rudy, Kathleen Margaret, 'North European responses to Holy Land pilgrimage, 1453–1550', unpublished PhD dissertation, Columbia University, 2000 (AAT 3005788), www.lib.umich.com/dissertations/fullcit/3005788.

Ruh, Kurt (ed.), *Die deutsche Literatur des Mittelalters: Verfasserlexikon* (Berlin and New York: Walter de Gruyter, 1977–).

Runciman, Steven, *The Kingdom of Acre and the Later Crusades*, in *A History of the Crusades*, 3 vols (Cambridge: Cambridge University Press, 1954), iii.

Rykwert, Joseph, *The Idea of a Town: The Anthropology of Urban Form in Rome, Italy, and the Ancient World* (London: Faber and Faber, 1976).

——, *The Peaceful Liberation of the Holy Places in the Fourteenth Century*, Studia Orientalia Christiana Monographiae, 3 (Cairo: Franciscan Center for Oriental Studies, 1990).

Scafi, Alessandro, *Mapping Paradise: A History of Heaven on Earth* (London: The British Library, forthcoming).

——, 'Il Paradiso Terrestre di Fra Mauro', *Storia del'Arte*, 93–4 (May–December 1998), 411–19.

——, 'Mapping Eden: Cartographies of the Earthly Paradise', in Denis Cosgrove (ed.), *Mappings* (London: Reaktion, 1999), pp. 50–70.

——, 'Paradise: The essence of a mappamundi', in Harvey (ed.), *The Hereford World Map*.

Schein, S., 'Bridget of Sweden, Margery Kempe and women's Jerusalem pilgrimages in the Middle Ages', *Mediterranean Historical Review*, 14:1 (1999), 44–58.

Schein, Sylvia, *Fideles crucis: The Papacy, the West and the Recovery of the Holy Land, 1274–1314* (Oxford: Clarendon Press, 1991).

Scott Stokes, C., 'Margery Kempe: Her life and the early history of her *Book*', *Mystics Quarterly*, 25:1–2 (1999), 9–68.

Setton, K. M. (gen. ed.), *A History of the Crusades*, 6 vols, 2nd edn. (Madison, WI: University of Wisconsin Press, 1969–89).

Seymour, Michael C., *Sir John Mandeville*, Authors of the Middle Ages, 1 (Aldershot: Variorum, 1993).

Sinor, D., 'The Mongols and western Europe', in Hazard (ed.), *The Fourteenth and Fifteenth Centuries*, pp. 513–44.

Sommerfeld, Martin, 'Die Reisebeschreibungen der deutschen Jerusalempilger im ausgehenden Mittelalter', *Deutsche Vierteljahrsschrift*, 2 (1924), 816–51.

Stargardt, U., 'The Beguines of Belgium, the Dominican Nuns of Germany, and Margery Kempe', in Heffernan (ed.), *Popular Literature*, pp. 275–313.

——, 'The influence of Dorothea von Montau on the mysticism of Margery Kempe', PhD dissertation, University of Tennessee, 1981.

Stenton, F. M., 'The road system of medieval England', *The Economic History Review*, 7:1 (1936), 1–21.

Stern, Samuel, 'A collection of treatises by 'Abd al-Latif al-Baghdadi', *Islamic Studies*, 1 (1962), 53–70.

Stopford, J. (ed.), *Pilgrimage Explored* (York: York Medieval Press, 1999).

Sumption, J., *Pilgrimage: An Image of Medieval Religion* (Totowa, NJ: Rowland and Littlefield, 1975).

Swanson, R. N., *The Church and the Book* (Woodbridge: The Boydell Press for The Ecclesiastical History Society, 2004).

—— (ed.), *The Holy Land, Holy Lands, and Christian History*, Studies in Church History, 36 (Woodbridge: The Boydell Press for The Ecclesiastical History Society, 2000).

Taylor, Barry, 'Los libros de viajes de la Edad Media hispánica: Bibliografía y recepción', in *Actas do IV Congresso da Associação Hispânica de Literatura Medieval* (Lisboa: Cosmos, 1991–93), i, pp. 57–70.

Thorndike, Lynn, *A History of Magic and Experimental Science*, 4 vols (New York: Columbia University Press, 1923–34).

——, *The* Sphere *of Sacrobosco and its Commentators* (Chicago: University of Chicago Press, 1949).

Tooley, Marian J., 'Bodin and the medieval theory of climate', *Speculum*, 28 (1953), 64–83.

Toorawa, Shawkat M., 'Language and male homosocial desire in the autobiography of 'Abd al-Latif al-Baghdadi (d. 629/1231)', *Edebiyât: The Journal of Middle Eastern Literatures*, new series, 7:2 (1997), 45–59.

——, 'Patronage', in Meisami and Starkey (eds), *Enayclopedia of Arabic Literature*, ii, pp. 598–9.

——, 'Selections from the autograph notes of 'Abd al-Latif al-Baghdadi', in Dwight F. Reynolds (ed.), *Interpreting the Self: Autobiography in the Arabic Literary Tradition* (Berkeley: University of California Press, 2001), pp. 156–64.

——, 'The educational background of 'Abd al-Latif al-Baghdadi', *Muslim Education Quarterly*, 13:3 (1996), 35–53; revised as 'A portrait of 'Abd al-Latif al-Baghdadi through his education and instruction', in Joseph E. Lowry, Devin Stewart and Shawkat M. Toorawa (eds), *Law and Education in Medieval Islam: Studies in Memory of George Makdisi* (Oxford: Oxbow Books for the Gibb Memorial Trust, forthcoming).

Touati, Houari, *Islam et voyage au Moyen Age: Histoire et anthropologie d'une pratique lettrée* (Paris: Seuil, 2000).

Turner, V. and E. Turner, *Image and Pilgrimage in Christian Culture: Anthropological Perspectives* (New York: Columbia University Press, 1978).

Tyerman, Christopher, *The Invention of the Crusades* (Toronto: University of Toronto Press, 1998).

——, 'Marino Sanudo Torsello and the last crusade: lobbying in the fourteenth century', *Transactions of the Royal Historical Society*, 5th series, 32 (1982), 57–73.

Vantini, G., *Christianity in the Sudan* (Bologna: EMI, 1981).

Vat, O. van der, *Die Anfänge der Franziskanermissionen und ihre Weiterentwicklung im Näher Orient und in den mohammedanischen Ländern während des 13 Jahrhunderts* (Werl im Westfalen: Franziskus-Druckerei, 1934).

Vaughan, Richard, *Matthew Paris* (Cambridge: Cambridge University Press, 1958).

Voaden, R., *God's Words, Women's Voices: The Discernment of Spirits in the Writing of Late-Medieval Woman Visionaries* (York: York Medieval Press, 1999).

——, 'Beholding men's members: The sexualizing of transgression in *The Book of Margery Kempe*', in Biller and Minnis (eds), *Medieval Theology and the Natural Body*, pp. 175–90.

Wallace, D., *Chaucerian Polity: Absolutist Lineages and Associational Forms in England and Italy* (Stanford: Stanford University Press, 1997).

Wasserstein, D., 'Eldad ha Dani and Prester John', in Beckingham and Hamilton (eds), *Prester John*, pp. 213–36.

Webb, D., *Pilgrims and Pilgrimages in the Medieval West* (London: IB Tauris, 1999).

Wessells, C., *Early Jesuit Travellers in Central Asia, 1603–1721* (The Hague: M. Nijhoff, 1924).

Wessley, Stephen, 'The role of the Holy Land for the early followers of Joachim of Fiore', in Swanson (ed.), *Holy Land, Holy Lands*, pp. 181–91.

Westrem, Scott D., *Broader Horizons: A Study of Johannes Witte de Hese's* Itinerarius *and Medieval Travel Narratives* (Cambridge, MA: The Medieval University of America, 2001).

——, *The Hereford Map* (Turnhout: Brepols, 2001).

—— (ed.), *Discovering New Worlds: Essays on Medieval Exploration and Imagination* (New York and London: Garland Publishing, 1991).

—— 'A medieval travel book's editors and translators: managing style and accommodating dialect in Johannes Witte de Hese's *Itinerarius*', in Roger Ellis and Ruth Evans (eds), *The Medieval Translator*, 4 (Exeter: University of Exeter Press, 1994), pp. 153–80.

Whitfield, P., *The Image of the World: 20 Centuries of World Maps* (London: The British Library, 1994).

Wilken, Robert L., 'Christian pilgrimage to the Holy Land', in Rosovsky (ed.), *City of the Great King*, pp. 117–35.

Williams, David, *Deformed Discourse: The Function of the Monster in Mediaeval Thought and Literature* (Montreal and Kingston: McGill-Queen's University Press, 1996).

Wiseman, Peter, 'Julius Caesar and the Hereford world map', *History Today*, 37 (1987), 53–7.

Wittkower, Rudolf, 'Marco Polo and the pictorial tradition of the Marvels of the East', in Rudolf Wittkower (ed.), *Allegory and the Migration of Symbols* (London: Thames and Hudson, 1977), pp. 75–92.

——, 'Marvels of the East: A study in the history of monsters', *Journal of the Warburg and Courtauld Institutes*, 5 (1942), 159–97; also in Rudolf Wittkower (ed.), *Allegory and the Migration of Symbols* (London: Thames and Hudson, 1977), pp. 45–74.

Wolf, Armin, 'News on the Ebstorf world map: Date, origin, authorship', in Monique Pelletier (ed.), *La géographie du monde au Moyen Age et à la Renaissance* (Paris: Editions du Comité des Travaux Historiques et Scientifiques, 1989), pp. 51–68.

Wolf, Gerhard, 'Die deutschsprachigen Reiseberichte des Spätmittelalters', in Brenner (ed.), *Der Reisebericht*, pp. 81–116.

Wolf, Norbert Richard (ed.), *Wissensorganisierende und wissensvermittelnde Literatur im Mittelalter: Perspektiven ihrer Erforschung: Kolloquium 5.–7. Dezember 1985* (Wiesbaden: Reichert, 1987).

Womersley, David, review of Leaske, *Curiosity and the Aesthetics of Travel Writing*, *Times Literary Supplement* (19 July 2002).

Woodward, David, 'Medieval *mappaemundi*', in Harley and Woodward (eds), *History of Cartography*, i, pp. 286–370.

——, 'Reality, symbolism, time and space in medieval world maps', *Annals of the Association of American Geographers*, 75:4 (1985), 510–21.

——, 'Roger Bacon on geography and cartography', in Hackett (ed.), *Roger Bacon and the Sciences*, pp. 199–222.

——, 'Roger Bacon's terrestrial co-ordinate system', *Annals of the Association of American Geographers*, 80:1 (1990), 109–22.

——, 'The image of the world in the Renaissance', in David Woodward, Catherine Delano-Smith and Cordell Yee, *Plantajements i objectivos d'una història universal de la cartografia:*

*Approaches and Challenges in a Worldwide History of Cartography* (Barcelona: Institut Cartogràfic de Catalunya, 2001), pp. 133–52.

Wright, J. K., *The Geographical Lore of the Time of the Crusades: A Study in the History of Medieval Science and Tradition in Western Europe*, American Geographical Society Research Series, 15 (New York: American Geographical Society, 1925); republished with additions (New York: Dover Publications, 1965).

Young, M. J. L., *et al.* (eds), *Religion, Learning and Science in the 'Abbasid Period* (Cambridge: Cambridge University Press, 1990).

Zacher, Christian K., *Curiosity and Pilgrimage: The Literature of Discovery in Fourteenth-Century England* (Baltimore: Johns Hopkins University Press, 1976).

——, 'Travel and geographical writings', in A. E. Hartung (gen. ed.), *A Manual of the Writings in Middle English, 1050–1400* (New Haven, CT: Academy of Arts and Sciences, 1967–), vii (1986), XIX, pp. 2235–54.

Zacour, N. P. and H. W. Hazard (eds), *The Impact of the Crusades on the Near East*: Setton (gen. ed.), *A History of the Crusades*, v (Madison, WI: University of Wisconsin Press, 1985).

# Index

◖◗

Note: page numbers given in *italic* refer to figures; 'n.' after a page number indicates the number of a note on that page; tr. = travelled.